WORLD WIDE WEB BIBLE

By Bryan Pfaffenberger

MIS: PRESS

A Subsidiary of
Henry Holt and Co., Inc.

First Edition—1995

Pfaffenberger, Bryan
    World Wide Web bible / Bryan Pfaffenberger.
        p.   cm.
    Includes index.
    ISBN 1-55828-410-9
    1. World Wide Web (Information retrieval system) 2. Internet
(Computer network) I. Title.
    TK5105.888.P43   1995
    005.75--dc20   95-7111
                                                             CIP

Printed in the United States of America.
10 9 8 7 6 5 4 3 2

MIS:Press books are available at special discounts for bulk purchases for sales promotions, premiums, fund-raising, or educational use. Special editions or book excerpts can also be created to specification.

For details contact: Special Sales Director
                        MIS:Press
                        a subsidiary of Henry Holt and Company, Inc.
                        115 West 18th Street
                        New York, New York 10011

Editor-in-Chief: Paul Farrell   **Managing Editor:** Cary Sullivan
Editor: Debra Williams Cauley   **Technical Editor:** Michael Zang
Copy Editor: Elissa Keeler   **Production Editor:** Anthony Washington

Dedication

For Suzanne, always

Acknowledgments

This book was written with one overriding aim, to make sure that its readers would possess the knowledge, skills, and tools they will need to become part of the Web's future. It was not a solitary crusade, as I was quick to discover. Many true believers joined the quest, including Bob Denny, the author of the splendid WinHTTPD server software that's included with this book; David Wall, an extraordinary University of Virginia English major who co-authored substantial portions of Part Five of this book; Mike Zang, a University of Virginia UNIX wizard who created the SmartPages (another goodie included on this book's disk), and David Beach, Web document designer extraordinaire and resident guru of the underground music archive scene. Inspiring the entire venture, as always, was Debra Williams Cauley, my editor at MIS Press, whose good humor and patience helped me through many a trying deadline. I would also like to thank my agent, Carole McClendon.

As this book went into production, MIS Press's great team went to work. Elissa Keeler combed through all that follows with care, ensuring not only its clarity but also making a number of valuable technical contributions. And don't you think the book looks great? Id like to thank Anthony Washington for the cool icons and design, and Shari Chappell and Brian Oxman for their patience and contributions to production.

Most of all, I'd like to thank my family for putting up with prolonged writing sessions and my long, rambling dinner discourses on the wonders of the Web. These must have struck ·a chord; with five computers in the house and three modems now, we're fighting to see who gets the SLIP connection!

Table of Contents

PART 1:
GETTING INTO THE WEB

PART 2:
CONNECTING TO THE WEB

PART 3:
BROWSING THE WEB

PART 4:
ADVANCED STRATEGIES
FOR WEB NAVIGATION

PART 5:
EXPLORING THE WEB

PART 6:
MAKING THE WEB YOUR OWN

PART 7:
WEB HORIZONS

INTRODUCTION

It's like the difference between the brain and the mind. Explore the Internet and you find cables and computers. Explore the Web and you find information.
—Tim Berners-Lee, European Center for Particle Physics

Tomorrow's history books may well mark the year 1993 as a milestone, the year that saw the birth of a global computerized information system.

It was in 1993 that the World Wide Web, a little-known Internet communication system based on hypertext principles, began to explode in popularity. The catalyst? The National Center for Supercomputer Applications' popular Mosaic software, an easy-to-use graphical program that enabled anyone to access Web (and other Internet resources) with ease.

Since then, the Web has experienced exponential growth. A recent forecast estimates that, by 1998, the Web will have 22 million users worldwide. By any standard, the Web is the fastest-growing communications system history has ever witnessed.

For you, the most important question about the Web's future is whether you'll be part of the action. This book's goal is to make sure that you will.

THE WORLD WIDE WEB DEFINED

KEY TERM

What is the *World Wide Web*? For starters, it's not the Internet, although it uses the Internet (and other networks) as a communication medium.

Basically, the Web is a way of creating a *geographically distributed* pool of information, so that people separated by short or long distances—even by continents—can make information available to others. In this sense, it doesn't differ from other Internet information pools, such as FTP or Gopher.

But what makes the Web special (and explains its rapid growth) is its incredible ease of use. Accessing nuggets of Internet information is as easy as pointing at an underlined phrase, and clicking the mouse button. These underlined phrases, called *hyperlinks*, contain information that tells your browser exactly how to go to the computer that contains the information you've requested. You might hook up to a computer in the next building, a different city, or a far-away country—all the mechanics are hidden from your view. Suddenly, the Internet's riches are at your fingertips (and you don't need a computer science degree to access them).

There's another reason for the Web's enormous popularity: It unlocks the Internet's multimedia capabilities. When you're browsing the Web with a graphical browser, you'll see beautiful fonts and attractive text layouts—and that's not all. Depending on the Web page you're accessing, you may also see graphics, watch movies and animations, or listen to sound recordings. This makes the Web a very potent tool for information discovery and learning. On the Web, you cannot only read about the first Apollo lunar landing, you can also hear it and see it.

With the word spreading fast about the Web's ease of use, growing numbers of people are setting off on Web journeys. You've probably heard how much fun it is to surf the Web, clicking hyperlinks to see what fun and useful stuff you can discover. You've probably also heard that the Web can be an incredibly valuable resource for all kinds of people, including parents and kids, educators and students, professionals in every line of work, hobbyists, job-hunters, consumers, and more. Just about everyone can find something of genuine value on the World Wide Web.

But what's really exciting about the Web is that it's a two-way medium. With the World Wide Web, ordinary people can become information providers as well as information consumers. All kinds of people—slick mail order businesses, giant computer firms, college students, non-profit organizations, hobbyists, writers, poets, artists, and more—are creating their own Web documents and making them available for access.

In sum, the Web is not only the fastest-growing communications medium in world history; it's also well on its way to becoming the most democratic. For my money, that's what makes the Web so wonderful. You'll find plenty of serious, useful information—the scoop on zero-coupon Treasury bonds, analyses of social change in eastern Europe, a primer on detecting early signs of common early childhood illnesses, and tons more. But you'll also find the weird, the wacky, the wild, and the just plain fun. The Web is fast becoming a riot of human creativity in addition to a building a mountain of information, knowledge, and wisdom. It's smart and fun—that's an unbeatable combination, isn't it?

WHY READ A BOOK ABOUT THE WEB?

The new graphical browsers, spearheaded by Mosaic, are very easy to use—if you're lucky enough to be viewing a document with lots of good hyperlinks. Anyone can learn to surf the Web in short order. To use the Web well, and even more to become a Web information provider, is a weightier matter that fully justifies a book such as this one. This book aims to provide the most comprehensive, useful, and practical resource that you'll find on the World Wide Web. My aim in these pages is to do no less than show you the way to absolute, flat-out mastery of the World Wide Web. Whether you're a complete beginner, a sometime surfer, or a would-be Web information provider, this is the book for you.

What does it take to become a Web maven? The following sections provide a quick overview, and they also tell you what's in this book. But I'd like to call attention to the theme of practicality—as you'll see, this book doesn't just tell you *about* the Web. It empowers you by providing information and software that can be of enormous practical value as you seek to achieve Web mastery. This book is packed with useful information, and wait 'til you find out what's on the disk!

Part One: Learning Hypertext Concepts

The World Wide Web is based on hypertext principles, which can be very confusing beyond the level of just clicking hyperlinks to see where you wind up. In Part One of this book ("Getting Into the Web"), you'll learn the fundamentals of hypertext, including what hypertext is, how hypertext systems are organized, and the strengths and shortcomings of hypertext as a medium for information retrieval. You'll learn how the Internet provides the staging ground for the emergence of the Web, and discover how the Web enables the delivery of hypermedia—hypertext documents that include multimedia resources.

By the end of Part One, you'll understand what hypertext is, what the Internet is, how the Web utilizes multimedia, and what a Web session looks like. You can go deeper, if you wish, to understand the technical philosophy that underlies the Web *protocols* (standards). Either way, you'll have a solid conceptual foundation for beginning your trek to Web mastery.

Part Two: Getting Connected to the Internet

Most books on the Web provide a superficial discussion of Internet connectivity, which is needed for Web access. But this book goes into this subject deeply, offering three solid chapters on Internet connectivity in Part Two, "Connecting to the Web."

You'll learn that there are some ways to connect to the Web that are much better than others. What's more, these chapters get right down to the nitty-gritty. You'll find full information regarding some of the best-kept technical secrets of Internet connectivity, such as writing SLIP/PPP scripts, and why ordinary dialup access isn't the best choice for Web users.

Here's a great example of this book's practicality. On the disk packaged with this book, you'll find some of the best Internet connectivity software you can find anywhere: Netmanage's Chameleon software for connecting a Microsoft Windows system to the Internet via a SLIP or PPP connection. (For more information on SLIP/PPP connections, see Chapter 8; for now, though, let's just say that it's a great way to get full Internet connectivity by means of an ordinary telephone line connection and a high-speed modem.)

Part Three: Mastering Graphical Browsers

Sure, Mosaic is easy to use. You just click hyperlinks. But wait 'til you get lost!

Mastering the Web requires pushing your knowledge of graphical browsers to the maximum. In Part Three, "Browsing the Web," you'll learn how to make full use of history lists, hotlists and bookmarks, memory caches, helper programs, and other advanced features of the best browsers.

Unlike any other book on the World Wide Web, this book documents commands and procedures for all of the most popular browsers: Netscape version 1.0 for Macintosh and Microsoft Windows, NCSA Mosaic for Microsoft Windows version 2.0a8, Enhanced NCSA Mosaic for Microsoft Windows version 1.1, and NetManage's WebSurfer.

If you don't have a graphical browser, this book comes with WebSurfer, which works with the Chameleon software that is also included. Although not as full-featured as Netscape or NCSA Mosaic, WebSurfer is a good graphical browser. What's more, it has some special features that make it ideal for use with systems connected to the Web by means of SLIP or PPP. Note, though, that WebSurfer will only work if you use the Chameleon software to connect to the Internet.

Part Four: Learning the Secrets of Finding Information on the Web

Using the Web effectively means more than just clicking around. It also requires knowing how to use the Web's facilities for information location and retrieval. Part Four, "Advanced Strategies for Web Navigation," three valuable chapters that present a comprehensive strategy for Web information retrieval, including using network starting points, subject trees, and search engines. I'll guarantee that you won't find better coverage of these subjects anywhere else—they're based on more than a decade of personal experience and research in the tools and techniques of computerized information retrieval.

Part Five: Learning How to Evaluate the Web's Offerings

The Web's a democratic medium, which means, unfortunately, that you'll find trash as well as treasures. In Part Five, "Exploring the Web," you'll find reviews of dozens of popular Web sites. Each review explains what's cool and what's clunky about an individual Web offering, allowing you to critically evaluate Web sites on your own. You'll see what works and what doesn't, and you'll know how to identify the best of the Web (and avoid the worst).

Part Six: Creating Your Own Web Documents

Once you've learned how to use your browser, navigate the Web, locate hidden information, and evaluate Web offerings, you're an expert Web user. But there's more. To customize your browser and make it your own, you can use this book's SmartPages, a series of default home pages in a variety of areas. You'll find the SmartPages on the disk included with this book. Part Six, "Making the Web Your Own," begins with an exploration of the SmartPages offerings.

By learning the HyperText Markup Language (HTML), you can add to your mastery by creating your own Web pages. If you've never done any computer programming, this might sound scary—but HTML is easy—it isn't even a programming language. Anyone can learn to create a new default home page in short order, and you'll find a complete, step-by-step tutorial in Part Six. In just a few hours, you'll learn how to create a page containing just the hyperlinks you want, that will automatically appear every time you start your browser.

To become a Web information provider, you must install and configure a Web *server*. A Web server is a computer running a program that accepts a browser's information requests, locates the desired document, and sends it out over the Internet. Until recently, obtaining and installing a Web server was an ordeal requiring substantial experience and programming expertise. But no longer. Included on

KEY TERM

the disk packaged with this book is an HTML document that accesses WinHTTPD for Microsoft Windows, a "point-and-click" Web server software package for Windows 3.1 and Windows for Workgroups 3.11 systems. It takes about five minutes to install WinHTTPD, and once you've done so, you can make your Web documents available for others! (*Note*: to create a Web server, you'll need a permanent Internet address with a unique IP address. To find out whether your connection qualifies, check with your Internet service provider; they can arrange the correct connection if you don't already have it.)

Part Seven: Understanding Web Issues and Futures

The World Wide Web is providing the foundation for a global information system, but it faces a number of challenges, including the inefficiency of the underlying Web protocols and the need for secure, encrypted communication of sensitive data (such as credit card information). Part Seven, "Web Horizons," will help you understand where the Web's headed.

A GUIDE TO THIS BOOK'S ICONS

To help you make efficient use of this book, you'll find icons that flag passages of special interest. Here's a guide:

HOME PAGE Beginners, look here for information that helps you get oriented.

KEY TERM Here's an important term, fully defined in plain English.

EXCELLENT A Web feature that's especially useful, cool, or well-conceived, such as WebSurfer's individual document cache capabilities. (This is a really great feature for people accessing the Web via modem.)

AWFUL Something that's unnecessarily difficult, cumbersome, boring, or dreadful, such as WebSurfer's inability to run with any TCP/IP package other than NetManage's.

**WISH
LIST**

Features or capabilities that the Web doesn't have but needs—developers, are you listening? For example, it would be very nice if browsers could incorporate sound and video decoding software so we wouldn't have to hassle with those shareware helper programs.

HOT TIP

Here's a tip that will help you increase your enjoyment and use of the Web.

**WEB
SECRET**

Little-known facts about the World Wide Web, exposed and explained.

🕷WEBMASTER

Information of interest to anyone thinking about setting up a Web server or putting information out on the Web.

**USEFUL
RESOURCE**

Storehouses of Web-related resources, such as icons, shareware programs, documents, tips and tricks, and more.

WHAT'S ON THE DISK?

Lots of books come with disks—and to be honest, they're not often worth the effort of seeing what's on them. That's why we've worked very hard to make sure that this book's disk is a very special one, as I think you'll agree. The 1.44 MB (IBM format) disk contains everything you need to get connected to the Web, to browse the Web, to attain mastery in Web navigation, and to create your own HTML documents. Here's what's included:

- **Internet Chameleon**. Contained in the disk is a selection from NetManage's award-winning Internet software, including everything you need to connect a Microsoft Windows computer to the Internet by means of a high-speed modem. Check out Appendix A for complete installation instructions, including all the information you need to establish a SLIP or PPP connection to an Internet service provider.

- **WebSurfer**. A graphical browser that's very similar to Mosaic and Netscape, this program stems from NetManage, the makers of Internet Chameleon, and is designed to work with their software, If you connect to the Internet with the Chameleon software included with this book, you're ready to browse the Web!

- **SmartPages**. Here's a mini-web that you can use as your browser's default home page, in place of the one that's preconfigured to display when you launch your browser. Instead of just one page, there are more than a dozen, and each is chock-full of useful and interesting Web sites for you to visit. And because they're stored on your computer, they load much faster than they would if you had to retrieve them from the network.

- **The Generic Web**. Want to put your own documents on the Web? Here's a very valuable set of linked, generic Web documents, which you can customize to create an impressive Web site in very short order. Everything's included—the HTML code, the in-line graphics, the study and work involved to make sure that these Web pages live up to the highest Web standards. With The Generic Web to help you, you'll establish your Web presence in short order.

THE OFFICIAL WORLD WIDE WEB BIBLE WEB SITE

Books go out of date, and that's particularly true of books about the World Wide Web! For the latest information, corrections, updates, and news about the Web, designed specifically for readers of this book, check out The Official World Wide Web Bible Web Site, at the following URL:

http://watt.seas.virginia.edu/~bp/wwwb.html

See you on the Web!

PART 1:
GETTING INTO THE WEB

CHAPTER 1

Understanding Hypermedia

The human mind...operates by association. With one item in its grasp, it snaps instantly to the next that is suggested by the association of thoughts...Man can not hope to duplicate this mental process artificially, but he certainly ought to be able to learn from it...[and] it should be possible to beat the mind decisively in regard to the permanence and clarity of items resurrected from storage...Consider a future device for individual use...any item may be caused at will to select immediately and automatically another....Wholly new forms of encyclopedias will appear, ready-made with a mesh of associative trails running through them.   —Vannevar Bush (1945)

The Word Wide Web marries two very new technologies—hypermedia plus the global computer nexus known as the Internet. This chapter introduces the first of these technologies, hypermedia. The next chapter introduces the Internet and shows how the marriage of hypermedia and Internet technologies produces the Web.

Hypermedia is a multimedia version of *hypertext*, a nonlinear method of viewing textual information. *Multimedia* refers to the use of graphics, sound, and video to supplement a texts meaning. The "nonlinear" part means that you can read the text in any order you wish. To do so, you use boldfaced or underlined "hot spots," called *links*, to jump from place to place (see Figure 1.1). In the sections to follow, you'll learn more about this new form of non-sequential writing—and the way it's the ideal information-retrieval system for the Web.

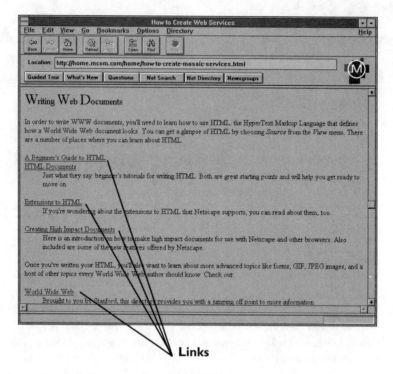

Links

Figure 1.1 Hyperlinks

What does the "hyper" in "hypertext" mean? Here's the scoop. Nineteenth-century German mathematician Felix Christian Klein (1849–1925) conceived a geometry of what he called "hyperbolick space"—a space with many more dimensions than the four we're used to (height, width, depth, and time). Almost impossible to conceptualize, hyperspace **WEB SECRET** nevertheless has known mathematical properties, which are now well understood. A century later, in 1967, computer visionary Ted Nelson did what many of history's greatest inventors have done: He transferred a known concept—here, hyperspace—to a new subject: text. Hypertext, in Nelson's view, is the *hyperspace of a text:* A hypertext is a multidimensional expansion of the concepts implicit in a text. The conceptual hyperspace of this paragraph would include the following dimensions (minimally): **Klein's hyperbolic space**, the **limits of human perception** that make it difficult to conceptualize more than four dimensions, the **known mathematical properties of hyperspace**, Ted **Nelson**'s life and career, Nelson's **definition of hypertext**, and **this list of concepts**. In hypertext, separate documents, linked to all the others, would explore each of these concepts.

WHAT IS HYPERTEXT? AN EXAMPLE

When you read an ordinary document, like this one, you read it sequentially, from the beginning to the end. There's nothing wrong with this idea, but it does cause some problems. As a writer, I'm constantly fighting the temptation to bring in all kinds of interesting side information. But, I have to resist this temptation. As a reader, you're trying to understand the ideas, and I've got to stick to the point to help you do this. To be sure, I can insert a cross-reference, like this one: "See below for more information on **hypermedia**"—but probably very few people will thumb through the book in search of the related passage. That takes a dedicated reader.

Enter the computer, which makes possible all kinds of things that print media can't—like hypertext. In a hypertext document, you can use a computer's mouse to click boldfaced or underlined words or phrases called *hyperlinks*. Usually boldfaced or underlined so that you can distinguish them from the surrounding text, links are basically just computer-activated cross-references. When you click the mouse button on a link, a new page appears, containing information about the topic you just clicked. You can then go back to the place you started, or you can continue exploring other links, as you please.

KEY TERM

It's difficult to convey the hypertext concept in a book, but here's an attempt. Suppose you're reading a hypertext document on your computer screen:

HOME PAGE

> North Carolina's Outer Banks, one of the state's premier tourist destinations, are **barrier islands.** Measuring only 7 to 12 feet above sea level, the islands are sometimes overwashed during violent storms, such as the **Halloween Storm** of 1991. In calmer weather, visitors flock to the Outer Banks to take advantage of its many **recreational opportunities.**

If you click **barrier islands**, here's what you see:

> A **barrier island** is a land form made up entirely of sand, without any underlying anchor of rock. Lacking such an anchor, barrier islands are subject to change by the forces of wind and sea. North America's most striking barrier islands are found in North Carolina's **Outer Banks.**

Clicking **Outer Banks** returns you to the original document. If you click **recreational opportunities**, you see the following:

> Vacationers love the Outer Banks for its fine **beaches**, excellent seafood **dining**, rich **history**, abundant **wildlife**, and quaint little **towns** with great **shopping.**

If you wished to continue exploring, you could click **Halloween Storm** to learn more about this destructive 1991 storm and its effect on the Outer Banks—or you could click any of the other links, and find out about all the fun things you can do there!

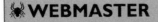

🕷 **WEBMASTER**

Should a hypertext system have a hierarchical structure? The Outer Banks document just described seems to have such a structure, as follows:

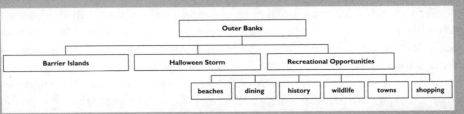

KEY TERM

Hypertext visionary Ted Nelson urges hypertext authors to avoid the hierarchy hang-up. "Hierarchies [are] false," Nelson asserts, "they are oversimplifications of reality." In place of a rigid hierarchical structure, Nelson advocates a *semantic net*, in which there are multiple connections and pathways among the topics.

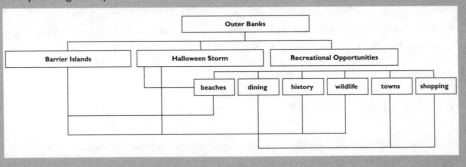

In a semantic net, the goal is to *multiply the interconnectedness* of the linked documents, not to force the information into a rigid model. That's the way the world is, Nelson argues—interconnected in ways that don't conform to rigid, linear models. Hypertext should reflect the disorganization and multiplicity of the world—even if that means creating links that end in odd cul-de-sacs and pathways that never get you back to the beginning point.

WHAT'S THE POINT OF HYPERTEXT?

Freedom. Hypertext frees you to read a document the way you want, instead of the way imposed upon you by the authors. If you really need more information on a subject, you can go get it—hypertext makes it easy. If you don't need the information, you can skip it. Hypertext doesn't fill up the text with verbose cross-references such as "For more information on veeblefitzers, see the discussion and commentary in Chapter 3, as well as the analysis in Chapter 9, and the definition in the Glossary."

HOME PAGE

Hypertext also encourages writers to think of new ways to organize their information. For starters, you don't throw tons of text at the readers—you give them a concise, one-screen page that provides a starting point for exploration.

The Outer Banks

North Carolina's Outer Banks, one of the state's premier tourist destinations, are **barrier islands**. Measuring only 7 to 12 feet above sea level, the islands are sometimes overwashed during violent storms, such as the **Halloween Storm** of 1991. In calmer weather, visitors flock to the Outer Banks to take advantage of its many **recreational opportunities**.

See what I mean by freedom? If you couldn't care less about the island's geology, you can go directly to "recreational opportunities" without having to wade through a long spiel about shifting sands.

EXCELLENT

Recreational Opportunities in the Outer Banks

Vacationers love the Outer Banks for its fine **beaches**, excellent seafood **dining**, rich **history**, abundant **wildlife**, and quaint little **towns** with great **shopping**.

Hungry? Let's click **dining**.

Fine Seafood Dining

The Outer Banks features dozens of fine restaurants specializing in seafood. Everywhere, you can find standard seafood entrees, either boiled or fried. But don't miss some Outer Banks specialties, such as **She-crab soup**, **soft shell crabs** (a springtime specialty), and **Outer Banks style clam chowder**.

HYPERTEXT TALK: BASIC TERMS

Now that you're familiar with the basics, you'll find it useful to go over some basic terms, which are bandied about in Web talk as if everyone knew just what they mean.

 KEY TERMS

Hypermedia refers to a hypertext system that includes sounds, graphics, animations, and video as well as text. The Web is a hypermedia system.

Nodes are the basic elements of a hypertext or hypermedia system. A node is simply one of the interconnected items. It could be a document, a picture, a sound, a movie, a database item, a pop-up box that contains clarifying information such as a definition or an animation. Most people don't have any idea what "node" means, though, so it's simpler just to use the term "document" instead.

Links (also called hyperlinks) provide the means by which you can go from one node to the next. When you activate a link, the computer makes a "jump through hyperspace" to the document to which the link is connected. The link might be embedded in the text, in which case it's indicated by some special formatting (a distinctive color, underlining, or boldface—or all three). It might also be embedded in a graphic or an on-screen button.

A hypertext system's **home page** is its Grand Central Station—the place you start your hypertext journey. You can take journeys from the home page, and return to it if you get lost.

Browsing refers to the process by which you read a hypertext document. As the term implies, this isn't necessarily a disciplined, organized process—you just click on a link, and away you go. Hope you can find your way back!

Navigation is more organized than browsing. Here, you use tools such as hotlists (a list of frequently accessed, favorite documents) that enable you to find your way through the hypertext system without getting lost. A **path history** list can help you retrace your steps. You also use searching tools that enable you to find documents of interest.

A **browser** is a computer program that helps you browse a hypertext system—and if it's any good, it will offer you lots of navigation tools.

Authoring refers to the process of creating hypertext documents. It's lots of fun and quite easy. This book introduces authoring as well as browsing and navigation.

LOST IN HYPERSPACE

Hypertext is useful and fun, but there *is* a down side. The very fact that a good hypertext system is nonlinear means that it's easy to get lost. The two most common exclamations of beginning hypertext users are "Wow, this is neat," followed by "Where am I?"

AWFUL

A well-designed hypertext system has many interconnections—and that can prove confusing. If you tried to construct your own map of the interconnections, you'd wind up with something that looks like a bowl of spaghetti! In fact, the term *spaghetti layout* is used, chidingly, to describe hypertext systems that don't provide the user with a means to conceptualize the system of linked documents.

Are there cures for that "lost in hyperspace" feeling? Well-designed hypertext systems help people navigate by providing *navigation buttons*, such as those shown in Figure 1.2. Also very useful is the use of a familiar metaphor to organize the documents. For example, a hypertext "library" could be organized like a real library, with a "card catalog," "reference desk," "newspaper room," "periodicals room," and other familiar features. In hypertext talk, the use of such a metaphor as an organizing principle is called a *museum view*.

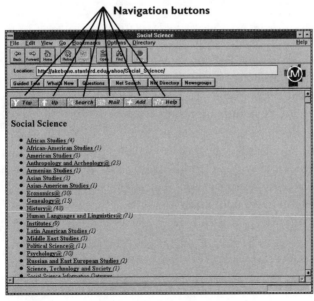

Figure 1.2 *Navigation buttons*

EXCELLENT

In Figure 1.3, you see a museum view layout of the Information Technology Communication server at the University of Virginia. A clickable organization chart provides a metaphor for browsing for information about ITC people.

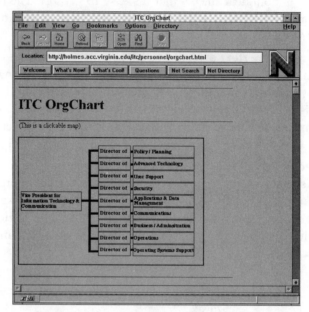

Figure 1.3 *Museum view layout (University of Virginia)*

Less helpful is the attempt made by some hypertext authors to let the reader see the spaghetti—er, the map (see Figure 1.4). Compare this map to one that uses a metaphor with which the reader is familiar. In Figure 1.5, for example, you see the remarkable Tree of Life, which organizes massive amounts of biological information according to the principles of biological classification.

One thing's certain—authoring a set of related hypertext documents is a very different matter from authoring a traditional, linear document. Given that most of the hypertext authors contributing to the Web have devoted precious little thought to easing the readers' navigational burden, you can expect to get lost pretty often. In Part III of this book, though, you'll find plenty of strategies for finding your way again.

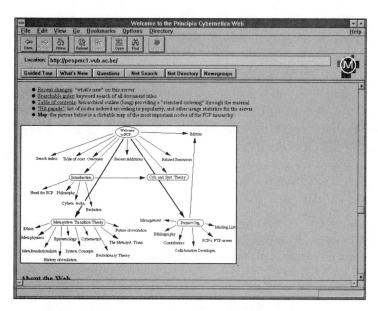

Figure 1.4 *Clickable map of hypertext links (Principia Cybernetica)*

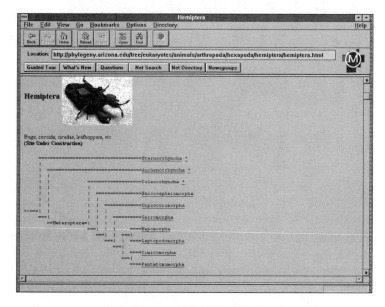

Figure 1.5 *The Tree of Life*

HYPERTEXT APPLICATIONS

How is hypertext best applied? Because hypertext is a nonsequential medium, it's best used for documents that are inherently nonsequential. Stories, which don't make sense unless you follow the plot sequence, are not a good bet. But don't rule fiction out—there are plenty of experiments going on right now with hypertext-based interactive fiction. Fiction aside, though, there are plenty of nonsequential document types, such as the following.

- **Reference Works.** Any encyclopedia article has extensive cross-references to other such articles, but it's a pain to flip to another page manually. A hypertext encyclopedia does the flipping automatically. Figure 1.6 shows a page from the Free On-Line Dictionary of Computing (FOLDOC), with plenty of links to other encyclopedia articles as well as resources outside the encyclopedia.

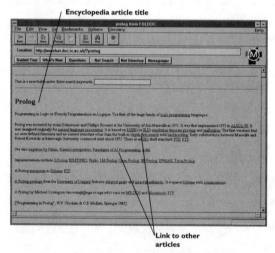

Figure 1.6 *Reference work (encyclopedia)*

- **Catalogs and Resource Guides.** Printed catalogs are expensive, and worse, they consume many resources. In the future, on-line hypertext catalogs will replace their printed predecessors—and you'll order on-line, too. Figure 1.7 shows the on-line hypertext catalog of Harrington's of Vermont. Other catalog and resource guide possibilities: university course listings, recipes, employment listings, personal ads, government documents, databases of college fellowships, telephone directories, yellow pages, showcases of travel information—and much more.

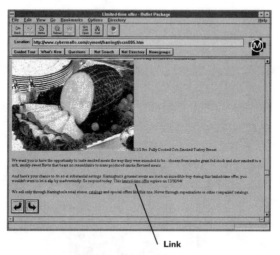

Link

Figure 1.7 Product catalog

- **Computer-Aided Instruction.** Hypertext systems can aid instruction by showing the relationships among subjects. In the Virtual Frog Dissection Kit, users see a graphic representation of a frog (Figure 1.8). After clicking on an organ, the user sees a description of the organ and its function.

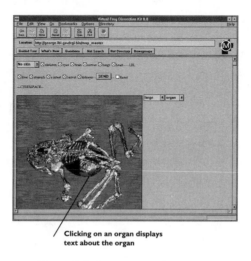

Clicking on an organ displays
text about the organ

Figure 1.8 Computer-aided instruction

- **Museum Exhibits.** If you can't travel to a distant museum, you can visit it on the Web! Hypertext techniques enable browsers to pick pathways through the exhibits as they please. Figure 1.9 shows the home page of the Krannert Art Museum, on the campus of the University of Illinois, Urbana-Champaign.

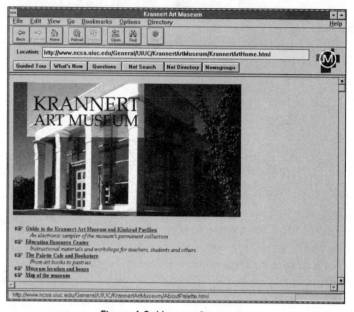

Figure 1.9 *Hypermedia museum*

EXCELLENT

- **Clickable Maps.** In a hypertext map, clicking one part of the map brings up a more detailed view of a particular seciton. Perhaps the most amazing exploration to date of this possibility is WebWorld, which lets you "beam down" to a world of Internet sites (see Figure 1.10). More prosaic examples include a clickable map of a city's tourist attractions and the office layout of big corporations' headquarters.

Figure 1.10 WebWorld

A GLOBAL HYPERTEXT MASS MEDIUM

Let your imagination run wild for a minute: What would a global hypertext mass medium be like? Imagine a global computer network, that would allow hypertext authors to write links that access documents stored on other computers. There'd be no question of reinventing the wheel—if somebody had already created a great frog dissection tutorial, and made it available on the system, your document could include a link to that tutorial. As thousands and then millions of people contribute their knowledge and resources to the emerging medium, it grows at a fantastic pace.

If this sounds like science fiction, you're wrong. This global hypertext mass medium already exists! It's the World Wide Web. In the next chapter, you'll learn how hypermedia concepts and Internet linkages have produced humanity's fastest-growing communications medium.

SUMMARY

Hypertext is a non-sequential medium in which document "chunks" are connected by hyperlinks. Browsing software enables you to read the document in the sequence you want. Not all documents are equally suited to hypertext; reference works, catalogs, and instructional texts are examples of documents that work well in the hypertext medium. Navigation can be a challenge unless the author provides navigation buttons, or other navigation clues.

FROM HERE

- New to the Internet? You'll find an introduction in Chapter 2.
- Like to know more about how multimedia works in the hypermedia environment? See Chapter 3.
- Take a look at the Web! See Chapter 4.

CHAPTER 2

Introducing the Internet

For 20 years, we have been hearing about the global village, a futuristic vision of how we will live in a wired world with instantaneous communication. Over the last two years, something remarkable has happened: The global village has become a reality. —Carl Malamud

If hypermedia is so great, why didn't hypermedia applications pop up everywhere, prior to the Web's arrival? The answer is simple: Creating a rich hypermedia system is too much work to do all by yourself. As this chapter explains, the amazing thing about the World Wide Web is that it enables *you* to create hypermedia documents that access *other peoples'* hypermedia documents, thus avoiding the common problem of reinventing the wheel. The result is an exponential explosion in information productivity.

An example should help to clarify the Web's significance. I teach ethics to engineering students, and it's an important job. To do it correctly, I need in-depth case studies. Most of the ones published in books or journals aren't useful for one reason or another—I need cases specifically written for undergraduate students. Until the Web came along, I thought I'd have to write them myself. But other engineering educators have been wrestling with the same problem, and they've put some great cases on the Web. All I have to do is create a one-page Web document for my students (and anyone else who'd be interested)—a document that contains hyperlinks to the contributions others have made!

How is this possible? The quick answer: The Internet. The marriage between hypermedia concepts and Internet connectivity is creating a global hypermedia system, and it's going to change the world. Sure, that's been said before, but most

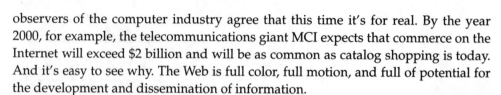

observers of the computer industry agree that this time it's for real. By the year 2000, for example, the telecommunications giant MCI expects that commerce on the Internet will exceed $2 billion and will be as common as catalog shopping is today. And it's easy to see why. The Web is full color, full motion, and full of potential for the development and dissemination of information.

HOME PAGE

This chapter introduces the Internet technology and Web protocols that make the emerging global hypermedium possible. It begins with an introduction to the Internet and continues with a survey of Internet resource discovery tools and an introduction to the *client-server model* that underlies Web transactions. Next, the chapter explains the two most fundamental technical concepts that underlie the Web: the HTTP protocol and the HTML programming language.

KEY TERM

Is there a simple way to sum up this chapter's basic points? You bet. The Internet is a network of dissimilar networks, and its key achievement is *interoperability*—the ability to operate a computer that may be as many as thousands of miles away and made by a completely different manufacturer than the one you're using. And the key achievement of the Web is the marriage of hypertext links and interoperability. In short, when you access a Web link, your Web browser originates a message that traverses the Internet, contacts a distant computer, and says, "Show me this document." As you browse the Web, you can access computers all over the world—and it's all totally automatic.

WHAT'S SO COOL ABOUT THE INTERNET?

I'm sure you've heard about the Internet but, like many people, you may not exactly grasp what it's all about. For starters, it's not a network. Rather, it's a way of linking networks together so that all kinds of computers can work together and exchange data, even if they're dissimilar from an electronic standpoint. This is called *interoperability*.

Arthur C. Clarke once commented that any sufficiently advanced technology is indistinguishable from magic—and using the Web, I'm convinced he's right. Interoperability is truly an amazing thing. Sitting here at my desk in Earlysville, Virginia, looking out at the horses grazing in the fields of Wakefield Farm, I'm connected to computers in Los Gatos (California), Trondheim (Norway), Paris (France), and Kyoto (Japan). And I'm sending requests for information that these computers are happy to answer—even though I'm "talking" to a Sun workstation, a DEC minicomputer, an overworked Windows NT system, and who knows what else.

Is interoperability such a big deal? You've probably already noticed that computers made by different manufacturers work in different ways. If you've ever tried to get data from a Macintosh disk into an IBM PC, you'll appreciate the difficulties involved. But the computer scientists who created the Internet's predecessor, called ARPANET, solved the problems of linking dissimilar networks very handily by creating the *Internet protocols*.

Protocols are communication standards for exchanging data so that different networks can work with it. If you prepare data according to the Internet protocols, you can send it out over networks of worldwide scope, and the computer on the receiving end, no matter whether it's a Macintosh or an IBM mainframe, can receive it, display it, and print it. That's the capability that makes Internet electronic mail so popular.

KEY TERM

But the Internet protocols let you do something even more amazing. You can actually control a distant computer, making it do things like cough up the data you want. For example, you can tell a computer that's 5,000 miles away to do the following: "Look for those cool photos of the comet Shoemaker-Levy 9 striking Jupiter, would you, and zap them over here to me." Of course, this only works if the people running that distant computer agree to make their resources, such as files and programs, publicly available for browsers-at-a-distance. But it's part of the Internet's spirit to share, and such resources are widely available.

TOOLS FOR INTERNET USE: CLIENT PROGRAMS

To make data on distant computers more accessible, Internet software tools called *clients* have been developed. These tools are programs that enable ordinary people to access distant computers and obtain files and other resources.

Here's a quick overview of the clients that preceded the World Wide Web:

- **Telnet**. This utility program lets you control a remote computer somewhere else on the Internet just as if you were sitting in front of it. You can launch programs and move or copy files (if you have the necessary access privileges). Telnet allows you to look at the file directories on another computer, which is why I group Telnet under "resource discovery tools. However, Telnet is not an efficient tool for hunting for information. More commonly, Telnet is used to access information services of various kinds, such as the card catalogs of major university libraries throughout the world.

- **FTP**. This program lets you send and receive files from one computer to another on the Internet. It also has some fairly crude capabilities for browsing file directories, but again, it isn't much fun to find resources this way unless you know exactly what you're looking for.

- **Archie**. This program tells you where copies of a given file are located, as long as you know all or part of the file's name. Once you find out where the files are located, you can get them with FTP.

- **Gopher**. A major improvement over Telnet, FTP, and Archie, Gopher lets you navigate the Internet via menus. You can search for resources using a Gopher utility called Veronica.

- **WAIS**. If people prepare data in the form of a certain kind of database, WAIS can find all the available databases, connect you to the one you want, search the database for you, and retrieve information.

**KEY
TERM**

Why are these programs called clients? A client is a program that runs on your computer but knows how to contact other programs on other computers that make resources available, such as text files, programs, or information in a database. The programs on the other computers are called *servers*. That's why the Internet resource discovery tools are often described as following the *client-server model*.

The term "client-server" is a little confusing because it plays fast and loose with the everyday meaning of these terms, but think of it this way. The client is your program, which works on your behalf. You tell it, "Client, I need some information." Obediently, the client goes hunting for the information by contacting different servers. Once the client finds the information, it is retrieved for you. It would be nice if computer people could come up with better terms for these two kinds of programs, but when asked for an alternate description for client, they suggested "agent." Better stick with client-server—at least lots of people have had to go through the painful ordeal of figuring out what they mean by this.

EXCELLENT

The client-server model has many advantages for computer networks. Because the client runs on your computer, it's your computer, and not the poor computer that everyone's trying to access, that does most of the processing. This reduces the drain on network resources when thousands (or even millions) of people are trying to access network-based information. The server doesn't have to do much work beyond spitting out a specific piece of information in response to each client's request, and then spitting out the next one. (A popular Web server in Pittsburgh receives a new client request about every ten seconds.)

A PRETTY PICTURE INDEED (GRAPHICAL CLIENTS)

There's no reason that clients can't be beautiful and easy to use as well as clever. In the old days (10 years ago!), almost everyone was using clients that ran on clunky old UNIX minicomputers with ASCII text displays. But then wonderful new UNIX workstations came along, with beautiful color graphics displays. Computer genius- es thought, "Hey! Why can't I create a client that looks nice?" Since the client runs on your own computer, it should, ideally, be able to take full advantage of everything your computer can do, like display fonts and detailed color graphics, or even play sounds and show video clips. Thus the GUI client ("gooey client") was born. GUI is short for *graphical user interface,* a method of relating to the computer using a mouse, pull-down menu, windows, and graphical images call *icons.*

KEY TERM

GUI clients are fully consistent with the Internet ideal of allowing dissimilar computers to communicate. As long as the actual data that's exchanged conforms to established Internet standards (protocols), the client can display the data any way it chooses. So why not create a client program that works the same way that your other applications do? A Macintosh user can use a client that looks and responds just like a Macintosh application, while a Windows user can use a client that works just like other Windows applications. Yet, the two can exchange text, graphics, sounds, and video through the Internet. The concept of the GUI client is the second of the two concepts that underlie the Web in general, and GUI-based browsers such as Mosaic and Netscape in particular, as you'll see in the following section.

PUTTING IT ALL TOGETHER, OR, VOILÁ!

OK, we've got two unrelated concepts—hypermedia, on the one hand, and the GUI Internet client on the other. Each of these concepts has a problem.

- **Hypermedia.** Creating a really rich hypermedia document is a huge job; you need tons of links, files, graphics, sounds, and video clips—too much for one person to collect in one place. Various ill-fated attempts to create rich hyper- media systems housed a single computer have fizzled out due to the high cost and amount of work involved.

- **GUI clients.** All the fonts, graphics, and colors in the world don't mean much if you still haven't insulated the user from the nuts-and-bolts mechan- ics of searching the Internet—that is, specifying exactly which computer to go to and exactly where a given file is located.

Now it's genius time. Tim Berners-Lee, a computer programmer working at the European Laboratory for Particle Physics (CERN), conceived of the single, brilliant idea that underlies the World Wide Web: Make a hypertext document, just like any other hypertext document, but take each hyperlink and place the specific information about where the referenced document is located on the Internet "under" the hyperlinked term. So if you're reading a Web document, and you click a hyperlinked word like CERN, the client reacts: "Hm, the user just clicked CERN. Let's see, I'm supposed to FTP to cern.info.ch and look for the file cern.info in the directory /WWW/info/CERN. OK, got it, here it is."

If you love computer terminology, here's how the Web is described: It's a *distributed hypermedia system*. The "distributed" part holds the key. Information consumers can also be information producers, and they can do this at the point of consumption (their own client computers can become servers, in other words). Just look at how brilliant this idea is—how it solves the problems both of hypermedia and GUI clients in one stroke:

KEY TERM

- People all over the world can create hypermedia documents and make them accessible to others browsing the Web. You don't have to cram all the data on one computer, and millions of people can participate.

- When you're using a Web client program, you don't have to worry about where a specific resource is located—just click the anchor. Information associated with it tells your client program where to hunt down the requested resource. All this takes place transparently, without your being aware of it. You just see a succession of beautiful documents on-screen. You may not realize that you started out in Charlottesville, went to Paris, stopped briefly in Kyoto, spent some time in San Francisco, and returned back home!

In sum, the World Wide Web is a worldwide distributed hypermedia system that uses GUI clients to hide the complexities of accessing distant computer resources. Simple enough once you know the background!

That's the basic idea of the Web. In the rest of this chapter, you'll learn some terms, such as HTTP, URL, and HTML, that pop up often in the Web and Mosaic contexts. Don't let these terms scare you, though—once you've understood the basic concepts of the Web, these secondary concepts are easy to grasp.

MAKING THE WEB WORK: THE HTTP PROTOCOL

To make dissimilar computers communicate with each other, the Internet uses standards called protocols. Web-related communication is governed by the *HyperText Transport Protocol* (*HTTP*).

KEY TERM

You don't need to know much about HTTP to use Mosaic and the Web effectively, since the purpose of a GUI client like Mosaic is to hide the internal complexities of what the linked computers are actually doing. All you really need to know about HTTP is that it defines the format for *Universal Resource Locators (URL)*.

A Universal Resource Locator (URL) is a statement, written according to strict rules of syntax, that specifies where a Web resource can be found. (URL, incidentally, is pronounced "you are ell"—I haven't heard anyone say "Earl" as yet, but I fear this is coming.) Anyway, a URL is what's buried "under" the anchors in Web documents.

Do you really need to know anything about URLs? Granted, Mosaic hides the specifics of logging on to other computers to retrieve resources. But as you'll soon find, you sometimes have to do a lot of clicking and navigating to get to the document you want. Sometimes it's easier just to hold your nose and type the URL directly. (You only have to do this once, as you can save the information for the next time you want to access that data.) Plus, every time you access a link, a graphical Web browser displays the URL that it's using, as shown in Figure 2.1. Understanding a little about URLs—enough to type one correctly, for example—can help save you time and give you important clues about what your browser is doing.

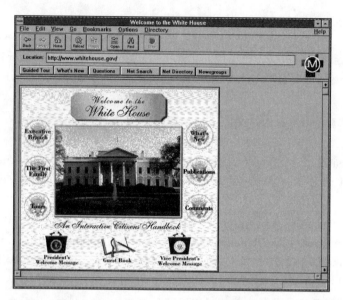

Figure 2.1 White House URL displayed by graphical Web browser (Netscape)

Don't let URLs put you off. A URL isn't any more complicated than the path statements you've probably seen in DOS commands, such as the following:

word c:\docs\poems\love.doc

This DOS command says, "Start the program called Word, and open the file on the C drive named LOVE.DOC in the directory \docs\poems." (A directory is a special section of a computer disk that's set aside for storing a particular kind of information—here, bad poetry.)

A URL is almost exactly the same kind of statement, except that it begins by saying which protocol to use. In Figure 2.1, the URL begins with the following:

http://

This part tells Mosaic that the resource should be accessed using the HTTP protocol for Web documents.

The second part of the URL specifies the name of the particular computer to be accessed—a computer somewhere on the Internet. In Figure 2.1, the computer in question is the following:

www.whitehouse.gov/

The third part of the URL, if there is one, specifies the name of the directory in which the resource is located, as well as the file name to be accessed:

http://www.whitehouse.gov/White_House/Family/html/First_Family.html

The file to which this URL refers is **First_Family.html**, and it's located in the directory **/White_House/Family/html/**. If you're used to DOS, note that UNIX uses forward slashes for directory names, while DOS uses backward slashes.

Here's another example of a URL (Netscape's home page):

http://home.mcom.com/home/welcome.html

This says, "Using HTTP, let's go to the computer called home.mcom.com, open the directory **/home/**, and access the document **welcome.html**.

The only time you'll need to use URLs is when you have to type one directly. This doesn't happen often—in Web documents, URLs appear as hyperlinks, which you can just click. So when do you need to type a URL? When you want to try a URL that you read about in an "old-fashioned," print-based book or magazine.

HOME PAGE

HTML

OK, one last acronym, and we're done. Another term that you'll run across frequently in the Web context is *HyperText Markup Language* (HTML). Basically, this is a standard for adding funny-looking symbols to documents so that, when accessed by Mosaic or any other HTML-capable viewer, they look good on-screen. Another thing that HTML does is hide those URLs so that you can't see them (all you see is the boldfaced or underlined anchor).

KEY TERM

You don't have to learn HTML to browse the Web. HTML is required only if you want to put your own documents on the Web. It's not difficult to learn the little HTML that's needed to do this.

HOME PAGE

HTML is a hypertext variant of *Standard Generalized Markup Language* (SGML), which deserves a few words. Basically, a *generalized markup language* is a way of marking a document's parts so that the computer can tell what they are. For example, you use a code to mark a title so that it's displayed as a title. Now the interesting thing about a generalized markup language is that it doesn't say exactly

KEY TERM

how the title should look—it just marks the title as a title. It's up to the client program to define exactly how the title should be displayed. Note that this is very different from the formatting capabilities of word processing programs or page description languages such as PostScript, which tell the printer to display exactly how the document should look.

Here's a quick look at the way it works. The beginning of an HTML document looks like this:

```
<html>
<header>
<title>Design Issues</title>
</head>
</header>
<body>
<h1>
Design Issues
</h1>
<p>
(etc....)
```

Figure 2.2 shows this document when viewed by a graphical Web browser (here, Netscape).

There's more to this document, but you get the idea. HTML gives you a way of "marking up" the document so that your client knows which part of the document is which.

HTML also gives you a way to "bury" URLs under the anchors so that, when the user clicks the anchor, the client goes hunting on the Internet. In Figure 2.2, for example, you see several document titles that appear with underlining, including "The Topology of Web Links." The line that produces this on-screen appearance looks like this in HTML:

```
<a>http://info.cern.ch/hypertext/WWW/DesignIssues/Topology.html</a>
```

Don't worry about what all this means; you don't have to learn HTML to use the Web! I'm just showing this to you so you can see that there's a URL buried in there.

In practice, all you need to know to use the Web is the proper operation of the mouse button!

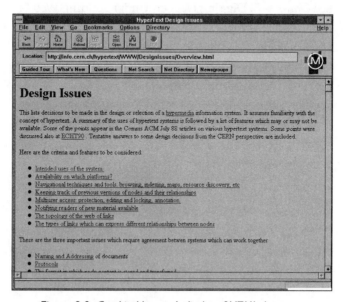

Figure 2.2 *Graphical browser's display of HTML document*

SUMMARY

The World Wide Web brings together two formerly separate ideas—using hypermedia documents for nonsequential access to multimedia information, and using GUI-based client programs capable of scouring a worldwide network in search of information. Because the Web can link dissimilar computers worldwide into a hypermedia network, it permits any Internet user to originate hypertext-based information and make it available to the world Web community. Summarizing the Web's significance, the president of the Massachusetts Institute of Technology, Charles M. Vest, recently described the Web as a significant leap toward a global information society. "The World Wide Web creates world-circling information bridges connecting Europe, America, and the rest of the world. It will mean that whatever brand of computer you use, wherever you live, you can have easy access to information services from all over the world."

FROM HERE...

- For more information on the HyperText Transport Protocol and how it works, see Chapter 5, Digging Deeper: Understanding Web Protocol.

- For an introduction to graphical browsers, see Chapter 9, Introducing Graphical Browsers.

- For a non-programmer's introduction to HTML, see Chapter 27, A Quick Intro to HTML: Creating Your Own Home Page.

CHAPTER 3

Hypermedia:
Engaging the Senses

The design of cyberspace is, after all, the design of another life-world, a parallel universe, offering the intoxicating prospect of actually fulfilling—with a technology very nearly achieved—a dream thousands of years old: the dream of transcending the physical world, fully alive, at will, to dwell in some Beyond—to be empowered or enlightened there, alone or with others, and to return.
—M. Benedikt, *Cyberspace: First Steps*

A hypertext system that includes multimedia resources, such as sounds, pictures, animations, and video, is a *hypermedia* system. One of the most astonishing things about the World Wide Web is its ability to deliver hypermedia across a bewildering variety of computer networks and computer hardware platforms. Whether you're using a Macintosh, Microsoft Windows, or a UNIX system, and whether your computer is connected via the telephone system or hard-wired to a computer network, the Web lets you view multimedia resources along with text.

This chapter introduces the multimedia resources you're likely to encounter on the World Wide Web. As you'll see, these resources are stored in files—generally, *large* files—which must be downloaded to be viewed, played, or heard. And therein lies the down side of multimedia, the lengthy time required to transfer large multimedia files. Still, the Web wouldn't be as engrossing as it is without multimedia. You'll find a comprehensive introduction to multimedia in this chapter, as well as a survey of the graphics, videos, animations, and sounds that you're likely to encounter while surfing the Web.

From a practical standpoint, the information in this chapter will be valuable when it comes to configuring your own Web browser to display multimedia files. For more information on configuring your Web browser, see Chapter 15.

WHAT'S MULTIMEDIA?

The term *multimedia* refers to the use of more than one communication medium to convey a message. Why would anyone want to? Because, as the saying goes, a picture is worth a thousand words. Once you've seen a complex concept illuminated by a vivid animation, you'll surely agree (to see what I mean, check out the Electronic Visualization Laboratory, http://www.ncsa.uiuc.edu/evl/html/gallery.html). If you're curious to know how atoms work, you'll find out.

Hypermedia systems typically incorporate the following multimedia resources:

- **Still Graphics.** Almost all Web documents include still graphics, which most Web browsers can display without the aid of a helper program. Most of the documents you'll see incorporate *in-line graphics*, which are pictures mixed with the text. Most of these pictures are small ones that browsers can display rapidly. Many also include hyperlinks to graphics files, which usually contain larger, more richly detailed pictures.

- **Full-Motion Video.** *Full-motion video* is a filmed or videotaped sequence that produces the illusion of smooth motion. The video consists of a series of still images that flash by at a rate of up to 30 per second, tricking the eye into seeing motion. After still graphics, full-motion video sequences are the most commonly-used form of multimedia on the Web, but you'll need a helper program to view them (see Chapter 13).

- **Animations.** An *animation* is a sequence of still graphic images, produced by an artist, that produces the illusion of motion. Very few Web documents exploit animation, since it is expensive and tedious to produce. To view animations, you'll need a helper program (see Chapter 13).

- **Sound.** Some Web documents contain links that, when clicked, download data containing a recorded sound, but you'll need a helper program to play the sound (see Chapter 13).

For comprehensive information on multimedia, check out the Index to Multimedia Information Sources at http://cui_www.unige.ch/OSG/MultimediaInfo /index.html. This amazing resource contains URLs covering the entire spectrum of multimedia, including:

- Bibliographies
- Commercial Services
- Companies
- Conference Announcements
- Current Events
- Digital Galleries
- Educational
- FAQs
- Hypertext and Hypermedia
- Magazines, Books and Journals
- Media Archives
- Media Delivery Services
- Miscellaneous Information
- Newsgroup Archives
- Publishers
- Ratings and Guides
- Research
- Software
- Standards
- The CD Family

THE BANDWIDTH PROBLEM

Multimedia sounds great, doesn't it? But there's one big problem—the size of multimedia files. Multimedia consumes a huge amount of network *bandwidth* (the amount of data transmission capacity available through a given channel). The chart in Figure 3.1 shows the size of typical computer files, beginning with one page of text—only 1.5 kilobytes or about 1500 characters and ending with a two-minute video clip (800 KB). With an average modem, the video clip could take several minutes to download. Note that the chart uses a logarithmic scale, which downplays the differences—if it weren't for this scale, you wouldn't even be able to see the first column on the graph!

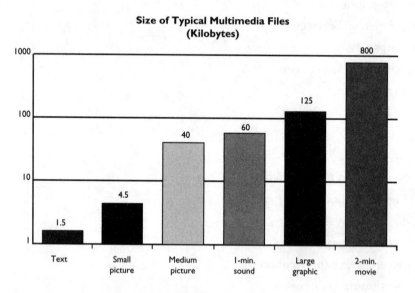

Figure 3.1 *Multimedia files are big!*

Why do computer-readable graphics, sounds, and movies take up so much disk space? Computers are very good at processing digitally-represented words and numbers. However, analog devices like televisions and VCRs can store and play sounds, graphics, and pictures much more efficiently.

The huge size of multimedia files explains why multimedia has been so slow to develop as a networked medium. The multimedia-rich World Wide Web requires high-speed computer networks and high-speed modems, which have only recently come into widespread use. Even so, a common complaint of Web users is that large graphics files take forever to display. For now, don't expect to view huge graphics, watch lengthy movies, or listen to hour-long recorded interviews on the Web; you'll see small pictures and brief videos, and hear sounds lasting a few seconds. However, that's enough to make things interesting.

The demand for faster, ubiquitous networking may usher in the much-heralded "Information Superhighway"—but let's hope they do it right. Cable and telephone companies want to deliver entertainment and charge you for it; they don't care very much about your ability to *originate* information for others to consume. For this reason, many early "Information Superhighway" plans call for more "downstream bandwidth" (data-carrying capacity *to* the information consumer) than "upstream bandwidth" (data-carrying capacity *from* the information producer). But the very heart of the Web is the notion that we can all be information providers as well as consumers! The ideal "Information Superhighway" technology would provide equal amounts of upstream and downstream bandwidth.

WISH LIST

HYPERMEDIA

According to the most widely-accepted definition, a *hypermedia system* is a hypertext system in which some of the links display graphics or play movies or sounds. There's a big difference, though, between well-thought-out hypermedia documents and those that merely employ multimedia links, or an in-line graphic or two, just to liven things up. Ideally, multimedia should enhance a presentation in ways that text just can't.

A great example of *real* hypermedia is found in the Virtual Frog Dissection Kit (see Figure 3.2). Here, there's a perfect marriage of hyperlink concepts and vivid graphics. This isn't just a picture of a frog; it's a hyperlink. To dissect the frog, you use the controls (the list boxes and check boxes) to select the items you want to see, and then you click on the graphic (see Figure 3.3 for the result). If you choose Organ from one of the on-screen list boxes, a one-sentence explanation of an organ's function will be displayed when you click on the organ.

EXCELLENT

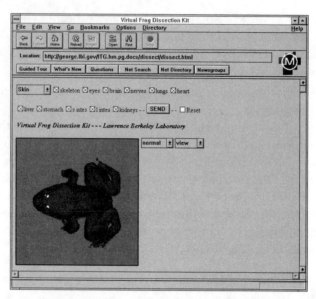

Figure 3.2 *"Real" hypermedia using a graphic as a hyperlink*

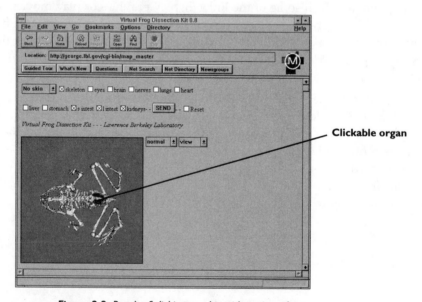

Figure 3.3 *Result of clicking graphic with settings shown*

Navigable resources such as this one are the exception, not the rule. Most Web authors use multimedia as an ancillary to hypertext, adding a picture here or there. But excellent efforts such as the Virtual Frog Dissection Kit show the possibilities.

🕷 WEBMASTER

Looking for examples of creative, "real" hypermedia? Try these sites:

- The **Klingon Language Institute** (http://www.kli.org/) includes a pronunciation guide to the Klingon language. Click on a transliterated letter of the Klingon alphabet, such as *ch*, to hear the correct pronunciation.

- Brigitte Jellinek's **Guest Book** is (http://www.cosy.sbg.ac.at/rec /guestbook/World.html a bit of web wizardry from the Mage of Salzburg (see Figure 3.4).

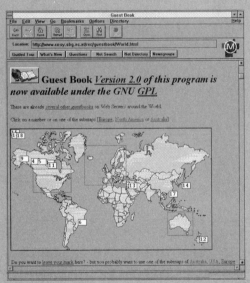

Figure 3.4 *Brigitte Jellinek's Guest Book*

- **Tarot** (http://cad.ucla.edu/repository/useful/tarot.html) contains an online tarot card reading, just for you!

- The **Dow-Jones Industrial Average** (http://www.secapl.com/secapl /quoteserver/djia.html) appears graphed on-screen, with just a five-minute delay from active trading.

- In **Current U.S. Weather** (http://www.mit.edu:8001/usa.html), click on an area for a more detailed forecast (see Figure 3.5).

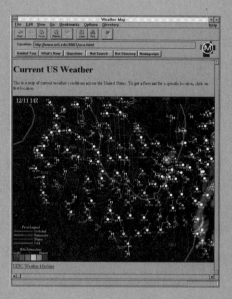

Figure 3.5 *Clickable map of U.S. weather*

- **Welcome to Switzerland!** is (http://heiwww.unige.ch:80/switzerland/) another clickable map, and very nicely implemented.

GRAPHICS

To display a graphic image on a computer, the graphic must be converted into digital form—a collection of 1s and 0s. Computer images are recorded and stored using standards called *graphics formats*. In order to use Web graphics, you'll need to understand a little about the differences among the available graphics formats.

Colors

Graphics can vary in the number of colors that they can assign to each pixel on your monitor. For example, a graphic containing 8 bits of information for each pixel can display a maximum of 256 colors. Because computers represent information using binary numbers, the maximum number of colors that you can represent with 8 bits is 256, since an 8-bit coding system gives you 256 different possibilities (28 = 256). Here's a quick overview of the relationship between the number of bits per pixel and the maximum number of colors that can be represented:

- **4-bit**. A 4-bit graphics format can represent only 16 colors, and requires only a very small file. However, the image's colors won't look like the original's.

- **8-bit**. An 8-bit graphics format can represent 256 colors. That's enough to provide a reasonable approximation of the original's colors, at least for screen display purposes. Most of the images you'll encounter on the Web are 8-bit graphics. You can display an 8-bit graphic on most computers without requiring special equipment.

- **16-bit**. A 16-bit graphics format is capable of representing 65,536 colors, which is common on Macintosh systems.

- **24-bit**. A 24-bit graphic can contain 16.7 million colors. 24-bit graphics files come closest to capturing the true colors of the original, but they require a great deal of storage space unless they're radically compressed.

Some graphics formats use a technique called dithering to make the image appear to have more colors than it does. In dithering, the colors of surrounding dots are adjusted to make up for discrepancies between the source color and the display color.

Compression

In addition to the number of colors, graphics vary according to the type of compression that's used. Compression is required because uncompressed graphics take up too much disk space and transmission bandwidth. Compression techniques fall into two categories, "lossless" and "lossy":

- **Lossless Compression**. A method of data compression that seeks to preserve all of the original data without alteration. Much of the data in a typical graphics file is redundant, and can be stored using a shorter code than the ones originally used to represent the graphics data. Some images can be compressed to a tenth of their original size without loss of image quality, but the image must be decompressed upon receipt before you can view it.

- **Lossy Compression**. A method of data compression that sacrifices some loss of the data in ways that are not immediately obvious to a person who is viewing the graphics file after it has been transmitted.

Everyone agrees that compression is desirable for Web graphics. But the jury's still out regarding which of these techniques is the best, and in fact, this very subject is likely to launch a flame war if you bring it up on graphics-related Usenet newgroups.

Here's a quick overview of the file formats you're most likely to encounter while browsing the Web, listed in the order in which you'll find them:

- **GIF** (Graphics Interchange Format). An 8-bit, 256-color graphics file format originally developed by CompuServe and widely used to facilitate the exchange of graphics files throughout the computer community, including bulletin board systems and the Internet. The GIF standard employs a lossless compression technique to reduce the size of graphics files for economical transmission. On receipt, the image must be decompressed by a graphics program that can read GIF files. Generally, GIF files are very large—some are a half megabyte or more in size—and can require several minutes to download via a 14.4 Kbps SLIP or PPP connection.

- **JPEG** (Joint Photographics Expert Group)/JFIF (JPEG File Interchange Format). This file format is based on the JPEG lossy compression technique for graphic images named for an International Standards Organization subgroup. JPEG achieves greater compression than can be obtained with lossless techniques—you can compress a 2MB file to 100K or less. The technique pulls this trick off by destroying some of the visual information beyond recovery, but you'll never know it. JPEG exploits the known limitations of the human eye, especially the fact that we don't notice small color changes as much as changes in brightness. The colors may be slightly altered, but they're far richer than those of the competing graphics standard, Graphics Interchange Format (GIF). JPEG graphics can store 24-bit color information, for a total of more than 16 million colors. GIF, in contrast, can store only 256 colors. GIF graphics may have been acceptable for yesterday's graphics hardware and monitors, but JPEG can take advantage of the high-resolution displays that are increasingly common in mid-range personal computers.

- **TIFF** (Tagged Image File). This graphics format permits you to store more than one graphic image per file and supports a variety of compression techniques, as well as 24-bit color. It's most commonly used for grayscale images, which provide an approximation of a black-and-white photograph. A commonly-used format is 256-color True Gray, which emulates the smooth gray scale gradations of a photograph and prints beautifully on laser printers.

- **Targa**. This graphics format, created by a vendor of high-resolution video equipment, supports 24-bit color but is not widely used.

Some graphics formats are specifically supported by Windows or the Macintosh:

- **Windows Bitmap**. Standard Windows Bitmap files (named with the *.bmp or *.dib extensions) can be saved in 4-, 8-, and 24-bit formats, and may be compressed (using a compression technique called RLE compression) or uncompressed. Because these files tend to consume large amounts of disk space, they're not often encountered on the Internet.

- **PICT**. This format is the Macintosh's standard format for storing graphics data. Most Macintosh applications can read PICT files, either directly or through an Import command.

In-Line Graphics

Most graphical browsers are equipped to decode in-line GIF images, such as those shown in Figure 3.6. This example, from Brigette Jellinek's interesting home page, illustrates the considerate use of in-line graphics: The graphic is small, informative, and quick to display. (Brigitte is an Austrian computer science student who has contributed some interesting material to the Web.) In-line graphics surrounded by borders, like the icons in Figure 3.6, are hyperlinks—you can click them to display something.

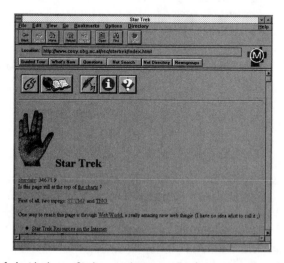

Figure 3.6 *An ideal use of in-line graphics—small, informative, and quick to display*

Viewing Larger Graphics Files

To view large graphics (more than approximately 20KB in size), most readers require a helper program, such as those discussed in Chapter 13. The graphic appears in a separate window, as shown in Figure 3.7.

Figure 3.7 *Large graphic displayed by helper program*
(Electronic Visualization Laboratory, University of Illinois)

If you're using Netscape, you won't have to worry about installing and using helper programs for large graphics as Netscape can read large JPEG and GIF graphics directly.

EXCELLENT

VIEWING MOVIES

When you're using a computer, you're looking at what appears to be a television screen, right? Superficially, yes. But computers display digital images, in which the image is constructed out of a very large number of bits of yes-no, on-off information. That's useful for certain purposes, but digital imaging requires a great deal more storage space than the analog techniques used to create an image on your TV set—as a rough measure, about 100 times as much.

Just how much? For example, a high-resolution digital version of Darth Vader boarding Princess Leia's vessel would consume a good portion of your computer's hard disk, although it's only a tiny piece of videotape. Here's why. To produce the appearance of smooth motion, a display device must be capable of displaying at least 15 frames per second. On your computer, each frame (or still picuture) might be as much as 10 MB a piece, so one second of video could be 300 MB! For one minute of high-definition, uncompressed computer video, then, we're talking about storing, processing, and displaying hundreds of megabytes worth of graphics files per minute. In other words, forget it.

But computer people have found ways to reduce the amount of disk storage (and transmission bandwidth) required to display animations and video clips on your computer screen. For one thing, you can reduce the size of the movie. (The first computer video standards got quite a laugh because the "movie" was about the size of a postage stamp!) or, you can use fewer frames per second, cutting the number of frames per second down to 12 or fewer, but this makes the motion look jerky, like those little "flip books" you had as a kid. You could reduce the length of the movie to just a few seconds—enough, maybe, to hear Martin Luther King say, "I have a dream," or to watch a Titan blast off. Or, you can also compress the image. Thanks to major advances in video compression technology, it's now possible to reduce the size of video file by a factor of 26:1. To be sure, there's some loss of image quality, but you still get a fairly good quality picuture.

In general, don't expect to find full-screen video on the Web. Movies are bigger than postage stamps—but not by much. Why the small size? The bigger the video, the more disk space—and transmission bandwidth—is required. A reasonably-sized and compressed video, appearing in a window approximately 3 inches square and running for just 2 minutes, can consume a megabyte of storage space. For most Web users, that's too much, as with SLIP/PPP (dialup IP) connections, or a slow network connection, videos of 500KB can take as long as 5 minutes to download.

There are many movie formats for computers, but you'll find the following most common when you browse the Web:

- **MPEG** (Motion Picture Experts Group). A standard for the digital representation and compression of video images defined by the Motion Picture Experts Group, a subgroup of the International Standards Organization. MPEG incorporates a lossy compression technique that is capable of realizing a compression ratio of 26 to 1 without objectionable loss in image quality.

- **QuickTime**. This is the standard Macintosh format for computer movies. It supports a variety of compression programs capable of compression ratios as high as 40 to 1.

- **Video for Windows**. This is the standard Microsoft video format for Microsoft Windows. Like QuickTime, it can be used with a variety of compression programs.

When you download a movie with a graphical Web browser such as Mosaic or Netscape, the program automatically detects the type of file you're downloading and starts the appropriate viewer (see Figure 3.8). Since most of the videos you'll download are MPEG videos, the following instructions pertain to viewing MPEG files with the viewers for each version of Mosaic.

Figure 3.8 *MPEG video (from the MPEG Movie Archive)*

ANIMATIONS

Requiring less disk space than videos, animations could figure prominently on the Web—if they weren't so time-consuming and difficult to produce. An important exception is in the field of scientific visualization, where rapid progress has been made. Programs such as Cornell University's DataExplorer enable scientific researchers to create complex graphics models of mathematical and natural phenomena.

Like to see some examples of well-conceived animations? Available on the Cornell Theory Center server (http://www.tc.cornell.edu/Visualization

EXCELLENT

/animations/animations.html) are animations including an enzyme that plays a key role in the human nervous system, the concentration of penguins and their prey in Antarctica, the effect of a tsunami (tidal wave) on Hilo Bay in Hawaii, and the motion of a walking Lego "spider". Like videos, animations require a helper program, usually the same one that plays videos (such as MPEGPlay).

SOUND

Like graphics and video files, sound files are stored in a number of differing formats. Some of these formats use 8-bit data storage, which provides the sound quality (roughly) of an AM radio, while others use 16-bit (CD-quality) storage techniques. Most of the recommended sound players can play two or more sound formats. Here's an overview of the sound file formats you'll find most commonly on the Web:

- **SoundBlaster .VOC file**. These files are designed to play through the popular SoundBlaster sound card, which works with IBM PCs and compatibles.
- **Sun/NeXT/DEC .AU files**. These files, used with UNIX workstations, employ an advanced storage approach to give the equivalent of 16-bit sound resolution even though only 8 bits of data are stored.
- **Windows .WAV files**. This is the standard sound format for Microsoft Windows systems. *.WAV files store sounds using both 8- and 16-bit techniques.
- **Sounder/Soundtools .SND files**. This is a standard sound format for Macintosh systems.
- **Amiga .8SVX .IFF files**. This is a standard sound format for Amiga systems., which is only capable of 8-bit storage.
- **Apple IFF**. This sound format was developed by Apple Computer and is based on, but incompatible with, the Amiga IFF format. This format is also used on Silicon Graphics workstations.

Just what you see on-screen when you activate a sound hyperlink depends on which sound player you've installed. Generally, you don't hear the sound immediately; instead, you see the sound player's dialog box, which lets you play the sound (see Figure 3.9).

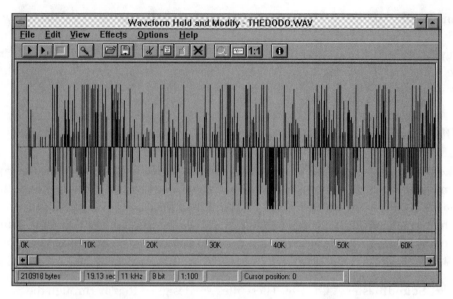

Figure 3.9 *Sound player (helper program for the IBM)*

DISPLAYING POSTSCRIPT DOCUMENTS

PostScript is a page description language that defines the precise appearance of a document, right down to the fonts, font size, and precise page layout. It's different from the generalized markup languages, such as HTML, that define Web documents, by defining the parts of a document (such as "title" or "normal text"), and leave the specifics of how to display those parts up to the client application.

For Web applications, generalized markup languages are clearly superior. They require less bandwidth to transmit, and what's more, you can display any HTML document using the fonts you've installed on your system. Nevertheless, you'll still find plenty of PostScript documents around. PostScript documents provided Internet users with a means to convey nicely-formatted documents before the Web originated. To display any PostScript documents you might encounter on the Web, you'll need a PostScript viewer (see Figure 3.10) such as GhostScript (see Chapter 13).

Figure 3.10 *PostScript viewer (helper program)*

SUMMARY

Multimedia resources—graphics, video, animation, and sound—can enhance hypertext, but multimedia alone does not hypermedia make. To qualify as hypermedia, a hypertext document must use the multimedia resources as something more than mere window dressing. Graphics that function as hyperlinks, clickable maps, and branching movies provide examples of true hypermedia.

Although hypermedia can enhance a hypertext system, it comes with a stiff price as multimedia files are much larger than text files. With slow network connections, multimedia-rich documents may take several minutes to download and view. Still, small graphics, brief sounds, and short videos can add depth and meaning to the text that still predominates on the Web.

FROM HERE...

- For more information on helper programs, see Chapter 13.
- For examples of the use of hypermedia in navigation, see the next chapter.

CHAPTER 4

Putting It All Together: A Web Tour

> Mosaic is doing for the Internet right now what Visual C, the proverbial
> killer application, did for the personal computer around 1980.
> —Bob Metcalfe, *InfoWorld*

Hypertext, the Internet, multimedia and hypermedia—these are the ingredients of
the World Wide Web. What unites them all is the Internet's "killer application,"
Mosaic (and its descendants, such as Netscape and WebSurfer). Now it's time to
see what the Web looks like, on-screen.

The necessary ingredients for a successful Web quest are curiosity and a little
practical knowledge. In this chapter, you'll join me in a quest for the very lively
presence of alternative music on the Web. Along the way, you'll learn the fundamentals of using graphical Web browsers such as Mosaic, as well as the basics of
navigating the Web. Parts Three and Four of this book return to all of the subjects
in this chapter in detail, so you can think of this as a preview of these important
sections of this book.

Mosaic, the program created by the National Center for Supercomputer
Applications (NCSA), is the graphical web browser that most people have heard
about. As you've probably heard, though, it has plenty of competition, including
Netscape, Air Mosaic, WebSurfer (the version of Mosaic included with this book),
and Enhanced NCSA Mosaic.

**KEY
TERM**

53

I've chosen to illustrate this chapter using Netscape, the best of the current crop of graphical browsers, and NCSA Mosaic, the original Web graphical browser. Most Web browsers work in much the same way, so if you're using Enhanced NCSA Mosaic, AirMosaic, or WebSurfer (included with this book), you won't have any trouble duplicating this quest on your own. Let's find some music!

**HOME
PAGE**

If you want to follow this quest with your graphical browser, make sure the program is installed correctly, including all the helper programs (see Chapter 13). You'll also need a direct Internet connection, either through an Internet-connected network or a SLIP/PPP connection. For more information, see Part Two.

STARTING YOUR BROWSER

**KEY
TERM**

Assuming you've got your browser installed, configured, and running on your system, and that you're connected to the Internet, just double-click the browser's icon to start the program. The first thing you'll see is the *default home page* (see Figure 4.1). A *home page* is the Web document that your browser is set up to display automatically. The default home page is the home page that your browser automatically displays when you open the program for the first time.

HOT TIP

Create your own home page! See Chapter 10 for easy instructions that show you how to change the default home page—or see Chapter 26 for information on the Smart Pages included with this book's disk and Chapter 27, which shows you how to create your own home page containing your favorite URLs.

Figure 4.1 *Default home page (Netscape Communications Corp.)*

EXPLORING THE SCREEN

As with any application program that you're learning, you should begin by exploring the features of the on-screen display.

Here's a quick overview of the features you'll see on a graphical browser's screen (see Figure 4.2). Just where you'll find these features varies among the various flavors of Mosaic, but each version has all these elements:

- **Menu Bar.** This bar contains the names of commands from which you can choose.

- **Tool Bar.** This bar contains icons or buttons you can click to navigate the Web and perform other tasks.

- **Program Icon.** When this icon displays motion, the browser is downloading a document. By clicking the icon, you can stop the download. This comes in handy if you've just clicked a hyperlink that you didn't mean to click.

- **Document Title.** This is the title of the document you're currently viewing in the Document View area. Most flavors of Mosaic display the document title on the title bar, but some have a separate area for this purpose.

- **Document URL.** This is the URL of the document you're currently viewing. You may not see this if your program is configured to hide the URL (see the tip following this list).

- **Document View Area.** Here, you actually see the current document. You can use the scroll boxes and scroll areas to display parts of the document that you can't see.

- **In-Line Graphic.** Most flavors of Mosaic can display these small in-line graphics without helper programs; Netscape can display large GIF and JPEG graphics without help.

- **Status Bar.** This area displays the URL of the hyperlink to which you're currently pointing. (It's blank if you're not pointing at a hyperlink.) Sometimes it displays additional information about what the program is doing.

HOT TIP

Don't see some of these features? Graphical browsers enable you to customize the screen to your heart's content. Some browsers hide some of these elements by default, in a kindly effort to save you from some of the Web's complexity. For example, Netscape doesn't automatically display the document URL; to turn it on, you must open the Options menu and choose Show Location. Personally, I like to see the URL, since you can often tell where the document is located from the URL's path information—and it might be in Sweden (.SE), the United Kingdom (.UK), Germany (.DE), Australia (.AU), or anywhere else!

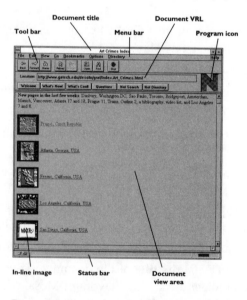

Figure 4.2 *Screen elements of a graphical browser*

ACTIVATING A HYPERLINK

A good home page contains many hyperlinks, which take you to other interesting and useful documents. Depending on how your browser was set up and what kind of monitor you use, you may see the hyperlinks in a distinctive color, with under-lining, or with both. (For example, on my monitor, the hyperlinks appear in blue underlined text.)

Every hyperlink contains a hidden URL. You can see this URL if you wish. Just move the mouse pointer over the hyperlink, as shown in Figure 4.3. With some browsers, the pointer changes shape over the hyperlink, as shown in the figure. The URL is displaced on the status line.

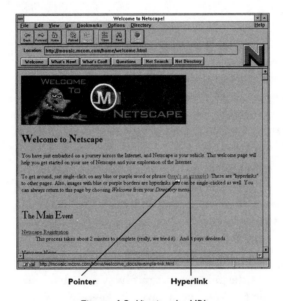

Figure 4.3 *Viewing the URL*

HOT TIP

To activate a hyperlink, you just move the pointer to it, and click. Yes, that's right—click *once*. Because many Macintosh and Windows functions are initiated by double-clicking something, you may have to un-learn the tendency to double-click. That second click may activate an unwanted hyperlink on the page that's about to be displayed, taking you to who-knows-where.

After you've activated a hyperlink, you see the page you've requested (see Figure 4.4).

Figure 4.4 *Page Displayed After Clicking hyperlink*

HOT TIP Some in-line graphics are hyperlinks that you can click to display another Web document. If there's a border around the graphic, it's probably a hyperlink. With most browsers, the border appears in blue. To check if the graphic is really a URL, move the prompt over it and see if a URL is displayed in the staus line.

NAVIGATION BASICS: NAVIGATION BUTTONS AND THE HISTORY LIST

KEY TERM After you've navigated through a few hyperlinks, you may feel as though you're getting lost. But don't despair—you can always get back to where you've been before. As you browse the Web, your browser keeps a record of all the documents you've displayed. This information is stored in the *history list*. To view the history list, you choose an option that displays the history list in a dialog box. The history list contains a record of all the URLs you have visited in the current session. If you wish, you can choose a URL from the history list. Alternatively, you can use the navagation buttons (called Back and Forward in most broswers)—but it's important to understand what these buttons do. Let's start with an example.

Suppose you start your Web session at Netscape's home page, http://mosaic.mcom.com/home/welcome.html (Figure 4.3). Then you try out the s ample hyperlink, and see the Congratulations! page shown in Figure 4.4. Your browser keeps a record of the documents you've displayed. The list looks like this:

Welcome to Netscape! http://mosaic.mcom.com/home/welcome.html

Congratulations! http://mosaic.mcom.com/home/welcome_docs/example-link.html

Going Back

At any time, you can go *back* in the history list, to display the document you've seen previously. To go back, you click the Back button. In the example history list just mentioned, if you're viewing "Congratulations," clicking Back displays the "Welcome to Netscape!" page.

The Document Cache

Notice how quickly your browser displays a page when you go back? That's because the program has stored this page in memory, where it can be re-accessed very quickly. The memory that's set aside for this purpose is called the *document cache* (pronounced "cash"), or just *cache* for short.

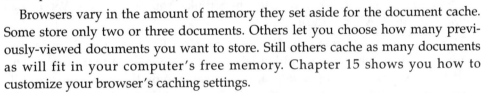

KEY TERM

Browsers vary in the amount of memory they set aside for the document cache. Some store only two or three documents. Others let you choose how many previously-viewed documents you want to store. Still others cache as many documents as will fit in your computer's free memory. Chapter 15 shows you how to customize your browser's caching settings.

You can tell how many documents your browser caches. Just click lots of hyperlinks, and then go back. When you get back to a document and find that it's being re-displayed much more slowly, you've come to the end of the cache. For more information on your browser's cache capabilities, see Chapter 15.

HOT TIP

Remember, if you want to go back to a document displayed some time ago, don't click Back several times. You can choose a document from the history list directly. In Netscape, for example, you open the <u>G</u>o menu and choose <u>V</u>iew History. When the history list appears, you just select the item you want, and click the Go to button. Most browsers eable you to select URLs from the history list in this way.

Going Forward

If you haven't gone back in the history list, the Forward button is dimmed and you can't choose it. Once you've gone back, the button becomes available, and you can use it to re-display a document you went back from.

Yes, I know, this is a little confusing. Just think in terms of the history list. Going back is like going *up* in the history list, to see a previously-displayed document. Once you've gone back, you can go forward (move *down* the history list) to see more recently-displayed documents.

AWFUL

Think of the example history list just discussed. Suppose you're viewing "Congratulations!" and you click the Back button. You see "Welcome to Netscape." If you click Forward, the program re-displays "Congratulations!"

WEB SECRET

Have you recently visited a hot URL? You shouldn't trust that you can return to it by using your history list, as described above. Most of the time, you can. But Web browsers will mysteriously drop items from their history lists, as you'll discover sooner or later. If you find a genuinely useful Web document, add it to your hotlist immediately. For more information, see "Adding Documents to your Hotlist," later in this chapter.

FINDING A COOL SITE

You've learned the basics. You can click hyperlinks. You can go back. You can go forward. Big deal! Where's the action?

AWFUL

There are riches galore on the Web. The problem lies in *finding* them. At last count, there were nearly one million URLs in existence—and that number will probably have increased by a substantial percentage by the time you read this book. But there's no search capacity built into the Web's underlying protocols. You'll have to rely on tips, books such as this one, and on-line subject indices and search engines, discussed later in this chapter.

EXCELLENT

Most browsers come with built-in menu options that take you to lists of interesting URLs, such as NCSA's "What's New" pages. With Netscape, you can open the Directory menu and choose What's Cool! (see Figure 4.5). This page will doubtless change by the time you access it—the Supreme Arbiter of Taste at Netscape is not known for constancy of opinion—but for now, it contains just what we're looking for: the Internet Underground Music Archive (http://www.iuma.com). Clicking this hyperlink brings up IUMA's first page (see Figure 4.6).

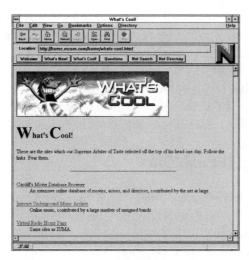

Figure 4.5 *Netscape's "What's Cool!" page*

Figure 4.6 *Internet Underground Music Archive*

HOT TIP

What if you're not using Netscape, or this URL isn't listed? With any graphical browser, you can type the URL directly. The easiest way to do this is to select the URL that's listed in the Document URL area, type the URL you want, and press Enter. You can also access a URL directly by using a menu command. With NCSA Mosaic, for example, you open the File menu and choose Open URL. Then, you type the URL in the dialog box that appears, and click OK. However you do it, make sure to type the URL correctly (http://www.iuma.com). Don't forget the two forward slashes after the colon, and don't put any spaces within the URL.

Can't access the Internet Underground Music Archive? There are several possible reasons. The server might be overloaded, or down temporarily for maintenance; try again later. IUMA may have moved, in which case you'll likely see a message informing you of this. Or it may have been withdrawn with no trace left behind. Remember that much of the material you find on the Web has been placed there by volunteers, with disk space donated by generous organizations. Under those circumstances, it's reasonable to expect URLs to come and go.

AWFUL

EXPERIENCING HYPERMEDIA

The Web's underground music sources, you'll find, aren't just *about* underground music. You can actually *hear* underground music recordings! Remember, though, that you need to configure your browser with *helper programs*—programs that show movies and play sounds—before you can fully experience the Web's hypermedia riches.

IUMA's Lotuspool page displays several music options, as shown in Figure 4.7. Note that each of the circles isn't just an in-line graphic; it's also a hyperlink, as indicated by the blue border (which, admittedly, doesn't show up very well in our black-and-white reproduction). When you click the Panel Donor offering, the Donor page appears (Figure 4.8).

Figure 4.7 *Lotuspool's on-line musical offerings (Internet Underground Music Archive)*

Figure 4.8 *Panel Donor (Internet Underground Music Archive)*

Because sounds take up large amounts of network bandwidth, considerate Web authors tell you how large the sound files are. In Figure 4.8, you see four offerings concerning the song Shiny Chrome Cells. The first two listings are full-length recordings of the song, and the last two are very brief excerpts.

To listen to the MPEG recordings, you'll need a helper program that's capable of playing X-MPEG sounds. To listen to the .au recordings, you'll need a helper program that's capable of playing sounds in that format.

How long does it take to download a complete, stereo song? On my system, with a SLIP connection and a 14.4 kbps modem, about 25 minutes. Ugh! On the plus side, it's free.

AWFUL

ADDING DOCUMENTS TO YOUR HOTLIST

If you find a really cool Web site during your travels, you may wish to return to it quickly without having to activate many hyperlinks to retrace your steps. You can save your link to that document by adding it to your hotlist. A *hotlist* is your own list of Web treasures that you've discovered on your journeys. In some graphical browsers, such as Netscape, the term *bookmarks* is used in place of hotlist.

To add a URL to your hotlist, you display the page that you want to store, and choose the appropriate command (with Netscape, you open the Bookmarks menu and choose Add Bookmark).

AWFUL

It's great to be able to store frequently-accessed items in a hotlist—but all too quickly, the list becomes lengthy and disorganized. Mine is a mess (see Figure 4.9).

Figure 4.9 *Disorganized hotlist with too many items*

HOT TIP

The cure for a disorganized and lengthy hotlist is to create your own home pages, as described in Chapter 27. When you start your browser, you'll see your favorite URLs in an organized format. This is a key part of making the Web your own, the subject of Part Six of this book.

USING SUBJECT TREES AND SEARCH ENGINES

KEY TERM

How are we doing on our quest for underground music sources? We found the Internet Underground Music Archive—but that was just good luck. How do you find interesting material on the Web, if you don't have Netscape's Supreme Arbiter of Taste around to help you?

The answer lies in *subject trees* and *search engines*, the subjects of Chapters 17 and 18.

- A *subject tree* is a subject-oriented catalog of URLs, organized by topic (such as "Astrology," "Astronomy," and "Astrophysics."). The "tree" part of the name comes from the catalog's hierarchical organization; under "music," for instance, you find "classical music," "folk music," "techno-rave music," etc.
- A *search engine* provides key word searching, enabling you to type in one or more search words (such as "Mars" and "pictures"). The search engine then tries to match these search terms against a database of URL names and topics.

Want to know the weakest aspect of the Web? Here it is, folks. There are hundreds of thousands of URLs out there and by the time you read this, there will be well over a million. But there's no good mechanism for *locating* information of interest. Subject trees require inordinate amounts of human energy and time to compile, while search engines rely on primitive searching methods that, more often than not, retrieve documents you *don't* want and skip the documents you *do* want.

AWFUL

Subject trees and search engines are imperfect, but they're better than nothing! Let's take a look brief look at both.

Using a Subject Tree: Yahoo

Subject trees vary in formality, with some of them attempting to approach the precision of a library catalog. One of the less systematic ones, Yahoo, is also (arguably) the most interesting—and certainly the most self conscious. The name "Yahoo" stands for Yet Another Hierarchically Officious Oracle.

WEB
SECRET

On Yahoo's help page, you'll find a pull-down box that lets you choose words other than "Officious," if you like, including "Obstreperous" and "Odiferous." Although Yahoo may be self-effacing, you'll probably supply another "O" word to describe it: Outstanding. (Actually, "Yahoo" means "a member of a race of brutes in Swift's Gulliver's Travels who have the form and all the vices of man," but surely this couldn't apply to Yahoo's creators—could it?)

When you first access Yahoo, the main subject tree (see Figure 4.10). In parentheses, you see the number of items listed under each category (under "Art," for instance, there are 443 items). Let's check out "Art," which lists an item called "Music." Clicking "Music" brings up the page shown in Figure 4.11.

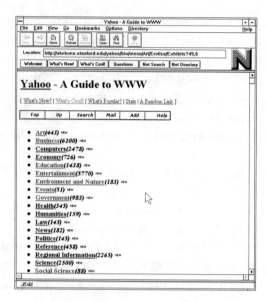

Figure 4.10 *Yahoo's main subject tree*

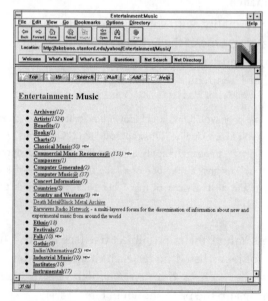

Figure 4.11 *Yahoo's ART subtree*

"Indie/Alternative" Sounds good, so click it! The Independent/Alternative page is displayed, shown in Figure 4.12. We're hunting for sound, and there are plenty of URLs to try (NrrrdTech Central, and the remarkable, even incomparable What The Cat Dragged In).

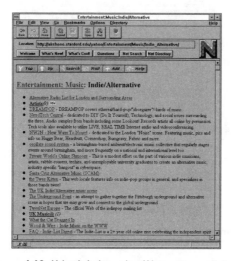

Figure 4.12 Yahoo's Independent/Alternative music page

Searching for URLs: The Lycos Search Engine

People make subject trees, computers don't. And that's why they're not very complete. In contrast, search engines use sophisticated net-searching algorithms to "crawl" throughout the web, finding and indexing new URLs. You can then search the database your search creates. The search results will be hit or miss (mostly miss), but sometimes you'll find the odd gem that couldn't have been discovered any other way.

Several search engines exist, but the best of them is the Lycos Search Engine, a project based at Carnegie-Mellon University. You'll learn more about Lycos in Chapter 18; I'll just mention here that Lycos, unlike other search engines, builds its key word indexes using part of the indexed documents' text, not just the titles and URL words.

To search Lycos, you type words that match your interests. We're hunting for musical excerpts, so the words in figure 4.13 provide a good starting point for the search. The result is a list of URLs that contain one or both of the search words—

and there are some interesting possibilities, including TeenBeat, the Vibe Box, the
Mudkats, and more (see Figure 4.14).

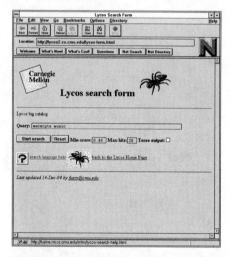

Figure 4.13 *Typing the search term (Lycos Search Engine)*

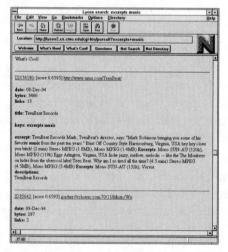

Figure 4.14 *URLs matching one or more search terms (Lycos Search Engine)*

SUMMARY

Curiosity and a few plain rules are the essential ingredients for a successful Web session. To avoid getting lost, understand how the history list works—and what happens when you click the Back or Forward buttons. To find interesting sites, you can use your browser's built-in menu options, which provide interesting starting points for Web navigation. When you find an interesting or useful document, add it to your hotlist. Subject trees and search engines can help find additional URLs of interest to you.

FROM HERE...

- For a quick start with Mosaic and Mosaic-related graphical browsers, see Chapter 10, World Wide Web: Quick Start.

- For more information on the display screen and what buttons and options do, see Chapter 11, Navigating the Web with Graphical Browsers.

- On navigation techniques, see Chapter 11, Navigating the Web with Graphical Browsers, and all the chapters of Part Four, "Strategies of Web Navigation."

- For help in finding interesting and useful Web sites, see Part Five, "Exploring the Web."

CHAPTER 5

Digging Deeper: Understanding Web Protocols

A good scientist is a person with original ideas. A good engineer is a person who makes a design that works with as few original ideas as possible.

—Freeman Dyson

The Internet, hypertext, hypermedia—put it all together, and you've got the World Wide Web. But what is the Web, exactly? In brief, the World Wide Web is a network of computers, all of which run software conforming to Web standards. In keeping with other Internet standards, these standards provide a simple, straightforward, and efficient means by which computers can operate one another even though they are geographically separated. The Web standards accomplish this feat in conformity to the hypertext model; when you click on a hyperlink, you originate a message that traverses the Internet and retrieves the desired document.

Among the several standards that support the Web is an Internet *protocol*, or communications standard—specifically, the HyperText Transport Protocol (HTTP). But equally germane to the Web are less official standards, including the definition of the HyperText Markup Language (HTML), the markup language used to prepare Web documents; and the Common Gateway Interface (CGI), is a set of standards specifying how Web servers access external resources, such as WAIS databases.

HOME PAGE

This chapter delves into the few original ideas that make the Web work so well. It's for those who are interested in the technical side of the Web, but it's not required reading if you just want to browse the Web. The chapter begins its exploration of the Web protocols by recounting the Web's birth at CERN, a European physics research laboratory, and continues by exploring HTTP, HTML, and CGI.

USEFUL RESOURCE

Want to explore Web technologies in the hypertext medium? Check out the Technical Details page at CERN, the Web's birthplace. Here's the URL:

http://info.cern.ch/hypertext/WWW/Technical.html

CERN: THE WEB'S BIRTHPLACE

Geneva, Switzerland, a lovely city nestled at the southwest tip of beautiful Lake Lemán, is surrounded dramatically by the Alps, and offers an unparalleled view of the Mount Blanc massif (see Figure 5.1). For Web enthusiasts, though, Geneva is more famous for the European Laboratory for High Energy Physics, the birthplace of the World Wide Web. (The acronym CERN comes from the center's earlier French name, Conseil Europeen pour la Recherche Nucleaire.)

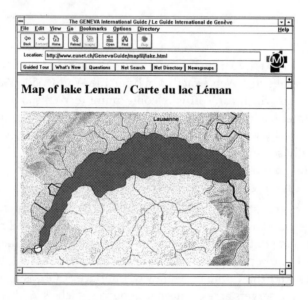

Figure 5.1 *Geneva International Guide*

Why would something like the Web come out of a physics think tank? Simple—at CERN, and at similar research institutes everywhere, scientists must cope with a deluge of printed information, including reports, experimental data, personnel data, electronic mail address lists, computer documentation, experiment documentation, and more. Most of this information is already in computer-readable form, but it isn't accessible as it's stored on a bewildering variety of computer systems using varied data storage formats.

For the CERN researchers, the problem of accessing documents was compounded by the international character of the high-energy physics research community. To stay on top of fast-breaking developments, physics researchers need to stay in touch. To promote communication, the physics community implemented the High-Energy Physics Network (HEPNet), using the Internet's TCP/IP protocols. HEPNet connected physics researchers at universities and research centers throughout Europe and North America, including CERN.

Pondering these challenges, Tim Berners-Lee, a document and text processing specialist, conceived the World Wide Web in the spring of 1989. "There is a potentially large benefit," he wrote, "from the integration of a variety of systems in a way which allows a user to follow links pointing from one piece of information to another one." The proposal listed the following objectives, which are here quoted from the source:

- To provide a common (simple) protocol for requesting human readable information stored at a remote system, using networks.

- To provide a protocol within which information can automatically be exchanged in a format common to the supplier and the consumer.

- To provide some method of reading at least text (if not graphics) using a large proportion of the computer screens in use at CERN.

- To provide and maintain at least one collection of documents, into which users may (but are not bound to) put their documents. This collection will include much existing data. (This is partly to give us first hand experience of use of the system, and partly because members of the project will already have documentation for which they are responsible).

- To provide a keyword search option, in addition to navigation by following references, using any new or existing indexes (such as the CERNVM FIND indexes). The result of a keyword search is simply a hypertext document consisting of a list of references to nodes which match the keywords.

- To allow private individually-managed collections of documents to be linked to those in other collections.
- To use public domain software wherever possible, or interface to proprietary systems which already exist.
- To provide the software for the above free of charge to anyone.

CERN photo

TIM BERNERS-LEE

Like Mosaic, the Web idea emerged from a high-powered academic think tank—in this case, the European Particle Physics Laboratory (CERN). (No, I didn't get my acronyms mixed up. "CERN" is an acronym for the French name for this institute.) Tim Berners-Lee, a graduate of Oxford University, came to CERN with considerable experience in computer-based communications, including a stint with Plessey Communications in England. Believing that high-energy physicists around the world needed a networked hypertext system to exchange fast-breaking research information, Tim led the development effort, beginning in 1989, that resulted in the Web protocols.

WEB SECRET

Berners-Lee's Web proposal is clearly focused on CERN's concerns, but a careful look at his objectives shows that he was thinking in broader terms. Knowing full well that open Internet protocols such as FTP and WAIS had led to the development of world-wide information access, he clearly foresaw that the Web protocol, available to all, would provide the basis for a world-wide hypertext system. But you won't find much about this in his proposal as research institutes want to know how a proposed project will benefit the institute, not the wider world.

In Berners-Lee's conception, the Web wasn't so much a network as a *protocol*, a standard for the exchange of information among dissimilar computer systems.

Using the Web protocol, a participating researcher would be able to access information stored on another computer system, and display this information using a program called a *browser*. The browser program would initiate requests that would travel to Web *servers*, which would then find the requested information and convey it back to the browser. The Web protocol, Berners-Lee proposed, would define the standards by which the browser-server communication would take place.

The proposed Web protocol, Berners-Lee wrote, would overcome the problems of accessing documents using existing Internet procedures. Unlike existing Internet protocols such as FTP or WAIS, the Web would not force users to go through a tedious log on procedure. In addition, it wouldn't force information providers to reformat their documents; the protocol would enable browsers to accessing existing WAIS-, FTP-, and Gopher-based information.

CERN asked Berners-Lee to resubmit the proposal, which was done in October, 1990 with the assistance of Robert Cailliau, a programmer. By November, 1990, a prototype Web browser had been created on a NeXT workstation, and work began on a *line-mode browser*, a program that would provide Web functionality to people using text-only VT100 terminals.

On May 17, 1991, the Web software was released to the CERN and HEPNet community—and the rest, as the saying goes, is history (see Chapter 31, Web Futures). Check out the following Web timeline for evidence of exponential growth: in March, 1993, Web traffic accounts for 0.1% of NSF backbone network usage, but six months later, in September, 1993, the amount grows to 1%—and a year later, in November, 1994, it amounts to 10%!

WORLD WIDE WEB TIME LINE

DATE	EVENT
March 1989	World Wide Web first proposed by Tim Berners-Lee, who writes paper entitled "HyperText and CERN."
October 1990	Revision of original project proposal, with assistance from Robert Cailliau.
November 1990	Tim Berners-Lee develops initial Web prototype browser on NeXT workstation.
November 1990	Nicola Pellow, a programmer with a degree from Leicester Polytechnic, begins work on a line-mode browser.
Christmas 1990	NeXT and line-mode browsers demonstrated.

WORLD WIDE WEB TIME LINE (continued)

DATE	EVENT
May 17, 1991	General release of World Wide Web software on central CERN machines.
August 1991	General release of World Wide Web software on the Internet via FTP.
February 1993	First version of Mosaic browser released by National Center for Supercomputer Applications (NCSA).
March 1993	Web traffic measures 0.1% of NSF backbone traffic.
September 1993	Web traffic measures 1% of NSF backbone traffic.
October 1993	Over 500 Web servers are known to exist.
December 1993	Web featured in *New York Times* business section.
January 1994	O'Reilly announces *Internet in a Box*.
March 1994	Marc Andressen and colleagues leave NCSA to form Mosaic Communications Corporation, later renamed Netscape Communications Corporation after NCSA objected to the use of the term "Mosaic."
May 1994	First International WWW Conference, CERN, Geneva.
June 1994	Over 1500 Web servers are known to exist.
July 1994	Massachusetts Institute of Technology (MIT) announces joint project with CERN to promote the development of the World Wide Web.
November 1994	Web traffic measures 10% of NSF backbone traffic.
November 1994	Over 150,000 Web servers are known to exist.

WEB SECRET

If you log on to CERN's server and view the Web documents, you'll see the three super-imposed letter "Ws" in very bright green (for a monochrome version, see Figure 5.2. Why? Robert Cailliau, one of the Web's inventors, is *synaesthetic*—that is, he's one of the 1-in-25,000 people whose brains are wired in such as way that two senses are linked. When Cailliau reads words, each letter has a distinctive color—For Cailliau, the letter W always looks green—and that's why they're green in all of CERN's pages.

Figure 5.2 *Those Ws are bright green—why?*

THE HTTP PROTOCOL: HOW THE WEB WORKS

At the heart of the World Wide Web is the HyperText Transport Protocol, the CERN-developed standard that has made the explosive growth of the Web possible. In essence, HTTP defines a standard way by which client Web applications can do the following:

- establish a connection with a server,
- make a request for information,
- receive information (an *object*) from the server,
- and close the connection.

Let's take a closer look.

Establishing the Connection

A client application using HTTP begins a Web link by establishing a connection with another Internet-linked computer. Normally, the connection process begins when you click a hyperlink.

Although HTTP can function over many kinds of networks, it's optimized for use on the Internet or other TCP/IP networks. As an example of this optimization, the HTTP protocol specifies the number of the *port* to be used by Web client applications. A port is a software-defined doorway that provides access to a server, providing a logical end point for a given application's information-seeking requests. HTTP's use of Internet ports enables a client's requests to proceed quickly to their destination.

The connection process goes by very quickly when you're using a Web browser—you see a message such as, "Connect: Host Contacted. Waiting for reply..." on the browser's status line. If the connection is made, your browser sends the request (see "Making the Request," the next section).

AWFUL

Woe unto you if the computer you're trying to contact isn't available for some reason. Nothing will happen for a long period of time as many as several minutes, depending on how your local network access is configured. What's happening is that your browser is waiting for a *time out*, a message that confirms the unavailability of the computer you're trying to contact. But it may take several minutes for the time out message to arrive. In the meantime, nothing happens—no message, no data. Experienced Web users know to click the browser's icon (Mosaic) or the Stop button (Netscape) rather than waiting around for the time out message to arrive.

Sending the Request

Once the connection is established, the client application sends the request, in the form of a *universal resource locater (URL)*. Essentially, a URL specifies the exact location of the *object* (usually, a file such as a JPEG graphic or an HTML document; an object can also be a piece of information, such as the result of a database search). Every URL has the following format:

    scheme://path

Here, *scheme* refers to the protocol that's used to retrieve the object, and *path* refers the location of the object within the computer's hierarchical file organization. The following example includes the scheme, and the path, which includes the name of the object.

    http://ds.internic.net/rfc/rfc1630.txt

A URL can be used to describe many kinds of objects available on the Internet.

In this example, the scheme is the Hypertext Transfer Protocol—in other words, the object to be accessed is a Web document. The document to be located, rfc1630.txt, is located at the computer named "ds.internic.net," in the directory /rfc.

Scheme Types in the HTTP Protocol

http	Hypertext Transfer Protocol
ftp	File Transfer Protocol
gopher	Gopher protocol
mailto	Electronic mail address
news	Usenet news
telnet, rlogin and tn3270	Reference to interactive sessions
wais	Wide Area Information Servers
file	Local file access

There's more to a request than just the URL. The request supplies additional information, such as the name of the client program being used, the server's location, and the URL of the document from which the request originated. In addition, the request can specify what the user wants done. Normally, the user wishes to get a copy of the object, but other options exist, including putting a new object into the server's storage area, posting a message to a Usenet newsgroup, and deleting an object from the server's storage area.

WEB SECRET

You'd best be aware of an unhappy fact: A Web site operator can quite easily compile a list of all the users who have accessed the system. Unbeknownst to you, your browser sends your electronic mail address along with every HTTP request you send. If you're using a computer at work, think twice before accessing that "X-Rated Video Archive" URL you've heard about!

Getting a Response

Once the request has been received, the server sends a response, including a message (which the client program displays) and the requested object, if it's available. You won't see these messages on screen in this precise form; Web browsers interpret them and, if necessary, display an alert box or dialog box.

Selected HTTP Server Response Messages

OK	Everything's cool; the requested object will be sent.
CREATED	The server posted a Usenet message or made a copy of the file in the server's storage area.
ACCEPTED	The request has been received, but further processing is needed to carry it out.
NO RESPONSE	The server can't find the object.
DELETED	The server deleted the object, as requested.
MODIFIED	The server modified the object, as requested.
MOVED PERMANENTLY	The object has a new URL.
MOVED TEMPORARILY	The object has been moved temporarily to the indicated URL.
BAD REQUEST	Something's wrong with the syntax of the URL.
UNAUTHORIZED	You're not authorized to use this server.
PAYMENT REQUIRED	Fork over the dough first, please. This message will be used to support commercial Web services in the future.
FORBIDDEN	Access denied.
SERVER ERROR	Something happened that prevented the server from fulfilling the request.
SERVICE UNAVAILABLE	The server is overloaded or is being maintained.
GATEWAY TIMEOUT	The server didn't respond in the allotted time.

The object that the server sends comes with a *header*, an area that contains information about the object. The header specifies the source of the document, its expiration date, and other information, but most important of all is its MIME type. MIME is an acronym for *Multi-purpose Internet Mail Extensions*, a list of standards for conveying multimedia resources via Internet connections. The header specifies what the object contains (text, graphics, sounds, videos, or PostScript files).

Closing the Connection

Once the client has received the requested object, the connection is closed. This isn't something you're aware of, though—when you're using a graphical browser such as Mosaic, the browser loads and displays the document, giving the impression that the connection still exists even though it doesn't. The document has been downloaded to your computer's memory, where you can page through it as you like. You can even save it to a local disk file, if you wish.

HTML: THE WEB'S MARKUP LANGUAGE

Another term that you'll run across frequently in the Web and Mosaic contexts is HyperText Markup Language (HTML). Basically, this is a standard for adding funny-looking symbols to documents so that, when accessed by a graphical browser such as Mosaic or any other HTML-capable editor, they look good on-screen. Another thing that HTML does is hide those URLs so that you can't see them (all you see is the boldfaced or underlined anchor). The Yahoo page, shown in Figure 5.3 and displayed by Netscape, is coded in HTML.

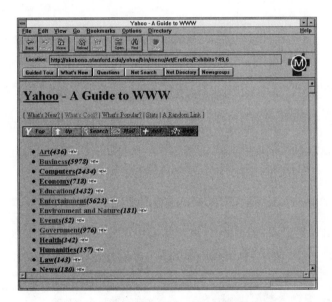

Figure 5.3 *Underlying Web pages is HTML coding*

HTML is a hypertext variant of Standard Generalized Markup Language (SGML), which deserves a few words. Basically, a generalized markup language is a way of marking a document's parts so that the computer can tell what they are. For example, you use a code to mark a title so that it's displayed as a title. Now the interesting thing about a generalized markup language is that it doesn't say exactly how the title should look—it just marks the title as a title. It's up to the client program to define exactly how the title should be displayed. Note that this is quite different from the formatting capabilities of word processing programs or page description languages such as PostScript which tell the printer and display exactly how the document should look.

You don't need to learn HTML unless you want to prepare your own Web documents—more about that in Chapter 27—but here's a quick look at the way it works.

An HTML document is basically a plain text document that has some codes added, using HTML's characteristic syntax. For example, you code a level 1 heading with the following codes:

- **<H1>** Turns the header format on
- **</H1>** Turns the header format off

A correctly-coded heading, then, looks like this:

```
<H1>Here's the heading</H1>
```

When a graphical browser such as Mosaic or Netscape reads this document, it translates the HTML codes into formats, as shown in Figure 5.4.

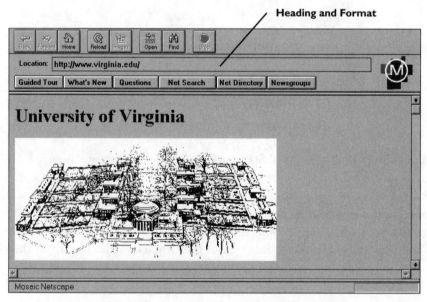

Figure 5.4 *Heading formats translated by HTML browser*

Is HTML a good language? It's easy to learn and produces fast results, but it's very limited. Currently, HTML gives you only very limited tools for specifying the components of a document. You can define headings, body text, and lists of various types, but no provisions are made for such features as tables or equations. In line with its declarative philosophy, too, there are very few provisions for specifying document design with graphics; most browsers align graphics at the left margin (see Figure 5.5), and there's little you can do about it, short of stacking all the graphics unattractively on one line (see Figure 5.6). The result is a rather boring and repetitive document design.

AWFUL

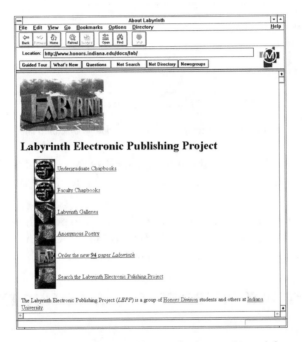

Figure 5.5 *Graphical browsers align small in-line graphics at left margin*

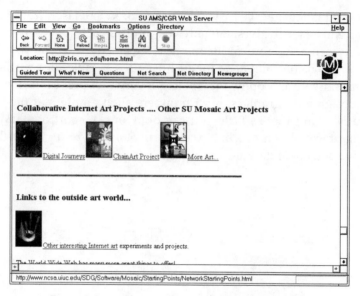

Figure 5.6 *You can place more than one graphic on a line*

A new version of HTML is in the works, called HTML Level 3 (formerly, it was called HTML+). This version enables you to define additional document elements, such as equations, tables, and footnotes.

WISH LIST

Further evolution of HTML will enable Web document designers to create more attractive and informative documents. Hint to HTML committees—it would be nice to have more control over the placement of graphics!

COMMON GATEWAY INTERFACE (CGI): ACCESSING EXTERNAL RESOURCES

As you know, Web browsers are designed to access HTML documents. In addition, most browsers can access FTP file archives and Gopher menus. To access other resources, additional programs called *scripts* are required. A script is a brief program that tells the server how to access a particular kind of information, such as a WAIS database. Scripts are also called *gateways*, because they provide a gateway to a type of information that your Web browser couldn't otherwise access.

As the Web evolves into an on-line transaction system, enabling people to order goods and services, the importance of gateways is growing. In particular, standards are needed to assure that Web browsers can perform searches of databases and display on-line forms correctly. To provide these standards, the Common Gateway Interface (CGI) standard is under construction. CGI specifies how scripts should be written so that they will work with Web graphical browsers, such as Mosaic and Netscape.

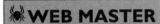

For more information on the Common Gateway Interface, including a hypertext-based tutorial, check out the following URL:

http://hoohoo.ncsa.uiuc.edu/cgi/

SUMMARY

At the heart of the Web is the Hypertext Transport Protocol (HTTP), which enables Internet users to access information quickly and easily by clicking hyperlinks. A creation of Tim Berners-Lee and his colleagues at CERN, a Swiss think tank, HTTP provides the standards that enable a Web browser to contact a Web server, send a request for information, obtain the response, and close the connection. HTML, the programming language used to format Web documents, is also an important component of the standards that make the Web possible, as is CGI, a scripting standard for accessing resources external to the Web.

FROM HERE

- See how the Web works in Chapter 10, World Wide Web Quick Start.
- Where are Web protocols headed? Check out Chapter 30, Web Issues, and Chapter 31, Web Futures.

PART 2:
CONNECTING TO THE WEB

CHAPTER 6

The Three Paths to Web Connectivity

> Forty years from now (if the human race survives) there will be hundreds of thousands of file servers—machines storing and dishing out materials. And there will be hundreds of millions of simultaneous users, able to read from billions of stored documents, with trillions of links among them. All this is manifest destiny. There is no point in arguing it; either you see it or you don't. Many readers will choke and throw down [this] book, only to have the thought gnaw gradually until they see its inevitability.
> –Ted Nelson (1981)

To understand what's needed to join the millions who access the World Wide Web, you must grasp some fundamental Internet concepts. Once you do, Web connectivity issues become simple and straightforward, and you can plan your Web access strategy intelligently. This chapter explains these concepts and the three basic ways you can connect to the Web: dialup access, dialup IP (SLIP/PPP), and network access.

To explain your Web connectivity options, and how they differ, this chapter begins with a nontechnical introduction to the way the Internet works. Armed with this knowledge, you'll fully understand the plusses and minuses of the three basic options for Web connectivity.

As you'll learn in this chapter, the best Web connection is one that directly connects your computer to the Internet—and that means you want dialup IP (SLIP/PPP) or network access. Unless you're lucky enough to have an Internet-connected network at your office, you'll want to get a dialup IP (SLIP/PPP)

HOME PAGE

connection, so study the sections on this topic carefully. For a list of dialup IP service providers, see Appendix B.

HOW THE INTERNET WORKS

You don't need to know the technical details of how the Internet works to use the World Wide Web, but a little background is useful when it comes to understanding your Web connectivity options.

KEY TERM

The Internet is a *packet switching network*. A packet switching network operates on very different principles from a *circuit switching network*, such as the telephone system. When you make a telephone call, the telephone system uses switches to create a single electrical circuit between your telephone and the one that you're calling. A packet switching network, in contrast, is called a *connectionless network* because it is not necessary for two linked computers to establish a physical connection before the transmission can take place.

So how the heck does a packet switching network work? Instead of establishing a direct connection, messages are chopped up into little sections called *packets*. Each packet contains a *header*—a part of the packet that indicates where the message came from, where it should be delivered, and how to reassemble the packets at their destination so that the message is recovered. The packets travel through the network independently, taking whatever route is freely available as they seek their destination. Think of the packets as if they were a flock of homing pigeons, each knowing its destination (but traveling together as need and chance arise).

How do packets get sent to their destinations? Devices called *routers* do this job. Each router examines each packet's destination address and decides how best to get the packet to its destination. At the end of each leg of the journey, a router is waiting to send the packet on its way.

At the final destination, the packets are reassembled, and if any were damaged or lost en route, the receiving computer automatically requests a retransmission.

🕷WEB MASTER

Many Internet users find the division of their messages (such as file transfers or electronic mail) into several or even dozens of packets somewhat disconcerting, but there is a good reason for this "chop-'em-up" approach—it's more efficient. Computer communications tend to be "bursty." A given computer might send a huge amount of data for a few minutes, and then not send any more for hours. So it doesn't make much sense to try to set up a single physical circuit for each pair of communicating computers because the line would only be used for infrequent bursts of activity. In a packet switching network, however, thousands of linked computers share a single high-speed line, which is often continuously occupied. The fact that each computer's data is broken up into hundreds or thousands of small packets makes it all that much easier to send them efficiently.

So what's the point of this brief excursion into the technicalities of a packet switching network? To get the most out of the Web, you need to connect your computer directly to the Internet's flowing streams of data packets. Otherwise, you can't take full advantage of the Web's multimedia capabilities.

THREE PATHS TO WEB ACCESS

You can connect to the Internet—and the Web—in three ways:

1. **Dialup Access.** Subscribe to a bulletin board system (BBS), an online information service, or an Internet service provider that offers a Web browser. You'll use a telephone line, a modem, and a communication program, which allow you to access the service's computer remotely. This is the cheapest and least satisfactory method of Web access because you won't be able to enjoy the Web's multimedia capabilities.

2. **Dialup IP (SLIP/PPP).** SLIP and PPP are Internet standards that allow Internet packets to traverse ordinary telephone lines. If your system is equipped with Internet support and SLIP or PPP capability, you can use multimedia browsers such as Mosaic, Netscape, or Cello to enjoy the Web's multimedia capabilities. But you'll need a high-speed modem (minimally, 14.4 Kbps) and a SLIP or PPP subscription from an Internet service provider.

3. **Network Access.** If you can connect your computer to a local area network (LAN) that has Internet access, you can enjoy the best Web access of all— you'll run browsers such as Mosaic at speeds of at least twice what you can expect from a SLIP or PPP connection. But, you'll need technical help to configure your computer properly.

The following sections explain each access method in detail.

DIALUP ACCESS

Dialup access is the cheapest, easiest, and least satisfactory way to access the Web. If you're just getting started with the Internet, though, it's a good place to start—and that's particularly true if you've already equipped your computer with the necessary equipment (a modem and a communications program).

KEY TERM

In dialup access, you dial into a computer that offers what's called a *login account* (also called a *shell account*). When you have a login account, you have the right to access a computer from a remote location, just as if you were sitting in the same room with it. This computer might be a UNIX minicomputer lodged in a college's academic computing center or at an Internet service provider's headquarters. Your communications program transforms your computer into a remote terminal of this computer—and that's the problem. You may be sitting in front of your computer, but you're really using the shell (the operating system) of the computer to which you've connected. You're operating that machine by remote control. And all those Internet data packets that you're trying to access are flowing to the distant computer, not your own.

Where can you obtain dialup access? Here's a brief overview (for more detailed information, see Appendix A):

- **Online Services** such as Delphi and Compuserve offer Internet access, which may (or may not) include Web access. This access is planned at most major services, but check with the service before subscribing.

- **Bulletin Board Systems (BBS)** sometimes offer limited Internet access, such as Internet electronic mail and a few newsgroups. A few offer Web access.

- **Internet Service Providers** such as Performance Systems International (PSI) offer login (shell) accounts at very reasonable rates. A few have nationwide 800 numbers, a big plus for those living in rural areas.

- **Freenets** are community bulletin board systems (BBS) that are usually housed in the local library and operates as a public service. Increasingly, freenets are offering limited Internet access. If there's a freenet in your area, it's worth checking out whether it offers access to the Web.

Dialup Access at a Glance

What you need

- A modem
- A communications program
- A subscription to a BBS or online service, or a shell account on a UNIX computer with Internet connectivity

The pluses

- It's cheap (some BBS systems offer free Internet access, and online services charge as little as $7.95 per month)
- Configuration is easy, especially if you've already set up your modem and learned how to use your communications program
- It's relatively fast (you'll browse the Web using a text-only browser, so you won't be waiting for large graphics files to download)

The minuses

- You can't run Mosaic, Netscape, Cello, or Enhanced NCSA Mosaic
- If you use the Web browser provided by your service provider, it will proirally be a text-only client such as Lynx, so you won't see inline graphics, hear sounds, or view videos
- Downloaded files don't come directly to your computer; they're stored on the computer on which you have an account. To get them to your computer, you must download them in a separate operation

Is it such a bad thing to use a text-based browser? In a pinch, it's okay. But look at what you're missing. Compare Figure 6.1, which shows the Internet Arts Museum for Free (IAMFREE) as viewed by Lynx, with the same page viewed by Netscape (Figure 6.2).

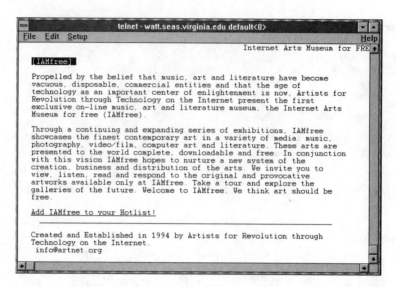

Figure 6.1 *Internet Arts Museum for Free (IAMFREE) viewed with Lynx (dialup access)*

Figure 6.2 *Internet Arts Museum for Free (IAMFREE) viewed with Netscape (SLIP/PPP access)*

HOT TIP

Do you have a UNIX account? Is so, you can use SlipKnot (http://www.interport.net/ slipknot/slipknot.html), a shareware program. SlipKnot is a graphical browser that does *not* require SLIP or PPP. You can see in-line graphics with SlipKnot, but you can't use on-line forms.

In sum, dialup access isn't the best choice for exploring the World Wide Web. To get the most out of the Web's multimedia capabilities, you must do the following:

- **Equip your system with TCP/IP capabilities**. This isn't necessary if you're using a UNIX workstation, since the TCP/IP capabilities are standard in most versions of UNIX. It *is* necessary if you're using a Macintosh or Windows 3.1 system (TCP/IP will be included in Windows 95, according to press reports).

- **Connect to the Internet via dialup IP (SLIP/PPP) or access the Internet through a local area network (LAN)**. Dialup IP uses a modem and telephone lines, like dialup access, but the Internet data packets reach your computer directly. SLIP and PPP are the two Internet protocols that govern dialup IP connectivity. They're explained in detail later in this chapter. Alternatively, you can connect your computer to a local area network (LAN), if one is available, that has an Internet connection.

DIALUP IP (SLIP/PPP)

Dialup IP enables computer users to achieve direct connections to the Internet by means of a modem and telephone line. You'll need to equip your system with TCP/IP support, as explained later in this chapter, and you'll also need a SLIP, CSLIP, or PPP subscription from an Internet service provider—a pricier proposition than dialup access (expect to pay at least $20 per month). But dialup IP has it all over garden-variety dialup access: You're directly connected to the Internet, and that means you can use graphical browsers such as Mosaic, Netscape, and Cello.

HOT TIP

Internet mavens who routinely access the Web through high-speed network access speak disparagingly of dialup IP, but don't believe them. Sure, it takes time—as much as a minute or two—to download large inline graphics with a SLIP connection at 14.4 Kbps. But having access to the graphical richness of the Web is well worth occasional downloading delays in my opinion.

Where can you obtain dialup IP service? Appendix B offers a list of service providers, but here's an overview:

- **Colleges and Universities:** If you're a student, staff person, or faculty member, check with the campus computing center to see if dialup IP (SLIP/PPP) service is offered. Chances are it's free.

- **Internet Service Providers:** Many providers offer dialup IP service nationwide and even internationally. But here's the catch: You'll have to call long distance if you're not within local dialing range of the provider's point of presence—usually large metropolitan areas.

DIALUP IP (SLIP/PPP) AT A GLANCE

What you need

- A high-speed modem (at least 14.4 Kbps)
- TCP/IP support for your computer
- SLIP/PPP software
- A SLIP, CSLIP, or PPP subscription to an Internet service provider

The pluses

- You can run graphical Web browsers such as Mosaic, Netscape, and Cello on your computer
- You can run other Internet sessions, such as electronic mail, Gopher, or Archie at the same time
- Downloaded files come directly to your computer

The minuses

- Inline graphics download slowly
- SLIP/PPP accounts are more expensive than dialup access (login account) subscriptions; expect to pay at least $20 per month

What's SLIP?

SLIP stands for Serial Line Interface Protocol, one of the older Internet protocols. SLIP outlines the procedure that sends Internet datagrams through your modem and Plain Old Telephone Service (POTS) lines—the ones that currently come into your house. SLIP tricks the Internet into thinking that your personal computer, temporarily connected through modems and phone lines to a terminal server at the service provider's headquarters, is actually a workstation connected to a local area network (LAN), a workstation that has a real, valid IP address. (An IP address is a unique numerical address required of every computer directly connected to the Internet.) The address is actually one of the many that belong to the terminal server to which you're connected. The terminal server assigns a unique IP address to each incoming SLIP line it handles. It moves all Internet packet traffic between the Internet proper and the connected computers, based on the IP addresses contained in each packet.

Compressed SLIP (CSLIP) is a variation of SLIP that is supported by most access providers. It improves the performance of Internet applications that generate large amounts of small packets, most notably Telnet, and in some cases the Web. Use CSLIP if your access provider and your TCP/IP software support it.

What's PPP?

PPP stands for Point-to-Point Protocol, a more recent Internet standard governing the transfer of Internet data via modems and telephone lines. Like SLIP, PPP hoodwinks the Internet into thinking your computer has a real IP address, allowing it to exchange Internet data with other Internet computers. But PPP is more up-to-date, offering data compression, data negotiation, and error correction to make the connection work more smoothly.

Which is Better?

The best dialup IP method is the one you can get. Chances are your service provider will give you SLIP, CSLIP, or PPP, but not all three—and chances are, it will be SLIP. The Chameleon Sampler included with this book can handle any dialup IP connection method—SLIP, CSLIP, or PPP. If you're lucky enough to have a choice, choose PPP because it offers automatic negotiation of such things as IP addresses, which you'd otherwise have to obtain through some devious scriptwriting. And if PPP isn't available, ask for CSLIP, because it provides better performance. SLIP is at the bottom of the list, but it will do if nothing else is available!

MCI AND NETSCAPE JOIN FORCES TO OFFER NATIONWIDE INTERNET ACCESS

If you live in a small town or rural area, Internet access now requires a long-distance telephone call to a service provider's point of presence (POP). Thanks to a major new Internet initiative by MCI Communications Corporation, one of the nation's largest long-distance telephone companies, Internet access will soon be available by means of a local telephone call throughout the United States. Currently planned are switched local, 800, and high-speed access methods.

The new service, called InternetMCI, is designed for the millions of computer users who have installed high-speed modems in their personal computers. Aided by point-and-click software, users can quickly install the necessary computer programs, which include Netscape Communication's highly regarded Web browser, Netscape Navigator. When accessing Netscape's business server software, Web browsers will be able to use their credit cards for online shopping without fear of losses from on line eavesdropping, thanks to MCI's implementation of RSA Data Security technology. By means of encryption, this technology assures what current Internet technology can't: That a call is actually from the person who owns the account, that no one is eavesdropping on the transaction, and that the server is a bona-fide business.

What's MCI doing in the Internet business? Most people don't realize that MCI has been busy for years positioning itself as a key player in Internet data communications. Today, almost 40 percent of Internet backbone traffic is carried on MCI's high-speed lines, which currently operate at 45 megabits per second. Next year, MCI will increase its backbone speed to 155 megabits per second, enough to transmit 10,000 pages in less than a second—or a 90-minute movie in just under three minutes.

Does MCI have the right leadership for its move? Directing MCI's Internet operations is Vinton G. Cerf, a member of the brilliant development team that is responsible for the Internet protocols. Internet MCI should be widely available by the time you read this book.

NETWORK ACCESS

By far the best Web access method is to connect your PC or Macintosh to a local area network (LAN) that has Internet access. This isn't a solution for individuals, since the necessary hardware and Internet connections are expensive: An Internet-connected LAN requires a router and a *dedicated line*, which can cost as much as $2,000 per month. But many organizations have Internet-connected LANs already in place, and it's possible you already have Internet connectivity at your office. Ask your network administrator!

NETWORK ACCESS AT A GLANCE

What you need

- A network interface adapter, which enables your computer to link with the network.
- A utility program called a *packet driver* and other network operating software.
- A direct connection to a local area network that is connected to the Internet
- TCP/IP support for your computer.
- Lots of help from someone who knows how the network works and how to configure computers for Internet access.

The pluses

- It's free, if the network to which you're connected already has Internet access.
- It's fast (a *dedicated* Internet connection is required to connect a LAN to the Internet, and dedicated connections start at 56 Kbps—twice as fast as the fastest modem).
- You can use graphical browsers such as Mosaic, Netscape, and Cello
- Your phone line isn't tied up.

The minus

- Installing and configuring the necessary software calls for skills and knowledge that go beyond the reach of most PC and Macintosh users.

SUMMARY

To get the most out of the Web, you need an Internet connection that lets your computer participate in the give-and-take flow of Internet data packets. Only then can you experience the Web's multimedia riches. Dialup access is inexpensive and widely available, but your computer isn't directly connected to the Internet, and you won't be able to enjoy graphics, sounds, animations, and video. Dialup IP (SLIP/PPP) is more expensive, but well worth it, as your computer is directly connected to the Internet, with full multimedia capabilities. However, it can take a minute or two to download large graphics or video files. The best Web access of all is network access, which is at least twice as fast as dialup IP. This is only available to those who are using a computer at work where there is an Internet-connected local area network (LAN). Most readers of this book will connect to the Web by means of dialup IP.

FROM HERE...

- For information on adding Internet (TCP/IP) capabilities to your computer, see Chapter 7.
- For more information on dialup IP (SLIP/PPP), see Chapter 8.

CHAPTER 7

Equipping Your System with TCP/IP Support

A TCP/IP connection to the Internet is like a Vulcan mind meld on *Star Trek*.   —Ed Krol

As the previous chapter explained, your best bet for Web connectivity is to connect your computer to the Internet directly, by means of dialup IP (SLIP/PPP) or network access. And that means you must equip your PC or Macintosh with TCP/IP support. This chapter explores your options for configuring your Microsoft Windows or Macintosh system for TCP/IP support. The chapter begins by explaining what TCP/IP stands for and continues by explaining why Macintosh and Windows systems need TCP/IP support for direct Internet access. It also lists some places to find the necessary software.

You don't need to read this chapter if you're accessing the Web by means of dialup access (a login account or shell account). For dialup access, TCP/IP support isn't needed. This chapter is for people who plan to connect to the Web using dialup IP (SLIP/PPP) or network access.

**HOME
PAGE**

HOT TIP

The disk included with this book contains NetManager's Chameleon software. This software provides TCP/IP support, as well as dialup IP with SLIP or PPP for Microsoft Windows systems. For more information on Chameleon, see Appendix A.

WHAT'S TCP/IP?

The term *TCP/IP* is an acronym for the two most important Internet standards, the Transmission Control Protocol and the Internet Protocol. But the acronym stands generally for all of the standards that are needed to connect a given computer to the Internet. To say "TCP/IP support," then, is synonymous with saying "Internet support." With TCP/IP support, your computer can "talk" to the Internet—and that's a precondition for full use of the World Wide Web.

EXCELLENT

Most PC and Macintosh users will need to purchase or obtain additional software to equip their systems with TCP/IP support, but that's about to change. The newest version of the Macintosh operating system, System 7.5, includes MacTCP, the software that provides TCP/IP support for Macs. Slated to include TCP/IP support is the much-awaited Windows 95 operating system from Microsoft.

Unless you've equipped your Mac with System 7.5 you'll need to equip your system with additional software to provide the needed TCP/IP support. This chapter explains why TCP/IP support is needed for Internet access and surveys the TCP/IP options available for Macintosh and Microsoft Windows systems.

WHY IS TCP/IP SUPPORT NEEDED?

Every computer "speaks" its own "language"—which is one reason why Macintosh software won't run on an IBM PC. In order to communicate with the Internet, your computer needs a translator program that knows how to translate between your machine's internal language and the language of the Internet.

There are two ways this translation can be done: by using a *proprietary utility* or an *application program interface* (API).

AWFUL

Proprietary utilities, programs that provided TCP/IP support only for the same vendor's programs, inconvenience the user. In the early days of TCP/IP connectivity for PCs and Macintoshes, the task of providing the needed translation was left up to the people who wrote Internet application programs, such as Telnet or Gopher clients. These programs worked by using a *terminate and stay resident* (TSR) utility, which started automatically when you started the client program. The program resided in memory until you rebooted, taking up precious memory space. Worse, the TSR utility would work only with the client program for which it was designed. If you purchased an Internet client program made by another software publisher, it wouldn't work unless you loaded that publisher's TSR utility. The result, as many found to their dismay, was a conflicting mess of utilities that could invade each other's memory space and cause the computer to crash.

To resolve the problems created by proprietary TCP/IP utilities, application program interfaces (APIs) for Internet connectivity were created for both the Macintosh and Windows systems. An API is a utility program that provides a common link between the computer's operating system and application software. As long as application programs are written to the API's specifications, they will work fine—even if the API and the application program are made by different software publishers. For Macintosh TCP/IP support, the API is provided by Apple Computer's MacTCP software. For Windows TCP/IP support, the API is provided by the Winsock 2.0 specification, an open standard created by a consortium of software publishers.

EXCELLENT

The creation of APIs for TCP/IP support has made it possible for growing numbers of Macintosh and Windows users to connect their computers to the Internet. With an API providing TCP/IP support, you can run Internet client programs made by a variety of software publishers, and they will all run—so long as they're compatible with the API's specifications. The next sections explore the details of TCP/IP support for Macintosh and Microsoft Windows systems.

If you're planning to connect to the Internet via dialup IP (SLIP/PPP), you'll need SLIP/PPP software and a dialer program in addition to the TCP/IP support discussed in this chapter. NetManage's Chameleon software included with this book provides TCP/IP support and a SLIP/PPP dialer. For more information on SLIP/PPP software, see the following chapter.

TCP/IP SUPPORT FOR THE MACINTOSH: MacTCP

MacTCP, an Apple product, provides TCP/IP support for all Macintoshes, including Power Macintoshes. MacTCP provides a common interface between the Macintosh's internal operations and the data pathways of the Internet—an interface that any Macintosh application program can use. All of the "hot" Internet applications, such as NCSA Mosaic and Netscape, and non-Web clients such as Fetch (an FTP client), make use of MacTCP.

HOT TIP

Before you pay $69 to buy MacTCP, consider upgrading to Version 7.5 of Apple's system software—MacTCP is included, for free! Alternatively, check out Adam Engst's book, *Internet Starter Kit for Macintosh* (Published by Hayden, it includes a disk containing MacTCP).

MacTCP is designed to work with Internet-connected Ethernet LANs and with dialup IP. If you're using dialup IP, you'll need additional software, such as MacSLIP or MacPPP (described in the following chapter).

A control panel device (CDEV), MacTCP must be properly installed and configured in order for your Macintosh to access the Internet—and there's the rub. It's easy enough to install MacTCP physically—you just drag it into the Control Panels folder—but the configuration requires Internet knowledge and experience. You'll need help and lots of information from your service provider to set up MacTCP correctly. For more information on what you'll need, see "Getting the Information You Need," in Chapter 8.

**WEB
SECRET**

Looking for help in configuring MacTCP? Here are some very useful URLs that contain step-by-step instructions and freeware (if you're not connected to the Internet yet, ask an Internet-connected friend to obtain the documentation for you):

- **http://beast.cc.emory.edu/MacTCP/Projects.HTML** These instructions walk you through the entire process of installing an Ethernet card, an Ethernet transceiver, and MacTCP, as well as configuring MacTCP for LAN access. The instructions are specific to Emory University, but you can make changes to suit your LAN's IP addresses.

- **file://ftp.tidbits.com/pub/tidbits/dominating-mactcp-draft.etx** Adam Engst, author of *Internet Starter Kit for Macintosh*, offers a Web-accessible update called "Dominating MacTCP." Anyone trying to configure MacTCP will want to have a copy of this indispensable document! Note that an update will soon appear, so this URL may change.

- **http://www.intac.com/njmug/MacTCP_Switcher_Doc.html** This document describes MacTCP Switcher, a freeware program that enables you to switch among multiple MacTCP configurations. This is especially useful for PowerBook owners who may access the Web from two or more service providers. The author, John Norstad, works at the Academic Computing and Network Services center at Northwestern University.

If you're planning to access the Internet by means of an Ethernet LAN, MacTCP gives you all you need. Macintosh users planning to use SLIP/PPP must obtain additional software, as explained in the box ("SLIP/PPP Software for the Macintosh," in Chapter 8).

TCP/IP FOR MICROSOFT WINDOWS 3.1: THE WINSOCK STANDARD

Connecting a Windows system to the Internet was virtually impossible outside of hacking circles before the 1992 development of the Winsock protocol. This standard defines a *dynamic link library* (DLL) file that provides TCP/IP support at the transport layer for Microsoft Windows applications. Previously, TCP/IP support programs for Microsoft Windows had used terminate and stay resident (TSR) programs that ran under DOS. There were two drawbacks to the TSR solution: TSRs consume conventional memory, of which there is seldom enough, and the TSR would support only those Internet access utilities made by the same manufacturer. By speficying standards for TCP/IP support in a DLL file, the Winsock specification provides support for any Winsock-compatible application. All of the hottest Web software, such as Netscape and Mosaic, is Winsock-compatible.

To put it briefly: If you want to access the Web with Windows, you need to equip your system with a WINSOCK.DLL file that's compatible with the Winsock 2.0 specification. It provides information and instructions needed by any application that needs to access the Internet. The Winsock specification is written in such a way that, in theory, no matter which software publisher actually created the WINSOCK.DLL file, any Internet application can access it and use it. In practice, as you'll see in a moment, that's not always true.

The Winsock protocol had its origins in a Birds Of A Feather session held at Interop, a major Internet trade conference, in late 1991. After a period of public debate, the standard was published as an open protocol in 1992. Since then, numerous programs have been developed that equip Windows with the necessary DLL file, and applications have been developed—such as Web—that require Winsock-compatible TCP/IP support.

WEB SECRET

An informative paper on the Winsock specification is available from Microsoft Corporation's World Wide Web server (http://www.microsoft.com/winsock/default.htm). The file is available in Microsoft Word, PostScript, and ASCII versions.

Microsoft Corporation has announced that it intends to fully support the Winsock specification (version 2.0), so that future versions of Microsoft Windows—including Windows NT and the much-awaited Windows 95—will fully support existing Winsock-compatible applications, including Web browsers such as Mosaic and

Netscape. Until Windows 95 comes along, most Windows users will need to add the WINSOCK.DLL file to their systems.

HOME PAGE

Looking for Winsock? You've already got it. The disk packaged with this book contains NetManage's version of Mosaic.

Although (in theory) any WINSOCK.DLL will work for any Internet application, you'll be well advised to use the WINSOCK.DLL file that's designed to work with the Internet access software you've chosen. Here's a list of your best options:

- **SLIP/PPP access.** The NetManage Chameleon sampler software included with this book features WINSOCK.DLL as well as a SLIP/PPP dialer.
- **LAN access.** Your best bet here is to use the Winsock support that's designed to work with the network operating system that you're using. Novell network users can upgrade to the latest version of the LAN Workplace network software (version 4.2), which includes a WINSOCK.DLL that's designed for Novell network access. If you're accessing a network through Windows for Workgroups' network support, you can obtain a free Microsoft utility called Wolverine.

AWFUL

Planning to connect via a network? Beware: Configuring TCP/IP support for LANs is a complicated business, one that's beyond the skills of most PC users. To configure your system for Internet access on a LAN, ask your network administrator for help.

Most readers of this book will access the Web through the fastest-growing type of Internet access: dialup IP (SLIP/PPP). In the next chapter, you'll learn how to configure your Macintosh or Windows system for direct Internet access using these dialup protocols.

SUMMARY

To get the most out of the Web, you need to equip your Macintosh or Windows system with TCP/IP support. This enables your computer to "talk" to the Internet. TCP/IP support is needed for dialup IP (SLIP/PPP) as well as network access. TCP/IP support will soon be a standard feature of computer operating systems. For Macs, the reigning standard is Apple's MacTCP utility, now included in System 7.5. For Windows, the Winsock 2.0 standard prevails, and it will be included in the forthcoming Windows 95.

FROM HERE

- For an introduction to your Web connectivity options, see Chapter 6.
- Planning to connect to the Web using SLIP or PPP? See Chapter 8.

CHAPTER 8

Connecting to the Web with Dialup IP (SLIP/PPP)

SLIP and PPP used to be the exclusive province of UNIX wizards, who mumbled
incomprehensible incantations over PCs and modems and somehow got the connection
to work. But a new generation of point-and-click SLIP/PPP programs is comming.
When they arrive, the information superhighway—still a dirt road for most
people—will get it's first coat of pavement.
Archibald Jones

The future of Web connectivity lies in dialup IP (SLIP/PPP). Throughout North
America and Europe, service providers are taking advantage of high-speed
modems, as well as the rapid spread of TCP/IP support in Macintoshes and PCs, to
offer dialup IP services at increasingly attractive rates. And many of the people getting dialup IP connections are doing it so they can access the Web—and for good
reason. Only with a direct Internet connection, as provided by dialup IP or network
access, can you access the multimedia riches of the World Wide Web (with plain
dialup access with a shell or login account, you're stuck with text only).

The pages to follow present the essentials of accessing the Web by means of
dialup IP, beginning with a discussion of why it's worth the hassle of installing and
configuring SLIP/PPP software. (If you're planning to use the Web on a networked
computer at work, you can skip this chapter.) Next, you'll find a discussion of the
high-speed modem that you'll need to access the Web at tolerable speeds. It continues with a discussion of Macintosh and Windows options for SLIP/PPP access and
explains the mysteries of the dreaded login script. You'll also learn how to obtain
the information you need to configure your SLIP/PPP software.

**HOME
PAGE**

Planning to use the Chameleon Sampler software included with this book? Read this chapter for a general introduction, and then flip to Appendix A for the specifics!

There's an excellent page devoted to Macintosh and Windows dialup IP programs and tools at http://www.dnai.com/programs.html. The page is provided by Direct Network Access (DNAI), an Internet service provider serving San Francisco and the East Bay area in California.

**WEB
SECRET**

ARE THE INSTALLATION AND CONFIGURATION HASSLES WORTH IT?

"Ordeal" is the best word to describe the hassle of installing and configuring a SLIP or PPP connection. Here's what's involved:

- **Obtaining Information from Your Service Provider.** You must obtain Internet addresses and other information, and type these into configuration dialog boxes. Unless you're a seasoned Internet pro, you won't have the slightest idea what you're doing—and if you're not careful, you might make some small mistake that will keep the configuration from working correctly.

- **Writing a Login Script.** A *login script* is a brief program that communicates with the server. It does simple things such as providing your login name and password and requesting SLIP access. To write a login script successfully, you must write instructions that anticipate the prompts that the service provider's computer displays. This isn't beyond the skill level of most Macintosh and Windows users, but that doesn't mean it's easy.

HOT TIP

Let someone else do the installing and configuring for you! If you're affiliated with a college or university, chances are that someone has created a document explaining how to configure popular SLIP/PPP packages (such as Trumpet Winsock) and written sample login scripts. Don't reinvent the wheel! If you're planning SLIP/PPP access through an Internet service provider, look for one that gives you "point-and-click" installation and configuration, and make sure you obtain a complete login script.

Is dialup IP worth the hassle? If you haven't experienced it, you won't believe the difference between ordinary dialup access and dialup IP. With dialup access, you're stuck (for the most part) with a clunky communications program and whatever text-based interface the connecting computer throws at you, and you can only do one thing at a time. With dialup IP, you can choose the applications you want.

And there's another good reason to try dialup IP. Imagine running several Internet client programs at the same time (see Figure 8.1). I'm running Netscape to browse the Web, of course, but also Eudora (a wonderful electronic mail client program), a terminal program that's displaying Gopher, and WinVN (a USENET newsreader)—all at the same time! How does this work? In Chapter 6, you learned that the Internet works by chopping data into little packets, each with its own address. These are reassembled at their destination. Along the way, these packets are mixed, helter-skelter, with packets from other applications. When you give your computer TCP/IP support, you give it the ability to reassemble the packets correctly on their arrival—even if they're coming from several different servers on the Internet.

EXCELLENT

Figure 8.1 *Running several Internet applications simultaneously with SLIP*

WHAT KIND OF MODEM DO I NEED?

In brief, a fast one—but here's some background. A modem is a computer accessory that permits your computer to communicate with other computers via the telephone system, which can't handle computer signals unless they're altered. The phone system, after all, was designed for the human voice, so it's optimized to carry the sound frequencies the human voice uses. To send computer signals, a modem modulates (changes) these signals into sounds within the frequency range of the human voice. It also demodulates incoming signals so the computer can understand them. The term *modem* is an abbreviation of MOdulator/DEModulator.

KEY TERM

What does "fast" mean in the modem world? Modems are rated by the number of *bits per second* (bps) the modem can transmit. (Sometimes this is referred to as the "baud rate" but technically that's incorrect—ask for the bps rate if you're shopping for a modem, just to make sure.) Today's high-speed modems operate at speeds of 14,400 bps (14.4 Kbps), which is reasonably fast, and 28,800 bps (28.8 Kbps), which is *very* fast. In general, you'll need a 14.4-Kbps modem for any form of dialup IP. 28.8-Kbps modems are now widely available, but check with your service provider to make sure it can handle that speed. (If you already have a 28.8-Kbps modem, but your service provider can't handle that speed, don't despair; a fast modem will automatically switch to the highest speed that the modem on the other end of the line can handle.)

KEY TERM

But speed isn't everything. To communicate with each other, the modems at the sending and receiving ends of the line must obey the same *modulation protocol*, a standard that specifies the modulation method. (When you see the word "protocol," just think "standard," and you'll understand the concept just fine.) It's wise to stick with modems that conform to the international protocols maintained by the International Telecommunications Union—Telecommunications Standards Section (ITU-TSS), an agency of the United Nations. The ITU-TSS, formerly called the CCITT (Comité Consultiv International de Télégraphique et Téléphonique), is responsible for all those "V-dot" standards you may have encountered, such as V.32*bis* and V.42. An ITU-TSS-compatible modem can "talk" to another ITU-TSS-compatible modem, even if it's made by a different manufacturer.

HOT TIP

If you're looking for a 14.4-Kbps modem, look for one that conforms to the V.32*bis* and V.42*bis* standards. For 28.8-Kbps modems, look for V.34 compatibility—and don't settle for a "V.FC" modem. The "V.FC" or "V.Fast Class" standard isn't an ITU-TSS standard at all; it's a preliminary V.34 standard created by manufacturers impatient with the ITU-TSS's very slow progress in publishing the V.34 standard. But once V.34 comes out, V.FC and its imitators will be history, and you may be stuck with a modem that you can't upgrade and that can't talk to your service provider's modem.

SLIP/PPP SOFTWARE FOR MACINTOSH AND WINDOWS SYSTEMS

To access the Web by means of dialup IP, you'll need software that provides TCP/IP support (see the previous chapter). You'll also need software that configures your computer for SLIP or PPP access, dials the access number, and handles the details of connecting to the service provider's computer. The following sections discuss SLIP and PPP software for Macintosh and Microsoft Windows systems.

For Macs, the TCP/IP and SLIP/PPP software are separate. MacTCP, an Apple product, provides the TCP/IP support. You'll also need a dialup IP program such as InterSLIP or MacPPP. For Windows systems, the TCP/IP support usually comes with the dialup IP software.

SLIP/PPP Software for the Macintosh

MacTCP, the Apple TCP/IP utility package for Macintosh systems, provides the Internet support that Macs need to access the Web. If you plan to use dialup IP, though, you'll need additional software (see the box, "Macintosh Software for SLIP/PPP Access").

HOME PAGE

MACINTOSH SOFTWARE FOR SLIP/PPP ACCESS

- **MacSLIP** (Hyde Park Software, $49.95) supports SLIP and CSLIP (but not PPP). Essentially, it's an extension of MacTCP.

- **InterSLIP** (InterCom Systems, freeware). InterSLIP is available with InterCom's complete networking product (TCP/Connect II), but InterSLIP is available separately, and for free, from InterCom's anonymous FTP server (ftp.intercon.com in InterCon/sales).

- **MacPPP** (Merit Network/University of Michigan, freeware) MacPPP is available from gopher://gopher.ethz.ch:1070/11/mac/ppp/macppp2.0.1-src.hqx.

SLIP/PPP Software for Microsoft Windows

Unlike the Mac products just surveyed, the SLIP/PPP packages for Microsoft Windows systems also include TCP/IP support in the form of a WINSOCK.DLL file. This will doubtless change when Microsoft incorporates full TCP/IP support in the forthcoming revision of Windows, Windows 95. For now, plan to obtain your TCP/IP support when you get your SLIP/PPP software. For a review of current offerings in this area, see the box entitled "Microsoft Windows Software for SLIP/PPP Access."

MICROSOFT WINDOWS SOFTWARE FOR SLIP/PPP ACCESS

- **Internet in a Box** (Spry, $149). Contained in the package is Spry's AIR NFS TCP/IP support for Microsoft Windows, the winner of *PC Magazine*'s coveted Editor's Choice award in a survey of a dozen commercial TCP/IP support packages. The package contains an NFS-compatible WINSOCK.DLL, a SLIP/PPP dialer, Air Mosaic, a variety of additional Internet navigation tools, and a copy of Ed Krol's *The Whole Internet*. If you're using one of the service providers that this package supports, installing all the software is easy: preconfigured point-and-click installation scripts take care of all the tedious configuration tasks.

- **NetManage Chameleon** (NetManage, $199). Like Internet in a Box, this package includes point-and-click installation and configuration for a variety of SLIP/PPP service providers. The package includes a Chameleon-compatible WINSOCK.DLL, NetManage's graphical Web browser (WebSurfer), a variety of additional Internet client applications, and the Instant Internet point-and-click configuration program. NetManage's Chameleon Sampler, which includes WebSurfer and software for SLIP/PPP access, is included on the disk with this book.

- **Trumpet Winsock** (Trumpet Software International, $40). If you don't go the commercial TCP/IP route, you can save some money—you can obtain shareware programs that will equip your computer with the needed TCP/IP connectivity. But be forewarned: You'll be on your own when it comes to writing a dialin script for SLIP/PPP service providers. Trumpet Winsock, the most respected shareware product for TCP/IP support and SLIP/PPP dialin, supports SLIP and PPP as well as Ethernet packet drivers. Trumpet Winsock, now available in Version 2.0, is wider, available by means of anonymous FTP (ftp.trumpet.com.au).

HOT TIP
If you're thinking of buying a point-and-click access kit such as NetManage Chameleon or Internet in a Box, you can save lots of time by using the preconfigured login scripts provided with these packages. Such scripts are provided for a variety of Internet service providers. But before plunking down your money, make sure you're within a local telephone call of the service providers. Generally speaking, these service providers have points of presence only in large metropolitan areas. If you live in a smaller city, a town, or a rural area, you may

find that the much-vaunted "point-and-click" installation does you no good whatsoever, unless you're willing to fork over big bucks for long-distance calls to the nearest access number. Caveat emptor!

A TYPICAL SLIP OR PPP SESSION

Here's an overview of a typical SLIP or PPP session:

1. You launch the dialer program, which is included among the programs in your SLIP or PPP package. This program accesses and configures your modem and then dials the service provider's number.

2. When the service provider answers, the dialer program plays a *script*. This script is a minicomputer program that communicates with the service provider's computer. If (and only if) the script is properly written, the SLIP or PPP connection is achieved.

3. The dialer program drops into the background, and you're ready to start using the Internet.

This is all pretty easy, with the exception of writing the script. With the SLIP/PPP software that's currently available, writing a script for error-free SLIP or PPP access isn't exactly a piece of cake. Happily, most service providers know this and provide prewritten scripts. If you can't get a preconfigured script, though, don't despair. The script needn't be any longer or more complicated than those little Lotus 1-2-3 macros that millions of PC users write without blinking an eye. This book gives you all the information you'll need to write scripts for both Windows and Macintosh IP connectivity.

HOT TIP If you're planning SLIP or PPP access with a particular service provider, don't buy SLIP or PPP software until you check with your service provider. Ask whether they have prewritten scripts for dialup IP access, and if so, which SLIP/PPP software package these scripts are designed to work with. Then, get that package and no other!

PREPARING YOUR SYSTEM FOR DIALUP IP (SLIP OR PPP)

To get your SLIP or PPP connection working, you must take the following preliminary steps:

1. Get an account with a service provider that offers SLIP, CSLIP, or PPP access using a high-speed modem.
2. Obtain information from your service provider that you will need in order to configure your software.

Getting an Account

Your first step is to contact an Internet service provider and set up an account. Look for the following:

- **Local telephone access**. You don't want to have to pay long-distance charges, if possible. Some service providers offer access by means of 800 numbers. This may be the best choice if you're trying to get connected from a rural location.

- **Flat rate billing**. If you shop around, you should be able to get a SLIP or PPP connection for as little as $29 per month for unlimited or practically unlimited usage. It's an increasingly competitive market.

- **Low up-front fees**. Watch out for high up-front fees, particularly if this is justified by giving you NetManage's Chameleon software. You've already got it!

- **Preconfigured software**. Ideally, your service provider can supply you with all the software you need for TCP/IP support and SLIP, CSLIP, or PPP access, including a preconfigured login script.

Installing and Configuring the Software

Ideally, the software you've obtained is preconfigured; you simply install the programs, click the icon, and you're connected! In practice, you may need to type information into dialog boxes, and—this is the worst-case scenario—you may have to write a login script. If you must configure the software, see the next section to find out what information you need from your service provider. If you must write your own login script, see "Writing a Login Script" later in this chapter.

Unless you're lucky enough to have obtained a completely preconfigured "point-and-click" package, you'll need lots of information from your service provider in order to get your SLIP or PPP connection to work. You will need to supply this information in configuration dialog boxes, such as the one shown in Figure 8.2.

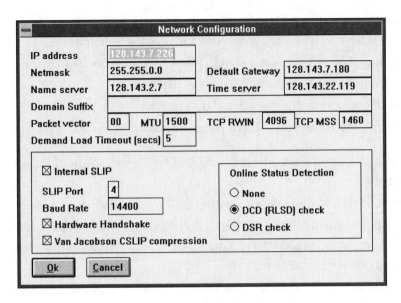

Figure 8.2 TCP/IP and SLIP configuration dialog box (Trumpet Winsock).

Here are the questions you should ask. (If you don't understand what all this stuff means, don't worry—you just need to type this information into the appropriate dialog box in your SLIP or PPP software and then you can forget about it.) You'll use the answers to these questions to set up your Windows or Macintosh system for dialup IP.

- **Type of Service.** Is the service based on the SLIP, CSLIP, or PPP protocol? If it's a SLIP service, what command must I type to initiate the SLIP connection when I log on?

- **IP Address.** How is the IP address determined? Is it permanent or dynamic (temporary)? If it's permanent, what's the address?

- **Domain Name.** What is the service provider's domain name?

- **Subnet Mask.** What is the subnet mask (also called net mask) that I should enter?

- **Domain Name Server (DNS) Addresses.** What is the IP address of the default Domain Name Server that I'll be using? Is there a second DNS server in case the first one's down or busy? A third?

- **Login Procedure.** What exactly do I type when I log on to your computer? Do I have to press Enter after making initial contact? (On all systems, you'll have to type your login name and your password. If you're using SLIP, you'll have to type a command that initiates the SLIP link.)

- **Dialup Access User Name (Login Name).** What is my login name?
- **Dialup Access Password.** What is my password?
- **SLIP command.** What command do I type to initiate the SLIP link?
- **Telephone Number.** What telephone number do I dial to access this service?

If you are also getting electronic mail and USENET service from this provider, ask the following:

- **E-Mail User Name.** What's my electronic mail address?
- **E-Mail Password.** What password do I type to access my electronic mail?
- **Mail Gateway Name.** What's the IP address of the computer where people send electronic mail to me?
- **Mail Server Name.** What's the IP address of the POP server where I access my electronic mail?
- **NNTP Server Name.** What's the IP address of the NNTP (USENET) server?

WRITING THE LOGIN SCRIPT

A *login script* is a brief computer program that tells the SLIP/PPP dialer how to interact with your service provider's login messages. The script performs vital functions such as providing your login name and password and initiating the SLIP or PPP link. You write the script with a word processing program, saving it to the dialer's directory so it's accessible to the dialer.

Do you really need to write a script? Some SLIP/PPP programs permit you to respond to the service provider's prompts manually. In some cases, this enables you to avoid writing the script—but you'll have to type your login name, password, and perhaps additional information every time you want to use the Web. Chances are you'll soon decide to write a login script, which handles these tasks automatically. Note, however, that manual login procedures won't work with dynamic IP addressing, in which your computer is assigned a temporary IP address every time you access the Web. With dynamic addressing, an important function of the login script is to "capture" the temporary IP address you've been assigned.

If your SLIP/PPP software does not come with a preconfigured login script, you'll have to write your own. Because many SLIP/PPP programs are inadequately documented, this task can prove tedious and frustrating. However, it's easier if you approach the task with a logical line of attack. Here's an overview of the procedure I recommend:

AWFUL

1. **Access the service provider with a communications program and print the results.** You'll see the messages that the service provider's computer displays when accessed.

2. **Study the scripting language.** Most scripting languages are very simple in that they do only two things: look for some specific set of characters (a *string*) and send characters in response. That's what enables the dialer program to respond to text such as "Please type your password."

3. **Obtain and modify a sample script.** Don't start from scratch. Chances are the program comes with several sample scripts. You can also find and download sample scripts from the Web, if you can arrange Web access on a friend's or colleague's computer.

4. **Test and revise the script.** Try logging on. It probably won't work, and you'll have to figure out why.

Accessing the Service Provider's Computer

By using a communications program to access the service provider's computer, you can find out what this computer displays on-screen. You need this information in order to write your script. In brief, your login script will be nothing more than a set of commands that detects incoming text and sends a response.

The following is an example of the information displayed on your screen after you contact a service provider's computer. In this example, you're contacting a SLIP service provider that uses dynamic IP addressing. Armed with the service provider's list of what you should type in response to the system's prompts, you use a communications program (or the manual dialer in your SLIP program) to contact the service provider's computer. The text sent by the service provider's computer is shown in ordinary type, while the text you type to access the system is shown in bold:

```
CONNECT 14400
Welcome to Cyber City!
Login name: wmi2x
Password:2tuff2type
Cybercity>SLIP DEFAULT
Initiating SLIP mode.
Your IP address is 129.70.222.10
Matching headers to your compression.
```

AWFUL

If you're accessing a SLIP service provider that uses dynamic addressing, typing responses manually—as shown in the above example—won't fully establish the SLIP connection. Why? Because you need to "capture" the IP address that the system has temporarily assigned your computer. You could do this by copying the IP address and entering it into the appropriate configuration dialog box, but that's a tedious procedure that will have to be followed every time you log on. The solution? Write a login script.

Study the Scripting Language

The term *scripting language* refers to the *statements* (typed commands) and *syntax* (rules for typing commands) that you use to write a login script. Unfortunately, there's no "standard" scripting language—each program uses its own unique commands and has its own rules of syntax. Yet there are similarities. Each scripting language must be able to detect certain incoming character patterns, called *strings*, and respond by sending the appropriate text (such as a password). In most scripting languages, then, there are two basic kinds of statements that you'll type:

KEY TERM

- **Expect Statements**. You type the word or the characters that the dialer program is supposed to wait for. For example, you can tell the dialer program to wait for "name:" before it sends information.
- **Send Statements**. These follow the expect statements and tell the dialer program what to send. An example is a statement that says, in effect, "send the login name and then press Enter."

Expect statements require that you type some of the text that the dialer waits to match. In the following table, you see examples from two scripting languages (NetManage Chameleon and Trumpet Winsock) that would match text sent by the "CyberCity" service provider.

Examples from Two Different Scripting Languages

	NetManage Chameleon	Trumpet Winsock
Expect login name	login name:	input login name:
Expect password	password:	input password:

Send statements require that you type a command and, in some cases, the text that you want the dialer to send (such as the login name and password). In the following table, again based on the "CyberCity" example, you see examples from the same two scripting languages. Chameleon gets the login name and password automatically from a configuration dialog box that you've filled out, while Trumpet Winsock requires that you add this text to the login script.

Example Send and Expect Statements

	NetManage Chameleon	Trumpet Winsock
Send Enter	$r	\r
Send login name	$u	Output wmi2x
Send password	$p	Output 2tuff2type
Initiate SLIP	$c	Output SLIP DEFAULT
Get IP address	address -i	address

The login script itself is a text file that you can create with any word processing program or text editor. It consists of a few simple expect and send statements. The tough part is making sure that you've typed everything correctly and that you've followed the rules of syntax.

Obtain and Modify a Sample Script

Don't try to start from scratch. Chances are that your SLIP/PPP software comes with one or more "generic" scripts that you can study and modify.

Here's an example of a simple NetManage Chameleon login script that would work with the CyberCity example:

```
SCRIPT=name: $u$r password: $p$r City> $c$r address -i
```

This script says, in English, "Wait until the service provider's computer sends the text **name:**. Then send the login name and press **Enter**. Now wait until **password:** is received, send the password, and press **Enter**. When the prompt **City>** is received, send the SLIP command and press **Enter**. Wait for the text **address** and get the IP address."

In Trumpet Winsock, the same script looks like the one in the following example. Note that Trumpet Winsock, unlike Chameleon, requires you to include modem commands. The numbers refer to the time (in seconds) that the program is instructed to wait for expected text.

```
output atdt*70,9825084\13
input 50 Login name:
output wmi2x \r
input 30 Password:
output 2tuff2type \r
input 30 CyberCity>
output slip \r
input 40 address
address 30
```

Scripts can get much fancier than these simple examples. Here's a wish list of advanced features for login scripts:

- **Error Trapping.** What happens if the service provider's line is busy? What if SLIP failed to initiate? A complex login script can jump to subroutines (optional sections of the program) if something goes wrong.

- **Prompting the User for the Password.** If you embed your password in the script, anyone can use your computer to get onto the Internet. For this reason, it's best to write the program so that it prompts you to type your password each time you log on.

**WEB
SECRET**

Trying to write an advanced login script? Don't reinvent the wheel! If you can't get your hands on a preconfigured login script, check out these sample scripts available on the Web:

- **MacSLIP** (Macintosh). For a general introduction, see the MacSLIP FAQ available at http://www.intac.com/njmug/files/MACSLIP.TXT. A detailed sample, keyed to a specific service provider but easily adapted for other uses, is found at http://www.intac.com/njmug/files/INTAC.script

- **InterSLIP** (Macintosh). A very thorough and well-written introduction to InterSLIP scripting is found at http://www.intac.com/njmug/files/scr-interslip-dialscript

- **MacPPP** (Macintosh). A thorough introduction is available at ftp://merit.edu/pub/ppp/mac/macppp.txt.new. A detailed sample, keyed to a specific service provider but easily adapted for other uses, is found at http://www.intac.com/~jvafai/macppp_tcp.html

- **Trumpet Winsock** (Windows). This shareware program comes with excellent documentation. For tips and hints, you'll find a thorough exploration of Trumpet Winsock installation issues at http://tbone.biol.scarolina.edu/~dean2/kit/winsock.html

Testing and Revising the Script

In computer programming, the term *debugging* refers to the laborious process of figuring out why a program doesn't work correctly. Chances are good that your login script won't work correctly the first time you try it. Here's a list of possible reasons:

KEY TERM

- In expect statements, you must type the expected text precisely. Did you include all the necessary punctuation? As far as Chameleon is concerned, "login name" and "login name:" are two different strings (the difference lies in the colon at the end of the second string).

- You must follow the syntax rules. In Chameleon, for example, every expect statement must be followed by a send statement.

- Did you put spaces where they're supposed to be—or leave them out where they're not required?

- Did you use the correct statements?

- Are the statements in the correct order?

Don't beat your head against the wall if you can't get your login script to work—get help from somebody who's done it successfully. Computing is supposed to be fun and rewarding!

HOT TIP

SUMMARY

Dialup IP lets you work with two or more Internet applications at once, including Web, and once you've experienced it you will never go back to dialup access. It's simple to work, once you've got everything set up. You just launch a dialer program, which executes an automatic script. In less than a minute, you're connected, and you can start using theWeb.

Your best source of guidance for SLIP, CSLIP, or PPP connectivity is the service provider you're planning to use. Chances are the service provider will give you preconfigured software that's ready for you to install and run. If not, Windows users can run the Chameleon Sampler that's included with this book, and Macintosh users can obtain a free program called InterSLIP that will do the trick (but for SLIP only).

When you establish your account with the service provider, you'll need lots of information so that you can configure your software correctly. If you must write your own login script, this chapter provides a step-by-step formula for success.

FROM HERE...

- For information on installing and configuring the Chameleon software that comes with this book, see Appendix A.

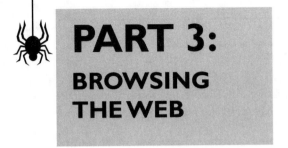

PART 3:
BROWSING THE WEB

CHAPTER 9

Introducing Graphical Browsers

Mosaic is driving the next stage of evolution of the global Internet.
What emerges will be a new form of life on-line.
—Joseph Hardin, National Center for Supercomputing Applications

Created at CERN in 1989, the World Wide Web was initially little more than an Internet curiosity—until graphical browsers came along. Combining the multimedia capabilities of the Internet with the hypertext metaphors of the World Wide Web, graphical browsers fueled the Web's explosive growth. And it's becoming clear that graphical browsers are well on their way to becoming *the* client application of choice for *all* Internet services, including FTP, WAIS, Gopher, and more.

In most peoples' minds, the terms "graphical browser" and "Mosaic" are all but synonymous—in much the same way that "cola" and "Coke" or "photocopy" and "Xerox" have become interchangeable. But there are many versions or flavors of Mosaic, including products that look and work very much like Mosaic (but go by different names). In this chapter, you'll enter the world of Web browsers, and learn to distinguish among the many browsers available, including NCSA Mosaic, Cello, Air Mosaic, Enhanced NCSA Mosaic, Netscape, and WebSurfer. Before going into these specific programs, this chapter looks at the ideal graphical browser. Then we'll see how these specific offerings measure up.

THE IDEAL GRAPHICAL BROWSER

**WISH
LIST**

What's the ideal graphical browser? After testing all of the graphical browsers currently available, I'd like to see a browser that has all of the following features.

- **Graphical User Interface (GUI).** The program should conform to prevailing GUI standards so that users do not have to learn new techniques to use the program. The interface should use a mouse and employ pull-down menus with underlined accelerator keys, dialog boxes with familiar controls (such as radio buttons and list boxes), and toolbar icons that selection of frequently-accessed commands quickly.

- **Fast Operation.** The program should download in-line images quickly and efficiently. Preferably, it should download the text prior to the images, so that you can read the text while the images are taking shape.

- **Efficiency.** The program should not consume inordinate amounts of memory or disk space.

- **Navigation Buttons.** The user should be able to click on-screen navigation buttons (located on the toolbar) to display previous documents (back), to return to newer documents (forward), and to return home.

- **History List.** As the user browses the Web, the program should keep a list of all the URLs that have been visited. Additionally, the user should be able to return to a previously-visited URL by displaying the list and selecting a URL from it.

- **Hotlist.** The user should be able to add an interesting or useful URL to a hotlist, that can be accessed by using a dialog box or a pull-down menu. The user should be able to organize the hotlist easily by creating folders (sometimes known as submenus).

- **Subject Trees/Search Engines.** The program should come with built-in buttons or hotlist items that point the user to subject trees and search engines, which are necessary tools for Web exploration.

- **Easy Configuration.** The program should provide easy-to-use dialog boxes or other controls that enable the user to identify helper pages, to select new home pages, and to choose other configuration options.

- **Multimedia.** The program should be able to display GIF and JPEG graphics quickly, preferably without relying on helper programs. If it can't play sounds and movies directly, it should start helper programs.

- **Document Styles.** The program should provide easy-to-use controls for choosing fonts, font sizes, emphases, and other attributes. It should enable the user to make full use of all the font resources available on the user's system.

- **Annotations.** The program should allow the user to add private annotations to displayed documents.

- **Document Cache.** To speed re-display of recently-accessed documents, the program should store these documents in RAM. If the user elects to re-display these documents (for example, by clicking the Back button), the browser should not have to retrieve them again from the network. The best browsers let the user cache documents on disk, where they can be kept during browser sessions.

Does the ideal browser exist? In brief, no—but Netscape comes close. Let's get down to the details.

NCSA MOSAIC

What do the graphical user interface (GUI), the mouse, laser printers, Ethernet LANS, what-you-see-is-what-you-get word processing programs, and most recently, Mosaic have in common? They're all the products of academically-oriented think tanks. The user interface technology that's so familiar to millions of Windows and Macintosh users comes from Xerox Corporation's Palo Alto Research Center (XEROX PARC). The Web itself is a product of the European particle physics think tank, CERN, while Mosaic—the latest rage in computing—comes from the National Center for Supercomputing Applications, a computer science think tank affiliated with the University of Illinois.

The Think Tank Advantage

What is it about think tanks such as PARC and NCSA that produces such innovative technology as GUI and the WEB browser? It's simple. High-powered researchers find themselves drowning in information, strapped for time, and hard-pressed to share information. They spend a lot of time thinking about how such things could be done more efficiently. If they're let loose to create technology, chances are they'll do what comes naturally—create exactly what they want. And they don't have to worry about marketing; their research is supported in the hope of scientific gains that may have big commercial payoffs down the road.

What do scientific researchers want? Increasingly, they want to visualize their data—to see graphics and animations that show them the patterns inherent in the data they're analyzing. And they also want to break down the geographic barriers to collaboration. Clearly, the technology's available to do this. Says Joseph Hardin, NCSA's associate director for the Software Development Group, "It's now possible to create a tool for digitally-based collaboration across space and time."

EXCELLENT

Interested in what scientists are up to with visualization? Take a look at *Visualization of Natural Phenomena* by Robert S. Wolff and Larry Yaeger of Apple Computer Inc., published by TELOS: The Library of Science (a division of Springer/Verlag, Inc., New York, 1993). The text can be tough going if it's been a while since your last physics class, but the graphics are great—and, if you're tired of reading, you can pop the enclosed CD-ROM into your Macintosh. NCSA contributions include a foreword written by NCSA Director Larry Smarr.

In NCSA's case, what research scientists wanted was a way to make supercomputer power accessible to geographically-distant researchers. Formerly, researchers had to travel hundreds or even thousands of miles to visit NCSA, give the supercomputer operators a disk with their data, sit around while the program runs on the supercomputer, and then view the analyzed data on a graphics terminal. It costs money and time to send people to NCSA, and there's no real reason to do so.

With the right software, researchers can upload their data via the Internet for supercomputer analysis. The results, expressed in charts, diagrams, and animations, are transmitted back to the researcher, again via the Internet, and viewed on the researcher's workstation. No travel, negligible cost, no pollution! All that was missing was the software, and a graphics-capable Web browser seemed ideally suited to the task. Tim Berners-Lee had already demonstrated the potential of the Web to link scientific researchers, so a graphics-capable Web browser offered what appeared to be an ideal solution to NCSA's needs.

Mosaic: A Tool for Digital Collaboration

NCSA has developed a variety of programs that address this solution, including Collage, a program that fosters long-distance, interactive visualization of supercomputer data. But Mosaic has proven to be by far the most useful of these tools. Mohan Ramamurthy, a professor of atmospheric sciences at University of Illinois, recalls: "[NCSA Mosaic] solved a series of problems when it came out. We were doing interactive multimedia, but not across the network. We wanted to set up some sort of digital library that provides access to real and retrospective databases, to educational modules, and so on. In one shot, Mosaic allows us to do that."

NATIONAL CENTER FOR SUPERCOMPUTING APPLICATIONS (NCSA)

Think tank, research institute, supercomputer center, and birthplace of Mosaic—it's all these, and more. With a common mission to develop and disseminate high-performance computing technology, NCSA fosters collaboration among some of the country's most talented scientists, engineers, social scientists, artists, humanists, and educators. A staff of 180 caters to their needs—and the results are evident everywhere in the Center's pathbreaking work.

NCSA was founded in February 1985 with assistance from the National Science Foundation, the state of Illinois, the University of Illinois at Urbana-Champaign (UIUC), corporate partners, and other federal agencies. By 1994, the center had provided high-performance computing resources and services to more than 6,000 users at more than 380 universities and corporations.

Why is the Center necessary? Today, the problems facing scientists and engineers are so complex that they can't be modeled by physical systems—the expense would be too great. By simulating complex systems on the computer, and then observing the behavior of these systems in graphical simulations, scientists are making important new discoveries. And the results are affecting our lives—more efficient automobile engines, less pollution, safer aircraft, more accurate weather forecasts, and much more.

NCSA Mosaic was originally designed and programmed for the X Window (UNIX) platform by Marc Andreessen and Eric Bina at NCSA. Version 1.0 was released in April, 1993. In December, 1993, the Macintosh and Microsoft Windows versions of Mosaic were released. Figure 9.1 shows the screen appearance of the Windows version of NCSA Mosaic for Windows, version 2.0a8.

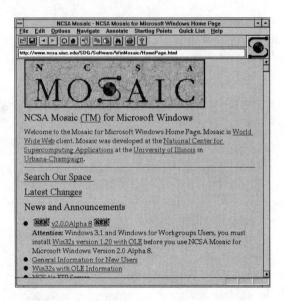

Figure 9.1 *NCSA Mosaic for Windows (version 2.0a8)*

Mosaic Takes Off

Originally created to foster scientific collaboration on the World Wide Web, NCSA's Mosaic is obviously useful for other Internet users as well. For this reason, NCSA decided to make Mosaic available via **anonymous FTP** (a form of file transfer) as well as traditional snail-mail channels. NCSA is committed to providing a free, public-service version of Mosaic to advance the program's research and educational uses.

Available for Microsoft Windows, Macintosh, and X Window/Motif systems, NCSA Mosaic is available on a "free with copyright" basis, which means the following:

- The program is copyrighted. The NCSA Mosaic logo (the spinning globe) is a trademark owned by the University of Illinois, and the program code itself is copyrighted, with the copyright again held by the University.

- The program is free for use by individuals, by academic institutions, and by companies for internal business.

- Commercial use of NCSA Mosaic requires a license from NCSA. In general, commercial use means the following: (1) distributing the program to clients or customers outside the firm for business purposes; (2) using the source code for derivative products that are offered for sale; (3) installing Mosaic as a for-profit service; or (4) distributing the program on disks or CD-ROM disks. Other uses may be judged to be commercial as well.

The widespread availability of Mosaic on the Internet led to the Web's explosive growth, and caused problems for NCSA. Deluged by electronic mail, phone calls, and letters, the NCSA staff realized that they were not in a position to support a program that had quickly attained an installed user base of two million. The decision was made to license the Mosaic code for commercial development, as described in the following section.

Although NCSA decided to license Mosaic for commercial development, the organization has clearly affirmed its intention to continue the distribution of the free version of the program. Individuals, academic institutions, and businesses may still obtain and use the free versions of NCSA Mosaic, as long as they do not use the program for commercial purposes.

EXCELLENT

Obtaining NCSA Mosaic

If you're an individual who wants to use Mosaic for non-commercial purposes, you can still obtain the free version of the program, in versions for Microsoft Windows, Macintosh and UNIX workstations.

It's free, but remember the Ferengi Rule of Acquisition #218: "Sometimes what you get for free costs entirely too much." NCSA Mosaic is downright *slow*. Designed in a high-speed networking environment, NCSA's creators gave little thought to the millions who would try to use the program with slow SLIP or PPP dialup connections—and it shows. Worse, the Windows version has been notoriously buggy; one of its least-loved features is a memory leak that consumes more and more of your memory while the program's running.

AWFUL

NCSA MOSAIC SYSTEM REQUIREMENTS

NCSA Mosaic for the Macintosh The Mac version will run on any Macintosh with at least System 7 or later, MacTCP 2.0.2 or later (version 2.0.4 or later is recommended), and 4 MB or more of RAM, with at least 2MB free.

To obtain NCSA Mosaic, you can use NCSA's beleaguered FTP server, or one of the many unofficial **mirror sites** (FTP servers located elsewhere that try to maintain a copy of all the files available at NCSA's server).

Here are the URLs for NCSA's FTP server:

NCSA Mosaic for the Macintosh:
ftp://ftp.ncsa.uiuc.edu/Mosaic/Mac

NCSA Mosaic for X Windows:
ftp://ftp.ncsa.uiuc.edu/Mosaic

NCSA Mosaic for Microsoft Windows:
ftp://ftp.ncsa.uiuc.edu/Mosaic/Win

Here are the unofficial mirror sites:

USA:

site: sunsite.unc.edu

location /pub/packages/infosystems/

Australia:

site: miriworld.its.unimelb.edu.au

location: /pub/clients/

Europe:

site: ftp.luth.se

location: /pub/infosystems/www/

Review

NCSA Mosaic for Windows (version 2.0a8) set the standard for graphical browsers. The program's interface beautifully implements the best Windows standards, and has been widely—and deservedly—imitated. A suite of advanced features such as user-configurable hotlists and menus, annotations, a history list, and more make the program come very close to the ideal, as outlined earlier in this chapter. But NCSA Mosaic is still difficult to configure, requiring the user to access a text-based configuration file in order to specify the helper programs. Another example of the power-at-a-price problem occurs when you create menus and submenus containing your hotlist items, since the built-in Menu Editor is very cumbersome to use. In addition, the program is far from ideal for users of dialup SLIP/PPP connections—it's just too slow.

CELLO

Developed in March of 1993 by Thomas R. Bruce, an "accidental computer guy" working alone at Cornell University Law School, Cello was designed as a hypertext browser for lawyers and law researchers. Its applications go far beyond the legal world, though, and Cello may be used as a general-purpose Web browser. Copyrighted by Cornell University, Cello is free to individuals who wish to use the program for research and educational purposes. The program is available for Microsoft Windows (but not for Macintosh or X Window systems).

Introducing Cello

Anyone familiar with NCSA Mosaic will experience sensory deprivation when beholding Cello's screen, as there's no graphical toolbar (although there are three navigation icons), and the program doesn't look as polished as NCSA's stylish offerings (Figure 9.2). But the program is still worth a second look.

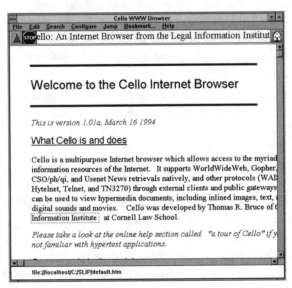

Figure 9.2 Cello

Cello was the first Web browser designed for Microsoft Windows, and may have inspired the National Center for Supercomputer Applications (NCSA) staff to get going on their Mosaic for Windows offering. But Cello stems from a very different ancestry than Mosaic—it derives from late-1980s research into ways of putting legal references on CD-ROM. Legal documents are very well suited to hypertext formats, since, for example, one decision may cite several other cases as precedent or relate to works of legal theory. Rather than having to look up references by hand or do several searches on a computer, hypertext allows legal researchers to easily locate laws, regulations, and opinions. Prior to the advent of Cello, there were hypertext browsers for UNIX and Macintosh platforms but not for Windows machines, which are standard equipment in law offices. Cello deserves recognition as the first successful Web browser for Microsoft Windows.

EXCELLENT

Cello was designed from the beginning with slow dialup IP connections in mind—a reasonable design goal, considering that few attorneys have, direct Internet connections. Its caching capability, or ability to store lots of Web data on your hard disk and recall it when needed, cuts down on the need to tie up a phone line transmitting text and graphics more than once.

For example, you may come across a Web page containing an image of Pablo Picasso's "Guernica" and text about the Spanish Civil War. If you move from that page to another one that also shows "Guernica," but instead features a description of the artist's technique, your computer can fetch the painting from its own memory, not from a distant Web server. Your computer will use the phone line to get anything it doesn't already have in its cache. The cache files are deleted from your hard disk when you exit Cello. You can also download documents onto your hard disk independent of the cache, and have them available for retrieval until you use a file manager to delete them.

Cello's chief advantage does have a down side: it consumes huge amounts of disk space while it's running. It isn't advisable to use Cello unless you've got several megabytes of free space on your hard drive. If you have less, you can tell Cello to leave about half a megabyte on your hard disk empty.

By contrast, NCSA Mosaic employs a caching scheme better suited for computers with an Ethernet (i.e., high-speed, hard-wired) link to the Web. Mosaic saves only the last two or three documents accessed, so it won't tie up your hard disk with its cache file during a session, but makes your computer reload HTML pages more often than Cello does. In short, Mosaic is not as well suited as Cello for use on a dialup connection unless you rarely return to pages you've already viewed. Mosaic also lets you download and store documents you think you'll want to look at again later.

What are the other points of comparison between NCSA Mosaic and Cello? In brief, Mosaic offers you greater opportunity to customize its many functions, while Cello allows greater control over the appearance of documents. For example, Mosaic sticks you with "blah gray" backgrounds, while Cello lets you define a background color by choosing from a palette, or "mixing" your own.

In comparison to Mosaic (version 2) and Netscape, Cello has one enormous drawback—it can't handle on-screen forms. Increasingly, forms are appearing all over the Web; right now, they're permitting users to provide feedback to Webmasters, access WAIS databases, and search Web documents. Soon, they'll let you order goods and services via authenticated secure linkages. Cello's lack of forms-related features puts it out of the running for most Web users.

AWFUL

Another small but distinct advantage of Mosaic over Cello is the globe icon in the upper-right corner of the Mosaic screen that spins whenever the program is looking for something on the Web. Though it changes the mouse cursor from an arrow to the word "NET" enclosed in a box when it goes off to follow a hyperlink, Cello gives you no indication that the program has not hung when it spends a long time waiting for network access. This can get frustrating—as you think, "Is the Net hung up, or should I keep waiting?

Obtaining Cello

You can obtain Cello via anonymous FTP from the following server: ftp:/ /ftp.law.cornell.edu/pub/LII/Cello/.

Review

Cello—and, arguably, NCSA Mosaic—are early efforts that have been surpassed by more recent Web browsers. Still, Cello has many contented users, particularly in the legal environment. If you're just getting started with the Web, though, I'd recommend that you use a more advanced browser.

AIR MOSAIC

By the summer of 1994, NCSA had distributed more than 2 million copies of Mosaic—by any standard, that's a smash hit in the software market. Clearly, there's money to be made from Mosaic, and venture capitalists were soon to take notice. NCSA's charter, however, forbids the research institute from engaging in profit-seeking business ventures.

The solution to this problem was found in licensing schemes, in which commercial vendors are given a license to use and develop derivative products based on NCSA's code. Of the several licensees that developed commercial versions of Mosaic, Spry, Inc., a Seattle firm, was one of the first to make a major impact on the market. Spry's version of NCSA Mosaic, called Air Mosaic (Figure 9.3), is a capable Web browser that addresses many of NCSA Mosaic's shortcomings.

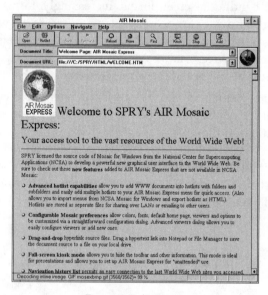

Figure 9.3 *Air Mosaic*

Air Mosaic is the creation of Chris Wilson, the author of the first version of NCSA Mosaic for Windows, and William Perry, author of a character-based UNIX browser. The product is available for Macintosh computers and UNIX workstations as well as Microsoft Windows.

Obtaining Air Mosaic

Air Mosaic sells for $29.95, but you can download a free demo version from the company's Web site. The demo is a fully functional version of Air Mosaic, but limits the number of hyperlinks to six. When you've displayed the sixth document in a session, you see a message inviting you to purchase the full version of the product.

USEFUL RESOURCE

Looking for Spry's demo version of Air Mosaic? Check out Spry's Web site at http://www.spry.com/. While you're there, click the Spry City button to display a nicely-conceived, clickable "city."

You can also purchase Air Mosaic through Spry's *Internet in a Box*, available widely in bookstores. Included is Spry's Air Series software (including Winsock-compatible TCP/IP support, electronic mail, Gopher, FTP, and a Usenet newsreader). The package also includes a PPP dialer, as well as a copy of Ed Krol's *The Whole Internet* (O'Reilly). But be forewarned: This package isn't cheap, and you may not need everything that's in it. However, it has one advantage over obtaining the program via FTP—you don't have to worry about installing and configuring the viewers and players for multimedia information as it's all done for you.

 If you already have TCP/IP support and Internet software for your computer, you'll be better off downloading Air Mosaic and paying the $29.95 fee, as described in the previous section.

HOT TIP

Do you live in a rural area? Internet in a Box provides point-and-click login for SprintLink access via an 800 number. You'll pay $8.95 per month, with an additional $8.95 charge per hour of Net surfing. Another access possibility is a recently-announced deal with CompuServe that will make Internet access available for *Internet in a Box* customers through CompuServe's 400 points of presence worldwide.

EXCELLENT

Review

Air Mosaic for Microsoft Windows (version 1.0) directly addresses almost all of the shortcomings of NCSA Mosaic. While sharing that program's trend-setting user interface, it offers advanced hotlist capabilities (you can quickly organize your hotlist items into folders and subfolders). The program is faster and more efficient than NCSA Mosaic, but it doesn't give the user much control over basic configuration options. Missing are some advanced NCSA Mosaic features, such as annotations. On the positive side, the program includes a kiosk mode, which lets you hide the program's menus; all the user sees is the document, making the program very useful for on-screen demonstrations or presentations.

ENHANCED NCSA MOSAIC

Although NCSA had issued several licenses to the Mosaic code to a variety of firms, including Spry, a decision was reached in the fall of 1994 to limit future licensing to only one firm. This would enable NCSA's staff to concentrate on their main mission, developing software for scientific visualization. Anyone wishing to license Mosaic would have to approach the officially-appointed firm, which would handle all the details.

The right firm was already in existence. In January of 1990, a company called Spyglass had been formed to enhance and commercialize technology from NCSA. Spyglass is a privately-held company located in Naperville, Illinois, not far from NCSA. Spyglass' co-founder and Vice President of Research & Development, Timothy Krauskopf, and many of Spyglass' software developers formerly worked at NCSA. Krauskopf was the developer of NCSA Telnet, an Internet client program now in use by an estimated two million people.

Initially launched to create enhanced versions of NCSA's scientific visualization tools, Spyglass provided the perfect channel for the distribution of an enhanced, commercial version of Mosaic. In May of 1994, NCSA and Spyglass signed a commercial licensing agreement for the distribution of Mosaic. In September, 1994, NCSA announced that Spyglass would be Mosaic's sole commercial licensee. Spyglass's version of Mosaic is called Enhanced NCSA Mosaic (Figure 9.4). Versions of the program are available for users of Microsoft Windows, Macintosh, and X Window/Motif systems.

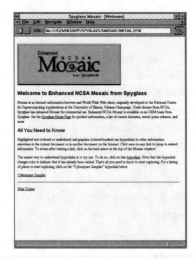

Figure 9.4 *Enhanced NCSA Mosaic*

A Better Mosaic

The deal is good news for NCSA Mosaic fans. NCSA's agreement with NCSA calls for Spyglass to make much-needed improvements to the original Mosaic code, such as fixing NCSA Mosaic's notorious memory leak problems, the program's frequent crashes due to General Protection Faults, its limited documentation, its sluggish performance, and NCSA's inability to provide technical support. Spyglass promises to remedy all these deficiencies. Another plus is that even though Spyglass will sell the product commercially, it also promises to make improved versions of the product available for distribution on NCSA's server.

Spyglass subsequently released its product, called Enhanced NCSA Mosaic, but not to the general public. The firm grants licenses to software resellers and book publishers, who include the program in commercial distributions of their products. Version 2.0 of Enhanced NCSA Mosaic was released in November, 1994.

ENHANCED NCSA MOSAIC SYSTEM REQUIREMENTS

Mosaic for Microsoft Windows/Windows NT
Any Intel-based 386SX-based PC (or better) running Microsoft Windows or Windows NT. 8MB of RAM is recommended.

Mosaic for the Macintosh
Any color-capable Macintosh with System 7.0 or later; 4MB of RAM is recommended.

Mosaic for X Windows
This version of Mosaic will run on virtually any UNIX-based workstation, including Sun SPARCstations, IBM RS/6000, DEC RISC, Silicon Graphics IRIS, and HP 9000 series.

20 Million Users By 1995?

How popular is Spyglass's Enhanced NCSA Mosaic? By December, 1994, Spyglass had licensed 12 million copies of the product, and predicted that 20 million people would be using the program by the end of 1995. Some licensees and product names are listed below:

- Digital Electronic Corporation (DEC) calls its product Pathworks for Windows.

- IBM calls its version Web Explorer, and packages the program with OS/2 Warp.

- Luckman Interactive Inc., a Los Angeles-based firm, distributes Super Mosaic, an easy-to-use, "point-and-click" version of Enhanced NCSA Mosaic. The program, to be packaged with a number of Internet-related books, comes with preconfigured multimedia helper programs, a SLIP/PPP dialer, and a month of free Internet access.

- Spry, Inc. announced in December, 1994 that its Air Mosaic products would be integrated with Enhanced NCSA Mosaic.

Although millions of copies of Enhanced Mosaic are in existence, most of them have been packaged with TCP/IP networking software and Internet how-to books. It's far from clear that Enhanced NCSA Mosaic will succeed in establishing itself as *the* Web browser. The program faces very stiff competition from Netscape, which is discussed in a following section.

Enhanced NCSA Mosaic's Security Provisions

Enhanced NCSA Mosaic was developed for commercial purposes. Ideally, companies could distribute the program under license from Spyglass, and then their customers could use the Web to browse on-line catalogs and make credit card orders. But there's one big problem—the Web provides precious little security for such transactions.

Put bluntly, the Web is a security nightmare. Suppose you're ordering a compact disk player from an on-line Web vendor. How do you know if the vendor is really a bona-fide electronics store on the Internet, or if it's a couple of crooks collecting your credit card numbers for a scam? And who will observe your credit card number, expiration date, and address while it's en route via the Web? And look at the problem from the store's point of view, too. How do you know that the people placing an order are really who they say they are?

With Enhanced NCSA Mosaic 2.0, secure Web transactions have finally become possible. The program includes a security and payment-processing framework, called Mosaic Security Framework, that allows a variety of business transactions to take place without risk. Mosaic Security Framework allows users to select the security level that's appropriate for their transactions. The program provides the following levels of security:

- **Basic Authentication.** A password travels in non-encrypted form over the Internet with minimal security. Basic authentication is suitable for exchanging non-confidential information, such as technical   support information or software demos. This level is appropriate only for non-sensitive applications, such as obtaining catalogs or documents.

- **Enhanced Authentication.** Data Encryption Standard (DES) encryption is used to verify customers' identities without requiring the use of passwords. This level of security is acceptable where it is vital to confirm the identity of the person accessing the Web site.

- **Secure HTTP.** The highest level of authentication uses public-key authentication technology from RSA Data Security, Inc. Secure HTTP is a proposed extension to the HTTP protocol that can encrypt sensitive data such as credit card numbers and expiration dates, without requiring a prior arrangement to establish the code.

Review

Version 1.0 of Enhanced NCSA Mosaic fixed many of NCSA Mosaic's irritating bugs and nasty habits, but at a price. Spyglass deleted features, such as Annotations, that weren't working very well. The result was a smoothly-functioning subset of NCSA Mosaic's features, but a subset nonetheless. Version 2.0 should remedy these deficiencies and bring Enhanced NCSA Mosaic up to the level set by its chief competitor, Netscape.

NETSCAPE

Bob Metcalfe, publisher of *InfoWorld* magazine, visited NCSA in the summer of 1994 to present NCSA with the magazine's coveted Industry Achievement Award. Metcalfe hoped to present the award to Mosaic's creators, including Eric Bina and Marc Andreesen, but they didn't show up. They were in California, busily setting up a company that they hoped to call Mosaic Communications Corporation—until, NCSA objected, forcing a change of name to Netscape Communications Corporation. The University of Illinois and Netscape formally buried the hatchet in December, 1994, in an agreement that absolved Netscape of wrongdoing so long as the new company did not use the name Mosaic.

Netscape, founded in April 1994 by Andreesen and James Clark, the founder of Silicon Graphics, is giving Spyglass a run for its money. With the seemingly unstoppable advantage of possessing the sole future licensing rights to NCSA, Spyglass appeared to be ideally positioned to make significant money as the Web becomes an avenue of commerce. But it's Netscape, not Spyglass, that's getting the lion's share of the attention from businesses planning Web ventures, thanks to

Netscape's well-conceived line of secure Web products. Approximately seven out of every ten people navigating the Web at this writing were doing so with Netscape's browser, called Netscape Navigator, which is available in versions for Microsoft Windows, Macintosh, and X Window systems.

Netscape's Products

Netscape offers a suite of Web products that work together to provide secure online transactions capability including:

- **Netscape Navigator.** A graphical Web browser that looks very much like NCSA Mosaic (Figure 9.5), Netscape Navigator was actually rewritten from scratch to avoid copyright infringements. It's a full-featured browser that's fast and efficient. The program incorporates Netscape's security schemes for secure on-line transactions.

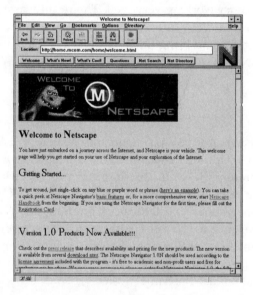

Figure 9.5 *Netscape Navigator*

- **Netsite Communications Server.** This software provides fast, efficient, and easy-to-use Web server facilities for firms that do not need advanced security protection. Included is basic-level access authorization, that enables users to access the site by typing a password. The software runs on a variety of UNIX workstations. A future version is planned for Windows NT.

- **Netsite Commerce Server.** A version of Netsite Communications Server that provides "bullet-proof" security, this software employs public-key encryption technology developed by RSA Public Key Cryptography.

AROUND THE CORNER: NEW WAYS TO MAX OUT YOUR CREDIT CARD

Bank of America, the largest merchant bank in the United States, announced in late 1994 that the bank will provide businesses with a secure means for electronic commerce on the Internet using Netscape Communications' secure client/server software. Businesses that want to conduct commerce via the Internet will be able to accept consumers' Visa, MasterCard, Discover, Diners Club, Carte Blance, JCB Card, or American Express Cards via Web transactions.

Is it really secure? Sharif Bayyari, a senior vice president of Bank of America commented: "We researched payment options available for the Internet and found that Netscape Communications is providing the fastest, most secure, and most open environment for online payment processing. Other payment options on the net come with high transaction risks, bypass bank payment systems, and open the way to fraud and consumer liability. This approach eliminates those concerns and allows companies and consumers to feel comfortable and confident conducting business on the Internet."

Bank of America's business customers can now create their own Internet presence or virtual storefront using the Netsite Commerce Server, and then enroll in the service through Bank of America. Consumers using Netscape Communications' Netscape Navigator can then access and establish a secure link with the server, enabling credit card information to be sent securely over the net. The card information is then processed and verified by Bank of America while the customer is still online.

Netscape Navigator: How Good?

The other flavors of Mosaic have their proponents, to be sure, but many believe that Netscape is simply the best graphical browser available today, and that's especially true if you're using a dialup SLIP/PPP connection. Compared to its predecessors, Netscape is fast, efficient, easy, and fun to use.

The program's exceptional performance on slow dialup lines is deliberate. According to Paul Koontz, vice president of marketing at Netscape: "The NCSA prototype [of Mosaic] was written in a research environment for research environments, and they had access to high-speed communications, T1 and T3 lines. Quite logically, the guys who wrote Mosaic didn't spend a lot of time architecting for lower-speed lines. As a result, it's not suitable for the general population, those people without T1– and T3–class bandwidth." Netscape is expressly designed to run at the maximum possible speed, thanks to the inclusion of several very desirable features.

EXCELLENT

- **Multiple, simultaneous image download.** You don't have to wait for the images to be downloaded one-by-one; instead, you see a "Venetian blind" effect, as multiple in-line graphics download line-by-line. After a few passes, the images snap into focus even if they're not fully downloaded yet.

- **Continuous document streaming.** The text appears even while the program's still downloading the graphics; if you don't feel like waiting for the in-line images, you can read the document.

- **Document and image caching.** Netscape takes full advantage of the additional RAM in your system by enabling you to specify the size of the memory cache, where documents you have just accessed are stored for speedy retrieval. In addition, you can specify the size of a disk cache, where documents are stored between sessions so that they don't have to be re-accessed via the network.

- **Native JPEG image decompression.** You don't need a helper program to decode JPEG graphics—which, incidentally, are up to 50% smaller than the same picture in a GIF format.

NETSCAPE NAVIGATOR'S SYSTEM REQUIREMENTS

Netscape Navigator for Windows

At least a 386SX with 4MB of RAM; a 486 with 8 MB is recommended; Windows 3.1; 5 MB of disk space. Versions are available for 16-bit versions of Windows (Windows 3.1 and Windows for Workgroups 3.1) as well as for 32-bit versions (Windows NT).

NETSCAPE NAVIGATOR'S SYSTEM REQUIREMENTS (continued)

Netscape Navigator for Macintosh

At least a 68030 Macintosh with 4MB of RAM; 8 MB is recommended; System 7.0 or later; 5 MB of disk space.

Netscape Navigator for UNIX

A UNIX workstation with at least 16 MB of RAM; 5 MB of disk space. OS options include Digital Equipment Corporation (OSF/1 2.0), Hewlett-Packard (HP-UX 9.03), Silicon Graphics (IRIX 5.2), IBM (AIX 3.2), Sun (Solaris 1.0 & 2.3, SunOs 4.1.3)

Netscape Navigator: Free?

When the first beta versions of Netscape Navigator hit the net, Netscape officials insisted that their client software would be "free for individuals"—the firm would make its money selling servers. With the release of version 1.0, however, the company changed its tune, setting off a hue and cry in Usenet discussion groups related to the Web (such as comp.infosystems.www.misc). Here's a description of the license for version 1.0 from a Netscape press release:

> Netscape Navigator for free evaluation, academic or non-profit use can be obtained via anonymous FTP from ftp.mcom.com. Free evaluation use allows individuals to use the software for the purpose of determining whether they want to purchase an ongoing software license. Academic and non-profit use means that students, faculty and staff of educational institutions and employees of non-profit organizations have unlimited free use of the software. Educational institutions and non-profit organizations can also obtain a license free of charge to redistribute Netscape Navigator to these individuals. Organizations or individuals wishing to use Netscape Navigator for commercial purposes can purchase supported, licensed copies of Netscape Navigator directly from Netscape Communications. Pricing starts at $39 for a single user license, and volume discounts are available for right-to-copy licenses for multiple users.

Can individuals still use the software for free? According to Netscape officials, the answer depends on whether the software is to be used for commercial purposes. If your company gives everyone a copy of Netscape and expects the program to be used for business-related purposes, then the company must purchase user licenses. But if an individual uses Netscape for non-business purposes, even at work, this user

can "evaluate" the software for an indefinite period of time. Users at educational institutions and non-profit organizations can use the product without a license.

Review

Most Web users will readily agree that Netscape is pretty close to the cat's pajamas, as far as Web browsers are concerned. Even on a slow 14.4 Kbps connection, it's fast and efficient. User-configurable memory and disk caches enable the user to store frequently-accessed documents for rapid re-display. Overall, Netscape offers a beautiful implementation of Mosaic, designed around the needs of people who must access the Web through slow SLIP/PPP connections. The product's tight integration with highly secure servers will usher in a huge wave of commercial activity on the Web.

Is there a down side to Netscape? The program doesn't offer all the bells and whistles that NCSA Mosaic does—for example, there's no provision for annotations. Compared to most other browsers, Netscape provides only very limited control over fonts, font sizes, and other document styles. For example, you're stuck with just one font for headings as well as body text. But these drawbacks haven't kept Netscape from becoming the browser of choice for most Web users. According to one survey, more than 80% of all the users contacting the site did so with Netscape.

WEBSURFER

NCSA Mosaic and its successors, from Air Mosaic to Netscape, have clearly demonstrated the viability of the graphical browser concept. What's also clear is that a software publisher doesn't necessarily need to pay licensing fees to Spyglass in order to bring out a Mosaic-like browser, as long as you're content to use a name other than Mosaic. WebSurfer, the Web browser included with this book, is a home-grown product of NetManage, Inc., which offers the program as part of its Internet Chameleon package. The program, and the Internet Chameleon software, works only with Microsoft Windows.

Introducing WebSurfer

On-screen, Websurfer (Figure 9.6) looks very much like Mosaic, Air Mosaic, and Netscape, except that there are fewer menus. You soon discover that's a sign of decreased functionality. For example, WebSurfer's hotlist capabilities are the least developed of all the products reviewed in this chapter.

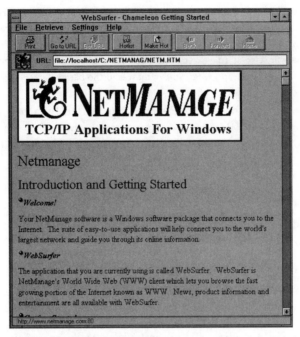

Figure 9.6 *Websurfer (NetManage)*

WebSurfer isn't the star of the graphical browser show, but don't be put off by the program's simplicity. It's a competent program that provides an excellent introduction to the World Wide Web. And here's a plus—it's designed for use with slow dialup SLIP/PPP connections.

Like Netscape, WebSurfer keeps a copy of each document that you access on disk, so that the program doesn't have to reload the document from the network should you return to it later in the same session. By default, WebSurfer erases the cached documents when you quit the program. If you wish, though, you can select an option that saves the cached documents so that they're available in the next session. You can even change the properties of individual documents so that they're cached in this way.

EXCELLENT

In addition to its excellent document caching capabilities, WebSurfer offers superb control over your document's appearance on-screen. You can easily select document styles, such as headings, and choose fonts, font sizes, font colors, and emphases (such as boldface or italic).

HOT TIP

WebSurfer doesn't offer all the bells and whistles that a full-featured browser such as Netscape does. For example, you can define only one hotlist, and you can't organize the list in any way (except by removing URLs you no longer want). But the program's simplicity is itself a benefit. Use it to get started with the Web, and then switch to a full-featured browser such as Netscape when you've mastered the basics.

AWFUL

If your computer already has TCP/IP support provided by a publisher other than NetManage, forget using WebSurfer—the program requires NetManage's Internet Chameleon software. Should you try to run WebSurfer with TCP/IP software other than NetManage's, the program won't start.

Obtaining WebSurfer

WebSurfer is included with the Internet Chameleon software provided with this book. Note that you must install the Chameleon software in order to run WebSurfer.

Review

WebSurfer isn't the most feature-packed browser available, but it's an excellent starting point for readers who will access the Web by means of slow dialup IP connections, no other Web browser provides so much control over cache operations on disk. However, after you've learned the basics of the Web, you'll run into WebSurfer's shortcomings—particularly the simplicity of its hotlist capabilities. I recommend that you learn the Web with WebSurfer, and then download a copy of Netscape.

MORE GRAPHICAL BROWSERS

This section briefly examines additional graphical browsers, including one—MacWeb—that should prove of special interest to Macintosh users.

WinWeb

WinWeb (Figure 9.7) stems from the efforts of the Enterprise Integration Network (EINet) group at Microelectronics and Computer Technology Corporation (MCC). As Figure 9.7 shows, WinWeb is a simple browser with few bells and whistles. A serious shortcoming is the lack of a "Forward" button. Even more serious is that you can't access a URL by typing it directly. Still, it's relatively stable, which is more than one can say about many of the browsers discussed in this chapter. And like other browsers designed for fast operation on dialup IP lines, WinWeb uses a disk cache so that recently-accessed documents won't have to be retrieved from the network, should you wish to view them again.

Figure 9.7 *WinWeb (EINet)*

To obtain WinWeb, use ftp://ftp.einet.net/einet/pc/winweb. WinWeb requires Windows 3.1, 4MB of memory, and 5MB of free disk space.

MacWeb

Long-suffering Macintosh users know that sometimes the Windows versions of software products have more "bells and whistles" than their Macintosh counterpart, but that's not true in this case. MacWeb, the Macintosh cousin of the WinWeb program just discussed, is a much better browser. It's good enough, in fact, to warrant serious consideration as an alternative to Netscape Navigator for Macintosh or NCSA Mosaic for Macintosh.

EINet MacWeb is available at ftp.einet.net/einet/mac/macweb. (You'll need StuffIt Expander to decompress this file. To run MacWeb, you'll need System 7, MacTCP 2.0.2 (2.0.4 or higher is recommended and at least 4MB of RAM.)

NetCruiser

Netcom, one of the largest Internet service providers, distributes a Web browser with their NetCruiser "point-and-click" connection software. The program provides a unified interface to the Internet, and comes with preconfigured viewers and players. The catch here is that you can't use NetCruiser unless you're connected to Netcom.

Even if you are connected to Netcom, you might want to think about using a different browser, as NetCruiser's Web browser can't handle forms. You won't be able to search document indexes, access WAIS databases, or send information to the authors of a Web document. That's a serious deficiency which puts NetCruiser (like Cello) out of the running.

SO WHICH BROWSER IS THE BEST?

This chapter opened with a discussion of the ideal browser. Let's see how the current generation of browser offerings measures up!

- **Graphical User Interface (GUI).** GUI literacy is high these days, and all the Web browsers reviewed in this chapter (save Cello) make effective use of the Windows interface.

- **Fast Operation.** For slow dialup IP connections, Netscape is by far the fastest Web browser available. WebSurfer's advanced disk cache capabilities come in second, and one should give a nod to Cello here, even though the program will eventually consume much of the free space on your hard drive.

- **Efficiency.** Overall, Netscape is the clear winner here, followed by Enhanced NCSA Mosaic.

- **Navigation Buttons.** All the browsers discussed in this chapter (save Cello) provide toolbars with well-designed icons.

- **History List.** All the browsers discussed in this chapter compile a history list; Netscape's is somewhat confusing to use as the items appear in reverse chronological order.

- **Hotlist.** Air Mosaic provides the best tools for hotlist revision and organization, followed by Netscape. But none of the browsers provide tools that enable the user to conveniently reorganize already-noted hotlist items into new folders or submenus. Developers, please note that we'd like to be able to restructure our existing hotlist items as easily as Macintosh users can restructure folders and documents using the Finder.

**WISH
LIST**

- **Subject Trees/Search Engines.** Most browsers include hotlist items that point to various subject trees and search engines; Air Mosaic does a great job here, while Netscape provides an on-screen button for this purpose. Still, the lack of effective, built-in search capabilities must be judged a serious shortcoming of the current generation of Web browsers.

- **Easy Configuration.** All of the browsers discussed here do an adequate job, except NCSA Mosaic, which requires the user to edit the MOSAIC.INI file. Netscape's configuration menus are loaded with options but can be confusing.

- **Multimedia.** Netscape sets the pace here with its built-in capability to decode JPEG graphics. Why can't sound and video decoding become part of the browser, too, so the poor user doesn't have to fiddle with helper programs?

WISH
LIST

- **Document Styles.** The best job here is done by WebSurfer; developers should take a look. Netscape is at the tail end of the pack with its limited font control options.

- **Annotations.** NCSA Mosaic is the only browser that currently offers this feature.

- **Document Cache.** Creating a disk cache sounds like a great idea, but it's hard to implement. If you cache every document the user downloads, the program gobbles up enormous amounts of disk space. Cello "solves" this problem by letting you set a "low water mark," the amount of disk space you want Cello to leave untouched. Netscape addresses the problem by letting you specify the upper limit of the disk cache size. In both these approaches, a problem arises: you must delete ("flush") the cache when it reaches its maximum size, since newly-downloaded documents can't be placed into it. WebSurfer solves this problem handily by letting you mark *individual* documents for storage in the cache.

SUMMARY

Most people think of Mosaic as the graphical Web browser *par excellence*, but NCSA Mosaic has been left in the dust by better-funded corporate efforts. Enhanced NCSA Mosaic and Air Mosaic offer improved versions of NCSA Mosaic's buggy, memory-hungry offerings, while Netscape and WebSurfer show the merits of starting from scratch with new, freshly-conceived products. For dialup users, browsers with advanced disk cache capabilities are clearly preferable. The current generation of browsers falls short, however, in two key areas: hotlist organization and subject tree/search engine integration. Avoid any browser that can't handle forms.

FROM HERE

- Get going with your graphical browser! Chapter 10, World Wide Web Quick Start, shows you how to browse the Web with the browser you're using, whether it's NCSA Mosaic, Enhanced NCSA Mosaic, Netscape, or WebSurfer.

- Learn how to navigate the Web with your graphical browser in Chapter 11, Navigating the Web with Graphical Browsers.

- Master the procedures of displaying, saving, and printing Web documents in Chapter 12, Working with Web Documents.

- Configure your browser for multimedia in Chapter 13, Using Helper Programs.

- Make full use of non-Web resources, such as FTP, Gopher, and WAIS, by reading Chapter 14, Accessing Other Internet Resources.

CHAPTER 10

World Wide Web Quick Start

A journey of one thousand miles must begin with a single step.
—Lao Tzu

This chapter introduces almost everything you need to know about browsing the Web with Mosaic and its successors, Enhanced NCSA Mosaic, Netscape (Netscape Communications Corporation), and WebSurfer (NetManage). To get started, you'll learn how to understand the screen features that graphical browsers display, and how to change the default home page so that you don't have to wait for slow network connections every time you log in. The chapter continues with a tour of the essentials of Web navigation, including using hyperlinks, accessing URLs by typing them, handling in-line images, using history lists, and using hotlists.

In this chapter and the remaining chapters of Part Three, you will find complete instructions for the use of all five of the most popular graphical browsers. Look for the following icons:

HOME PAGE

This icon signals instructions for NCSA Mosaic for Microsoft Windows (version 2).

NCSA MOSAIC

This icon signals instructions for Enhanced NCSA Mosaic for Microsoft Windows (version 1).

ENHANCED NCSA MOSAIC

This icon signals instructions for both the Microsoft Windows and Macintosh versions of Netscape Navigator. (*Macintosh users*: please ignore the underlined accelerator keys, which Windows users can use to gain quick keyboard access to menu commands).

NETSCAPE NAVIGATOR

This icon signals instructions for NetManage's WebSurfer application, which is included on the disk packaged with this book. The program runs on Microsoft Windows systems on which NetManage's TCP/IP software has been installed.

WEBSURFER

To get the most out of this chapter, try working through it with your browser on-screen.

HOT TIP

Remember, you can't use your graphical browser until you've equipped your system with TCP/IP support. For more information see Chapter 7.

AWFUL

UNDERSTANDING YOUR BROWSERS' SCREEN FEATURES

As explained in Chapter 4 ("Exploring the Screen"), you should understand the screen features of the program you're about to use.

Here's a quick overview of the features you'll see on a graphical browser's screen. Figure 10.1 shows how these features are arranged on NCSA Mosaic's screen, while Figure 10.2 displays Netscape's features, and Figure 10.3 displays those of WebSurfer.

- **Menu Bar**. The three programs' menus are organized somewhat differently, but they all offer essentially the same options.

- **Tool Bar**. Most of the tools enable you to choose navigation options quickly, including Back, Forward, Home, and Reload.

- **Program Icon**. When this icon displays motion, the browser is downloading a document.

- **Document Title**. All the flavors of Mosaic except Air Mosaic display the name of the current document on the window title bar. With Air Mosaic, you see a separate Document Title area, next to the Document URL area.

- **Document URL**. This is the URL of the document you're currently viewing.

- **Document View Area**. Here, you see the current document. You can use the scroll boxes and scroll areas to display parts of the document that you can't see.

- **Status Bar**. On all the programs, you'll find the status bar at the bottom of the program's window.

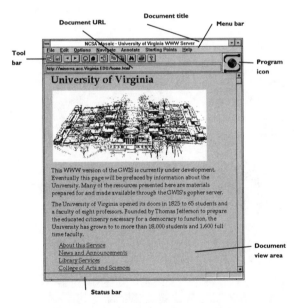

Figure 10.1 *NCSA Mosaic's screen features*

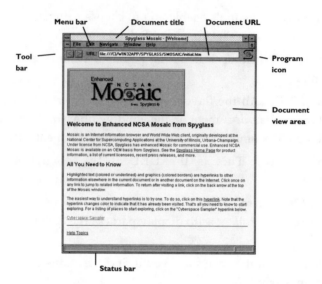

Figure 10.2 *Enhanced NCSA Mosaic's screen features*

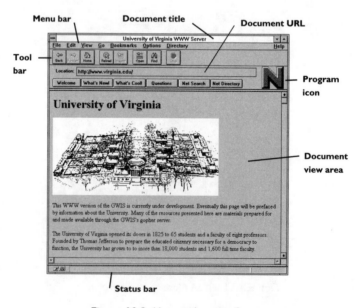

Figure 10.3 *Netscape's screen features*

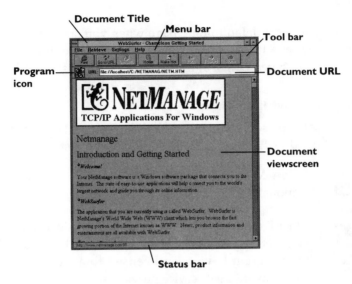

Figure 10.4 WebSurfer's screen features

Note that all three of the graphical browsers discussed here use a set of standard buttons on their toolbars. All Web browsers work pretty much the same way. You'll find buttons for going forward, for going back, and for going home, as explained later in this chapter. You'll also find buttons for common tasks such as printing, accessing a URL by typing its address, reloading a document, and finding text within a document.

Whatever your feelings about the over-exuberant icon bars of some Windows products, you'll find your browser's toolbars to be indispensable. It's much faster to click a button than to choose a command from the menu.

EXCELLENT

Prefer to use the keyboard? See the end of this chapter for a handy list of the keyboard shortcuts enabled by each of the discussed programs.

HOT TIP

FUNDAMENTALS OF WEB NAVIGATION

It's easy to browse the Web with a graphical browser, but you can get lost very fast if you just click a lot of hyperlinks. This section introduces some basic concepts that will help make your Web experiences less disorienting. It starts by explaining why you see a default home page when you start your program, and tells you how to change it to something more useful. It continues by exploring hyperlinks, manually-typed URLs, in-line images, history lists, and hot lists.

KEY
TERM

Understanding the Default Home Page

Every Web browser is preset to display a *default home page*, the home page that the program is configured to display when you start it for the first time:

NCSA
MOSAIC

NCSA Mosaic displays the NCSA Mosaic home page at the National Center for Supercomputer Applications.

ENHANCED
NCSA
MOSAIC

What **Enhanced NCSA Mosaic** displays depends on how it's been set up—and by whom. More than 10 million copies of the program have been licensed to a variety of vendors, including Internet service providers.

NETSCAPE
NAVIGATOR

Netscape displays the Netscape home page at Netscape Communications Corporation's headquarters in Silicon Valley.

WEBSURFER

WebSurfer displays a local file.

HOME
PAGE

Lost? You can always re-display the default home page by clicking the Home button on the toolbar.

AWFUL

Can't get to the default home page? With millions of copies of Mosaic and Netscape in circulation, it's no wonder. To get to a home page, you may need to change your default home page, as explained in the following section.

Changing the Default Home Page

A good home page lists many interesting and useful URLs. As your mastery of the Web grows, you'll want to create your own home page, as explained in Chapter 27, "A Quick Introduction to HTML: Creating Your Own Home Page." To do so, however, you will need to learn some HTML. For now, you'll be wise to choose a link-rich home page that will serve as a good launching point for your Web exploration.

Ideally, a good home page should contain the following.

- Links to exemplary Web sites to show you what the Web can do.
- Subject guides to Web resources.
- Starting points for Web exploration.
- Links to Web search engines.

Hundreds of people have put their home pages onto the Web, so that others can benefit from their legwork. A few of my favorites:

- **John December's Index Page.** (http://www.rip.edu:80/~decemj /index.html). John is a Ph.D. candidate in technical communication at Renssalaer Polytechnic Institute (RPI), and is an acknowledged expert on new forms of computer-mediated communication (CMC). You'll find plenty of interesting material here!

- **Meng Weng Wong's Home Page.** (http://www.seas.upenn.edu/~meng wong/meng.html) Another Web expert, Meng has designed a home page loaded with interesting URLs. See Figure 10.5 for an example.

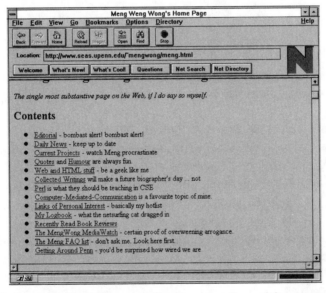

Figure 10.5 *Meng Weng Wong's home page (http://www.seas.upenn.edu/~mengwong/meng.html)*

- **Planet Earth Home Page** (http://white.nosc.mil/info.html) Lots of great starting points and Web information.

USEFUL
RESOURCE

Looking for cool home pages? Check out the The Complete Home Page Directory at http://web.city.ac.uk/citylive/pages.html (see Figure 10.6). And when you finish Chapter 26 and learn how to put your own documents on the Web, add your home page to the Complete Home Page directory (check out the "How To Add Your Own" button).

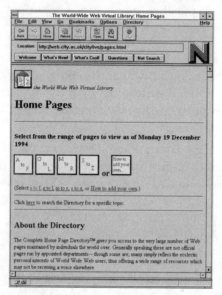

Figure 10.6 *The Complete Home Page Directory (http://web.city.ac.uk/citylive/pages.html)*

To change the default home page:

NCSA
MOSAIC

Use the Windows Notepad text editor to open the file C:\WINDOWS\MOSAIC.INI. In the [Main] section, look for the Home Page line. Delete the current URL, and carefully type the URL of the new home page you want to use. Save the file and exit.

ENHANCED
NCSA
MOSAIC

From the Edit menu, choose **Preferences.** In the dialog box, type the URL in the Home Page area and click the **OK** button.

NETSCAPE
NAVIGATOR

From the Options menu, choose **Preferences.** In the list box, choose **Styles.** In the Start With area, select Home Page location, and type the URL. Click **OK** to confirm.

WEBSURFER
Open the Settings menu, choose **Preferences.** In the Startup Document area, type the URL of your new home page in the URL box, and click **OK.**

Activating a Hyperlink

To activate a link in any of the three Web browsers, move the pointer to the hyperlink, and observe the status line where you'll see the URL of the link to which you're pointing. Click the link once to activate the link.

While the program accesses the hyperlink, watch the Mosaic logo. As Mosaic downloads the document you requested, the logo flashes or shows activity. The document you requested is then displayed on-screen, and you see the document's title on the title bar (and in the Current Document URL area, if it's visible).

Going to a URL By Typing It

Many times you will want to access a Web document that you've heard about or read about, but can't find a hyperlink for it. For example, this book contains many URLs for interesting, useful, and fun Web sites. To access many of these, you will need to type the URL directly.

URLs must be typed correctly. Be sure that you don't include any spaces. Also, URLs are case-sensitive—You must type the exact pattern of capital letters that you see in the original URL. (To avoid case sensitivity problems, almost all URLs are typed, by convention, in lower-case letters, but there are exceptions). Be sure to check your typing carefully!

AWFUL

To go to a URL by typing it:

NCSA MOSAIC
Select the current URL in the Document URL box, and type the new URL (this will erase the previous one). Check your typing carefully, and make corrections, if necessary. When you are certain the URL is correct, press **Enter.**

ENHANCED NCSA MOSAIC
Select the current URL in the Document URL box, and just start typing the new URL (this will erase the previous one). Check your typing carefully, and make corrections, if necessary. When you are certain the URL is correct, press **Enter.**

NETSCAPE NAVIGATOR
Select the current URL in the Location box, and just start typing the new URL (this will erase the previous one). Check your typing carefully, and make corrections, if necessary. When you are certain the URL is correct, press **Enter.**

WEBSURFER

Select the current URL in the Location box, and just start typing the new URL (this will erase the previous one). Check your typing carefully, and make corrections, if necessary. When you are certain the URL is correct, press **Enter**.

AWFUL

If you see an error message after typing a URL, check your typing carefully. Correct the mistake, and try again. Still see an error message? The site's server may be down temporarily—try again later.

HOT TIP

If you see an interesting URL in a document you're reading, you can copy it to the clipboard and paste it into the URL box. With Netscape and Enhanced NCSA Mosaic, just select the URL on-screen and press **Ctrl-C** to copy the URL to the Clipboard. With NCSA Mosaic and WebSurfer, you must display the source document, from which to copy the URL. With Mosaic, open the File menu and choose **Document** source. With Websurfer, open the Retrieve menu and choose **Edit HTML**. To paste the copied URL with any of the four programs, position the insertion point in the URL text box and press **Ctrl-V**.

Turning Off In-line Images

In-line graphics are attractive, but they take time to download. If you're using a graphical browser on a sluggish connection, whether it's a slow SLIP link or an overloaded network, you can speed things up considerably by turning off the default display of in-line images.

After you turn off in-line images, you see placeholders where the graphics would have appeared (see Figure 10.7).

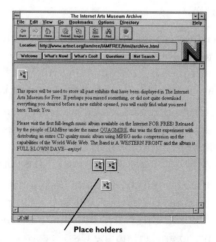

Place holders

Figure 10.7 *In-line image placeholders*

To turn off the display of in-line images:

NCSA MOSAIC

Open the Options menu, and deselect the **Display In-line Images** option.

ENHANCED NCSA MOSAIC

From the Options menu, choose **Preferences**. Deselect the **Load Images Automatically** check box and click **OK**.

NETSCAPE NAVIGATOR

Open the Options menu, and deselect the **Auto Load Images** option.

WEBSURFER

From the Settings menu, choose **Preferences**. In the Preferences dialog box, choose the **Defer Image Retrieval** option, and click **OK**.

HOT TIP

To see the in-line images, you can instruct your browser to download individual graphics in a document, as explained in the following instructions. If you're using a slow SLIP connection, this is a great technique to learn; you can turn off the slow downloading of graphics and then view just the graphics that you're really interested in seeing (see Figure 10.8).

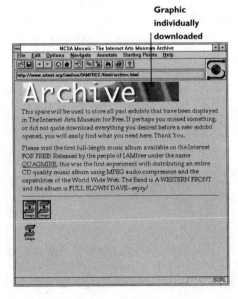

Figure 10.8 *In-line image individually downloaded*

To display an individual in-line graphic:

NCSA
MOSAIC

Point to the placeholder for the graphic you want to see, and click the **right** mouse button.

WEBSURFER

Point to the placeholder for the graphic you want to see, and click the **right** mouse button.

AWFUL

Netscape and Enhanced NCSA Mosaic won't let you load graphics individually. To view a graphic, you must re-load all of them.

To reload all the in-line graphics:

ENHANCED
NCSA
MOSAIC

From the <u>N</u>avigate menu, choose **Load Missing Images**.

NETSCAPE
NAVIGATOR

Click the **Images** button on the toolbar.

In-Line Images as Hyperlinks

In some documents, in-line graphics may function as hyperlinks. These graphics are surrounded by a blue border, as shown in Figure 10.9. Click one of these navigation buttons, and you see a related page. Clicking a bordered in-line image is the same as clicking a hyperlink.

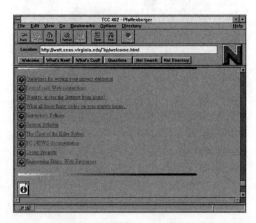

Figure 10.9 In-line images as hyperlinks (note the border around the images)

WEBMASTER

Check out those big, nifty navigation buttons in Figure 10.9. Unlike the cryptic icons you'll find in many Web documents, these are legible (the text explains what the buttons do, just in case you can't figure out what the icon means). And they're nice and big, too, meaning that you don't have to have the skills of a neurosurgeon to point to the button and click it. Figure 10.9 is from Internaut's Online Encyclopedia, located at http://www.zilker.net/users/internaut/toue.html.

Stopping the Download

If you've just accessed a document or graphic only to find that it isn't of interest, you can save time by stopping the downloading procedure.

 Use the following procedures if you're trying to access a site that won't respond right away. You can try again later.

HOT TIP

To stop downloading a document or graphic:

 Click the **NCSA Mosaic** icon.

NCSA MOSAIC

 Press **Esc**.

ENHANCED NCSA MOSAIC

 Click the **Stop** button. You can also press **Esc**.

NETSCAPE NAVIGATOR

 You can't stop downloading, but you can click the **Back** button to display the previous document.

WEBSURFER

WebSurfer provides no way to stop downloading—a serious drawback. However, you can use the Back or Forward buttons to display another document while downloading occurs.

AWFUL

Using the History List

After you've navigated through a few hyperlinks, you may feel as though you're getting lost. If you've been clicking away at hyperlinks and have no idea how you got where you are, you can look at the history list, shown in Figure 10.10. This list displays all the documents you've visited, one after the other, with the most recently-accessed document at the bottom of the list. To view any of the previously-accessed documents, select the document and click the mouse button that confirms your command.

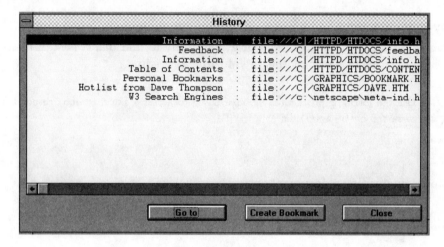

Figure 10.10 *History list (Netscape)*

To display the history list and choose a document from it:

NCSA
MOSAIC

From the Navigate menu, choose **History**. The NCSA Mosaic-History dialog box will be displayed. Select the URL you want to view, and click the **Load** button. (To cancel, click **Dismiss**.)

ENHANCED
NCSA
MOSAIC

From the Navigate menu, choose **History**. Select the URL you want to view, and click the **Go** to button.

NETSCAPE
NAVIGATOR

From the Go menu, choose **View History**. Select the URL you want to view, and click the **Go To** button (or just press **Enter**). You can also choose recently-accessed documents from the lower portion of the Go menu.

WEBSURFER

From the Retrieve menu, choose **History**. In the WebSurfer-History dialog box, select the URL you want to view, and click the **Go To** button (or just press **Enter**).

Using Hotlists

If you find a really cool Web site during your travels, you may wish to return to it quickly without having to activate many hyperlinks to retrace your steps. You can save your link to that document by adding it to your hotlist. A *hotlist* is your own list of Web treasures that you've discovered on your journeys. EXCELLENT

To add an item to your hotlist:

NCSA
MOSAIC

Click the **Add to Hotlist** button.

ENHANCED
NCSA
MOSAIC

In the Hotlist dialog box, click the **Add Current** button to add the current document to the hotlist, and click the **Close** button to return to the document.

NETSCAPE
NAVIGATOR

From the Bookmarks menu, choose **Add Bookmark**.

WEBSURFER

Click the **Make Hot** button.

Choosing an Item From Your Hotlist

Once you've added items to your hotlist, you can retrieve them quickly. This is much more convenient than having to wade through a series of hyperlinks to get back to something you saw previously. And you can find it again easily the next time you launch the program.

To choose an item from your hotlist:

NCSA
MOSAIC

From the Starting Points menu, choose the document that you saved as a hotlist item.

ENHANCED
NCSA
MOSAIC

From the Navigate menu, choose **Hotlist**, and double-click the item you want.

NETSCAPE NAVIGATOR

From the Bookmarks menu, choose the document that you saved as a bookmark.

WEBSURFER

Click the **Hotlist** button. In the WebSurfer - Hotlist - Favorite Places dialog box, double-click the document that you saved as a hotlist item.

USING KEYBOARD SHORTCUTS

If you prefer to use the keyboard for choosing menu commands, you will find that all four of these programs make several available. The following table lists the keyboard shortcuts for each of the programs discussed in this chapter.

NCSA Mosaic	Keyboard Shortcut
Close the application	Alt+F4
Copy selection to the Clipboard	Ctrl+C
Open a URL by typing it	Ctrl+O
Paste selection from the Clipboard	Ctrl+V
Print the current document	Ctrl+P
Save the current document	Ctrl+S
Enhanced NCSA Mosaic	
Close the application	Alt+F4
Close the current window	Ctrl+F4
Copy selection from the Clipboard	Ctrl+C
Cut the current selection	Ctrl+X
Display hotlist	Ctrl+H
Find again	Ctrl+G
Find text in the document	Ctrl+F
Go back	Ctrl+B
Open a local file	Ctrl+O
Open a new window	Ctrl+N

Open a URL by typing it	Ctrl+U
Paste selection from the Clipboard	Ctrl+V
Print the current document	Ctrl+P
Reload document from network	Ctrl+R
Select all	Ctrl+A

Netscape

Add to hotlist (bookmarks)	Ctrl+A
Close application	Ctrl+W
Copy selection to the Clipboard	Ctrl+C
Display history dialog box	Ctrl+H
Find text in the document	Ctrl+F
Go back	Alt+<
Go forward	Alt+>
Mail document	Ctrl+M
Open local file	Ctrl+O
Open new window	Ctrl+N
Open URL by typing it	Ctrl+L
Paste selection from the Clipboard	Ctrl+V
Reload document from network	Ctrl+R
Save document as	Ctrl+S
Stop downloading	Esc
Undo previous action	Ctrl+Z
View hotlist (bookmarks)	Ctrl+B

WebSurfer

Copy text to Clipboard	Ctrl+C
Open a local file	Ctrl+O
Paste from the Clipboard	Ctrl+V
Print the current document	Ctrl+P
Save the current document	Ctrl+S

SUMMARY

Every session with a graphical browser begins with your default home page. From there, you navigate hyperlinks to display additional documents. To speed up slow downloads, you can temporarily switch off the display of in-line images.

After you've wandered the Web for a while, you might start feeling lost. If so, check out the history list. It tells you where you've been, and what's more, you can go back to any of the documents you've previously visited by just choosing the document from this list. Click the Home icon to get back to the home page quickly.

When you find a document you wish to revisit, add its name to your hotlist. Later, you'll be able to go directly to this document by choosing its name from the hotlist.

FROM HERE...

- Become an expert in Web navigation! Check out the tips and strategies in Chapter 11, Navigating the Web with Graphical Browsers.

- Save and print those Web documents! You'll learn how in Chapter 12, Working with Documents.

- Install, configure, and use helper programs! For the lowdown, see Chapter 13, Using Helper Programs

- For assistance in accessing additional Internet resources such as FTP, Gopher, and WAIS with your graphical browser, see Chapter 14, Accessing Other Internet Resources

- Make your browser work the way you want! See Chapter 15, Customizing your Browser.

CHAPTER 11

Navigating the Web with Graphical Browsers

The biggest problem in hypertext systems, which most of us admit in footnotes toward the end of papers extolling the virtues of our systems, is ... getting lost.

—P.J. Brown

Navigating the Web can be a bit frustrating when you're first learning to use a graphical browser such as Mosaic, Netscape, or Websurfer. If you're trying to find your way back to a document that you saw previously, it can seem like finding your way back to a well-hidden campsite in a confusing, featureless forest. After navigating an endless series of documents using hyperlinks, you may give up in disgust. But that's because you don't know how to take full advantage of the features of graphical browsers that let you mark your way.

This chapter presents a cornucopia of navigation tips and tricks, building on the basic knowledge introduced in the previous chapter. You'll learn how to make the most of hyperlinks, history lists, and hotlists (also called bookmarks).

If you're just starting with your graphical browser, read Chapter 10 (World Wide Web Quick Start). In that chapter, you'll learn the basics of Web navigation, including using navigation buttons, typing URLs directly, and other essentials.

HOME PAGE

HYPERLINK TIPS AND TRICKS

Hyperlinks are easy to use—and I'm sure you've already used quite a few of them. Here are some points to keep in mind about hyperlinks.

- Click the hyperlink only once. GUI interface users are accustomed to double-clicking on-screen controls to open something, but this can lead to unwanted consequences with graphical browsers—the first click activates the hyperlink, while the second may do something you don't expect in the new document that's displayed!

- Hyperlinks do different things. Some just display a different part of the same document, or another document on the same computer as the one you're currently browsing. Others display a graphic or video that can't be shown without the aid of a helper program. Still others forge a connection with a computer that might be thousands of miles away.

- When you move the pointer over a hyperlink, it changes into a hand. (Unless you're using Enhanced NCSA Mosaic). Look at the status bar to see the URL that's "hidden" under this hyperlink.

- Remember that in-line images are hyperlinks. These images have a border. When you click an in-line image hyperlink, you initiate a jump, just as if you clicked a text hyperlink.

KEY TERM

- Most browsers compile a *global history list* that keeps track of all the documents you've visited while using Mosaic. This list permits the program to distinguish between *visited hyperlinks* (hyperlinks you've already accessed) and *unvisited hyperlinks* (hyperlinks you've never accessed). To distinguish the two, they're shown in differing colors on-screen (Figure 11.1).

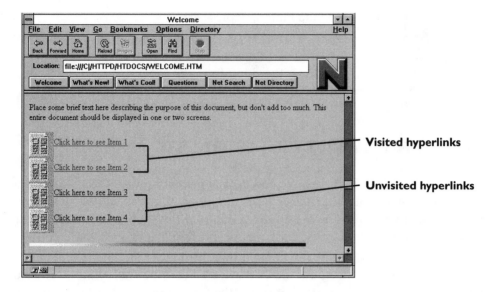

Figure 11.1 *Visited and unvisited hyperlinks.*

STOPPING AN UNWANTED DOWNLOAD

If you've just clicked a hyperlink, only to find that you're downloading a huge document that you don't want, you can stop the download.

HOT TIP Site not responding? If you don't see results within 15 seconds of clicking a hyperlink, there's probably something wrong with the connection—and you'll be sitting there for several minutes until the network times out. To return to the current document so that you can try another link, stop the download, as described in the following steps.

To stop the download:

NCSA
MOSAIC

Click the **Mosaic icon**.

ENHANCED
NCSA
MOSAIC

Press **Esc**.

NETSCAPE NAVIGATOR

Click the **Stop** button, or press **Esc**.

WEBSURFER

You can't stop the download, but you can click **Back** or **Forward** to display previouisly-accessed documents.

STILL CONFUSED ABOUT THE HISTORY LIST?

Welcome to the club. Of the many aspects of hypertext browsers that people find hard to understand, the history lists takes first prize. If you're still having trouble understanding what the history list is all about, read this section. It presents a way of thinking about the history list that many people find helpful.

Let's say you're browsing a document that introduces the instruments in the orchestra. You begin with **About the Orchestra**, so your browser places this document in your history list (actually, it places the URL in the list, but for the sake of simplicity, let's use the document name):

About the Orchestra

You click a hyperlink that displays a document called **Strings**. Now your history list has two entries:

About the Orchestra
Strings

Then you access several more documents. Now your history list looks like this:

About the Orchestra
Strings
Violins
Violas
Cellos
Wind Instruments
Flute
Percussion Instruments
Timpani

If you think of the history list in this way, clicking the **Back** button is the same as going back "up" in the history list, while clicking **Forward** is the same thing as going "down" in the history list:

- **Going Back**. The Back button (or its menu equivalent) takes you *up* the history list to see previously-viewed documents. For example, suppose you're looking at "Flute." When you click **Back**, you see "Wind Instruments."

- **Going Forward**. When you use the Forward button (or its menu equivalent), you go *down* the history list to see more recently-retrieved documents. Naturally, you can only do this if you've gone back (up in the list) so there's something to go forward to (down the list).

Why is the Forward button sometimes dimmed? Don't get frustrated—this really *does* make sense. When you're viewing the most recently-accessed document, in other words, you're at the *bottom* of the history list. You can't go Forward until you've gone Back.

USING NAVIGATION ICONS

The ideal Web page presents a manageable "chunk" of information—no more than one or two screens. For this reason, most Web offerings include more than one page. The Internet Underground Music Archive (IUMA), for instance, presents more than a dozen pages.

In line with current Web usage, these multi-page presentations are referred to as a *Web site*. A typical Web site includes a *welcome page*, which provides a table of contents and jumping-off-point for the various available documents. Thoughtful Web authors provide *navigation icons* to help you find your way among the various documents of a Web site. Navigation icons help you find your way among the various documents.

KEY TERM

HOT TIP

If you find a site with navigation buttons, by all means use them (instead of the Back and Forward buttons). You'll find it much easier to make sense of the relationships among the linked documents.

HOTLIST TECHNIQUES AND TRICKS

When navigating the Web with your graphical browser, you'll want to add items to your hotlist, the stored list of URLs you've found particularly useful or appealing. By storing a URL in a hotlist, you can get back to it quickly just by choosing the item from the hotlist—you don't have to renavigate the Web to find your way back.

HOME PAGE

For an introduction to hotlists, see "Adding an Item to Your Hotlist" and "Choosing an Item from Your Hotlist" in Chapter 10.

This section provides additional information about the specifics of using hotlists in the four "flavors" of Mosaic that this book discusses, NCSA Mosaic, Air Mosaic, Netscape, and WebSurfer.

As you'll see, this is the area in which you'll see the greatest variation among the flavors of Mosaic. The current version of WebSurfer is the weakest here; you can't do much with its hotlist besides adding new items and removing unwanted ones. NCSA Mosaic, Netscape, and Air Mosaic offer many more options, such as the ability to create more than one hotlist.

KEY TERM

You'll also find some terminology discrepancies. In NCSA Mosaic, Enhanced NCSA Mosaic, and WebSurfer, the term *hotlist* is used to denote favorite or useful document titles that you've added to the list, while Netscape uses the term *bookmarks* for the same thing. Of the two, I prefer bookmarks, since there's less chance of confusing the term with *history list*.

Creating a New Hotlist

To create a new hotlist, follow the steps for the program you're using.

NCSA MOSAIC

From the Navigate menu, choose **Menu Editor**. The Personal Menus dialog box will be displayed. In the Menus area, select the first blank line, and click **Insert**. The Add item dialog box will appear. In the Title area, erase the existing text, if any, and type the menu title you want. Click **OK** to confirm your new menu name, and click **Close** to return to Mosaic.

ENHANCED NCSA MOSAIC

With Enhanced NCSA Mosaic, you're stuck with the one, default hotlist.

From the Bookmarks menu, choose **View Bookmarks**. In the Bookmark List dialog box, click the **New Header** button. In the Name box under this button, delete the text "New Header" and type the hotlist name you want to use. Click **OK** to return to Netscape.

With WebSurfer, you're stuck with the one, default hotlist.

Adding a URL to a Specific Hotlist

To add a URL to a specific hotlist:

From the File menu, choose **Open URL**. In the Open URL dialog box, click the **Current Hotlist** list box, and choose the hotlist to which you want to add new URLs. Confirm your choice by clicking **OK**.

With Enhanced NCSA Mosaic, all the URLs you add go to the default hotlist.

From the Bookmarks menu, choose **View Bookmarks**. In the Bookmark List dialog box, click the **Edit** button. In the Add Bookmarks Under list box, select the bookmark name you want to use, and click **OK** to return to Netscape.

With WebSurfer, all the URLs you add go to the default hotlist.

Changing the Title of a Hotlist Item

To change the title of a hotlist item:

From the Navigate menu, choose **Menu Editor**. In the Menus area, select the hotlist item you want to rename, and click the **Edit** button. In the Edit Item dialog box, edit the name, and click **OK** to confirm.

From the Navigate menu, choose **Hotlist**. In the Hotlist dialog box, select the hotlist name, and click the **Edit** button. In the dialog box that appears, change the name, and click **OK**. Click **Close** to exit.

NETSCAPE NAVIGATOR

From the Bookmarks menu, choose **View Bookmarks**. In the Bookmark List dialog box, select the bookmark name you want to change, and click the **Edit** button. Edit the name in the Name box, and click **Close**.

WEBSURFER

From the Retrieve menu, choose **Hotlist**. Select the hotlist item, and click **Properties**. Edit the title in the Title box and click **OK**.

Deleting a Hotlist Item

To delete a hotlist item:

NCSA MOSAIC

From the Navigate menu, choose **Menu Editor**. In the Menus area, select the hotlist item you want to delete, and click the **Delete** button. Click **OK** to confirm the deletion.

ENHANCED NCSA MOSAIC

From the Navigate menu, choose **Hotlist**. In the Hotlist dialog box, select the document name, and click the **Delete** button. Click **Close** to exit.

NETSCAPE NAVIGATOR

From the Bookmarks menu, choose **View Bookmarks**. In the Bookmark List dialog box, select the bookmark name you want to change, and click the **Edit** button. Click **Remove Item**, and click **Close**.

WEBSURFER

From the Retrieve menu, choose **Hotlist**. In the Hotlist dialog box, select the document name you want to delete, and click **Remove**. Click **OK** to exit.

Restructuring a Hotlist

To change the order of hotlist items:

NCSA MOSAIC

There's no convenient way to change the order of hotlist items, but try this if you're desperate. From the Navigate menu, choose **Menu Editor**. In the Menus area, select the hotlist that contains the item you want to move. In the Items area, select the name of the item you want to move, and click **Copy Item**. Then select the item where you want the copied item to appear, and click **Insert**. After inserting the copied item, delete the original by selecting it and clicking **Delete**.

ENHANCED
NCSA
MOSAIC

You're stuck with the order in which the hotlists were created; when you create a new hotlist file, Air Mosaic puts it at the bottom of the list.

NETSCAPE
NAVIGATOR

From the <u>B</u>ookmarks menu, choose **View <u>B</u>ookmarks**. In the Bookmark List dialog box, select the hotlist item you want to move, and click the **Up** or **Down** butons. Click **Close** when you are finished.

WEBSURFER

You're stuck with the order in which the hotlist items were created.

Adding a Hotlist to the Menu Bar

To add a hotlist to the menu bar:

NCSA
MOSAIC

"Creating a New Hotlist," earlier in this section. NCSA Mosaic's hotlists appear on the menu bar by default.

ENHANCED
NCSA
MOSAIC

From the <u>F</u>ile menu, choose **<u>H</u>otlists**. In the Hotlists dialog box, select the hotlist name, and activate the checkbox entitled **Put this Hotlist** in the menu bar. Click the **Close** button to return to Air Mosaic.

NETSCAPE
NAVIGATOR

In Netscape, hotlists appear on the Bookmarks menu only. By default, this menu shows all the bookmark lists. To change this setting, choose **View <u>B</u>ookmarks** from the Bookmarks menu. In the Bookmark List dialog box, click the **Edit** button. In the Bookmark Menu list box, choose the name of the bookmark menu that you want to appear, and click **Close** to return to Netscape.

WEBSURFER

You can't add the hotlist to the menu bar.

Creating an HTML Local File From Your Hotlist

To create an HTML local file from your hotlist:

NCSA MOSAIC

You can't save your hotlist to a file with NCSA Mosaic. However, note that this program saves your hotlists in the file MOSAIC.INI. If you would like to copy the URLs, you can do so by opening the file with a text editor (such as the Windows accessory program called Notepad).

ENHANCED NCSA MOSAIC

From the _N_avigate menu, choose **Hotlist**. Select the hotlist you want to save to an HTML file, and click the **Export** button. In the Save As dialog box, type a file name, and click **OK**. Click **C**lose to exit.

NETSCAPE NAVIGATOR

From the _B_ookmarks menu, choose **V**i**ew B**ookmarks. In the Bookmark List dialog box, click the **Edit** button. Click **View Bookmarks** to create the HTML document with the default file name BOOKMARK.HTM. To create a bookmark file with a different name, click the **Export Bookmarks** button; when the Save dialog box appears, type a file name and click **OK**. If necessary, click the **Close box** to return to Netscape.

WEBSURFER

You can't create a local HTML version of your hotlist with WebSurfer.

SUMMARY

The history list, manually-typed URLs, and the hotlist can help you find your way through the Web's many trails. Make sure you know how the history list works, and choose documents directly from the list rather than going back or forward through a long series of hyperlink jumps. Add useful documents to your hotlist so that you can go to these items directly the next time you use Mosaic.

FROM HERE...

- For more information about working with Mosaic documents, see the next chapter.
- Learn to work with Mosaic's helper programs in Chapter 13.
- Explore Internet resources with the aid of Chapter 14.
- Customize your browser, with Chapter 15's help.

CHAPTER 12

Working with Documents

The vast, mostly uncharted wilderness of data stored "somewhere on the Internet,"
once accessible only with extensive "inside information" about their location
and format, can now be explored with powerful "browsing" tools such as Mosaic...
—A. Lyman Chapman (Bolt, Beranak, and Newman)

Sooner or later, you'll want to do something more with the Web documents you'll
find than surf around in them—you'll want to store them on disk so that you can
retrieve them quickly, print them, or copy and paste graphics from them into other
documents. These and other document-management techniques are covered in this
chapter, with detailed instructions for all four of the most popular browsers (NCSA
Mosaic, Enhanced NCSA Mosaic, Netscape, and WebSurfer).

DETERMINING THE SIZE OF THE MEMORY CACHE

Graphical browsers would be tedious to use if it weren't for the *memory cache*, a
portion of your computer's memory that the program sets aside. This memory is
used to store previously-accessed documents. If you click the Back button, the
cached documents are re-displayed much more quickly than your browser could
retrieve them from the Web.

**KEY
TERM**

Most browsers let you choose the number of documents to be cached. If you
have lots of memory in your computer (more than 8 MB), you may wish to increase
the default memory cache size.

To change the default memory cache size:

NCSA MOSAIC

Quit Mosaic. Use the Windows Notepad editor to open the file WIN.INI, and locate the [Document Caching] area. Find the line with the text "Number=2." Carefully delete the "2" and type a larger number—Start with 10. Save the file and quit Notepad.

ENHANCED NCSA MOSAIC

You can't change the size of Enhanced NCSA Mosaic's memory cache.

NETSCAPE NAVIGATOR

From the Options menu, choose **Preferences**. From the drop-down list box, choose **Network, Images and Security**. In the Memory Cache box, type the number of bytes you want to set aside for the memory cache. Click **OK** to confirm your choices.

You can't change the size of WebSurfer's memory cache.

WEBSURFER

CACHING DOCUMENTS ON DISK

The memory cache speeds your browser's performance considerably, but unfortunately, when you exit the program, the cache is erased. The next time you access the same URLs, they'll have to be loaded from the network.

KEY TERM

A *disk cache* provides a way around the shortcomings of the memory cache. In a disk cache, accessed documents are stored in disk files. The next time you access the URL, your browser automatically retrieves the document from the disk file rather than the network.

AWFUL

Disk caching sounds like a great idea, but it's hard to implement in practice. Just consider Cello, the first Web browser to implement disk caching. The more you use the program, the bigger the disk cache gets—until it threatens to swallow up your entire hard disk. Cello addresses this problem by allowing you to set a "low water mark"—the amount of disk space you want to defend from Cello's territorial aggression. Netscape addresses the issue by letting you define the maximum size of the disk cache—a setting that, unfortunately, Version 1.0 ignores, presumably due to a bug in the program's code. In both applications, though, the solution for a full disk cache is unsatisfactory; sooner or later, you must delete (or "flush") the cache, so all documents will have to be downloaded from the network again when they're re-accessed. It would be better if you could selectively delete documents you'll probably not access again.

The only Web browser that addresses this problem intelligently is WebSurfer, which permits you to mark individual documents for disk caching. With WebSurfer, you can cache just those frequently-accessed documents that you know you're going to display time and again.

EXCELLENT

Note that disk caching differs from loading documents to a local file (discussed in the following section). When a browser caches a document on your hard disk, you can access it by choosing it from your hotlist (or clicking a hyperlink in any Web document)—your browser "knows" to access the disk version of the document rather than the net version. If you load a document to a disk file, you must open it using a special command—the document won't be accessed automatically should you click a hyperlink to the network version of the document. For this reason, disk caching is much more convenient.

To activate or adjust the default disk cache:

NCSA MOSAIC

NCSA deletes the disk cache when you exit the program.

ENHANCED NCSA MOSAIC

Enhanced NCSA Mosaic deletes the disk cache when you exit the program. To change this, open the SMOSAIC.INI file, and locate the Delete_Temp_Files_on_Exit line. Delete "no," and type **yes**. Save the file and exit.

NETSCAPE NAVIGATOR

From the _O_ptions menu, choose **Preferences**. From the drop-down list box, choose **Network**, **Images** and **Security**. In the Memory Cache box, type the number of bytes you want to set aside for the memory cache. Click **OK** to confirm your choices.

WEBSURFER

From the _S_ettings menu, choose **Preferences**. In the Preferences dialog box, activate the **Save Cached Documents Between Sessions** check box. Click **OK** to confirm your choice. This activates the disk cache for all documents.

If you're using WebSurfer, you can cache documents individually rather than caching all documents. To store a displayed document in the disk cache, begin by deactivating the **Save Cached Documents Between Sessions** option in the Preferences dialog box; this option caches all the documents you download. From the _R_etrieve menu, choose **Properties.** Activate the **Save Cached Document Between Sessions**, and click **OK**.

LOADING DOCUMENTS TO A DISK FILE

When you access Web documents, your browser keeps them in your computer's memory or in a temporary disk file. When you quit your browser, the document's lost. If you want to save the document to disk, however, you can do so. Ordinarily, browsers save a document in HTML format, which means you can later reload the document with your browser. You'll see the document on-screen, just as if you accessed it from the Web.

AWFUL

Loading documents to a disk file works just fine for text-only documents, but don't count on getting in-line graphics. In HTML documents, in-line graphics are handled by placing into the document coded references to graphics files, which are normally stored on the remote system's disk drive (along with the original copy of the document). These references say, in effect, "Get the graphic file called such-and-such that's located in the same directory." When you load the document to a file on your disk drive, these references no longer work correctly; the browser goes looking for the graphics, but can't find them.

WISH LIST

Developers, please note: How about a "load to disk" command that automatically scans the document for references to inline graphics, and downloads them too?

To load a document to disk:

NCSA MOSAIC

Display the document. From the Options menu, choose **Load to Disk**. From the Navigate menu, choose **Reload**. When the Save As dialog box appears, use the name that Mosaic proposes for the file, and click **OK**. Deselect the **Load** to **Disk** option (in the Options menu) if you don't want to continue downloading files. Here's a neat mouse shortcut: to download a graphic associated with a hyperlink, hold down the **Shift** key and click the hyperlink. Instead of activating the hyperlink, Mosaic will download the document to a file.

ENHANCED NCSA MOSAIC

Display the document. From the File menu, choose **Save As**. In the Save As dialog box, type a file name, and click **OK**.

NETSCAPE NAVIGATOR

Display the document. From the File menu, choose **Save As**. In the Save As dialog box, type a file name, and click **OK**.

WEBSURFER

From the Retrieve menu, choose **Edit HTML**. WebSurfer starts the Windows Notepad accessory. From the File menu, choose **Save**. In the Save As dialog box, type a file name, and click **OK**. From the File menu, choose **Exit** to return to WebSurfer.

VIEWING THE SOURCE DOCUMENT

If you would like to see the HTML code that underlies the document you are viewing, you can do so with some of the graphical browsers discussed in this book. Figure 12.1 shows an HTML document as displayed normally by Netscape; Figure 12.2 shows the same document's source.

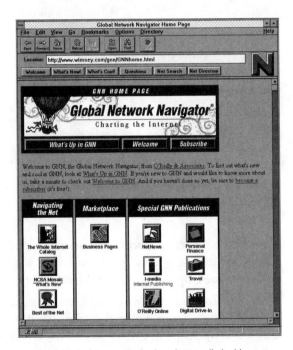

Figure 12.1 *Document displayed normally by Netscape*

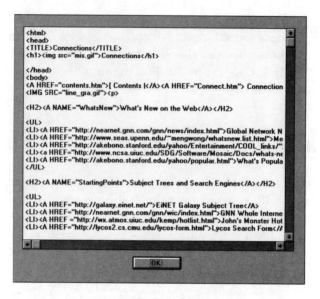

```
<html>
<head>
<TITLE>Connections</TITLE>
<h1><img src="mis.gif">Connections</h1>

</head>
<body>
<A HREF="contents.htm">[ Contents ]</A><A HREF="Connect.htm"> Connection
<IMG SRC="line_gra.gif"><p>

<H2><A NAME="WhatsNew">What's New on the Web</A></H2>

<UL>
<LI><A HREF="http://nearnet.gnn.com/gnn/news/index.html">Global Network N
<LI><A HREF="http://www.seas.upenn.edu/~mengwong/whatsnew.list.html">Me
<LI><A HREF="http://akebono.stanford.edu/yahoo/Entertainment/COOL_links/"
<LI><a HREF="http://www.ncsa.uiuc.edu/SDG/Software/Mosaic/Docs/whats-ne
<LI><A HREF="http://akebono.stanford.edu/yahoo/popular.html">What's Popula
</UL>

<H2><A NAME="StartingPoints">Subject Trees and Search Engines</A></H2>

<UL>
<LI><A HREF="http://galaxy.einet.net/">EiNET Galaxy Subject Tree</A>
<LI><A HREF="http://nearnet.gnn.com/gnn/wic/index.html">GNN Whole Interne
<LI><A HREF ="http://wx.atmos.uiuc.edu/kemp/hotlist.html">John's Monster Hot
<LI><A HREF="http://lycos2.cs.cmu.edu/lycos-form.html">Lycos Search Form</A
```

```
[ OK ]
```

Figure 12.2 *Document source*

To view the source document:

NCSA MOSAIC

From the File menu, choose **Document Source.** You'll see the document in a new window, from which you can save it, or copy it to the Clipboard. To exit the window, click **OK.**

ENHANCED NCSA MOSAIC

From the Edit menu, choose **View.** You'll see the document in a new window, from which you can save it, or copy it to the Clipboard by pressing **Ctrl-C.** To exit the window, click **OK.**

NETSCAPE NAVIGATOR

From the View menu, choose **Source.** You'll see the document in a new window. To copy some or all of the text to the Clipboard, select the text, and press **Ctrl-C.** To exit the window, click **OK.**

WEBSURFER

From the Retrieve menu, choose **Edit HTML**. WebSurfer starts the Windows Notepad accessory. You can use Notepad's menus to save, copy, or edit the file. In the Save As dialog box, type a file name, and click **OK**. From the File menu, choose **Exit** to return to WebSurfer.

OPENING A LOCAL DOCUMENT

Once you've saved an HTML file to your local disk drive, you can open it with your browser. You see the document on-screen just as if you downloaded it from the Web. Note, however, that the in-line graphics probably won't appear. (If they do, it's because the URLS referencing these graphics point to graphics stored outside the directory in which the document was originally stored—and that's a rarity.)

To open a local document:

NCSA MOSAIC

From the File menu, choose **Open Local File**. In the Open dialog box, specify the file name, and click **OK**.

ENHANCED NCSA MOSAIC

From the File menu, choose **Open Local**. In the Open dialog box, specify the file name, and click **OK**.

NETSCAPE NAVIGATOR

From the File menu, choose **Open File**. In the Open dialog box, specify the file name, and click **OK**.

WEBSURFER

From the Retrieve menu, choose **Open Local File**. In the File Open dialog box, specify the file name, and click **OK**.

FINDING TEXT IN A DOCUMENT

If you are viewing a lengthy document, you don't have to page through the document manually to find the text or hyperlink you're looking for—let your browser do it for you. The search is restricted to the document you're viewing.

To search for text in a Web document:

NCSA MOSAIC

From the Edit menu, choose **Find**, or click the Find tool. In the Find What box, type the word or phrase you're looking for. If you like, click the **Match Case** check box. Click **Find Next** to find the next occurrence of the word or phrase. If there aren't any more occurrences of this text, you'll see a dialog box informing you that the string (the characters for which you're searching) isn't found. Close the Find dialog box by clicking **Cancel**.

ENHANCED NCSA MOSAIC

From the Edit menu, choose **Find**. In the Find box, type the word or phrase you're looking for. If you like, click the **Match Case** check box. Click **OK** to find the next occurrence of the word or phrase. If there aren't any more occurrences of this text, you'll see a dialog box informing you that the string (the characters for which you're searching) isn't found. Close the box by clicking **OK**.

NETSCAPE NAVIGATOR

From the Edit menu, choose **Find**, or click the Find tool. In the Find dialog box, indicate the direction of the search. To match the case of the search string, activate the **Match Case** check box. Type the text you want to match in the Find What box, and click **OK**.

WEBSURFER

WebSurfer lacks a Find command. However, you can open the document source, and use Notepad's Search command to search for text. From the Retrieve menu, choose **Edit HTML**. WebSurfer starts the Windows Notepad accessory. From the Search menu, choose **Find** in the Find dialog box, indicate the direction of the search. To match the case of the search string, activate the **Match Case** check box. Type the text you want to match in the Find What box, and click **OK**. From the File menu, choose **Exit** to return to WebSurfer.

PRINTING DOCUMENTS

You can print the document that your browser is displaying. Most browsers offer a print preview option (Figure 12.3), which lets you view your document's printed appearance on-screen.

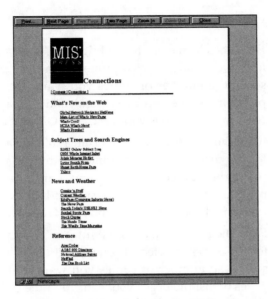

Figure 12.3 *Print Preview option (Netscape)*

To display the print preview:

NCSA
MOSAIC

From the File menu, choose **Print Preview**. In the Print Preview window, you can click buttons to display two pages at once or one page; zoom in or zoom out; view the next or previous pages; or begin printing. To exit the window, click **Close**.

ENHANCED
NCSA
MOSAIC

No print preview is available

NETSCAPE
NAVIGATOR

From the File menu, choose **Print Preview**. In the Print Preview window, you can click buttons to display two pages at once or one page; zoom in or zoom out; view the next or previous pages; or begin printing. To exit the window, click **Close**.

WEBSURFER

From the File menu, choose **Print Preview**. In the Print Preview window, you can click buttons to display two pages at once or one page; zoom in or zoom out; view the next or previous pages; or begin printing. To exit the window, click **Close.**

To print the document:

WEBSURFER

From the File menu, choose **Print**. You'll see a print dialog box for the currently-selected printer. With most printers, you can select the number of copies you want, the page range (all pages or just the pages you want), and the paper source. After choosing the options you want, click **OK** to start printing.

ENHANCED NCSA MOSAIC

From the File menu, choose **Print**. You'll see a print dialog box for the currently-selected printer. With most printers, you can select the number of copies you want, the page range (all pages or just the pages you want), and the paper source. After choosing the options you want, click **OK** to start printing.

NETSCAPE NAVIGATOR

From the File menu, choose **Print**. You'll see a print dialog box for the currently-selected printer. With most printers, you can select the number of copies you want, the page range (all pages or just the pages you want), and the paper source. After choosing the options you want, click **OK** to start printing.

WEBSURFER

From the File menu, choose **Print**. You'll see a print dialog box for the currently-selected printer. With most printers, you can select the number of copies you want, the page range (all pages or just the pages you want), and the paper source. After choosing the options you want, click **OK** to start printing.

ANNOTATIONS (MOSAIC ONLY)

When you're reading a book, sometimes it's nice to take notes. With Mosaic, you can make your own notes on a Web document that you're viewing in the document view window. The annotations are stored on your computer and are accessible only to you. You can view, alter, and delete them whenever you wish.

You create your annotation in an annotation window. After you create your annotation, an annotation marker is displayed at the bottom of the annotated document.

To add an annotation to a document:

Display the document. From the Annotate menu, choose **Annotate** to see the Annotate Window; Mosaic has automatically added your email address and the default title "Personal Annotation by Mosaic User." If text appears in the window from the last annotation you made, you can erase it by clicking the **Clean Slate** button. If you'd like to include a file, click the **Include File** button and use the dialog box to indicate the name and location of the file you'd like to include. Type the annotation text, and click **Commit** to save your annotation.

To display an annotation:

Click the annotation mark as if it were a hyperlink. You'll see the annotation in a new document.

To edit an annotation:

Display the annotation. From the Annotate menu, choose **Edit this Annotation**. You'll see the Annotate Window. Edit the annotation, and choose **Commit** to save it.

To delete an annotation:

Display the annotation. From the Annotate menu, choose **Delete this Annotation**. You'll see the Annotate Window. Click **Delete** to remove the annotation.

SUMMARY

You can save wear and tear on your patience—and conserve Internet bandwidth—by downloading frequently accessed documents to files and browsing them on your own system. To locate text quickly within a lengthy document, use your browser's text searching capabilities. If you'd like to save the document for non-hypertext uses, you can save it in a variety of file formats. You can even save the original HTML text, which is useful if you want to learn how to code documents in HTML. If you're using Mosaic, you can add annotations, to indicate your reactions to the document's you're viewing.

FROM HERE...

- In the next chapter, learn how to configure your browser to use helper programs.

- For information on navigating Internet resources with your browser, see Chapter 14.

- Chapter 15 introduces the art of customizing your browser, so that it looks—and acts—the way you want.

CHAPTER 13

Using Helper Programs

> When I read, I forget. When I see, I remember.
> —Ancient Chinese proverb

Most graphical browsers can display in-line images without difficulty, but the programs need help when you download PostScript files, high-resolution graphics, movies, or sounds. You must equip your system with *helper programs*, Which step in to handle data types that your browser can't handle on its own.

**KEY
TERM**

Currently, one of the worst aspects of Web graphical browsers is that they leave it up to you to obtain, install, and configure the helper programs. This isn't so difficult if you've got plenty of guidance and help, but it's still a tedious job. Tomorrow's graphical browsers will include the ability to display all kinds of files and graphics, as well as play movies and sounds—but that's still a year or two away.

AWFUL

If you're not sure how to obtain programs with anonymous FTP and don't know a subdirectory from a sub sandwich, get someone to help you with the nettlesome tasks of obtaining, installing, and configuring helper programs. Chances are there's someone in your office who has done this before, and can do it again with a minimum of effort.

**HOME
PAGE**

WHAT YOU NEED

Most graphical browsers need help with the following data types:

- **Graphics.** Although most browsers can display in-line GIF images, they need help with larger GIF files and JPEG graphics. (For more information on

191

graphics file types, see "About Graphics File Formats" later in this chapter.) Netscape users, you're in luck: Netscape can handle GIF and JPEG graphics without any help.

- **Video.** Animations and videos require the assistance of a player that can handle MPEG video files. You may wish to obtain a player for videos stored in the QuickTime format as well. For more information on these formats, see "Video Formats" later in this chapter.

- **Sound.** To hear sounds, your computer must be equipped with sound circuitry and speakers. Windows users will need a sound card such as a SoundBlaster. You also need a helper program that can deal with a variety of sound file formats (see "Sound File Formats" later in this chapter).

- **PostScript documents.** To display documents stored in the PostScript page description language, you'll need a viewer that can decode the PostScript commands and display the document on-screen. PostScript is explained later in this chapter.

- **Telnet sessions.** Much interesting information is available from mainframe computers that aren't directly compatible with the World Wide Web. These include on-line library card catalogs and other goodies. To access this information, you need a Telnet helper application that can open a new window and enable you to exchange commands with the mainframe computer.

AWFUL

So here's the bad news: To use the full multimedia potential of your browser, you may need to obtain, configure, and install as many as six additional programs. If you want to be able to deal with every multimedia file that might come your way, you may need more. For example, most MPEG video players can't handle QuickTime videos, so you'll need a different player for these files.

WISH LIST

Software developers, are you listening? Web users want full multimedia capability built into graphical browsers. At the very minimum, you should distribute browsers with the necessary helper applications, together with an installation utility that automatically configures the utilities for the users' systems.

HOT TIP

Do you already have some of the helper programs you need? If you're using TCP/IP package such as Internet Chameleon, the answer may be "Yes." Most of these packages include a Telnet helper application. You should be able to configure your browser to start and use.

HOW HELPER PROGRAMS WORK

To exchange multimedia information on the Internet, a standard called *Multipurpose Internet Mail Extensions* (MIME) was developed. This standard enables Internet users to exchange multimedia messages containing enhanced character sets, PostScript formatting, recorded sounds, GIF and other graphics, and digital video. The World Wide Web takes advantage of MIME standards.

For a good overview of MIME, check out Mark Grand's "MIME Overview," which you'll find at ftp://ftp.netcom.com/pub/mdg/mime.txt.

USEFUL RESOURCE

KEY TERM

In brief, MIME works by defining a set of standards for the exchange of multimedia data. MIME defines a set of multimedia data types, such as PostScript text files and JPEG graphics files, so that your application knows what kind of data it's receiving. Each data type is associated with an *extension*, a two- or three-letter code that identifies the type of data a file contains.

That's all you really need to know about MIME. When your browser encounters a URL that isn't an HTML document, it then looks at the file's extension. Suppose, for example, that the URL points to a Microsoft Windows file. Next, with the WAV extension it will look for a helper program that can deal with this data. It will start the program, and pass the file to the helper program. The helper program then displays or plays the multimedia file.

For all this to happen, you must do the following:

1. **Obtain the helper program**. Most of the available helper programs are freeware (copyrighted but free for individual use) or shareware (you must pay a registration fee if you want to continue using the program). This section surveys what's available at this writing, but bear in mind that new, more capable programs may come along in the future.

2. **Decompress the helper program.** If you're using Microsoft Windows, you'll need PKUNZIP.EXE. WinZIP, a Windows interface for the PKZIP software package is also strongly recommended.

3. **Install the helper program on your computer's hard disk**. This is easy enough, so long as you understand how your computer's storage system is structured (folders, if you're using a Macintosh, or directories, if you're using Windows).

4. **Tell your graphical browser where the helper program is located**. With most browsers, you do this by typing the program's location in a dialog box.

HOT TIP

There are dozens of helper programs and many graphical browsers, so this chapter can't survey every conceivable variant on the tasks of obtaining, installing, and configuring helper applications. However, you'll find full coverage of the most popular helper programs and browsers.

WEB SECRET

For each of the graphical browsers discussed in this book, you'll find a list of recommended helper programs. Such lists are generally accessible through the browser vendor's Welcome page, the browser's on-line documentation, or public FTP sites such as XXX.

Can you use helpers other than those recommended? In general, the answer is yes, provided that the helper program can start and open a file at the same time. When your browser starts a helper program, it sends a message that launches the application and tells it which file to display. Most helper applications can handle this without difficulty.

OBTAINING HELPER PROGRAMS

To obtain helper programs, your best bet is to use the FTP site maintained by the vendor of your graphical browser, since the vendor tests to make sure the program works with your browser before it's made available. Here's a list of the FTP sites maintained by vendors of graphical browser:

- **Cello** ftp://law.cornell.edu/put/LII/Cello
- **NCSA Mosaic** http://www.ncsa.uiuc.edu/SDG/Software/WinMosaic /viewers.html
- **Netscape** http://home.mcom.com/MCOM/tricks_docs/helper_docs /index.html

HOT TIP

You can also look for helper programs in FTP shareware archives, such as CICA and SimTel. By far the best way to do this is to search the Virtual Shareware Library (Shase) This search service scans the major shareware libraries for files, enabling you to search by descriptor words as well as file names (http://www.fagg.uni-lj.si/SHASE/)

A GUIDE TO HELPER PROGRAMS

Helper programs come and go, and there will be new versions of many of these programs available by the time you read this book. Nevertheless, here's a quick guide to the best of the current crop of helper programs.

The following helper programs are currently recommended for Windows graphical browsers:

- **WPLAYER.EXE.** This utility is included with Microsoft Windows. It plays sound files with the MIME type video/x-mswindows.

- **MPEGPLAY** (version 1.0). A shareware program by Michael Simmons, (the registration fee is $25, payable to Michael at 34 Shillington Way, THORNLIE WA 6108, AUSTRALIA) that plays MPEG videos and animations but not QuickTime.

- **LView Pro.** Version 1.0 is the latest version of the highly-regarded LView graphics viewer. Created by Leonardo Haddad Loureiro (1501 East Hallandale Beach Boulevard #254, Hallandale, FL, 33009), LView Pro is a shareware program. However, you need not pay the registration fee if you use the program for leisure purposes only. The program can display GIF, PCX, TIFF, JPEG, and Targa graphics.

- **WPLANY.EXE.** This freeware sound player was created by Bill Neisius. It can play just about any sound file format that you'll find on the Web. One drawback of WPLANY is that you can't repeat or save the sounds you hear.

- **Waveform Hold and Multiply (WHAM).** Created by Andrew Bulhak, this shareware program plays a variety of sound file formats (though not as many as WPLANY). Unlike WPLANY, you can replay, save, and manipulate the sounds you've downloaded. To register, send $20 to $30 to Bulhak at 21 The Crescent, Fertree Gulley, Victoria 3156, Australia.

- **Ghostview for Windows.** This program permits you to display and print the PostScript files that you may encounter on the Web. Created by Russell Lang, it's a freeware program (copyrighted but freely redistributable for non-profit use).

- **Adobe Acrobat.** Lets a computer user print a document to a file using the Portable Document Format (PDF), which captures fonts, colors, and graphics. With the help of Adobe Acrobat, a recipient of a file can open it and display it—with all the graphics and text intact—on any Windows or Macintosh system. Note, you probably won't find Adobe Acrobat in most of the browser vendor's FTP sites. A free version of the Adobe Acrobat reader is available from Adobe's Acrobat page (http://www.adobe.com /Acrobat/Acrobat0.html).

CONFIGURING YOUR BROWSER TO USE HELPER PROGRAMS

Once you've obtained the helper programs you want to use, you need to tell your browser where they're located on your hard drive. To do so, you'll use a dialog box (unless you're using NCSA Mosaic, in which case you'll have to edit MOSAIC.INI manually). In this dialog box, you associate a given MIME data type with a specific helper program, and you also tell your browser where the helper program is located on your hard disk. To do this, Windows users will find it helpful to refer to Table 13.1.

Table 13.1 Recommended Helper Programs for Windows Browsers

MIME type	Recommended Player
application/postscript	GSVIEW.EXE
audio/basic	WPLANY.EXE
audio/wav	WPLANY.EXE
audio/x-wav	WPLANY.EXE
image/gif	LVIEWP1A.EXE
image/jpeg	LVIEWP1A.EXE
image/tiff	LVIEWP1A.EXE
video/mpeg	MPEGPLAY.EXE
video/x-msvideo	WPLAYER.EXE

To configure your browser to use helper programs:

NCSA MOSAIC

To configure NCSA Mosaic for helper programs, you must make changes to the MOSAIC.INI, which you'll find in the \Windows directory. Locate the [viewers] section. Locate the viewer type, such as video/mpeg, and type the helper program's path after the equals sign. Type a space and add **%ls.** Enclose the expression with quotation marks as follows:

video/mpeg = "c:\helpers\mpegplay.exe %ls" Save the file and exit.

**ENHANCED
NCSA
MOSAIC**

The venders who package this program preconfigure it for use with the helper programs they provide.

**NETSCAPE
NAVIGATOR**

From the <u>O</u>ptions menu, choose **Preferences**. In the Preferences dialog box, select **Helper** applications from the drop down list box. Select the MIME type that you want to configure. Click **Browse** to find the application. Select application. Click **OK**. You'll see your selection in the list of MIME types. Repeat this operation until you've selected helper applications for all the helper programs you want to use. To configure your Telnet viewer, select **Directories, Applications, and News** in the drop down list box. Use the Browse button next to the Telnet applications box to add your Telnet application to the configuration. Click **OK** when you are finished configuring Netscape.

WEBSURFER

Websurfer does not work with the helper program.

DISPLAYING GRAPHICS

About Graphics File Formats

Computer images are recorded using standards called graphics formats, which dictate the precise procedure for storing the image on disk so that it can be retrieved and displayed. Graphics formats vary in the technical method that's used to store the images, but let's leave that to the computer wizards. For users, what matters is the format's ability to represent color information (gauged by the number of bits stored for each dot on the screen), and the method used to compress the data.

Graphics formats vary in the number of colors they can represent. For example, a format that's capable of representing 8 bits of information for each dot on the screen (pixel) can display a maximum of 256 colors. Because computers represent information using binary numbers, the maximum number of colors that you can represent with 8 bits is 256, since an 8-bit coding system gives you 256 different possibilities (28 = 256). Here's a quick overview of the relationship between the number of bits per pixel and the maximum number of colors that can be represented:

- **4-bit**. A 4-bit graphics format can represent only 16 colors, but requires a very small file. However, the image's colors won't look like the original's.

- **8-bit**. An 8-bit graphics format can represent 256 colors. That's enough to provide a reasonable approximation of the original's colors, at least for screen display purposes. Most of the images you'll encounter on the Web are 8-bit graphics. You can display an 8-bit graphic on most computers without requiring special equipment.

- **16-bit**. A 16-bit graphics format can represent 65,536 colors, a capability that is common on Macintosh systems.

- **24-bit**. A 24-bit graphics format can represent 16.7 million colors. 24-bit graphics files come closest to capturing the true colors of the original, but they require a great deal of storage space unless they're radically compressed.

KEY TERM

Some graphics formats use a technique called *dithering* to make the image appear to have more colors than it does. In dithering, the colors of surrounding dots are adjusted to make up for discrepancies between the source color and the display color.

Make sure your display is matched to the color depth of the graphics you're displaying. Most monitors can run in more than one video mode. For example, the monitor I'm using right now can be switched between 256; 65,536, and 16.7 million colors. A graphic with 16-bit (65,536, colors) information will display more slowly on a display at 256 colors because the graphics software will have to compensate by translating the colors.

In addition to the number of colors that graphics formats can represent, they vary according to the type of compression that's used. Compression is required because uncompressed graphics take up too much disk space and Internet transmission bandwidth. Compression techniques fall into two categories, *lossless* and *lossy*:

- **Lossless Compression**. A method of data compression that seeks to preserve all of the original data without alteration. Much of the data in a typical graphics file is redundant. This redundant data can be stored using a shorter code than the ones originally used to represent the graphics data. Some images can be compressed to a tenth of their original size without loss of image quality. The image must be decompressed upon receipt before you can view it.

- **Lossy Compression**. A method of data compression that sacrifices some loss of the data in ways that are not immediately obvious to a person who is viewing the graphics file after it has been transmitted.

Everyone agrees that compression is desirable for Web graphics. But the jury's still out regarding which of these techniques is the best, and in fact, this very subject is likely to launch a flame war if you bring it up on graphics-related Usenet newgroups!

Here's a quick overview of the file formats you're most likely to encounter while browsing the Web with your graphical browser, listed in the order in which you'll find them.

- **GIF (Graphics Interchange Format)**. An 8-bit, 256-color graphics file format originally developed by CompuServe and widely used to facilitate the exchange of graphics files throughout the computer community, including bulletin board systems and the Internet. GIF files, stored with the .GIF extension, are compressed to shorten transmission times. The GIF standard employs a lossless compression technique to reduce the size of graphics files for economical transmission. On receipt, the image must be decompressed by a graphics program that can read GIF files. Generally, GIF files are very large—some are a half megabyte or more in size—and can require several minutes to download via a 14.4 Kbps SLIP or PPP connection.

- **JPEG (Joint Photographics Expert Group)/JFIF (JPEG File Interchange Format)**. This file format is based on the JPEG lossy compression technique, named for an International Standards Organization subgroup, for graphic images. JPEG achieves greater compression than can be obtained with lossless techniques—you can compress a 2MB file to 100K or less. The technique pulls this trick off by destroying some of the visual information beyond recovery, but you'll never know it. JPEG exploits the known limitations of the human eye, especially the fact that we don't notice small color changes as much as changes in brightness. The colors may be slightly altered, but they're far richer than those of the competing GIF standard. JPEG graphics can store 24-bit color information, for a total of more than 16 million colors. GIF, in contrast, can store only 256 colors. GIF graphics may have been acceptable for yesterday's graphics hardware and monitors, but

JPEG can take advantage of the high-resolution displays that are increasingly common in middle-of-the-run personal computers.

- **TIFF (Tagged Image File Format)**. This graphics format permits you to store more than one graphic image per file and supports a variety of compression techniques. It's most commonly used, though, for gray scale images, which provide an approximation of a black-and-white photograph. A commonly-used format is 256-color True Gray, which emulates the smooth gray scale gradations of a photograph and prints beautifully on laser printers.

- **Targa**. This graphics format, created by a vendor of high-resolution video equipment, supports 24-bit color but is not widely used.

Some graphics formats are specifically supported by Windows or the Macintosh include:

- **Windows Bitmap**. Standard Windows Bitmap files (named with the *.bmp or *.dib extensions) can be saved in 4-, 8-, and 24-bit formats, and can be compressed (using a compression technique called RLE compression) or uncompressed. Because these files tend to consume large amounts of disk space, they're not often encountered on the Internet.

- **PICT**. This format is the Macintosh's standard format for storing graphics data. Most Macintosh applications can read PICT files, either directly or through an Import command.

To sum up this section on graphics formats, most of the graphics you'll encounter on the Web are 8-bit GIFs, 24-bit JPEGs, or 8-bit TIFF True Gray files.

USING LVIEW PRO

LView Pro, the recommended graphics helper program for Microsoft Windows browsers, is a capable program. It enables you not only to display the graphics you download but also to print, copy, resize, crop, enhance, and print them.

Displaying Graphics

When your graphical browser detects that you're downloading a graphic that the program can't display, it starts LView Pro. The program appears in a new window and displays the downloaded graphic (see Figure 13.1). If the picture is too large for the program's window, you can use the scroll bars to bring additional parts of the document into view.

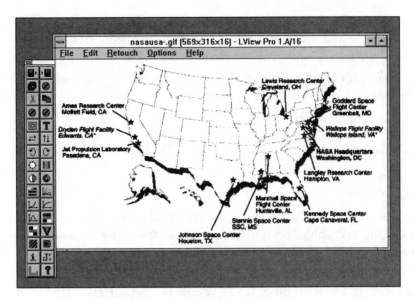

Figure 13.1 *LView Pro*

Printing a Graphic

Unless you have an expensive color printer, your downloaded color graphics will look better on-screen than when printed with a 300 dot per inch (dpi) laser or ink jet printer. Quality improves substantially with 600 dpi laser printers, if you're lucky enough to have one.

To print the graphic you've downloaded:

1. From the File menu, choose **Print**.
2. In the print dialog box for your current printer, click **Print** to begin printing.

Copying a Graphic to Other Applications

If you'd like to copy the graphic to another application, you can copy the whole graphic or just a portion of it.

To copy the whole graphic, choose **Copy** from the Eidt menu or press **CTRL**-C.

To copy a portion of the graphic:

1. Move the pointer over the graphic until it changes to the crosshair shape.

2. Move the crosshair to the upper left corner of the area you want to copy, and drag right and down until you've selected this area. (You'll see a selection band around the area you've defined in this way.)

3. When you've finished selecting the area you want to copy, release the mouse button.

4. From the Edit menu, choose **Copy**, or press **Ctrl-C**.

You can then paste the graphic to the desired application.

Resizing a Graphic

You can resize a graphic that's too large or too small for your screen. However, note that enlarging a graphic too much reveals the "paint-by-numbers" effect that underlies the graphic's realistic appearance. What appear to be smooth gradations are, when examined closely enough, little squares of solid colors.

When you resize a graphic, try to retain the aspect ratio (the ratio of the horizontal to the vertical measurement). If you change the aspect ratio when you resize the graphic, you could introduce unwanted distortion in the image.

To enlarge a graphic:

1. From the Edit menu, choose **Resize**. The Resize dialog box will be displayed.

2. Make sure the **Preserve Aspect Ratio** check box is selected.

3. You can choose from several resizing options, including Fit to Desktop and several others based on the screen resolution of typical Windows systems (640 x 480, 800 x 600, 1024 x 768, and 1280 x 1024). Choose one of these options.

4. Click **OK**. (Note: The Redimension option on the Edit menu changes the size of the LView window, not the size of the graphic.)

Cropping a Graphic

Cropping a graphic means to discard all the area around a rectangular portion of the graphic. Cropping is done to emphasize the portion of the image to which you want to call attention by removing unwanted information.

To crop a graphic:

1. Move the pointer over the graphic until it changes to the crosshair shape.

2. Now move the crosshair to the upper left corner of the area you want to crop, and drag right and down until you've selected this area. (You'll see a selection band around the area you've defined in this way.)

3. From the Edit menu, choose **Crop**.

Enhancing a Graphic

You can enhance a graphic image in a number of ways. Some of these enhancements require technical knowledge of computer graphics to use intelligently, but others are as simple as the controls you use on a color television set, such as brightness, color balance, and contrast.

To adjust the brightness of the image:

1. From the Retouch menu, choose **Gamma Correction**.

2. In the Gamma Correction dialog box, use the scroll bars to change the brightness of the red, green, and blue colors as you wish.

3. Click **OK** to confirm your settings.

To adjust the color balance:

1. From the Retouch menu, choose **Color Balance**.

2. In the Color Balance dialog box, adjust the Red (R), Green (B), and Blue (B) colors until you're happy with the balance.

3. Click **OK** to confirm your choices.

To change the contrast:

1. From the Retouch menu, choose **Contrast Enhance**.

2. In the Contrast Enhance dialog box, use the scroll bars to raise or lower the contrast.

3. When you're satisfied with the result, click **OK**.

Saving the Downloaded Graphic

If you would like to keep a copy of the downloaded graphic, use the Save command to write a permanent disk file.

To save the downloaded graphic, choose **Save** from the menu or press **Ctrl-S**.

Saving a Graphic to a Different File Format

Most programs permit you to save the graphic you've downloaded to a format other than the one in which it is currently displayed. You may find this useful in the following situations:

- You would like to open the graphics file with another application, but the application does not support the current graphics format. For example, suppose you've just downloaded a beautiful GIF picture of a distant galaxy. If you convert this to a Windows Bitmap file, you can use Windows' Control Panel to define this graphic as wallpaper so you'll see it on the desktop at all times.

- You would like to print the graphic file using a laser printer, which can handle 256 True Gray images, but does a poor job on JPEG graphics.

- You would like to transfer the file to another computer, which can't read the current graphics format.

To save the file to a different graphics format:

1. From the File menu, choose **Save As**.
2. In the Save As dialog box, open the **Save File as Type** list box.
3. Click the file type you want to use.
4. Type a new name for the file.
5. Click **OK**.

VIEWING MOVIES

When you're using a computer, you're looking at what appears to be a television screen, right? Superficially, yes. But computers display digital images, in which the image is constructed out of a very large number of bits of yes-no, on-off data.

AWFUL

"Digital" sounds great, but imaging requires a great deal more storage space than the analog techniques used to create an image on your TV set—as a rough measure, about 100 times as much. A high-resolution digital version of Darth Vader boarding Princess Leia's vessel would consume a good portion of your computer's hard disk. To produce the appearance of smooth motion (full-motion video), a display device must be capable of displaying at least 15 frames (still pictures) per second, in which each still picture shows a slight movement. For one minute of high-definition, uncompressed computer video, then, we're talking about storing, processing, and displaying dozens of megabytes worth of graphics files per minute. In other words, forget it.

But computer people have found ways to reduce the amount of disk storage (and transmission bandwidth) that's required to display animations and video clips on your computer screen. You can reduce the size of the movie, for one thing. (The first computer video standards got quite a laugh because the "movie" was about the size of a postage stamp!) You can use fewer frames per second, cutting the number of frames per second down to 12 or fewer. This makes the motion look jerkier, like those little "flip books" you had as a kid that made Donald Duck appear to walk. You can also reduce the length down to just a few seconds— enough, maybe, to hear Martin Luther King say, "I have a dream," or to watch a Titan blast off. Or, you can compress the image. Thanks to major advances in video compression technology, it's now possible to reduce the size of video file by a factor of 26:1. But don't count on VCR-like quality, lengthy videos, or full-screen pictures.

Video File Formats

There are many movie formats for computers, but you'll find the following most commonly when you browse the Web:

- **MPEG (Motion Picture Experts Group)**. A standard for the digital representation and compression of video images defined by the Motion Picture Experts Group, a subgroup of the International Standards Organization (ISO). MPEG incorporates a lossy compression technique that is capable of realizing a compression ratio of 26 to 1 without objectionable loss in image quality.

- **QuickTime**. This is the standard Macintosh format for computer movies. It supports a variety of compression programs capable of compression ratios as high as 40.1.

- **Video for Windows**. This is the standard Microsoft video format for Microsoft Windows. Like QuickTime, it can be used with a variety of compession programs.

When you download a movie with your graphical browser, the program automatically detects the type of file you're downloading and starts the appropriate viewer. Since most of the videos you'll download are MPEG videos, the following instructions pertain to viewing MPEG files with the viewers for each version of your graphical browser.

With standard players such as the recommended Windows player (MPEGPLAY), the movie is displayed in a still frame, ready to go (see Figure 13.2). If the image doesn't look right, you may need to change the dithering method. You then start the movie, which you can rewind if you wish. You can also view the movie in a continuous loop. The following sections detail the use of MPEGPLAY.

Figure 13.2 *Video ready to go (MPEGPLAY)*

Using MPEGPLAY

MPEGPLAY is a full-featured MPEG player that lets you view the movie, rewind it, view it with continuous looping, change the window size, choose a different dithering method, and save the video to disk. The following sections discuss these procedures.

Starting the Movie

Click the VCR-like Play button to play the movie. As it's playing, you can stop the movie to freeze the action, if you wish, and advance the movie one frame at a time.

To play the movie:

- From the Movie menu, choose **Play**, or click the **Play** button (the big triangle that faces right).
- To stop the movie before it finishes, open the Movie menu and choose **Stop**, or click the **Stop** button (the square).
- To advance the action one frame at a time, open the Movie menu and choose **Advance**, or click the **Advance** button (the little triangle that faces right).

Rewinding the Movie

When the movie finishes, it stops playing. To view the movie again, you must "rewind" it.

To return to the beginning of the movie from the Movie menu, choose **Rewind**, or click the **Rewind button** (the big triangle that faces left).

Turning on Continuous Looping

You can choose to view the movie in a continuous loop, repeating over and over. The movie will continue running until you choose the command to stop it.

To play the movie in a continuous loop, choose **Loop** from the Options menu.

Adjusting the Window Size

You can make the viewing window bigger, if you wish, but only at the cost of image quality. The smaller the window, the faster the frame rate that the player can achieve, and the more smoothly the movie will play.

To adjust the window size:

- From the Options menu, choose **Stretch to Window**.
- Click on the bottom right window corner and drag to the desired size.

Choosing the Dithering Method

The MPEG format defines the means by which the image is compressed, but leaves open several possibilities for the precise method used both to encode and decode the video images. The viewer attempts to determine which dithering method is correct, but you may have to experiment with different dithering options to get the movie to look right.

To change the dithering method open the Dither menu and choose a different dither method. Repeat this procedure until you find a dithering technique that gives the best results.

Saving the Downloaded Movie

When your graphical browser downloads a movie so that you can view it, the program doesn't keep a permanent copy of it. If you would like to keep a copy of the downloaded movie, use the Save command to write a permanent disk file.

To save the downloaded movie, from the File menu, choose Save, or press Ctrl-S.

LISTENING TO SOUND FILES

Like graphics and video files, sound files are stored in a number of differing formats. Some of these formats use 8-bit data storage, which provides the sound quality (roughly) of an AM radio, while others use 16-bit (CD-quality) storage techniques. Most of the recommended sound players can play two or more sound formats. Here's an overview of the sound file formats you'll find most commonly on the Web:

- **SoundBlaster .VOC file**. These files are designed to play through the popular SoundBlaster sound card that works with IBM PCs and compatibles.
- **Sun/NeXT/DEC .AU files**. These files, used with UNIX workstations, employ an advanced storage approach to give the equivalent of 14-bit sound resolution even though only 8 bits of data are stored.
- **Windows .WAV files**. This is the standard sound format for Microsoft Windows systems. *.WAV files store sounds using both 8- and 16-bit techniques.
- **Sounder/Soundtools .SND files**. This is a standard sound format for Macintosh systems.
- **Amiga .8SVX .IFF files**. This is a standard sound format for Amiga systems. It's capable of 8-bit storage only.
- **Apple IFF**. This sound format was developed by Apple Computer and is based on, but incompatible with, the Amiga IFF format. This format is also used on Silicon Graphics workstations.

Just what you see on-screen when you activate a sound hyperlink depends on which sound player you've installed. WPLANY doesn't show up at all; it just plays the sound and quits. The Windows sound player MPLAYER.EXE displays a window with VCR-like controls, as does WHAM. The following instructions pertain to WHAM, one of the recommended sound players for Windows systems.

Playing the Sound

The sound doesn't start until you click the play button.

To play the sound, click the **play** button (the one with the right-facing triangle). To play just part of the sound, select the part of the sound you want to play, and click the **play selection** button (the right-facing triangle with the vertical line after it).

Adjusting the Volume

If you can't hear the sound very well, you should first turn up your computer sound level or use your sound card's software to adjust the speaker volume upward. If the sound is markedly fainter or louder than comparable sounds on your system, you can adjust its volume by using the sound player.

To adjust the volume:

- From the Effects menu choose **Volume**, or just click the **Rewind** button (the big triangle that faces left).
- When the submenu appears, choose **Increase** or **Decrease**, and play the sound again.

Saving the Sound

When your graphical browser downloads a movie so that you can view it, the program doesn't keep a permanent copy of it. If you would like to keep a copy of the downloaded sound, use the Save command to write a permanent disk file.

To save the downloaded sound, from the File menu choose **Save** or press **Ctrl-S**.

DISPLAYING POSTSCRIPT DOCUMENTS

PostScript is a page description language that defines the precise appearance of a document, right down to the fonts, font size, and precise page layout. It's different from the generalized markup languages such as HTML that define your graphical browser documents. Generalized markup languages define the parts of a document (such as "title" or "normal text"), and leave the specifics up to the client application (such as your graphical browser).

For Web applications, HTML is clearly superior. It requires less bandwidth to transmit, and what's more, you can display any HTML document using the fonts you've installed on your system. Nevertheless, you'll still find plenty of PostScript documents around. PostScript documents provided Internet users with a means to convey nicely-formatted documents before the Web originated.

To display and print PostScript documents, you'll need a PostScript viewer, one of the essential helper programs that you install along with your graphical browser. The recommended PostScript viewer for Microsoft Windows is Ghostview for Windows.

When you download a PostScript document, your graphical browser automatically detects the document's format and starts Ghostview. You see the document in Ghostview's window, as shown in Figure 13.3, which illustrates the Windows version of Ghostview. You can then page through and print the document.

Figure 13.3 *PostScript file displayed by Ghostview*

The document you're seeing is a bit-mapped representation of the PostScript document. That's how it appears on-screen, and that's how it will print. This is convenient for quick viewing.

USING GHOSTVIEW FOR WINDOWS

Paging Through the Document

While Ghostview is displaying a PostScript document, you see only one page at a time. The scroll bars function only to display parts of the page that aren't visible in the current window. You must use special commands to display additional pages, if any.

Ghostview may not display a document's pages correctly if the document doesn't conform to Adobe's Document Structuring Conventions (DSC). If the paging commands don't work, it's probably because the document doesn't follow the DSC guidelines.

To view the next page, choose **Next Page** from the File menu, or press the gray plus key.

To view the previous page choose **Previous** from the File menu or press the gray minus key.

To go to a page number you specify:

- From the File menu, choose **Goto Page**. You'll see the Select Page dialog box.
- Click the page number you want to display.
- Click **OK**.

Printing the Document

When you print a document with Ghostview, you're printing a bit-mapped representation of the document, so don't expect miracles. Still, you'll see the fonts and layout as the author intended them to look.

To print a PostScript file:

- From the File menu, choose **Print** (or press **Ctrl + P**).
- If the document has more than one page, you'll see the Select Pages dialog box. Select the page you want to print. To select more than one page, hold down the Ctrl key and click the pages you want to print. You can also click

the Odd, Even, or All buttons to print just the odd pages, just the even pages, or the whole document.

- Click **OK** to confirm you page choices.
- In the Print dialog box, select the MSWIN printer driver, and click **OK**.
- In the Printer Setup dialog box, just click **OK** to confirm printing with your current default printer.

SUMMARY

Most of the graphics you'll find on the Web are 8-bit GIFs, 24-bit JPEGs, or 8-bit TIFF True Gray files. With your graphics helper program, you can print the downloaded graphics, copy them to other applications, resize or crop them, enhance them, and save them to disk, in their original or in a different file format. You can repeat, modify, and save the movies and sounds that you download (unless you're using an unenhanced X Window system). For PostScript documents, use the Ghostview viewer, which can display and print these documents without very attractive results.

FROM HERE...

- Learn how to access additional Internet resources, such as WAIS databases and FTP file archives, in Chapter 14.
- Customize your browser with the information you'll find in Chapter 15.

CHAPTER 14

Accessing Other Internet Resources

> In the high-tech world, if you're not on the Net, you're not in the know.
> —*The Economist*

The World Wide Web grows at an astonishing rate, with thousands of new URLs appearing every month. Even so, the Web represents only a fraction of the information resources available through the Internet. Apart from Web documents, there are huge archives of publicly-accessible files that can be found through tools such as FTP, Gopher, and WAIS.

In the past, you had to learn how to use several different tools to access these non-Web resources. For example, you needed to learn how to use WAIS search software to access WAIS databases fully, just as you needed to learn how to use an FTP client to get the most out of file archives.

But today's graphical browsers have made it unnecessary to learn a series of different tools, as they can access file archives and Gopher menus directly, as well. They can access other Internet resources, such as Archie and WAIS databases and X.500 white pages directories, through *gateways*. A gateway is a Web page that serves as an intermediary between Web browsers and Internet resources that aren't directly accessible to the Web.

KEY TERM

This chapter shows how you can use your browser to access non-Web resources on the Internet. Even if you don't know exactly what FTP file archives or WAIS databases are, read on—your graphical browser hides the complexity of these services, making them accessible and useful.

HOME PAGE

SEARCHING FOR FILES WITH ARCHIE

KEY TERM

Archie is the name of an Internet resource discovery tool that is designed to help you locate files that can be obtained by anonymous FTP. It's called *anonymous* because no login name or password is required to gain access to the computer system that contains the archive.

AWFUL

A major drawback of Archie is the need to know all or part of the file's exact name. Archie doesn't search the brief descriptions that are sometimes attached to file names in UNIX directories. Archie is most useful when you've heard or read about a specific file, and you're just trying to locate it in a publicly-accessible archive.

Using an Archie Gateway

Web browsers can't directly access Archie. To perform an Archie search, you need to contact an Archie gateway. Several are currently in existence. Figure 14.1 shows the Archie gateway at the Centre Universitaire d'Informatique, University of Geneva (CUI). To find a file, you must type the name of the file you want, or part of the file's name (to find winword.fnt, for example, you could type **winword** or **winword.fnt** or **fnt**.

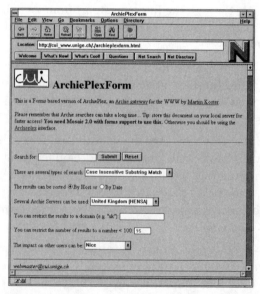

Figure 14.1 *ArchiePlex gateway (http://cui_www.unige.ch/.archieplexform.html)*

The result of the search is a new document, listing the archives that contain files that match your search terms (Figure 14.2), and the names of the files these archives contain. To download a file, just click the name. (*Note*: With some browsers, you must first choose the Load to Disk option.)

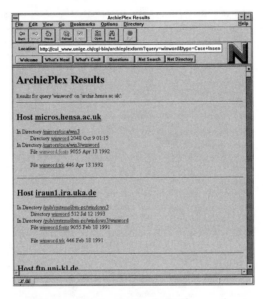

Figure 14.2 *Result of an ArchiePlex search*

Searching for Software with SHASE

If you're looking for software but don't know the exact name of a file, there's a wonderful gateway called The Virtual Software Library, also known as SHASE (short for "shareware archives search engines") that can help. SHASE (Figure 14.3) isn't an Archie gateway; instead, it provides a search engine for searching the file directories of a number of publicly-accessible shareware archives, such as SIMTEL, CICA, and GARBO.

SHASE currently indexes over 60,000 files, but the best thing about it is that its database index contains descriptions as well as file names. If you want to see a list of all the Word for Windows macros available in shareware archives, you can do so easily with SHASE.

EXCELLENT

To search SHASE, fill out the well-designed search form. You can select up to three shareware archives, and you can enter two search words. You can also indicate a term that you do *not* want to match (a useful tool if a search retrieves many unwanted items), as well as the date of the oldest file you want to retrieve. To further control the retrieval of files, you can specify a directory name, and SHASE will exclude all files that aren't stored there. After you submit the search request, SHASE generates a list of files. If you find a file that seems to meet your criteria, click it to begin the downloading procedure (*Note*: on some browsers, you must first choose the Load to Disk option).

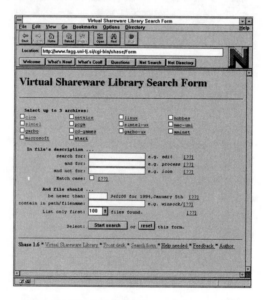

Figure 14.3 *Virtual Shareware Library (SHASE)*

ACCESSING FTP FILE ARCHIVES

One of the most useful things about the Internet is the availability of files you can use on your personal computer. There are literally thousands of public domain, freeware (copyrighted but free), and shareware programs available for your use, spanning the gamut from scientific software to some of the hottest games going, such as Doom. Many FTP client programs are available, including some very nice GUI-based efforts, such as Fetch (for the Macintosh). But once you've accessed an FTP archive with Mosaic, you won't want to do it any other way.

To access an FTP archive with your graphical browser, use a URL that begins with the ftp:// code, as in the following (fictitious) example:

ftp://ftp.cdrom.com/pub/cica/winword/

If you've run across a hyperlink that references the FTP archive, just click it to see the archive on-screen. As Figure 14.4 shows, graphical browsers display the archive's directory structure in a way that is easy to understand. If you click one of the folders you see lists of files and perhaps additional subdirectories.

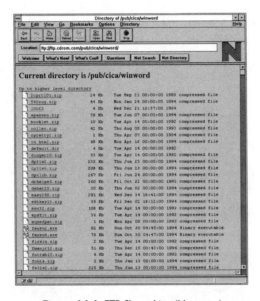

Figure 14.4 *FTP file archive (Netscape)*

In the file lists, some browsers use icons to show you what the various items represent. The following icons are displayed by NCSA Mosaic:

 A subdirectory that you can open to display more items.

 A binary file that you can download.

A text document that you can read on-screen.

A sound that you can listen to or download.

A graphic image you can display.

HOT TIP

Not sure what's in an FTP file directory? Look for an item called INDEX, and click it. You'll see a list of the files and a brief description of the files' contents (see Figure 14.5).

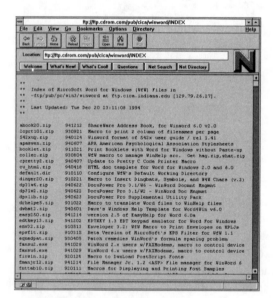

Figure 14.5 INDEX *file contents summary*

Changing Directories

FTP file archives are organized into directories and subdirectories, much like the directories and subdirectories on a DOS hard disk. The terms directory and subdirectory, incidentally, are best understood as relational—a subdirectory is a directory that's subordinate to an encompassing directory, which is called the *parent directory*.) At the top of the directory structure is the *root directory*, symbolized by a slash mark (/). Within the root directory you'll typically find a README or INDEX file, and several subdirectories, as in the following example:

The files you're looking for will probably be found in the pub directory, which may have its own README and INDEX documents and numerous subdirectories:

With a graphical browser, the sometimes confusing task of navigating through the directory structure becomes simple. The directory you're currently examining is listed at the top of the document view area (see Figure 14.4). To open a subdirectory, click its subdirectory name. To go back to the parent directory, click the hyperlink titled "Up to Parent Directory" or "Up to Higher Level Directory"

You can also use the Back and Forward buttons to navigate among the directories you've already displayed. Remember, these buttons take you to the previous and next documents on your history list; they don't necessarily take up up or down the directory structure.

HOT TIP

Automatically Decompressing Downloaded Files

You can set up your graphical browser so that the program automatically decompresses the files you download, if they're stored in a commonly-used compression format such as PKZIP (Windows), StuffIt (Macintosh), or compress (UNIX). To set up your browser to do this automatically, you must link a specific program to one of the compression document types, such as Zip or Binhex.

To tell your browser which decompression program to use:

NCSA MOSAIC

Using the Windows Notepad accessory, open the file MOSAIC.INI, which you'll find in the Windows directory. In the [Viewers] area, locate the item **application/zip=**. and carefully add the following (include the quotation marks): **"C:\pkzip\winzip.exe %ls"** (when you're done, the line should look exactly like this: application/zip="C:\pkzip \winzip.exe %ls"). Save the file and exit.

ENHANCED NCSA MOSAIC

You cannot configure this program to unzip a file. Instead, it will prompt you to save the compressed file to your hard disk, where you can decompress it using your decompression program.

NETSCAPE NAVIGATOR

From the Options menu, choose **Preferences**. Select the Helper Applications option from the drop down list box. In the list of MIME data types, select application/**x-compressed**. Click the **Browse** button. Navigate the directory tree to locate WINZIP.EXE. Click **OK** to confirm your choice.

WEBSURFER

With WebSurfer, you can't select a default compression program. You must download the file to your hard disk and run the decompression program from Program Manager.

Displaying Documents

With the exception of binary files, you can access documents directly just by clicking on their names. Text documents appear in a new document view window, as shown in Figure 14.5, earlier in this chapter. Other items may require helper programs, such as a PostScript viewer, a graphics viewer, a sound player, or a decompression utility such as PKUNZIP.

Downloading Files

To download a file that you've found in an FTP archive, you must first select the option that downloads the data to your disk drive. Then click the name of the file you want.

To download a file from an FTP archive:

NCSA
MOSAIC

From the Options menu, choose **Load to Disk**. Then click the item you want to download. You'll see the Save As dialog box. Type a filename or accept the one that Mosaic proposes. Click **OK** to save the file. When the item has been downloaded, open the Options menu and turn off **Load to Disk** by choosing it again

ENHANCED
NCSA
MOSAIC

Just click the file you want to download. You'll see a save dialog box, enabling you to save the file.

NETSCAPE
NAVIGATOR

Just click the file you want to download. If you've configured Netscape to run WinZip, you'll see the WinZip dialog box showing the files in the downloaded archive.

WEBSURFER

Just click the file you want to download. You'll see a save dialog box, enabling you to save the file.

BROWSING GOPHER MENUS

Gopher is a resource discovery tool that permits you to browse for diverse Internet resources, such as files, graphics, WAIS databases, or phone books, by using on-screen menus (lists of items). Gopher is easy to use, but graphical browsers make Gopher even easier by letting you access Gopher menus directly. You can also access the two Gopher search tools, Veronica and Jughead. The following sections detail these points.

Accessing Gopher Menus

To access a Gopher menu with Mosaic, you use a URL that begins with the gopher:// code, as in the following fictitious example:

gopher://gopher.leviathan.gvc.edu/library

If you've run across a hyperlink that references a Gopher site, click it to see the Gopher menu on-screen (see Figure 14.6). You can also type the URL directly.

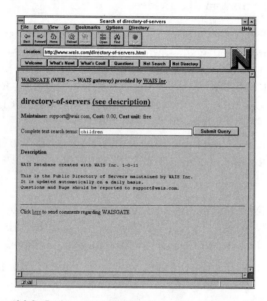

Figure 14.6 *Gopher menu displayed by graphical browser (Netscape)*

KEY TERM

Gopher menus list two basic items: **directory titles** and **resources**. Directory titles are preceded by an open folder icon, while resources are preceded by icons that indicate the type of data they contain:

 Click here to see another Gopher menu.

 Click this item to display and read a text document.

Click this item to display a graphic.

 Click this item to search a WAIS database.

 Click this item to start a Telnet session.

 Click this item to obtain a binary file.

Navigating Gopher Menus

Gopher menus are easy to use. When you choose an item from a Gopher menu, you tunnel "down" into a Gopher "hole." After browsing the resources available there, you can go back "up" to the previous menu.

Grahical browsers implement Gopher navigation through the use of the menus and the Back button. To go "down" into a Gopher hole, click the **Gopher menu** item (which looks like a hyperlink). To go back "up" to the previous menu, click the **Previous** button.

Displaying Gopher-Accessible Resources

To access any of the resources you find on Gopher menus, simply click them, just as you would click a hyperlink. Here's an overview of the procedures you follow to access specific Gopher resources with Mosaic:

- **Text Files**. To read the file on-screen, click the item. If you would like to download the file, activate the Load to Disk option before clicking the item.

- **Binary Files**. To download the file, use the same procedures you would use to download a file from an FTP archive. (For example, with Netscape, you just click the name of the item.)

- **Graphics Files**. To view the graphics file on-screen with the appropriate viewer, click the item. If you would like to download the file, activate the Load to Disk option before clicking the item.

- **Searchable Indexes**. If you click a searchable item, you'll see a form that prompts you to type one or more search words. Fill in the form and press Enter to proceed with the search. If the search is successful, the result will be another Gopher menu that contains one or more items conforming to the search request you made.

- **Telnet Sessions**. If you click a Telnet item, Mosaic looks for the Telnet terminal helper program (see Chapter 13), starts it, and opens a Telnet terminal window. From then on, you're back in the world of text-based terminal interfaces. For more information, see "Running a Telnet Session," later in this chapter.

Searching with Veronica and Jughead

Veronica is a search engine that's designed to find resources in Gopherspace (the world of accessible Gopher items). To do so, Veronica scans an automatically-compiled index of titles of Gopher directory titles and resources. Note that this index does not include words found within the text of these files. Jughead is essentially a version of Veronica that searches for directory titles only, ignoring the names of the files they contain.

Tightly integrated with Gopher, Veronica and Jughead appear to your brower as if they were ordinary Gopher resources. Normally, they're positioned at the top level of most Gopher menus where a list of Veronica servers are displayed. Click the name of a server to begin your search. Enter your search term in the dialog box that appears then click **OK** to initiate the search. The result of the search is another Gopher menu, listing the items that match your search word.

If you can't find Veronica elsewhere, try gopher://veronica.scs.unr.edu/11/veronica.

HOT TIP

EXCELLENT

Don't expect too much from a Veronica search: The resources in Gopherspace are extremely heterogeneous, and include tons of Usenet postings that are of very little value. Worse, Veronica servers are notoriously overloaded, and you may not be able to get through until the wee hours of the morning. See Chapters 17 and 18 for information on using more sophisticated Web subject searching tools.

WAIS

WAIS (pronounced wayz) is an acronym for Wide Area Information Server. It's a resource discovery tool designed for retrieving documents from full-text databases (such as collections of articles, newspapers, electronic texts, or Usenet postings). With a graphical Web browser, you can access WAIS databases in two ways: Through a gateway to a specific WAIS database, or through a gateway to the WAIS Directory of Servers. Before describing these gateways, though, let's take a closer look at WAIS.

Understanding WAIS

Unlike the search tools included with Gopher (Veronica and Jughead), which only search the names of Gopher directories and resources, WAIS bases its retrieval on the content of documents found in its databases. The term "database" is normally defined too rigidly to capture the diversity of WAIS resources. Some WAIS-accessible databases are generally databases in that they offer information grouped in tables or records, but most are collections of text files that have been grouped and indexed for WAIS retrieval.

Like other full-text retrieval systems, WAIS uses keyword searching. You type one or more search words that describe the topic in which you're interested. However, WAIS does not necessarily employ Boolean operators (AND, OR, and NOT), as do most key-word searching systems. WAIS retrieves documents based on a numerical score, which is computed according to how many times the search word or words appear in the document. The score is weighted so that words appearing in the document's title count ten times more than words in the document's body. (This is logical, considering that words appearing in the title are very likely to describe the document's content.) The highest-scoring document's score is always normalized to 1,000.

SEARCHING A WAIS DATABASE

Many Web documents present forms that let you type words that you want to match in a search, and most of these are, in fact, gateways to specific WAIS databases. For example, SHASE—the shareware library search engine discussed earlier in this chapter—searches a database of shareware files and descriptions.

To access a WAIS database, you need a forms-capable graphical browser. Assuming your browser can handle forms, you'll see an on-screen form after you access the gateway document (For example, the SHASE search form shown in Figure 14.5.) You simply type any key words that you think describe the topic separated by spaces. The server then consults an inverted file, a list of all the significant words (words longer than two letters) in each document contained in the database, and computes a score for each document. The document that contains the greatest instances of the search terms is given a score of 1,000, and appears at the top of the list of the retrieved documents.

ACCESSING THE WAIS DIRECTORY OF SERVERS

Another way to access WAIS is to choose a database from a *directory of servers*, a list of all known publicly-accessible WAIS databases. There are hundreds of such databases in many fields of knowledge, particularly computers, health, and the environment. The directory of servers also includes text drawn from short descriptions of the database content, so you can find the database you need quickly and easily.

There are several Web gateways to the directory of servers:

- NCSA maintains a WAIS directory of servers gateway at http:/ /www.ncsa.vivc.edu/SDG/Software/Mosaic/Interfaces/wais/wais-inter face.html

- WAIS, Inc., maintains a WAIS directory of servers gateway at http:/ /www.wais.com/directory-of-servers.html

To search the directory of servers, access one of the gateway documents (see Figure 14.7), and type your search terms. You'll see a list of databases pertaining to the subject you typed (see Figure 14.8).

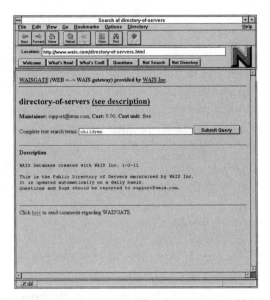

Figure 14.7 *WAIS directory of servers gateway (http://www.wais.com/directory-of-servers.html)*

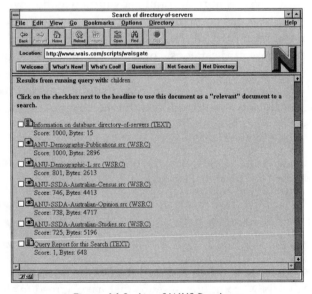

Figure 14.8 *List of WAIS Databases*

TELNET

To let you access resources that aren't accessible by the likes of FTP, Gopher, and WAIS, your browser can start a Telnet (terminal) application. To be sure, you're back in the world of text-based interfaces, but sometimes this is the only way you can access information resources that aren't directly navigable by Mosaic.

To start a Telnet session, your browser must be able to access a Telnet helper program on your computer. For more information, see Chapter 13.

When you initiate a Telnet session with Mosaic, you use a URL that begins with the Telnet:// code, as in the following example:

    Telnet://law@western.uili.edu:23

A Telnet URL like this one could be hidden under a hyperlink, or you can type it directly.

After you choose a Telnet URL, your browser starts the Telnet helper program that you've installed. What you see in this program's window depends on the Telnet service you're accessing, but you can count on seeing a text-based interface. What's more, your browser's normal commands for navigation won't work; you'll need to learn how to use this particular service's commands for doing things. For example, on-line library card catalogs are among the many available Telnet resources. To search these card catalogs, you must use the commands specific to the particular system you're accessing. Fortunately, most of these systems provide on-screen menus to make navigation easier. When you're finished using the Telnet resource, log off the Telnet resource and exit the helper program to return to your graphical browser.

If you can't figure out which command to use to exit the Telnet session, just close the Telnet window. This terminates the session.

HOT TIP

USENET

KEY TERM

Usenet isn't a computer network per se, and it's not the same as the Internet. It's a network of (mostly UNIX) computer systems that have agreed to share and propagate a huge (and growing) set of electronic discussion groups, called *newsgroups*, each focusing on a specific area of interest. The network is designed so that a message posted to a newsgroup on one system will eventually propagate throughout the network, with each machine eventually having a copy of the original message. With an estimated 5,000 newsgroups in widespread use by more than 5,000,000 people, Usenet has become by far the most popular computer discussion or bulletin board system ever devised. You can read Usenet newsgroups with NCSA Mosaic, but by far the best browser for Usenet purposes is Netscape, which lets you post messages as well.

AWFUL

Usenet is lots of fun, but whether it's a useful tool is another matter. It's easy to get distracted by controversial discussions, which often generate more heat than light! Still, many Internet users find that, when carefully used, Usenet can help them in their information seeking strategies. For example, if you post a well-worded question to the right Usenet news group, you may receive several replies electronic mail that may contain information that would otherwise have been impossible to obtain.

AWFUL

Using WebSurfer? Unfortunately, this program can't access Usenet. But you can use WebSurfer to download an excellent Usenet browser called WinVN, which is widely available from shareware file archives. For more information on finding shareware files with your Web browser, see the section titled "Accessing FTP Archives."

Understanding Usenet Newsgroups

KEY
TERM

Newsgroups are organized into two broad categories: the *world newsgroups*, which are automatically distributed to all Usenet sites, and the *alternative newsgroups*, which are distributed only to sites that request them.

Within each category, newsgroups are further subdivided into classes called hierarchies, which make up the first part of the newgroups' name (for example, comp.binaries.ibm-pc is one of the many newsgroups within the comp hierarchy). Within the world newsgroups, the standard hierarchies are the following:

- comp (computers and computer applications)
- news (newsgroups about Usenet itself)
- rec (hobbies and sports)
- sci (the sciences generally)
- soc (social issues and socializing)
- talk (no-holds-barred controversy)
- misc (anything that doesn't fit into the other categories)

Of the alternative newsgroups, the flagbearer is the alt hierarchy, a huge and fascinating collection of newsgroups created by people who wanted to bypass the world newsgroup voting procedures for creating new groups. Other alternative newsgroups include:

- bionet (biology and the environment)
- biz (business discussions and advertising)
- ClariNet (a do-it-yourself on-line newspaper consisting of feeds from major wire services, such as UPI)
- K12 (primary and secondary education)

Within a newsgroup, individual messages (called *articles)* fall into two categories:

- **Posts.** An original message, with a new topic, that somebody contributed.
- **Follow-up Posts.** A reply to the original message, which usually contains some quoted text from the original message. The title of a follow-up post usually echoes the original post's title, with the addition of "re:" at the beginning of the title.

To contribute to Usenet, you can post original messages, write follow-up posts, or respond to a post by electronic mail.

HOT TIP Don't get flamed for making a posting error. Post a new message only to the appropriate newsgroup. Post a follow-up reply if what you have to say would prove of interest to anyone reading the group; if not, respond via electronic mail.

To read Usenet effectively, it's important to understand that Usenet software generally has three distinct "levels":

- **Newsgroup Level.** At this level, you select the newsgroup that you want to read (from a list of 5,000 or more). Web browsers do not implement this level.
- **Article Title Level.** At this level, you see a list of titles of current articles in the newsgroup that you've selected. Web browsers show you these titles.
- **Article Level.** By clicking an article title, you go to this level, where you see the text of the article you selected. You can stay at this level to see the next or previous articles, if you wish, or you can go back "up" to the article title level.

Configuring Your Browser to Access Usenet

If you would like to browse Usenet messages with your graphical browser, you must configure the program to do so. (An exception is Enhanced NCSA Mosaic, which may have been preconfigured to access Usenet. Check the manual that came with your copy.) You'll need to know the Internet address of your service provider's NNTP news server. For example, if your service provider's news server is daily.provider.com, you need to supply this information to your browser.

To configure your browser to access Usenet:

Use the Windows Notepad utility to open MOSAIC.INI, and locate the line that starts with NNTP_Server. Carefully delete the current settings, if any, and type the new address within quotation marks (as in NNTP_Server=**"news.cso.vivc.edu"**).

From the Options menu, choose **Preferences.** From the drop-down list box, choose **Directories, Applications, and News.** In the News (NNTP server) box, type the name of your news server. Click **OK** to confirm.

Accessing a Newsgroup

Once you've configured your browser to access Usenet, you can access a news-group, as long as you know its exact name.

To access a Usenet newsgroup:

In the Document URL area, type **news:** followed by the name of the newsgroup, and press **Enter.**

From the Directory menu, choose **Go to Newsgroups**. In the Subscribe to This Newsgroup box, type the name of the newsgroup you want to access, and click the **Subscribe** button. When the newsgroup name appears, click it to download the newsgroup's current messages.

What you'll see is a list of article titles. If your browser is Usenet-savvy (like Netscape), they'll be sorted into *threads* (all the articles with the same topic are grouped together, showing the patterns of response, as shown in Figure 14.9). If not, you'll see the list of articles in the chronological order in which they were added to the newsgroup.

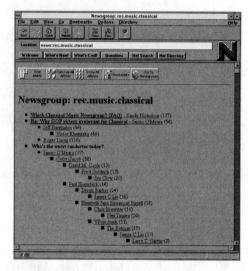

Figure 14.9 *Article titles displayed showing "thread" of discussion (Netscape)*

Reading Articles

To read one of the articles, just click its title. You'll see the article as if it were a new Web page (see Figure 14.10).

Figure 14.10 *Article displayed by Netscape*

Navigating at the Article Level

Just how you navigate within a newsgroup at the article level depends on your browser.

NCSA Mosaic displays a list of related articles as hyperlinks at the top of an article; you can click one of the hyperlinks to see other articles with the same topic.

Netscape uses navigation icons, which appear at the top and bottom of an article. Here's a brief description of what they do:

 Display the first article in the previous thread.

 Display the first article in the next thread.

 Display the next article in this thread.

 Display the previous article in this thread.

 Mark all of the articles in this thread as read, so that they do not appear again in the article title list.

 Go to the article title list.

 Go to the list of subscribed newsgroups.

 Create a follow-up post on the currently-displayed article.

 Send an email reply to the person who posted the currently-displayed article. Your message will not appear in the newsgroup.

Posting a New Message with Netscape

Of the current crop of graphical browsers, only Netscape lets you post your own articles. (In fact, Netscape compares very favorably with the best Usenet software in most respects.)

EXCELLENT

To post an article on a new subject using Netscape, display the article titles, and click the Post Article button. (You may have to scroll to the top or the bottom of the article title list to display this button.) You'll see the Usenet News Posting document, shown in Figure 14.11. Type a subject line, and type your message in the text box. When you are finished, click the Post Message button.

Changed your mind? Just click the Back arrow to cancel your post.

HOT TIP

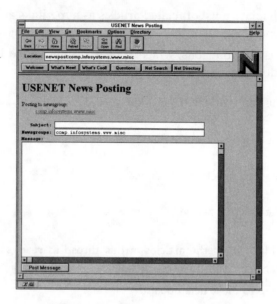

Figure 14.11 *Posting a new message*

Posting a Follow-up Message with Netscape

To post a follow-up message with Netscape, display the article to which you want to respond, and click the **Post Followup** button. (You may need to scroll to the top or the bottom of the article to access this button). You'll see a new page that closely resembles the one shown in Figure 14.12, except that Netscape has filled in the subject and quoted the article's text. Type your message in the text box. When you are finished, click the **Post Message** button. To cancel, click the **Back** button.

Posting an Email Reply

If your reply would prove of interest only to the person who posted the message, you should respond by email instead of posting to the newsgroup.

To post an email reply with Netscape, display the article to which you want to respond, and click the **Reply to Sender** button. (You may need to scroll to the top or the bottom of the article to access this button.) You'll see a Mail Document dialog box, where you should type a subject. If you would like to quote the document text, click the **Include Document Text** button. Type your message in the text box. When you are finished, click the **Send Mail** button. To cancel, just click the **Cancel** button.

Searching Today's Usenet Postings with Netscape

If you're looking for specific information on Usenet, you can easily go nuts trying to manually search through the thousands of postings that appear each day. Why not let the computer do it for you? A gateway document Search Today's Usenet News lets you do just that. It's accessible at http://ibd.ar.com/News /About.html (see Figure 14.12). The result of your search is a new page listing the results, which you can directly access by clicking the listed hyperlinks.

EXCELLENT

Figure 14.12 *Searching Today's Usenet news (http://ibd.ar.com/News/About.html)*

Searching Usenet FAQs

The day-to-day hue and cry on Usenet may be of debatable value, but Usenet's treasure-trove of Frequently Asked Questions (FAQs) is another matter entirely. Hundreds of newsgroups maintain these documents, which are frequently dozens of pages in length. Covering every conceivable subject, they constitute an education in themselves.

EXCELLENT

Usenet FAQs are text documents that you can access through subject trees as well as Usenet (see Chapter 17). Utrecht University in the Netherlands maintains a very good Usenet FAQ search engine (Figure 14.13). This amazing resource includes a database of the full text of the current crop of Usenet FAQs. When you search for a term (such as "Laserwriter"), a new page is displayed detailing the FAQs where the term appears. Since the references are listed as hyperlinks, you can go to the FAQs simply by clicking one of them.

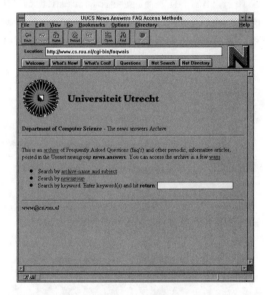

Figure 14.13　Usenet FAQ search engine (http://www.cs.ruu.nl/cgi-bin/faqwais)

SEARCHING FOR PEOPLE WITH WHITE PAGES

White pages are computer versions of the white pages section of a phone book, listing individuals, their telephone numbers, and their electronic mail addresses by name. There are a number of Internet services that let you search white pages for email addresses, and they're accessible through Web gateways.

If you're looking for a single, unified phone book system for the Internet, forget it—there isn't one (yet). To be sure, there are many organizational white pages available, which are often available through an organization's Gopher server. But there's no single database that collects all this information in a single standardized server. That would be a monumental job, considering how often people move and the problems of incompatible database standards.

AWFUL

Still, there are several experimental programs underway that are seeking ways to make white pages information more accessible. An example is Netfind, which is accessible through a Web gateway at http://alpha.acast.nova.edu/netfind.html.

To use Netfind, you'll need to begin with the person's last name, followed by the city and state where you suspect the person is located. In the search box that appears when you access the Netfind gateway, you type a name and location like this:

> O'Shanahan Los Angeles California

The result of a search such as this one is a long list of known white pages listings—and for L.A., we're talking about hundreds of these—one for each organization that has its own Internet domain. You then select one that looks like a likely prospect. You're much more likely to get useful results if you know exactly where the person is working, so you can choose the correct white pages directory.

A much-needed initiative is Four 11 Directory Services, a white pages service provided for the benefit of Internet users by SLED Corporation (http://www.four11.com/Sled.html). Free services include self-listing and searching the service's database of some half million Internet users. What's in it for SLED? For $20 per year (at this writing), members get additional benefits such as hot links to personal Web pages, encryption-based security and authentication, and search agents that scour the Internet for email addresses.

EXCELLENT

SUMMARY

Beside providing a wonderful way to explore the riches of the World Wide Web, your Web browser is also a great way to access FTP file archives, Gopher menus, WAIS databases, and Usenet newsgroups. Most of these are very well integrated into the Web way of doing things, in fact, you can often forget that you're navigating anything other than a Web page.

FROM HERE...

- Customize your browser with the information in Chapter 15.
- Master the techniques of Web navigation in Part Four.

CHAPTER 15

Customizing Your Browser

There are toys for all ages.
—Old English proverb

Now that you've mastered the essentials of your graphical browser, it's time to think about customizing the program to suit your preferences. With most browsers, this is a relatively straightforward matter of choosing a few toolbar and URL display options.

With the best browsers, you have full control over the display of a wide range of document formats. HTML, after all, is a generalized markup language, it doesn't specify exactly how Web documents should appear on-screen—that's up to your browser. The best browsers provide font control over the full range of HTML-defined document formats, including titles, paragraphs, headers, lists, and more. If you have fonts that you like installed on your system, you can make Web documents look just the way you want. So play on!

BROWSER DISPLAY OPTIONS

Most browsers provide options that control the display of the toolbar, the document URL, and the document title. The following sections detail these customization procedures.

Choosing Toolbar Options

Unlike the confusing toolbars of many Windows applications, a graphical browser's toolbar is useful and handy. For example, you'll need to click the Back and Home buttons frequently. Browsers display the toolbar by default, but you may wish to hide the toolbar if you're using a standard VGA (640 by 480) screen.

To hide the toolbar:

NCSA
MOSAIC

From the Options menu, choose **Show Toolbar** so that the check mark disappears.

ENHANCED
NCSA
MOSAIC

This program's minimal toolbar can't be customized.

NETSCAPE
NAVIGATOR

From the Options menu, choose **Show Toolbar** so that the check mark disappears. Choose this option again to re-display the toolbar.

WEBSURFER

You can toggle between a "Smart Buttons" view (where a brief text description of the button's function appears beneath the button's icon) and a regular view (where there's no descriptive text.) From the Settings menu, choose **Smart Buttons** to toggle the text display on and off.

Displaying the Document URL

Most browsers display the document URL by default, which is helpful! You can see what kind of document you're viewing (whether it's an HTML document or an FTP file archive, for instance), and get some hints about where it's from. Too, you can directly type a URL into the document URL text area. However, you may wish to hide the document URL if you're short on screen space.

To hide the document URL:

Normally,

NCSA
MOSAIC

From the Options menu, choose **Show Current URL** so that the check mark disappears.

ENHANCED NCSA MOSAIC

You can't hide the document URL with this program.

NETSCAPE NAVIGATOR

From the Options menu, choose **Show Location** so that the check mark disappears. Choose this option again to re-display the document URL.

WEBSURFER

From the Settings menu, choose **Dialog Bar** to toggle the document URL display on and off.

Turning Off the Display of In-line Images

If you're using your browser on a slow, 14.4 Kbps dialup line, you may wish to turn off the automatic display of in-line images so that documents load faster. If you want to see the graphics, you can selectively re-display them (with NCSA and Enhanced NCSA Mosaic), or redisplay all of them (Netscape).

To turn off automatic downloading of in-line images:

NCSA MOSAIC

From the Edit menu, choose **Display Inline Images** so that the check mark disappears.

ENHANCED NCSA MOSAIC

From the Edit menu, choose **Preferences**. Deselect the **Load Images Automatically** check box and click **OK.**

NETSCAPE NAVIGATOR

From the Options menu, choose **Auto-Load Images** so that the check mark disappears. To turn the automatic display of in-line images on, choose this option again.

WEBSURFER

You can't turn off the display of in-line images with WebSurfer.

To redisplay individual in-line images:

NCSA MOSAIC

Right-click the image you want to use.

**ENHANCED
NCSA
MOSAIC**

Right-click the image you want to see.

N

**NETSCAPE
NAVIGATOR**

You can't selectively load individual in-line images. To re-display in-line images for the current document, open the Options menu, and choose **Auto-Load Images**. Then click the **Reload** button.

CHOOSING FONTS

HTML is a generalized markup language, which means that it only specifies parts of the document (such as "title" or "list"); it doesn't specify fonts, alignments, or other aspects of the document's on-screen and printed appearance. When you open an HTML document with your graphical browser, the program uses its built-in default font settings to format and display the downloaded text.

EXCELLENT

By letting you decide just how to display a document, HTML pulls off a neat trick. Richly-formatted documents, can be displayed without requiring all users to equip their systems with exactly the same fonts and display capabilities.

For most styles, you can change the following:

- **Font**. The typeface name, such as Times Roman, Courier, or Helvetica. Note that fonts fall into two broad categories: monospace and proportionally spaced. Monospaced fonts take up more room, but they preserve the author's spacing intentions. Proportionally-spaced fonts use only as much horizontal space that each character requires, permitting more characters to be packed in a single line. Mosaic can use any of the fonts that have been installed on your system.

- **Font Style**. You can choose from normal (no emphasis), bold, italic, and bold italic.

- **Font Size**. Font sizes are measured in printer's points (72 to the inch). For most reading purposes, standard font sizes are 10 points and 12 points.

You can choose fonts for the following document styles:

- **Header 1 through Header 7.** Defines titles, headings, and subheadings. Heading 1 is the first value of the heading and normally corresponds to the document's title, displayed in the document area. You should use a large font for Heading 1. Subsequent headings should use successively less conspicuous fonts and font sizes. A document rarely has more than three or four heading levels, but HTML lets you define up to seven of them.

- **Normal**. Affects all the text that's not in titles or headers, including the text in anchors, bulleted lists, and numbered lists.

- **Bulleted List**. Affects text placed in bulleted lists.

- **Definition List.** Affects text placed in lists of defined terms.

- **Numbered List.** Affects text placed in numbered lists.

- **Menu List**. Affects text placed in lists of items called menus.

- **Directory List.** Affects the names of files and directories in file listings.

- **Address.** Used for the author's electronic mail address, which is often placed at the beginning or end of a document.

- **Block Quote.** Used for lengthy, indented quotations that appear blocked off from the rest of the text. You might wish to use a smaller font size than the normal font.

- **Example (also called Sample).** Used for a brief example line (for instance, an example of a URL or something else that the user is supposed to type).

- **Preformatted.** Permits the document's author to define spacing and line breaks. Use a monospace font such as Courier so you don't lose the author's spacing intentions.

- **Listing (also called Code).** Used for programming code examples, URLs, and other material that should look as though it's appearing on a computer screen. Be sure to use a monospace font such as Courier.

In addition to these document styles, you can also choose emphases such as bold face or italic for the following character styles, which can be used by HTML authors to give words or phrases special emphasis. There's little reason to change them the defaults reflect tasteful choices.

- **Citation**. By default, this is set to italic.

- **Emphasis**. By default, this is set to bold.

- **Strong**. By default, this is set to bold. You may wish to choose bold and italic to give this format additional emphasis.

- **Variable**. By default, this is set to italic.

EXCELLENT

By far the best implementation of HTML font control is found in WebSurfer, the Web browser included with this book. You can select any of the many HTML document formats and emphases, and control the font, font size, foreground color, background color, and style (bold, italic, or underline). Web software developers, please take a look.

Why don't all browsers let you choose document background colors, as does WebSurfer? Personally, I get tired of looking at the boring grey background which makes text difficult to read. To be sure, some people believe that HTML documents are aesthetically designed to be viewed against a grey background, but I don't buy it—very few HTML documents are designed with aesthetics in mind, period.

To change the font for one of the document styles:

NCSA
MOSAIC

From the Options menu, select **Choose Font**. You'll see a submenu, from which you can select the document style you want to change, choose the style. Then you'll see the Font dialog box. In the Font area, choose the typeface name you want to use. In the Font Style area, choose the emphasis you want to use. In the Size area, choose a font size. The Sample area shows what your font choice will look like on-screen. When you're satisfied with your choices, click **OK**.

ENHANCED
NCSA
MOSAIC

From the Edit menu, choose **Preferences**. In the style sheet list box, choose the styles you want (you can choose from Serif, Sans Serif, or Mixed, in small, medium, and large sizes). Choose **OK** to confirm your choice.

NETSCAPE
NAVIGATOR

Netscape provides only very limited control over document fonts. From the Options menu, choose **Preferences**. Select **Styles** from the dropdown list box. You can change the proportional font or the fixed font typeface—and that's it. To change one of these, click the button. In the **Choose Base Font** dialog box, select a font and font size. Click **OK**.

WEBSURFER

From the Settings menu, choose **Style Schemes**. From the list of HTML formats, click the format you want to modify. Choose the styles you want, such as font, font size, and color. To modify another format, click the format in the list of HTML formats, and choose styles for this format. When you're finished choosing formats, click **OK**.

SUMMARY

You can turn Mosaic into a personal statement in many ways, beginning with font choices. The program can use any of the fonts available on your system. If you get carried away, you can always restore the rather conservative default fonts. With the Windows version, and soon the Macintosh one, you can define custom menus that contain just the URLs you access most frequently. To get the program running at top speed, you can switch off the display of in-line images.

FROM HERE...

- Master Web navigation in Part Four.
- Explore intriguing Web Sites in Part Five.
- Create your own Web pages in Part Six.

CHAPTER 16

Using Web Starting Points

The longest part of the journey is said to be the passing of the gate.
—Marcus Terentius Varro 116-27 BC

When you're getting started with the Web, you might feel overwhelmed by the huge numbers and the equally daunting variety of the Web documents people have made available. Page after page goes by—underground music, Arabian horses, recent UFO sightings, some little Montana town's civic page, travel guides to Tazmania, San Francisco Bay Area kosher restaurants.... and disorientation sets in. But don't despair—read on.

This chapter begins a three-chapter mini-course in Web information retrieval. You'll learn how to use a variety of powerful tools: starting points pages, subject trees, and search engines. Let's get started with an overview of Web searching strategy, covered in the following section. This chapter continues with a detailed look at starting points pages; Chapter 17 examines subject trees, while Chapter 18 explores search engines.

**HOME
PAGE**

A WEB INFORMATION-SEEKING STRATEGY

If you're interested in finding Web resources on a given topic, you'll need to search for them—unless you're lucky enough to find a document that exhaustively sums up everything that's available. You can make use of the following search techniques:

247

- **Using Starting Points Documents.** These documents do not try to be comprehensive. Instead, they provide a number of useful points of entry into the Web. Some of these documents may contain information pertaining to the subject you're searching for, but don't count on it. For searching purposes, a starting points document's usefulness is sharply limited.

- **Subject Tree Searching.** Subject trees try to catalog Web resources by subject; you'll find a list of alphabetically-organized headings (such as "Anthropology," "Art," "Astronomy," etc.), with subheadings—and possibly additional levels of subheadings. As you burrow down into the subheadings, you'll eventually find lists of hyperlinks. Will the list be comprehensive? It all depends on how much time and energy were available—and since the work is almost exclusively done by volunteers and Web enthusiasts, don't count on finding an exhaustive list. Subject trees are discussed in this chapter.

KEY TERM

- **Key Word Searching with Search Engines.** A *search engine*, also called a *spider*, "crawls" the Web looking for new URLs—and adds them to a database when it finds them. You can search the database using key words. For example, suppose you're looking for Web resources pertaining to astrophysics. You can type "astrophysics" into the search engine's on-screen form, and you'll see a new page listing URLs that contain this word (usually in their titles). By any standard, these search engines are primitive, and it's all too likely that you'll fail to find relevant sources. It's just as likely that you'll get a long list of irrelevant ones, in which the key word is mentioned peripherally. Search engines are discussed in the next chapter.

- **Surfing.** Surfing the Web—following newly-discovered hyperlinks in search of something interesting—can be a useful searching technique. Just as a visit to the library stacks often turns up titles that you didn't notice in the card catalog, surfing often results in the discovery of a gem that you didn't know about. Surfing is discussed in the next chapter.

HOT TIP

What's the best Web search strategy? Combining all of them. Begin by scanning a good starting points document, such as the Planet Earth Home Page, and check out one or more subject trees. As you find URLs relevant to your interests, add them to your hotlist. Then try a key word search—chances are, you'll find still more documents of interest. Finally, surf around in these documents, checking out their hyperlinks to documents you haven't yet discovered.

INTRODUCING STARTING POINTS PAGES

To help Web users find their way in a more orderly fashion, several organizations have made *starting points pages* available. A starting points page provides a number of interesting and useful URLs to explore, ranging from the utilitarian to the ultra-cool. Among the organizations making such pages available are official Internet organizations, such as the Network Information Center (NIC); vendors of Web browsing software, such as Netscape, Air Mosaic, and NCSA Mosaic; and private individuals. This chapter surveys some of the most popular starting points pages.

KEY TERM

What's the difference between a starting points page and a subject tree? In a word, scope. To be sure, many starting points pages are actually mini-subject trees, with headings that group hyperlinks by subject (such as "Business Sites," "Weather," "Arts and Humanities," and more). But a starting points page doesn't try to list every available resource on a subject, as a subject tree does. It provides a few entry points for the beginning of your Web adventure, as well as hyperlinks to subject trees and search engines, which are discussed in the next chapter.

And what's the difference between a starting points page and an individual's home page, which has been made available for public use? The line's rather fuzzy, but individual's home pages usually contain documents that a particular individual has found appealing—and that's a supremely subjective matter. In a starting points page, some effort (at least) has been made to think through the information-searching needs of the typical Web beginner. That said, there are plenty of individuals' home pages (such as Meng Weng Wong's) that are justly celebrated as excellent starting points for Web navigation.

Please be aware that Web pages come and go. The starting points pages described in this chapter may have changed, moved, or disappeared by the time you read this book.

AWFUL

STARTING POINTS PAGES: INTERNET ORGANIZATIONS

Most of the organizations that play key roles in the Internet's development maintain starting points pages. Note, though, that these organizations lack the staff time and resources to develop these page fully. In general, they're less useful than the exuberant efforts of Web browser vendors and even some private individuals, whose starting points pages are discussed later in this chapter.

CERN

The birthplace of the World Wide Web provides an obvious place to get started with your Web exploration, but don't expect too much. Titled "General Overview of the Web," CERN's starting points page is brief (see Figure 16.1). Of chief interest is the document's link to CERN's Virtual Library, one of the subject trees to be discussed in Chapter 17.

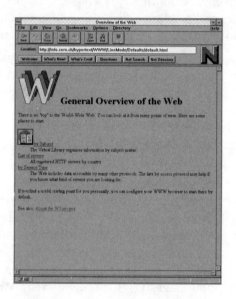

Figure 16.1 *CERN starting points page*
(http://into.cern.ch/hypertext/WWW/LineMode/Defaults/default.html)

NCSA

EXCELLENT

Much more useful than CERN's diffident effort is the National Center for Supercomputing Applications' Starting Points page (Figure 16.2), one of the best available. Here' a brief rundown of what you'll find:

- **Introductions to the Internet and to the Web** including CERN's starting points pages, InterNIC information that will prove useful to Internet beginners, and NCSA's home pages (including references to the Mosaic pages).

- **Other home pages** containing selection of organizational welcome pages from around the world, including the famed Honolulu Home Page.

- **Gateways to other Internet services** including WAIS, Gopher, Veronica, FTP, Usenet, Finger, HyTelnet, and white pages.

- **A selection of interesting Web pages,** with a pronounced slant toward the academic (Zippy the Pinhead excepted).

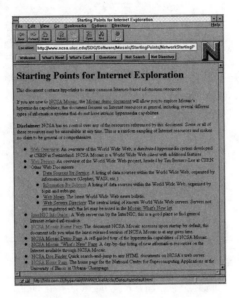

Figure 16.2 *NCSA's Starting Points Page*
(http://www.ncsa.vivc.edu/SDG/Software/Mosaic/StartingPoints/NetworkStartingPoints)

InterNIC

The InterNIC is a consortium of three organizations that provide networking information services to the Internet community, under contract to the National Science Foundation (NSF). These organizations provide three areas of service: networking information (from General Atomics), directory and database services (from AT&T), and network registration (from Networking Solutions, Inc.). The three organizations collaborate to make the Internet more easily accessible to researchers, educators, and the general public.

As you might expect, InterNIC has established its presence on the Web. The InterNIC InfoGuide is a good place to start, especially if you're just getting started with the Internet as well as with the Web.

The InfoGuide (Figure 16.3) offers a picture of the InterNIC InfoNaut, a wired being about to begin a tour of cyberspace. Available on the InfoGuide page are the following documents (clickable hyperlinks are shown underlined):

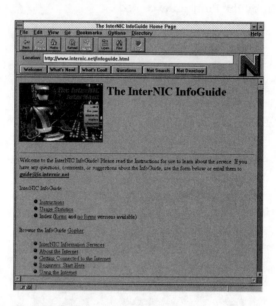

Figure 16.3 *InterNIC InfoGuide (http://www.internic.net/infoguide.html)*

- **InterNIC InfoGuide.** This section contains grouped documents that tell you how to use the InfoGuide, interesting statistics on Web usage, and a searchable index of InterNIC documents.

- **Browse the InfoGuide Gopher.** This section contains links to Gopher menus of interest to Internet beginners. You'll find information on getting connected to the Internet, how beginners should get started, and general information about InterNIC.

EXCELLENT

- **InterNIC Web Picks.** Here's the hidden jewel. Click here to find an excellent selection of subject trees and search engines, conveniently grouped on one page.

STARTING POINTS PAGES: INTERNET SERVICE PROVIDERS

Internet service providers are organizations that provide Internet access or communications links. A variety of service providers offer Internet access at the international, national, regional, and local levels, and offer a variety of access methods (ranging from high-speed dedicated access, for organizations and large local area networks, to dialup IP and dialup access for personal computer users.) Increasingly, they're setting up Web starting points pages to provide assistance to their customers.

Do you have to subscribe to one of these organizations' access services to use their starting points pages? Nope. They're accessible to any Web user, and some of them are gems. Of the dozens of examples, I've chosen two: Performance Systems International (PSI) and Netcom.

Looking for a list of Internet service providers? Check out the Yahoo list (http://akebono.stanford.edu/yahoo/Business/Corporations /Internet_Access_Providers/); hyperlinks take you directly to the welcome and starting points pages of most of the hundreds of providers listed.

USEFUL
RESOURCE

Performance Systems International (PSI)

Performance Systems International (PSI) is a major Internet service provider located in Herndon, Virginia. Vendors of the InterRamp service that offers point-and-click Internet access from any of the firm's more than 300 points of presence, PSI maintains a List of Cool Net Sites (Figure 16.4) that you'll want to add to your hotlists. To access the List of Cool Net Sites, use http://WWW.interamp. com/cool/cool.html.

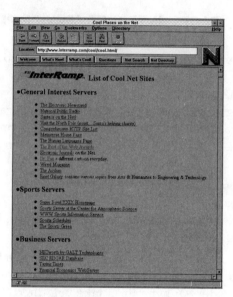

Figure 16.4 *PSI starting points page*

Here's a brief rundown on what's available:

- **General Interest Servers.** A very mixed, very fun collection of fun and interesting sites, including National Public Radio, Wired Magazine, and the over-the-top Dr. Fun.

- **Sports Servers.** Everything for the sports fan, including the Sporting Green on-line, the WWW Sports Information Service, and sports schedules.

- **Business Servers.** Stock quotes, lists of interesting business sites, and more.

- **Weather Servers.** Here's where to look for a national weather report.

- **Games on the Net.** Lists of games, including MUDs and interactive games.

- **Arts and Humanities.** The chestnuts here are Le WebLouvre and other popular on-line museums.

- **Stores and Malls.** Several Internet shopping malls are listed here, including the Internet Shopping Network.

- **Movies, Images, and Sounds.** Only one entry currently—Buena Vista MoviePlex Marquee.

NETCOM

NETCOM On-Line Communication Services, Inc., is a major Internet service provider, with points of presence in over 200 U.S. cities. An innovative feature of NETCOM's services is the WebCruiser software, which provides Web and Internet browsing capabilities to the firm's customers (WebCruiser doesn't work if you're using other service providers).

Some features of interest from NETCOM's starting points page (Figure 16.5) are the following:

- **NetCruiser Home Port Home Page.** On this page you'll find hyperlinks for subject trees ("Guided Tours"), international pages, and a mini-subject tree.

- **Favorite Internet Destinations.** This list was compiled by NETCOM users.

- **Internet Assistance and Information.** Hyperlinks to a variety of useful information sources for beginners.

- **Best of the Web Awards.** See for yourself; the list includes hyperlinks.

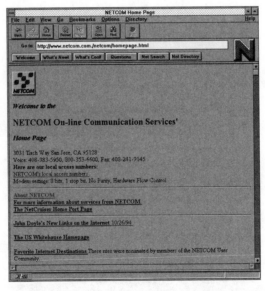

Figure 16.5 *Netcom's starting points page (http://www.netcom.com/netcom/homepage.html#ABOUT)*

STARTING POINTS PAGES: WEB SOFTWARE VENDORS

It makes sense that Web software vendors create their own starting points pages. After all, these firms usually set up their Web browsers to log on to their corporate server as the default home page. Of the several vendors of Web browsers that offer starting points pages, two are described here: Netscape and Spry (the makers of Air Mosaic). As with service providers' starting points pages, you don't have to use the vendor's browser to access these sites.

Netscape

Netscape Communications Corporation, the vendors of Netscape Navigator (see Chapter 9), offers a series of brief, usable starting points pages that can be accessed from Netscape Navigator's menus. However, you can access these starting points pages even if you're using another graphical browser.

Netscape's starting points pages are nicely organized into the following documents, all of which can be accessed from Netscape's Welcome page (Figure 16.6):

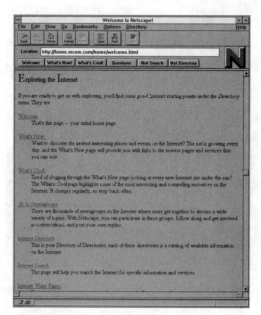

Figure 16.6 Netscape's Welcome page (http://home.mcom.com/home/welcome.html)

- **What's New!** The latest additions to the Web's fast-growing list of URLs. Organized month-by-month, this information isn't sorted any other way, and you may find it a bit overwhelming.

- **What's Cool!** A selection of interesting URLs, brought to you by people who surf the net for a living. Plan on wasting at least six hours here.

- **Internet Directory.** An excellent compilation of subject trees.

- **Internet Search Engines.** An equally excellent compilation of search engines.

- **Internet White Pages**. Ways to find someone's electronic mail address.

- **About the Internet.** General information about the Internet, for beginners.

- **How to Create Web Services.** An introduction to creating a Web site so that others can access your Web documents.

Spry, Inc.

The vendors of Air Mosaic, Spry, Inc. offers what is perhaps the most visually appealing starting points page yet surveyed in this chapter: Spry City (Figure 16.7). By clicking on one of the "buildings," you see lists of interesting and useful URLs that are pertinent to the category you've clicked. To access Spry City, use http://www.spry.com/sp.city/sp.city.html.

Figure 16.7 Spry City (http ://www.spry.com/sp_city/sp_city.html)

Here's a brief summary of what's available in each of Spry City's "buildings":

EXCELLENT

- **Art Museum.** One of the best quickie indexes to arts-related hyperlinks that you'll find on the Web. Comics and humor, television, the on-line magazine Netboy, Gopher Joke menu, Andy Warhol Museum, GIF Image directory, horror and the grotesque, arts index pages, clip art servers, on-line books, movie and film reviews, poetry, Star Trek, on-line magazines, and much more.

- **Travel Agent.** A few hyperlinks, organized by city and country. A highlight is the U.K. Guide, an interactive map.

- **Computer Source.** A varied collection of hyperlinks, including the National Public Telecomputing Network, Kaleidospace, Internet tools and information, Gopher Jewels, the Net-Happenings List archive, Usenet newsgroup links, computer vendors' home pages and tech info libraries, and much more.

- **School House.** An uneven collection of college and university home pages, sources organized by academic topic, and a few items of interest to K-12 educators.

- **Business Center.** Lots of documents pertinent to business and law, with an emphasis on reference sources, such as Supreme Court decisions, the Uniform Commercial Code, West's Legal Dictionary, and the National Trade Data Bank. You'll also find a smattering of interesting commercial Web sites.

- **City Hall.** A selection of documents pertaining to business and government, organized by country. Lots of links to U.S. government agencies and a few non-government organizations, such as Greenpeace and the Berkeley College Republicans.

- **Sporting Goods.** Much more varied than the name suggests, this interesting selection includes documents related to computer games, cars, motorcycles, amateur radio, wine, coffee, and cooking as well as to sports (such as football and basketball).

STARTING POINTS PAGES: INDIVIDUAL EFFORTS

Of all the things the Web can do, one of the most interesting is the power it gives ordinary people to group Web resources. Knowledgeable Web users everywhere are creating their own starting points pages, which generally have a slant toward their personal interests. Of the many thousands of such pages, I've chosen to illustrate three. Among them is what I think is the best starting points page you'll find anywhere on the Web: the Planet Earth Home Page.

John S. Makulowich's Awesome List

John Makulowich, an Internet trainer, has assembled a list of "the glory and grandeur of the Internet, the *sine qua non* of Cyberspace, the main characters in the evolving drama ...," with special focus on the needs of journalists, trainers, and first-time Web users. Distilled down to the best of the Web, it's an excellent starting points document.

EXCELLENT

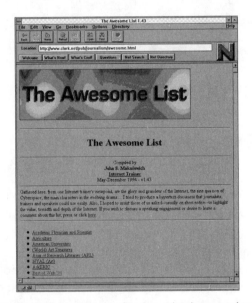

Figure 16.8 *The Awesome List (journalism/awesome.html)*

John's Monster Hotlist

Here's a gem. John's Monster Hotlist (Figure 16.9) incorporates an unusual, innovative interface: You click on one of the upper-case headings located at the bottom of the screen, and the pertinent hotlist items appear at the top (in the figure, you're looking at the Sounds items). You don't miss the graphics, do you?

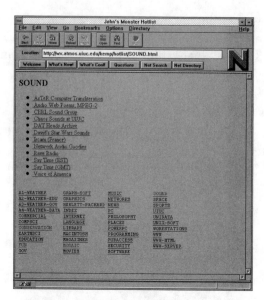

Figture 16.9 *John's Monster Hotlist (http://wx.atmos.uiuc.edu/kemp/hotlist/SOUND.html)*

Planet Earth Home Page

EXCELLENT

Of all the starting points pages on the Web, surely the most beautifully-implement-ed is the remarkable Planet Earth Home Page, based in San Diego, California. (Figure 16.10). Put simply, this is one of the most impressive pieces of HTML cod-ing and resource collocation that you'll find anywhere on the Web.

PEHP, as it's abbreviated, is the work of Richard P. Bocker, a physicist at the Naval Command, Control and Ocean Surveillance Center in San Diego, Far from a comprehensive subject tree—PEHP is eclipsed here by Yahoo and other subject trees that shoot for complete coverage—Bocker's effort is best seen as a wonderful starting points page. In fact, once you've looked at it, you'll probably make the page the default home page for your browser! (Please bear in mind, though, that if too many people do so, PEHP's server will become overloaded. You should make your own home page that contains the URLs you want to access.)

PEHP's offerings are organized into the following categories, which you select by clicking one of the on-screen buttons. After you do, you'll see additional pages crammed with graphics, URLs, and links to other resource-intensive pages. Here's a brief overview:

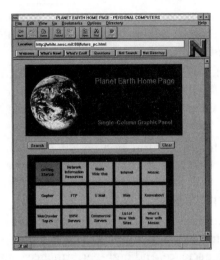

Figure 16.10 Planet Earth Home Page (http//white.nosc.mil:80/future_pc.html)

- **Getting Started.** General and introductory information about the Internet in general and the Web in particular. You'll find information resources about the Web, the Internet, Mosaic, Gopher, FTP. Email, WAIS, Knowabout, the WebCrawler Top 25, a comprehensive list of Web servers, commercial servers, list of new Web sites, and NCSA's What's New pages.

- **Search Engines.** Perhaps the most comprehensive list of search engines available. Included are Domestic Assistance, Comma Hotlist Database, CUIW3 Catalog, Product DA CLOD, External Infomation, WWW Search Engines, WWW Worm, Search the Web, SUSII II, Meta-Index, and JumpStation. You'll also find a Finger gateway, the movie database browser, and a voice synthesizer.

- **Information Sources I.** Included here are Britannica Online, EINET Galaxy, Global Network Navigator, Nova Links, Virtual Tourist, Virtual Library, Internet Web Text, Internet Tools, Information Sources, Index to Multimedia, Yahoo, Depth Probe, Ali Web, and Best of the Web 94.

- **Information Sources II.** More information compilations, with an emphasis on university welcome pages (including Rice, Colorado, Carnegie-Mellon, Stanford, and Caltech).

- **World Region I.** Here you'll find pages containing geographically-organized lists of Web servers, organized by region and country: Canada, the U.S.,

Mexico, Central America, the Caribbean, South America, Antarctica, Australasia, the Pacific Islands, Southeast Asia, the Indian subcontinent, China, Japan, and Korea.

- **World Region II.** More geographic information, including the Nordic countries, the British Isles, the Low Countries, Central Europe, France, the Iberian peninsula, Italy, Greece, Eastern Europe, Russia, the Middle East, Northern Africa, Central Africa, and Southern Africa.

- **Universities.** Reference information pertaining to colleges and universities, and academic subjects, including university White pages, Telnet links to libraries, dictionaries, and an on-line thesaurus. Also found here are reference guides to zip codes and area codes.

- **Sciences.** An excellent compilation of sources for science and technology, physics, chemistry, math, astronomy, earth science, ecology, biology, engineering, computer science, and high-performance computing.

- **Community.** A grab-bag of sources on economics, social trends, recreation and travel, sports, restaurants, museums, art, and more.

- **Multimedia.** Web resources related to multimedia, including database browsers, movies and video, music sources, television pages, newspapers, image processing, and more.

- **Government.** A guide to servers maintained by the U.S. and state governmental agencies.

EXCELLENT

Still looking for the ultimate starting points page? Check out the World Wide Web Power Index of Hot Lists (http://www.webcom.com/power/hotlists.html).

MORE INDIVIDUALS' STARTING POINTS PAGES TO TRY

Cashman's Hotlist (http://www.cs.odu.edu/~cashman/hotlist.html)

Doug's Hotlists (http://saul2.u.washington.edu:8080/hotlist.)

Honey's Hotlist (http://www.citi.umich.edu/users/honey/hot.html)

Karen's Organized Hotlist
(http://www.cs.cmu.edu:8001/afs/cs.cmu.edu/user/kcf/www/
me/newhot.html)

Marty's' Cool Links (http://garnet.acns.fsu.edu/~msalo/index.html)

Nadav's Hot Hot List (file://gauss.technion.ac.il/www/nyh.html)

SUMMARY

Starting points pages pull together a manageable list of places to start your Web journey. Some are provided by Internet service providers, others by the vendors of graphical browsers, and still others by individuals who have donated their time and energy in the Web's interest. A good starting points page includes some interesting sites, paired with a selection of subject trees and search engines, the subjects of the next chapter.

FROM HERE...

- For more information on subject trees, see Chapter 17.
- To use network search engines, check out Chapter 18.
- Looking for reviews of the hottest Web sites? Check out the Part Five, "Exploring the Web."

CHAPTER 17

Using Subject Trees

My library was dukedom enough.
—Prospero, in Shakespeare's *The Tempest*

The Web is jammed with amazing resources. But as you'll quickly discover, you'll be hard-pressed to find them through surfing techniques alone. That's why subject trees, the subject of this chapter, are an essential components of your strategy for Web mastery.

The use of a subject tree should be part of your overall strategy of Web information-seeking, discussed in the next section—in other words, it's best combined with other techniques, including the gentle art of Web surfing. Chapter 18 covers another essential aspect of your information-seeking strategy, the use of search engines ("spiders"). Here, the focus is one one indispensable element, the use of subject trees.

In brief, a *subject tree* is an alphabetically-organized list of Web resources, which is usually organized with major headings such as "Arts and Humanities," "Business," "Economy, "Government," and the like. Within each category are found subheadings, which in turn display pages listing specific hyperlinks. It's a "tree," then, because it has a trunk (the major headings) and branches (the subheadings and lists).

KEY TERM

As you'll see in this chapter, the Web sports several well-developed subject trees—but each of them embodies a slightly different philosophy of just how a subject tree ought to be organized, where the indexed material ought to come from, and what kind of materials should be indexed. One basic point to remember is that you should probably use at least two or three subject trees if you want to find as many resources as possible.

HOME PAGE

WHAT WILL YOU FIND?

The kinds of resources a subject tree can help you find, are simple to describe: jewels and junk. Here's why:

- As of this writing, there's no way to charge Web users for access to information—so don't expect valuable information to appear on the Web, except as an enticement to subscribe to a service. For example, *Information Week* lets you search the last three months of articles that have appeared in that magazine. If you want to search further back, though, you'll need to subscribe to the firm's on-line search service.

- Some of the documents referenced in subject trees, and that turn up in key word searches, aren't meant to contain subject-related information. A case in point: A search for "astrophysics" will turn up hyperlinks pointing to astrophysics departments here and there—and when you access these documents, you find a list of course offerings and the office phone numbers of department faculty. Big deal!

- Volunteers may take it upon themselves to create amazing Web-accessible resources—the Cardiff Movie Database is a case in point—but this is a work of love. In some areas, there's very little of value, because no one has cared to do the work.

Don't expect the World Wide Web to function as some sort of massive, unified repository of human knowledge, like the fabled Library of Alexandria. Information is a commodity, and a particularly valuable one at that. On-line information services such as Dialog make good money by selling access to technical, medical, and scientific databases at rates of up to $100 per hour. You're dreaming if you think that all this information is suddenly going to become available, for free, on the Web. Still, the Web is invaluable if you have an information-seeking strategy.

There's one other problem with Web information that you should keep in mind: There's no assurance that the information you find is correct, reliable, or up to date. No system of editorial or peer review exists to check the veracity and quality of Web-provided information. You'll have to judge for yourself whether the information you find is reliable.

INTRODUCING SUBJECT TREES

A *subject tree* is a Web document that lists Web resources using a hierarchically-arranged index, generally organized alphabetically. It's called a "tree" because of the index's hierarchical organization. When you click "Anthropology," for example, you see a page with subheadings and links pertaining to anthropology (see Figure 17.1) Main topics are the trunk, and subheading and links are the limbs and leaves.

KEY TERM

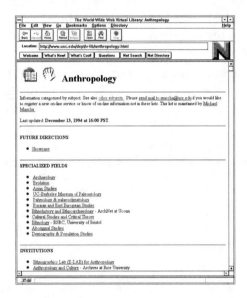

Figure 17.1 Anthropology resources on the Web (Virtual Library)

Are you looking at a huge repository of information, all stored on one gigantic computer? It may seem that way, but you're not. The further down in the subject tree you go, the more likely it is that you'll leave the subject tree's computer and venture out in the Web. Most subject trees are *distributed subject indexes*: some of the main headings reference subheadings that aren't actually stored on the site's computer; instead, they're hyperlinks that take you to subject guides stored elsewhere. And most, if not all, of the catalogued hyperlinks take you to other computers.

KEY TERM

Maintaining a subject tree is an arduous enterprise, and most subject trees depend on the work of volunteers. Don't count on a subject tree's comprehensiveness; there may very well be many new Web resources that haven't been indexed yet. Worse, subject trees do not usually conform to established library subject clas-

AWFUL

sification systems as volunteers tend to be computer people rather than librarians. The Web still awaits a sorely needed uniform system of subject classification In defense of the people who have labored long hours creating Web subject trees, though, remember that Web resources are transitory, of varied quality, and notoriously difficult to classify. You'll see this for yourself when you set off on a good, five-hour Web surf.

The Web brings together the efforts of thousands of individuals. Ideally, a subject tree ought to capture that same spirit of individual contribution—and some of them do. The Mother-of-All BBSs, for instance, permits users or anyone else to add their own hyperlinks to the database. It's as if a book's author or readers could put a card into a library's card catalog.

EXCELLENT

The pages to follow survey the most prominent subject trees, beginning with CERN's Virtual Library. For each, you'll find a table listing the tree's major subject headings.

Don't rely on one subject tree in your search. As you'll see, there are several subject trees in existence, and their coverage not only overlaps but also varies. One subject tree may miss several key documents that another one contains. Search at least two or three subject trees!

HOT TIP

THE VIRTUAL LIBRARY

CERN, the birthplace of the World Wide Web, maintains The Virtual Library, one of the first subject trees to be developed and still one of the most useful and comprehensive.

According to the Virtual Library's welcome page (http://ww10.w3.org/hypertext/DataSources/bySubject/Overview.html), this subject tree is a *distributed system*. By this is meant that the responsibility for maintaining the branches of the tree is delegated to individuals all over the world—people who have volunteered to keep their branch of the subject tree as current as possible. It's distributed in

KEY TERM

another sense, too—the hyperlinks you'll find in the Virtual Library's subject classification list take you to documents not at CERN, but here and there all over the Web. Just what you'll find when you click one of these hyperlinks (for example, "Fish" or Forestry") varies—there's no one set format to which the maintainers are forced to adhere. But that's a good thing. The library's maintainers, after all, are the people best prepared to figure out how to organize their branches of the tree. They're the experts (for an example see Figure 17.2).

What will you find in the Virtual Library? Table 17.1 lists the subject classifications available at the book's writing, and it's an impressive list. Even more impressive is what you'll find when you click one of the subject classification hyperlinks. You'll see a document crammed with additional hyperlinks, and organized in a way that makes sense, given the subject matter. If learning and knowledge mean anything to you, count on spending a few hours exploring the Virtual Library!

EXCELLENT

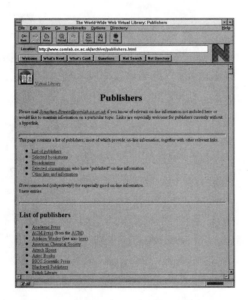

Figure 17.2 Virtual Library page maintained by Jonathan Bowen (Oxford University)

Table 17.1 Virtual Library subject classifications

Aboriginal Studies	Earth Science	Medicine
Aeronautics and Aeronautical Engineering	Education	Meteorology
Agriculture	Electronic Journals	Middle East Studies
Animal health, wellbeing, and rights	Encyclopaedia	Movies
Anthropology	Energy	Museums
Applied Linguistics	Engineering	Music
Archaeology	Environment	Oceanography
Architecture	Finance	Paranormal Phenomena
Art	Fish	Philosophy
Asian Studies	Forestry	Philosophy; Objectivism
Astronomy and Astrophysics	Fortune-telling	Physics
Aviation	Furniture & Interior Design	Politics and Economics
Beer & Brewing	Games	Prospectus
Bio Sciences	Geography	Psychology
Biotechnology	Geophysics	Publishers
Chemistry	German Subject Catalogue	Recipes
Climate research	History	Recreation
Cognitive Science	Home pages	Reference
Commercial Services	Human Computer Interaction	Religion
Communications	Human Factors	Russian and East European Studies
Community Networks	Human Rights	Secular Issues
Computing	Italian General Subject Tree	Social Sciences
Conferences	Landscape Architecture	Spirituality
Cryptography, PGP, and Your Privacy	Languages	Sport
Crystallography	Latin American Studies	Statistics
Culture	Law	Sumeria
Dance	Libraries	Telecommunications
Demography & Population Studies	Linguistics	Unidentified Flying Objects (UFOs)
Design	Literature	World-Wide Web Development
	Mathematics	

EINet GALAXY

EINet Galaxy, one of the most comprehensive subject trees available on the Web, was developed by the Enterprise Integration Network (EINet), a division of Microelectronics and Computer Technology Corporation. The motivation wasn't just to provide a service to Web users. Galaxy is a prototype for a commercial information system supported by significant corporate funding. In the years to come, EINet Galaxy will evolve into a subject tree with both free and fee-based access; users will pay fees to access specialized versions of the database. To access EINet Galaxy, use http://galaxy.einet.net.

Does this mean you'll be paying to access the Web subject tree in the future? No. EINet seeks to create the technology that will allow allied businesses to create information systems that transcend the boundaries of individual enterprises. Laser technology firms, for example, could create common—and mutually beneficial—databases of information concerning such matters as research results, suppliers, and parts availability. In the meantime, EINet Galaxy serves as a testbed for the development of EINet's information-classification technology.

The corporate backing shows. In contrast to The Virtual Library, EINet Galaxy offers advanced features—notably, the ability to search the subject tree using key words. In this sense, EINet Galaxy combines some of the characteristics of a search engine with those of a subject tree. The result is a unique and powerful search tool that is best demonstrated by example.

To begin a Galaxy search, you can browse the subject tree shown in Figure 17.3. Let's take a look at "Recipes" (see Figure 17.4). You see hyperlinks that have been manually added to the search subject. At the bottom of the screen, however, you see something you won't find in other subject trees: hyperlinks that enable you to carry out a key-word search using a set of default search terms. You can search Web, HyTelnet, Gopher, and WAIS resource databases with this feature. If you click the World Wide Web hyperlink, Galaxy begins a WAIS search of Web resources, and produces a list such as the one shown in Figure 17.5. (The next chapter examines WAIS searching in more detail). For now, note that the search results are numerically ranked. The top-scoring document (1,000) is the one that contains the greatest number of instances of the search terms.

Figure 17.3 *EINet Galaxy subject tree*

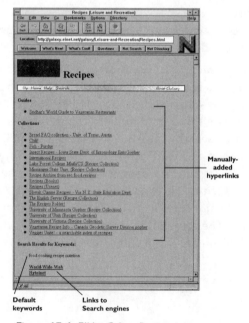

Figure 17.4 *EINet Galaxy Recipes page*

Figure 17.5 *EINet Galaxy search results*

This combined subject tree/search engine approach addresses—and overcomes—the limitations of both search techniques. The problem with subject trees is that they're not up to date. The problem with search engines is that they produce too many irrelevant documents. The combination of a list of high-quality documents that are known to be relevant to the subject category, together with a WAIS search that can retrieve new documents that haven't yet been added to the subject tree, guarantees that you'll find at least some useful information. A search form at the bottom of the page (see Figure 17.6) provides even more search flexibility.

EXCELLENT

Galaxy provides yet another feature—users can suggest URLs pointing to documents that ought to be included in the database. When you see a hyperlink entitled **You can add information to this page**, you can click it to display the form shown in Figure 17.7. The Galaxy staff will verify the information you submit.

Another unique and praiseworthy feature of EINet Galaxy is the service's attempt to classify indexed documents. Under the subject heading "Information Retrieval," for example, you find items indexed under "Documents," "Articles," "Books," "Guides," "Announcements," "Product Descriptions," "Collections," "Discussion Groups," "Directories," and "Organizations." These classifications help you to find the type of material you're seeking.

EXCELLENT

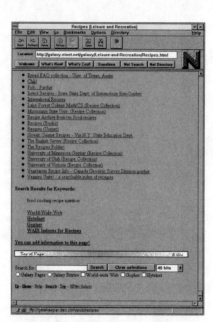

Figure 17.6 ElNet Galaxy search form

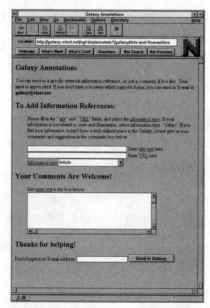

Figure 17.7 ElNet Galaxy user submission form

Table 17.2 ElNet Galaxy Subject Classifications

Arts and Humanities

Architecture

Language and Literature

Performing Arts

Philosophy

Religion

Visual Arts

Business and Commerce

Business Administration

Business General Resources

Company Organization and

Consumer Products and Services

Electronic Commerce

General Products and Services

Investment Sources

Management

Marketing and Sales

Community

Charity and Community Service

Consumer Issues

Crime and Law Enforcement

Culture

Education

Gender Issues

Health

Law

Liberties

Lifestyle

Networking and Communication

Politics

Religion

The Environment

The Family

The Home

The Workplace

US States

Urban Life

Veteran Affairs

World Communities

Engineering and Technology

Agriculture

Biomedical Engineering

Civil and Construction Engineering

Computer Technology

Electrical Engineering

Human Factors and Human Ecology

Manufacturing and Processing

Materials Science

Mechanical Engineering

Transportation

Government

Government Agencies

Laws and Regulations

Military

Politics

Public Affairs

Law

Administrative

Commercial

Constitutional

Criminal

Environmental

Intellectual Property

Legal Profession

Military

Personal Finance

Research

Societal

Tax

Leisure and Recreation

Amateur Radio

Beverages

Boating

Film and Video

Games

Gardening

Humor

Music

Pets

Pictures

Radio

Reading

Recipes

Restaurants

Speleology

Sports

Television

Travel

continued

Table 17.2 ElNet Galaxy Subject Classifications (continued)

Medicine	Conference Announcements	Physics
Community Medicine	Dictionaries etc	
Dentistry	Directories	**Social Sciences**
Exercise	Grants	Anthropology
History of Medicine		Economics
Human Biology	Internet and Networking	Education
Medical Applications and Practice	Library Information and Catalogs Publications	Geography
Medical Specialties		History
Medical Technologies	**Science**	Languages
Nursing	Astronomy	Library and Information Science
Nutrition	Biology	Psychology
	Chemistry	Sociology
Reference and Interdisciplinary Information	Geosciences	
Census Data	Mathematics	

WHOLE INTERNET CATALOG

Like ElNet, the Whole Internet Catalog (Figure 17.8) is one facet of a broader, for-profit enterprise developed by O'Reilly and Associates, of Petaluma, California, a leading publisher of books on computer topics. O'Reilly's Web presence, dubbed the Global Network Navigator (GNN), is one of the most impressive of all corporate Web presences, and contributes significantly to O'Reilly's reputation as a pacesetter in this area.

The Whole Internet Catalog is a much elaborated on-line version of the subject guide found in O'Reilly's best-selling *The Whole Internet* by Ed Krol. Like ElNet Galaxy, it's organized into major and minor subject headings, with much the same overall layout. But the Whole Internet Catalog lacks Galaxy's well-integrated search capabilities, which can discover resources that haven't yet been added to the subject tree. In compensation, GNN's staff spends more time hunting down new, interesting URLs and adding them to the subject tree.

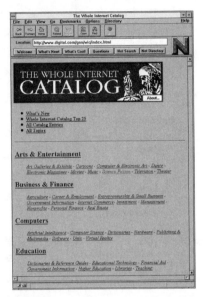

Figure 17.8 *Whole Internet Catalog (O'Reilly & Associates)*

Browsing the Whole Internet Catalog, one soon sees that the GNN staff were aiming for quality more than comprehensiveness—each of the hyperlinks has been checked out and, for the most part, they're the best the Web has to offer. In contrast to other subject trees that try to include any hyperlink that's even remotely relevant to the subject, the Whole Internet Catalog is a good place to search if you're interested in the highest quality sources. Table 17.3 lists the subject headings and subheadings that you'll find in the Whole Internet Catalog. To access the whole Internet catalog, use http://www.digital.gnn/wic/index.html.

Table 17.3 Whole Internet Catalog subject classifications

Arts & Entertainment

Art Galleries & Exhibits

Cartoons

Computer & Electronic Art

Dance

Electronic Magazines

Movies

Music

Science Fiction

Television

Theater

Business & Finance

Agriculture

Career & Employment

Entrepreneurship & Small Business

Government Information

Internet Commerce-Investment

Management

Nonprofits

Personal Finance

Real Estate

Computers

Artificial Intelligence

Computer Science

Dictionaries

Hardware

Publishing & Multimedia

Software

Unix

Virtual Reality

Education

Dictionaries & Reference Guides

Educational Technology

Financial Aid

Government Information

Higher Education

Libraries

Teaching

Government

Indexes to U.S. Government Resources

Executive Branch

Judicial Branch

Legislative Branch

U.S. Agencies

State & Local Government

Foreign and International Government

Health & Medicine

Alternative Medicine

Cancer

Disability

Family Medicine

Health Care Policy

Nutrition

Professional Medicine

Safe Sex

Substance Abuse

U.S. and International Health Organizations

Veterinary Medicine

Humanities

Classics

Languages

Literature

Online Book Collections

Philosophy

Religion & Belief

Internet

Community Networks

HTML

Internet User Guides

Netiquette, Ethics, and AUPs

Resource Indexes

Search the Internet

Security

Standards & Technology

Usenet

White Pages

Recreation, Sports & Hobbies

Cooking

Food & Drink

Games

Gardening

Genealogy

Hobbies & Crafts

Outdoor Recreation

Pets

Sailing & Surfing

Spectator Sports

Sports & Fitness

Table 17.3 Whole Internet Catalog subject classifications (continued)

Science & Technology	Oceanography	Economics
Aeronautics & Astronautics	Ornithology	History
Astronomy	Paleontology	Law
Aviation	Physics	Lesbian & Gay Studies
Biology	Psychology	Politics & Political Activism
Botany	Technology	Sociology
Chemistry	Transfer	Women's Studies
Engineering	Weather & Meteorology	
Environmental Studies	**Social Sciences**	**Travel & Culture**
Geography	Anthropology	Regional & Cultural Interest
Geology	Archaeology	Travel
Mathematics	Black & African Studies	

YAHOO

Decidedly hipper than the subject trees discussed thus far, Yahoo—short for Yet Another Hierarchically Odiferous Oracle—is the work of David Filo and Jerry Chih-Yuan Yang of Stanford University. Subject categories such as "Body Art," "Indie/Alternative Music," and "Cybersex" testify that you're very far from the librarian mentality. Web freaks themselves, Filo and Yang know how to get right to the point—options at the top of the welcome page let you see what's new, what's cool, and what's popular. If you're adventurous, you can even click link that takes you to a random URL! (When I tried it, I wound up at a gateway to—gulp—Internet Relay Chat.)

Yahoo (Figure 17.9) has its own unique twists, which set it apart from the two previous subject trees. For example, Filo and Yang don't have the manpower or funding of a EINet or GNN, so they add relatively few URLs manually. Most are submitted by users, or hunted down by a robot program, which scans the Web regularly for messages announcing a new Web site. Another very desirable feature is cross-links to related subject pages in other subject trees, including The Virtual Library.

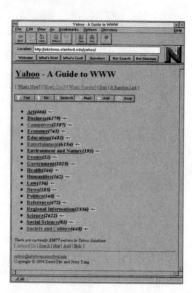

Figure 17.9 *Yahoo subject tree (top level)*

Like The Whole Internet Catalog, Yahoo provides limited searching capability. You can search the subject tree, but your query can't discover new resources that haven't been added to the database. You can suggest new URLs (see Figure 17.10, but if you do, make sure that the URL isn't already listed in Yahoo!

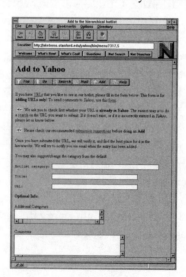

Figure 17.10 *Form for user submission of new URLS (Yahoo)*

Table 17.4 Yahoo Subject Classifications

Art(466)	Events(53)	Reference(473)
Business(6379)	Government(1025)	Regional Information(2556)
Computers(2597)	Health(366)	Science(2622)
Economy(743)	Humanities(162)	Social Science(93)
Education(1481)	Law(156)	Society and Culture(648)
Entertainment(6154)	News(185)	
Environment and Nature(193)	Politics(148)	

MOTHER-OF-ALL BBS

And now, as they used to say on Monty Python, for something completely different: The Mother-of-All BBS (Figure 17.11). Mother, as I'll abbreviate it, goes all the way down the road to user extensibility blazed by Yahoo—in fact, *everything* on Mother has been contributed by users. You can contribute a new URL, or even create a new subject category which, in Mother's terminology, is called a "bulletin board." This is it, folks—the people's subject guide. Unfortunately, it includes a fair number of pranks and cheesy commercial schemes as well as some very interesting documents.

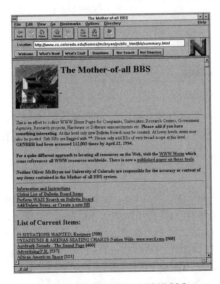

Figure 17.11 *Mother-of-All BBS*
(http://www.cs.colorado.edu/homes/mcbryan/public_html/bb/summary.html)

I won't list all the bulletin board titles here, as they'd take up several pages, but here's a selection, including the apparently normal, the quirky, the odd, the mad, and the downright bizarre.

Sample of Titles from the Mother-of-All BBS

Anarchy—Ideas & Action [192]

Bakhtin Centre, University of Sheffield, UK [357]

Bed & Breakfasts [256]

Best Places to Eat [28]

Bootleg Music [401]

Christmas on the Internet [422]

Community Networks [4]

Companies [9]

Cool Christmas Gifts [385]

Cyberpunk and Cypherpunk Info on the Web [23]

Darr's Dog World [362]

Disaster Relief and Emergency Services [379]

Do-It-Yourself Public Offering-Raise Up to $1 Million [580]

Drinking Establishments [269]

Fishnet [191]

Gay Lesbian Bisexual Transgender [245]

Godiva Online: Chocolate Bliss on the Web [517]

Grubbworm—Guitarist Todd Grubbs Info Server [461]

High Speed Rail [116]

IBERIAN CYBERSPACE PLEASURE MATRIX [414]

Japanese animation (anime) and comics (manga) [473]

Mr. Know-it-all [426]

New Star trek fans who feel left behind [389]

Sandoz Labs Better living through pharmacopia [323]

Sister Cities International—Atlanta Commission [87]

Tape Heads [434]

Teen Talk!...Age's 12 - 15... [396]

The Internet Extreme Ski Team [425]

The Offical Adult Movie Oddities Home Page[007] [572]

The PIT!!! [516]

The Realism/Antirealism Debate [511]

The Segue Foundation Newsletter—New Poetry and Prose [366]

The Unarius Academy of Science [459]

Travel Clubs [567]

TURQUOISE [339]

Twirl! A homepage with sugar on top! [415]

Unidentified Flying Objects [435]

Volleyball WorldWide [468]

Wizard of OZ and Big Little Books Page [410]

EXCELLENT

Who is responsible for such a strange and marvelous thing? None other than Oliver McBryan, a professor of computer science at University of Colorado at Boulder. A native of Ireland and the father of four children, McBryan is an expert in the field of parallel computing, and heads the university's Center for Applied Parallel Processing. In short, he sounds like a perfectly normal person—it's just that (1) he apparently loves what happens when you let people do creative things on the Web, and (2) he also apparently has a wonderful sense of humor.

WEB SECRET

If you'd like to get to know Dr. McBryan better, why don't you visit his home? The First Home on the Information Superhighway is located in Boulder, Colorado but you can get there using http://www.cs.colorado.edu/home/homenii/Home.html. McBryan's home is connected to the Internet by—get this—a 155 megabit per second ATM switch. You'll find plenty of information about future Information Superhighway applications, home pages for all of the family's members, and news of the family's doings—including notes about family member O.C. McBryan (age 12) addressing Senator Ben Nighthorse Campbell and 700 others from home at a recent Information Superhighway conference, and receiving his homework from his teacher at school, all by computer-based videoconference.

MORE SUBJECT TREES

- The W3 searchable catalog built from other sources here. A very useful tool.
- The UU_NNA wishes to create a fully accredited library over computer networks. This is their library.
- The Internet Services list (based on Yanoff's Internet List)
- The Whole Internet Catalogue from O'Reilly (updated from the bestselling "The Whole Internet Catalog User's Guide Catalog")
- The Clearinghouse for Subject-oriented Internet Guides in Michigan—you can browse or search.

SUMMARY

Subject trees provide a Web version of a library subject card catalog, but they have one huge drawback: they're manually updated, so there's no chance that they'll reflect the thousands of new documents added every month to the Web. Use subject trees along with other information-seeking tools, including key word searching with search engines and Web surfing.

FROM HERE

- Couldn't find what you're looking for in a subject tree? Learn to use search engines in Chapter 18.
- Look for information—and have fun doing it. Checkout the introduction to surfing the Web in the next chapter.

Search Engines and Surfing

One person's organization is another's chaos.
—Brian Pinkerton, author of *WebCrawler*

Subject trees, the subject of the previous chapter, try to catalogue existing Web resources under subject headings. The trouble with such efforts is that they do not "scale up" well, as Internet experts like to say. A solution that worked when there were 5,000 URLs in existence becomes less feasible when more than a million exist—or ten million. The work involved in maintaining a subject tree quickly overwhelms even a well-funded organization, let alone individuals who are volunteering their time. For this reason, subject trees are certain to lack some URLs that could prove very valuable to you.

How should you go about discovering information that isn't listed in subject trees? This chapter discusses three information-seeking approaches:

- **Using search engines.** Computer experts have devised automatic programs that "crawl" the Web, looking for new URLs and adding them to a database. These robot-like programs are called *spiders*, *robots*, or *wanderers*. These programs report back to their home base, and automatically update a database of URLs. You can then search the database using a *search engine*, which is usually a WAIS database system. There are several search engines in existence. All have imperfections that severely limit their use for information-retrieval purposes.

KEY TERM

- **Using geographical locators.** Several Web resources exist that permit you to find all the servers in a given geographical region, such as a city, a state, or a country. If you are attempting to locate a university's home page, this technique might prove much faster than subject trees, search engines, or surfing.

- **Surfing the Web.** This technique involves finding an interesting or useful document, and then exploring the chains of hyperlinks that flow from it. Although this technique can consume a great deal of time and frequently produces poor results, sometimes a Web surf produces a gem that could not have been discovered any other way.

HOME PAGE

Many of the search tools discussed in this chapter make use of WAIS database searches. If you haven't already done so, you may find it helpful to read Understanding WAIS Searches in Chapter 14.

EXCELLENT

Looking for a page that enables you to try lots of different search engines? Here are several:

- **CUSI.** Martijn Koster's Configurable Unified Search Interface, http:/-/web.nexor.co.uk/public/cusi/cusi.html.

- **Meta Index.** Probably the best meta-index of all, brought to you by Centre Universitaire d'Informatique, University of Geneva (http://cui_www.unige.ch /meta-index.html)

- **External Info** page at Twente Univ. in the Netherlands (http:// www_is.cs.utwente.nl:8080/cgi.bin/locl/nph-susi1.pl)

From these pages, you can initiate searches using most or all of the engines discussed in this chapter.

HOT TIP

Access CUI's Meta Index (http://cui_www.unige.ch/meta-index.html) save it to a local file, and make it your default home page! You'll have instant access to an incredible wealth of Web and Internet information, including subject trees, search engines, public domain software and shareware, Internet people, Internet documents, USENET FAQs ("Frequently Asked Questions"), Internet tools documentation, dictionaries of computer terms, and more.

SPIDERS AND SEARCH ENGINES

One of the hottest and most controversial areas in computer science concerns the creation of *agents*, robot-like programs that go out in search of information. In the future, you'll be able to sit down at your computer and say, "Computer, go out and bring back everything you can find on the Coonawarra wine-growing district in Australia." An hour later, you'll see a report from the agent, which has roamed the Internet looking for all related information on this subject, and for your convenience, it categorized and formatted for easy reading.

Such futuristic-sounding computer programs aren't available yet, although there are various experimental versions of them in development. However, less sophisticated agents are already roaming the web. Primitive but effective, their mission is simple: To locate every URL in existence, and to add all newly-discovered URLs to a huge and growing database. Web users can then search the database using a search engine—and hopefully, they'll find URLs that haven't been included in subject trees. These agents are known as wanderers, robots, or—as befits the Web—spiders.

WEB SECRET

Spiders are clever, but not every Web service provider is thrilled with their presence on the Web. Capable of duplicating themselves in their quest, these agents are in some respects like benign computer viruses, which gives some people qualms. A poorly-designed spider closely resembles a computer virus, as it can consume so much of the server's resources that it all but shuts the server down. An interesting paper by David Eichmann, a researcher at the University of Houston, attempts to specify guidelines for ethical spider behavior (http://www.ncsa.uiuc.edu/SDG/IT94/Proceedings/Agents/eichmann.ethical/eichmann.html).

WEB SECRET

If you're setting up a Web server, by all means take a look at Martin Koster's "A Standard for Robot Exclusion," http://web.nexor.co.uk/mak/doc/robots/norobots.html. This document describes a simple file that can be used to exclude unwanted resource-hogging robots from your server.

For more information on spiders, check out http://web.nexor.co.uk/mak/doc/robots/robots.html ("World Wide Web Robots, Wanderers, and Spiders"). You'll find a list of known spiders and guidelines for ethical spider constructions.

EXCELLENT

Are spiders the perfect solution to the problem of finding information on the Web? Far from it. Most spiders bring back only the titles of the newly-discovered URLs—that is, the text found within the <TITLE> </TITLE> codes at the top of

AWFUL

HTML documents. Unfortunately, most Web authors do not title their documents with information retrieval in mind. David Eichmann's excellent paper entitled "Ethical Web Agents," for example, would not be retrieved by a search for "ethics and spiders," even though it's probably the best thing that's available on the Web on this subject.

KEY TERM

To deal with the problems of retrieving documents by title text alone, some spiders retrieve some of the document text as well as the words in the title. This sounds like a great idea, but it raises a new problem—*false drops* in the list of retrieved items. A false drop is an item that superficially meets the search criteria, but is actually not related. For example, suppose you're looking for Web resources about backyard bird feeders. You type the key words "backyard," "bird," and "feeder," and launch your search—only to get a reference to a weird alternative music URL by the Backyard Birds, an unknown musical group, with a hyperlink to their MPEG audio file, "Bottom Feeder."

Do these limitations mean that search engines are useless? No. If you understand the limitations, and use this chapter's strategies for effective search engine use, you can vastly improve your potential to locate useful resources. In the following sections, you'll find tips and strategies for using the most popular search engines, beginning with the best of them all, Lycos.

AWFUL

Having trouble gaining access to a search engine? Welcome to the club. The more popular search engines are experiencing as many as a quarter of a million accesses per day. Keep trying—or, better yet, get up in the middle of the night to do your search.

HOT TIP
Each search engine embodies its own unique philosophy of just how a spider should work, what it should retrieve, and how the database ought to be searched, so you'll be well advised to try two, three, or more of them when you're hunting for information. As you'll see, the list of retrieved documents differs from search engine to search engine, sometimes dramatically.

HOME PAGE

Here's a quick guide to selecting a search engine:

- Looking for the maximum number of Web documents on your topic? Start with Lycos.

- Want to make sure you retrieve all documents that mention your search terms, even if they do so only peripherally? Search WebCrawler and Jonathan's JumpStation.

- Looking for high-quality sites only, with no extraneous junk in the list of retrieved items? Search the CUI W3 Catalog.
- Looking for graphics, video files, and other multimedia resources? Search with the World Wide Web Worm.

Using a Search Engine

No matter which search engine you choose, the overall process for using it is the same. Here's an overview:

1. **Understand the search engine's limitations**. Does it include Gopher, FTP, and Archie information, or just Web (http) documents? Does it index document content, or just document titles and URL text? Understanding what's in the database will help you devise more effective search terms. For example, if you know that the database contains text from URLs, you can find sounds, graphics, and other multimedia resources by typing file extensions (such as JPG, AU, and MPG).

2. **Access the search engine's URL.** You'll find these in this chapter, and they're cited on many starting points pages.

3. **Type one or more search words in the text box.** To avoid overloading the search engine, start with a fairly specific list—and type the most important word first (some search engines give greater weight to the first word in the query). To look for documents discussing the red wines of Oregon, for example, type "wine oregon white."

4. **Choose search options, if any are available.** Some search engines let you search different parts of Web documents, such as titles, document content, or hyperlink text.

5. **Click the "Start Search" or "Submit" button.** Clicking this button initiates the search.

6. **View the list of retrieved documents**. Most search engines rank the search results numerically, as does WAIS, with the first document having the highest score (1,000). If you find a document that looks like a good "hit," just click the cited hyperlink.

7. **Refine and repeat the search, if necessary**. Common problems include finding too many documents or too few. See "Search Engine Tips and Hints," the next section, for guidlines.

Search Engine Tips and Hints

No matter what search engine you're using, you'll find the following tips will help you search more effectively.

- **Check your spelling.** Before pressing Enter or clicking the Start Search button (or its equivalent), make sure you have typed the search terms correctly. If you find a spelling mistake, correct it before initiating the search.

- **Don't use commonly-occuring articles or Web terms.** Most search engines have a "kill list" that automatically deletes words such as "and," "the," and "http," but including such words could generate an error message, forcing you to repeat the search.

- **If the search retrieves too many documents, narrow the search.** To do so, try typing more search terms. For example, a search for "Windows" may retrieve thousands of URLs. If you're looking for documents describing Windows utilities software, type "Windows utility software."

- **If the search retrieves too few documents, widen the search.** Try reducing the number of search terms or truncating terms ("soc" will match "social," "sociology," "sociological," and more).

- **Don't worry about capitalization.** All the search engines discussed here are case-insensitive. The search words "Dixie" and "dixie" are identical, so far as the search engine is concerned.

HOT TIP
Search didn't work out? Don't give up. Think of more synonyms for your search terms, and try again. A search for "Norwegian environment" may not turn up items that are listed under "Norway ecology"!

Lycos

A project of the Carnegie Mellon University's Center for Machine Translation, the Lycos WWW search engine sets the standard for excellence in Web-based information retrieval. Late at night, the Lycos search engine prowls the Web, hunting down new Web, FTP, and Gopher documents—at last count, it added an average of about

5000 new documents per day. And for each one it finds, it adds the following information to the Lycos database:

- The words in the document title.
- The words in the document's headings and subheadings.
- The hyperlinks contained in the document.
- The 100 most important words in the document, retrieved using an algorithm that considers word frequencies and word placement within the document (for example, words in the title and the first paragraph are given more weight than others).
- The words in the first 20 lines of text.
- The size of the document in bytes.
- The total number of words the document contains.

How big is the database? In December, 1994, the database contained 1.49 million URLs. That's up from 1 million just three months previously.

Because Lycos retrieves so many words from the documents, it is much more likely to help you than Web spiders that retrieve only title information. Be aware that you'll get plenty of false drops, but thousands of people would readily agree that the irrelevant stuff is worth paging through, so long as you can find that one gem that's out there somewhere.

 Where does the name "Lycos" come from? It's from the spider family Lycosidae, and it's very apropos. The Lysosidae are large, fast-running ground spiders that hunt down their prey at night, rather than catching them in a web.

WEB SECRET

To start a Lycos search, access the Lycos search engine (http://lycos2.cs.cmu.edu /lycos-form.html). You'll see a forms-based search document (Figure 18.1). Note: Lycos requires that you use a forms-capable browser, like Mosaic v.2.0. To get started with the search, type the words you want to find in the Search Keywords text box. After you press **Enter**, Lycos searches the database, and generates a new document that contains the search results (Figure 18.2).

Type the search keywords here

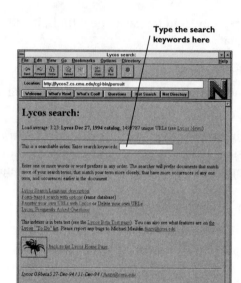

Figure 18.1 *Lycos Search Engine (http://lycos2.cs.cmu.edu/lycos-form.html)*

AWFUL

Like WAIS search engines, the Lycos retrieval software ranks documents with a numerical score; 1000 indicates a "perfect hit." But don't believe it. It's possible that a document ranked 1,000 will turn out to be a false drop. My search for information on the Coonawarra wine district in Australia produced a classic false drop—a document including many references to Wine, a program that emulates Microsoft Windows. In fairness to Lycos, the Web contains so many different kinds of documents—papers, hotlists, FTP archives, press releases, rants and raves, and more—that any retrieval list is bound to contain a good deal of useless junk.

But read on. The very next item, scoring .95032, is a beauty—the official home page of the Wine mailing list (Figure 18.3). Bingo!

Relevance score

**First of 20 documents
retrieved (false drop)**

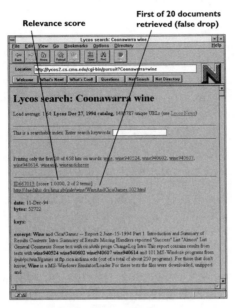

Figure 18.2 *Search results (Lycos)*

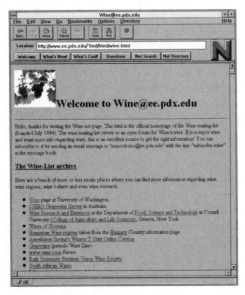

Figure 18.3 *Relevant document retrieved by Lycos*

To make the best use of Lycos, learn to use some of its advanced search functions. Here's a brief overview:

- **Exclude unwanted documents.** Bugged by retrieval lists that contain an unwanted term? Suppose, for instance, you're searching for "wine," and you keep getting documents on that Microsoft Windows emulator. Add the expression **-windows**. The hyphen tells Lycos to exclude documents containing that word.

- **Force an exact match.** By default, Lycos works with truncation—if you type **safety**, for example, you'll get safetycentre, safetyg, safetyicon, safetylock, and safetynet. To restrict the retrieval to safety, place a period before the word (**.safety**).

WebCrawler

Supported by the generous donations of DealerNet, Starwave Corporation, and Satchel Sports, all of Seattle, Washington, WebCrawler is a Web search engine housed at the University of Washington. Unlike the Lycos search engine, WebCrawler searches the entire text of the documents it finds—but this comes at a cost. To avoid consuming too many Internet resources, WebCrawler is programmed to crawl at a particularly slow pace. As of December, 1994, WebCrawler had indexed only 300,000 documents, only a fraction of Lycos' 1.49 million.

EXCELLENT

Because WebCrawler indexes the entire content of the documents it discovers, this search engine is much more likely to retrieve a document that contains a term buried somewhere in the depths of a Web resource—such as a file buried at the end of an FTP list, or a reference located in a lengthy bibliography.

To search WebCrawler, access the WebCrawler search page at http://webcrawler.cs.washington.edu/WebCrawler/WebQuery.html. Type your search terms in the text box (see Figure 18.4).

HOT TIP

WebCrawler implements limited Boolean searching. By default, WebCrawler uses "and" between the words in the search, meaning that no document is retrieved unless it contains all the words you type. (For example, if you type "Coonawarra wine," WebCrawler will not return documents that mention Coonawarra but not wine, or wine but not Coonawarra.) If you deselect the "And words together" check box, WebCrawler implements an "or" search, meaning that the program retrieves all the documents that mention one or more of the search terms (you see any document that mentions "Coonawarra," "wine," or "Coonawarra wine").

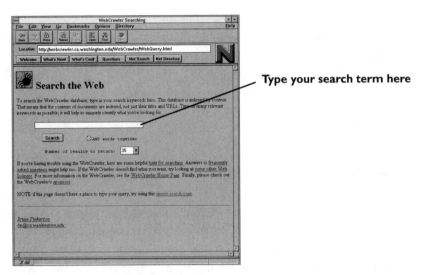

Type your search term here

Figure 18.4 WebCrawler search engine (http://webcrawler.cs.washington.edu/WebCrawler/WebQuery.html)

Revelance score

Document title

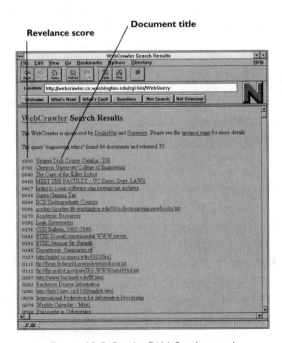

Figure 18.5 Result of WebCrawler search

The results of a WebCrawler search (see Figure 18.5) are a simple list of hyperlinks, listed with their numerical scores. Again, a rank of 1,000 means that the document is apparently a perfect hit, but don't count on it. You may have to try several variations on your search terms before meeting with success. If you don't find what you're looking for, remember that WebCrawler has indexed less than one quarter of the URLs known to exist.

CUI W3 catalog

Short for Centre Universitaire d'Informatique World Wide Web catalog, the CUI W3 catalog (Figure 18.6) is housed at the University of Geneva, Switzerland. To search the CUI catalog, use the URL http://cui_www.unige.ch/cgi-bin/w3catalog.

One of the most popular search engines on the Web, CUI W3 differs from the two just discussed in that it doesn't employ a spider. Instead, the search software consults the following manually-maintained lists. The result of a CUI search (Figure 18.7) is a list of retrieved items, which are sorted according to the URL source. The sources grouped under "nwn," for example, are from NCSA's "What's New" pages. Here's a list of the headings you'll find:

- NCSA What's new (nwn)
- NCSA's NCSA Starting Points (nsp)
- CERN's W3 Virtual Library Subject Catalog and selected sub-lists (cvl)
- Martijn Koster's Aliweb Archie-like Indexing for the Web (ali)
- Scott Yanoff's Internet Services List (isl)
- Simon Gibbs' list of Multimedia Information Sources (mis)
- John December's list of Computer-Mediated Communication Information Sources (cmc) and Internet Tools Summary (cmc)
- Marcus Speh's User Documents physics researchers (msp)

Although there are currently only about 13,000 entries, the CUI W3 catalog and searching system ensures that you will usually find high-quality documents.

Type your search terms here

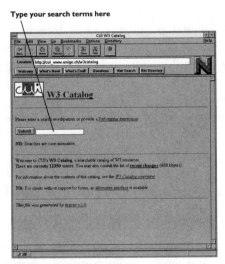

Figure 18.6 *CUI W3 Catalog (http://cui_www.unige.ch/w3catalog)*

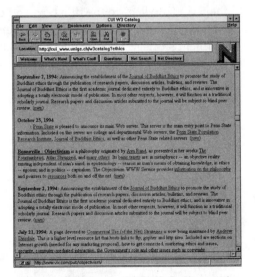

Figure 18.7 *Result of CUI W3 Catalog search*

JumpStation

Yet another Web search engine is maintained by Jonathan Fletcher, a systems programmer at Stirling University in Scotland. Based on a web-crawling spider, the JumpStation database is small by comparison to Lycos—just over 275,000 entries. Like WebCrawler, JumpStation's spider indexes all the words in the documents it finds, so it's a good choice if you're looking for words that might be buried deeply in a document (and not mentioned in the title or opening paragraph). To access JumpStation, use the URL http://www.stir.ac.uk/jsbin/jsii?jsii_doc_search.

A unique feature of the JumpStation's search software is that you can selectively search for words occurring in the document title, the header, or the document content, or any combination of these. Note the three text boxes in Figure 18.8 If you use just one of them, you can type more than one term. If you use two or more, JumpStation uses only the first term you type in each box.

The advantage of searching for title, header, and content words independently is that it allows you to focus your search. Suppose you search for documents containing "Mosaic" in the document content, and you get thousands of documents in the retrieval list. If you add the term "Mosaic" to the title box, and click the title delimitation check box, JumpStation retrieves only those documents that contain the word "Mosaic" in the document's title. Such documents may be more pertinent to your interests.

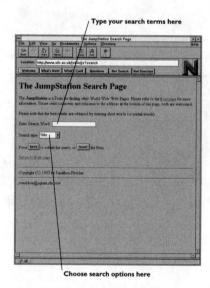

Type your search terms here

Choose search options here

Figure 18.8 *Jonathan's JumpStation search engine (http://www.stir.ac.uk/jsbin/jsii?jsii_doc_search)*

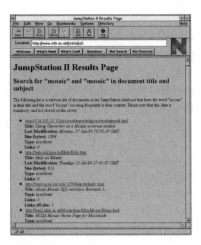

Figure 18.9 *Result of Jonathan's JumpStation search*

World Wide Web Worm (WWWW)

The creation of University of Colorado computer scientist Oliver McBryan, the World Wide Web Worm is another search engine with unique features. WWWW's spider roams the Web in search of new URLs, including graphics, video, and audio files. As of this writing, the spider had returned over 300,000 HTTP documents. To search WWWW, access the URL http://www.cs.colorado.edu/home/mcbryan-/WWWW.html (Figure 18.10).

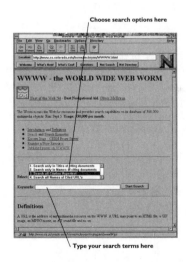

Figure 18.10 *World Wide Web Worm (http://www.cs.colorado.edu/home/mcbryan/WWWW.html)*

The World Wide Web Worm is unique because it doesn't index document content, as do WebCrawler and Jonathon's Jumpstation. Instead, it concentrates on URLs and hyperlinks containing URLs, many of which aren't links to documents. Among WWWW's 300,000 resources are many sound, video, and graphics files, which can be directly accessed through the search engine's retrieval list.

Another unique feature of WWWW is that you can choose the portion of the documents that you want WWWW to search. Here's the rundown:

- **Document Title.** Contains the text that shows up as the document's title on your graphical browser (the text between the <TITLE> and </TITLE> codes in an HTML document).

- **Document Name.** Contains the URL (such as http://www.cs.colorado.edu-/home/mcbryan/WWWW.html).

- **Citation Hypertext.** Contains the text of the hyperlink that refers to a document; unfortunately, this can be as simple as "here" (for example, many hyperlinks use this form: "The results of the Best of the Web 1994 competition are <u>here</u>"). When you search using this option, WWWW returns a list containing both the URL of a retrieved document and the URL of the document in which it was cited. (*Note*: The retrieval list may contain duplicates as many URLs are cited more than once.)

- **All Names of Cited URLS.** Returns a list showing both the URL of the retrieved document and the URL of the document in which it was cited, but it searches the URL text, not the citation hypertext. This list may also contain many duplicates.

HOT TIP

If you're searching with either of the citation options (Citation Hypertext or All Names of Cited URLs), turn off in-line image downloading before clicking the Start Search button. Many hyperlinks to sounds, images, and video URLs are in-line images. Since these retrieval options retrieve the citation as well as the document, you'll be downloading a lot of in-line images.

Other Search Engines

The previous sections examined the most popular Web browsers, but don't neglect some of the less-well-known search engines:

- **Nikos** (http://www.rns.com/cgi-bin/nomad). Formerly known as Zorbamatic, Nikos—short for New Internet Knowledge System—will soon become a major player in the search engine sweepstakes. Currently, about 100,000 documents are indexed, but Nikos aims to map 90% of the Web by the time this book appears. Nikos is jointly funded by Rockwell Network Systems and California State Polytechnic University, San Luis Obispo.

- **ALIWEB** (http://web.nexor.co.uk/public/aliweb/aliweb.html) doesn't use a spider. Instead, Web authors submit forms describing the content of their documents. ALIWEB adds these forms to the database, which you can then search. Unfortunately, ALIWEB does not collect the kind of information that could have made this project useful—it's limited to a brief description of content. ALIWEB is supported by NEXOR, a U.K. service provider.

- **Global On-Line Directory and News Service** (http://www.gold.net-/gold/search2.html). Provides free advertising for Web services and resources. Like ALIWEB, this service depends on Web authors' contributions., However, this service focuses on commercial Web sites, so it may get a better response than ALIWEB has. It's supported by CityScape Internet Services, Ltd., a U.K. service provider.

- **RBSE's URL Database** (http://rbse.jsc.nasa.gov/eichmann/urlsearch.html). Indexing slightly fewer than 40,000 documents at this writing, this spider-based database might be worth a try if you can't find a document by other means. It indexes the full content of the documents, so it's a good choice if you're looking for obscure information.

GEOGRAPHIC SEARCHES

Still can't find what you're looking for? If the information you're seeking pertains to a geographic area or city, you can use two very nice geographically-oriented searching tools, the Virtual Tourist and CityNet.

The Virtual Tourist (http://wings.buffalo.edu/world/), shown in Figure 18.11, is a beautifully-crafted page that is best accessed by forms-capable browsers. Based on a world map, the Virtual Tourist contains information about Web sites for each country, in addition to general information for that nation. Often, the country-related information is stored in offsite documents, and it's frequently of excellent quality.

To use Virtual Tourist, click on the area of the world you're interested in seeing. Another map will be displayed showing this area in greater detail. On-screen icons show what's available: maps of Web sites, lists of Web sites, and general information about the country. To see the information just click on one of the resource icons. A map, a list, or a document with country-related information will be displayed depending on what you clicked. Figure 18.12 shows the map of Web resources for Norway.

For information on specific cities, try City.Net (http://www.city.net/), a project of City Net Express of Portland, Oregon. To find information about a city, you can browse the subject tree or use the built-in search engine. Since City.Net contains hyperlinks to offsite documents, just what you'll find depends on what's available. If you're lucky, you'll find guides to tourist destinations, information about cultural events, maps of bus lines and subways, and more.

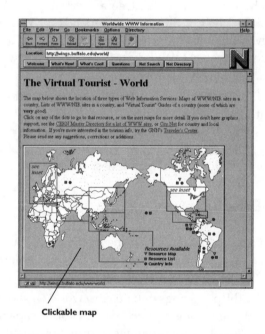

Clickable map

Figure 18.11 Virtual Tourist home page (http://wings.buffalo.edu/world/)

Figure 18.12 Web resources for Norway (Virtual Tourist)

THE GENTLE ART OF WEB SURFING

What is "Web surfing?" In a word, serendipity. You find a document, click a hyperlink, find another document, click another hyperlink, and so on (and so on!). Before you're done, you'll have obtained documents from the world over. It's all quite impossible to describe to someone who hasn't experienced it.

Web surfing is lots of fun. But is it useful as an information-seeking strategy? It can be. Here are some tips:

- **Start with a starting document, a subject tree, or a search engine**. Try to find one high-quality document in your area of interest, and explore its hyperlinks.

- **Keep the source document in its own window**. Once you've found a high-quality document from which to launch your surfing effort, keep it displayed in its own window (if your browser supports this), and surf in another. Why? Most browsers don't do a very good job of maintaining history lists. You wouldn't want to lose this document and not be able to find your way back.

- **Don't get sidetracked.** It's very easy to waste time by exploring exciting-sounding hyperlinks that aren't pertinent to your search. Avoid the temptation.

- **Set a time limit.** Don't spend the whole day surfing—if you haven't found anything in an hour, you probably won't.

- **Don't add too many documents to your hotlist**. Save disk space for the gems.

SUMMARY

Web search engines address the limitations of manually-updated subject trees by crawling the Web automatically looking for new URLs. Some of these "spider" programs retrieve Web documents only, while others also retrieve additional Internet resources, such as Gopher menu items and FTP file archives. Some retrieve document titles and URL text only, while others retrieve and index the entire document's text. Try using two or three search engines to make sure you've searched effectively. You can also find information by using geographic servers. Don't underestimate Web surfing as an information-seeking technique, but don't let it consume too much time!

FROM HERE

- Explore the Web—and try your hand at surfing! See Part Five, "Exploring the Web" for reviews of the hottest Web sites.

- Use this book's SmartPages—ready-to-use home pages that you can use with your graphical browser to get quick access to Web sites of interest. See Chapter 26, Using SmartPages.

- Create your own home page with just the URLs you want! See Chapter 27, Creating your own Home Page with HTML.

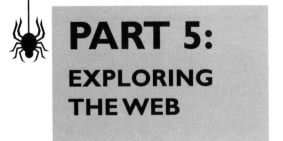

PART 5:
EXPLORING
THE WEB

CHAPTER 19

The Arts

Art postulates communion, and the artist has an imperative need to make others share the joy
which he experiences himself.

—Igor Stravinsky

The Web abounds with resources for those interested in the fine arts. Visiting documents dedicated to painting, drawing, music, dance, film, literature, and computer
graphics is a lot of fun, and those engaged in research in these areas can travel to
collections without leaving their computers.

Most intriguing of all, though, is the fact that the Web provides an outlet for
many artists who wouldn't otherwise have an audience for their work. Artists who
don't pursue their art full-time, or who lack the connections (and, in some cases,
the skills) to get their work displayed in traditional venues, can post their work to
the Web for all to see. The Web lets art aficionados follow fledgling artists long
before their work earns a place in even the lowliest local gallery, bar stage, or magazine. The quality ranges from atrocious to sublime, but a Web voyage with the arts
in mind can produce some very pleasant surprises.

EXCELLENT

Some sorts of art lend themselves to Web display more than others. It's not
difficult to post a TIFF file of a famous painting, but an audio file of an entire
symphony or an MPEG file featuring an hour-long ballet would choke any
personal computer. Therefore, the bulk of Web documents devoted to the arts focus
on the visual arts—painting, drawing, photography, and computer graphics. These
documents often include examples of the work discussed them. Most of the other

documents—the dance documents, for example—serve as clearinghouses for information. Visit these documents to learn about club meetings, exhibitions, and tour schedules. Often, these documents include references to FTP servers from which Web surfers can download files.

This chapter is a list of Web documents devoted to the arts. It is divided into sections devoted to a particular mode of expression, such as music, dance, or painting.

HOW THIS BOOK RATES WEB DOCUMENTS

Looking for cool Web documents? The documents discussed in this and subsequent Part Five chapters are rated on a scale of four stars. The ratings are as follows:

★★★★ A document rated four stars is one of the best on the Web, in any subject. Everyone should visit these documents—it doesn't matter whether you possess knowledge or even interest in the subject; you're sure to like what you see.

★★★ Anyone even remotely interested in a three-star document's subject should pay it a visit. They're the best in that field, but don't set trends for the entire Web, as four-star documents do.

★★ These documents have some unusual or meritorious features, but those who aren't interested in these documents' subjects would probably rather spend their Web time elsewhere.

★ One-star documents may prove useful to those doing research in the area they cover, but fall down in visual appeal, organization, or useability. Still, these sites are far from the "worst of the web"—they're of value to those devoted to the sites subjects.

VISUAL ARTS

The visual arts, including painting, drawing, photography, and computer graphics, lend themselves well to Web exhibitions. The markup language of Web documents, HTML, is well suited to embedding graphics. Furthermore, most personal computers can handle graphics files without a problem—there is no need for special hardware (as is the case with sound) or mega-fast processors, which are needed to run video files.

On-line visual art exhibits fall into two groups. First, there are documents that display art on which the copyright has expired. These works are typically at least 50 years old. The other group of exhibits typically include very new art—works of little known contemporary artists hoping to get exposure on the Web.

★★★ Krannert Art Museum

URL: http://www.ncsa.uiuc.edu/General/UIUC/KrannertArtMuseum/KrannertArtHome.html

Topic: On-line exhibition of fine art

Of Special Note: The Krannert's method of guiding visitors through its exhibits is one of the best I've seen.

The on-line exhibit of the Krannert Art Museum at the University of Illinois at Urbana-Champaign has benefitted from its affiliation with the National Center for Supercomputer Applications, also located on the UIUC campus. Though its collection of on-line art is not nearly as large as that at WebLouvre and the text that accompanies the art is not as elaborate, the Krannert Museum includes art from all over the world, and it has a more coherent scheme for guiding you through its various galleries.

You enter the Krannert Museum on-line at the welcome document which contains hyperlinks to several museum resources. Most of these links are to short informational documents about items like the operating hours of the museum and its cafeteria (this Web document apparently was designed with UIUC students in mind). The promising-sounding "Map of the Museum" link leads only to static images of the Krannert's floor plans; there is no clickable map.

The real appeal of the Krannert—its on-line exhibit—begins with the "Guide to the Krannert Art Museum and Kinkead Pavilion" hyperlink. This link leads to the museum guide document (Figure 19.1), from which you can jump to any of the exhibit documents or proceed through them in order. It's worth your time to start at the beginning and visit all the exhibits.

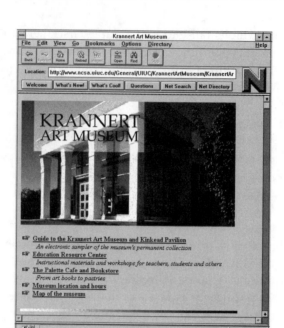

Figure 19.1 Krannert guide document
(URL: http://www.ncsa.uiuc.edu/General/UIUC/KrannertArtMuseum/Guide/GuideContents.html)

The Krannert Museum features collections of Asian, African, Middle-Eastern, and pre-Columbian American art. It also includes a collection of sculptures, pottery, basketry, and carved icons from around the world.

Each of the exhibit documents, analogous to rooms or halls in the museum, features from one to five thumbnail pictures of works of art, and their titles. By clicking on the title or the picture itself, you get a large rendition of the picture and some descriptive text about the art object. Unfortunately, the Krannert does not allow you to click on the pictures to download a copy.

Three navigational buttons appear at the bottom of each exhibit document (except those at the beginning and the end). One button is a hyperlink to the next exhibit, one leads to the previous exhibit, and the third is a link to the guide document. These buttons make it easy to see the entire collection or find the works you're interested in.

WISH LIST

With such a fantastic user interface, it's a shame that the Krannert doesn't have more of its collection available on the Web. One can only hope that the museum staff keeps adding works of art to the document.

★★ The Ohio State University at Newark Art Museum

URL: http://www.cgrg.ohio-state.edu/mkruse/osu.html

Topic: Art exhibition

Of Special Note: One of the best lists of on-line art resources available and a crude but intriguing periodic report of a live dance performance.

The exhibit at this museum is nothing to cheer about yet, though it has the potential to become more useful as more of the museum's exhibits are archived on the Web. As it is, there are only two "traditional" exhibits—those with GIF or JPEG files of the works of an artist and some accompanying text.

More interesting is the depiction of a live dance performance by Budoh dancer Ralph Rosenfield. Take a look at what happened here: On November 2, 1994, Rosenfield performed at the museum. Every four minutes, the museum staff posted pictures of his performance, along with descriptive text, to the Web, and they remain there for you to follow. The pictures are not great and the hurriedly typed text is full of errors, but the idea is interesting. You have to wonder why there are no video clips of the performance available, though. One of the Rosenfield screens appears in Figure 19.2.

Figure 19.2 *"Live" dance performance at OSU-Newark Art Museum*
(URL: http://www.cgrg.ohio-state.edu/Newark/ralph.html)

USEFUL
RESOURCE

The biggest attraction value of the OSU-Newark Museum is its list of on-line art resources. This document contains links to more than 400 exhibits, discussions, and archives, and should prove useful to anyone doing any sort of art research at all.

★★★★ OTIS

> **URL:** http://sunsite.unc.edu/otis/otis.html
>
> **Topic:** An exhibit of small-time artists' work
>
> **Of Special Note:** An eclectic collection of art from contemporary artists, ranging from the conventional to the patently bizarre. Also check out the Synergy documents, on which artists collaborate on projects.

The Vatican Exhibit described in the next session and the Krannert Museum are dedicated to displaying the works of established artists, while OTIS is designed to exhibit those of up-and-coming artists. It is a free-for-all exhibit, featuring works in media from pen-and-ink to photocopier art and body scarification. OTIS is the modern-day equivalent of the underground coffee shops where artists often got their first public exposure.

OTIS (which stands for "Operative Term Is Stimulate") is different in another way from the galleries for established artists. It encourages viewers of art to contact the artists and give them comments about their work. OTIS provides electronic mail addresses for many of the artists who display their work within its virtual walls, and keeps an archive of the sometimes lively critical debates that have taken place in the past.

🕷 WEBMASTER

Here's an idea for would be WebMasters who are wondering how to provide content: Let your users do it. Anyone who's interested in displaying their art on-line can post a document at OTIS. There's no real selection process, and because of this the OTIS collection is one of the most widely varied on-line exhibits.

When you first drop into the OTIS document, you're confronted with a collection of graphical links from which to choose. On your first visit, opt for the Gallery (Figure 19.3) and take a look at what some artists have posted. Works are cataloged by medium (i.e. photographs, ray-traces) and subject (i.e. landscapes, animals). A link to a list of artists also apears on the gallery document.

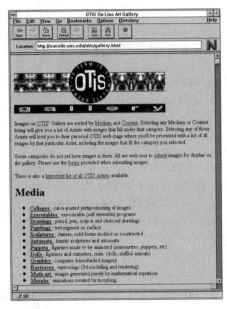

Figure 19.3 *OTIS gallery document (URL: http://sunsite.unc.edu/otis/gallery.html)*

Before leaving OTIS, return to the Welcome document and check out the link labeled "Synergy." The Synergy project allows artists to work together on projects, often with interesting results. For example, in the summer of 1993, OTIS artists collaborated on SYNERGY:ARCANA, an effort to redesign the deck of Tarot cards. Working together via email and FTP, the artists generated card images.

OTIS defines the on-line museum for mostly unknown artists. Its model of free access and open debate enables dozens of new artists to get exposure, and eliminates the cumbersome machinery of criticism that once stood between artists and exhibition of their products.

HOT TIP Using a slow dial-up connection to the Web? Use the Otis document at http://sunsite.unc.edu/otis/schmotis.html—it has no in-line images, so transmission is speeded up dramatically.

★★★★ Vatican Exhibit

URL: http://sunsite.unc.edu/expo/vatican.exhibit/Vatican.exhib   it.html

Topic: Art and manuscript exhibition

Of Special Note: Lots of old manuscripts, including Euclid's *Elements* and Aristotle's *Libri naturales*.

WISH LIST

Like WebLouvre, described in the next section, the Vatican Exhibit combines a huge collection of primary source material with excellent commentary and a slick Web interface. This exhibit isn't limited to the visual arts, since there are many works of literature and philosphy included, but some of the most interesting items in the collection fall into this category.

The Vatican Exhibit is the on-line version of an exhibit of Vatican treasures that appeared in the Library of Congress in 1993. It will remain on-line at SunSite indefinitely, but it is unlikely the curators will add any new material.

You arrive at the Vatican Exhibit's welcome document, which describes the efforts of the Vatican to accumulate knowledge over hundreds of years. The only link on this document goes to the Main Hall document. From there you can choose links to collections of material on various subjects, including mathematics, archaeology, and music. (The Mathematics exhibit appears in Figure 19.4). Each of these "rooms" contains thumbnail JPEG images that you can click to see a larger version. Yes, all of the document's displays are JPEGs—even the music exhibits, which are pictures of choir records and church ceremonies. It would be nice if the document's maintainers included audio files of liturgical chants or medieval hymns, or a small video clip showing how experts restored some of the artifacts on display.

The Vatican Exhibit is worthy of a visit from every Web user, particularly those with an interest in ancient history. It presents unique artifacts that most Web users would never otherwise see.

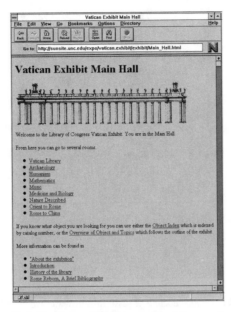

Figure 19.4 *The Vatican Exhibit is organized like a real museum*

★★ Vern's SIRDs

URL: http://www.cs.uidaho.edu/~vern/sirds/

Topic: Archive of random-dot stereograms

Of Special Note: Lots of links to other related documents

A Single Image Random Dot Stereogram (SIRDS) is a two dimensional image that, when stared at as if trying to focus behind the image, creates a stunning 3-D effect. You've surely seen them in bookstores and galleries. Now you can see them on the Web!

Vern Hart, a student at the University of Idaho, has composed a Web document dedicated to stereograms. His document (Figure 19.5) isn't especially stellar—it's mostly a list of archives at the University of Idaho and links to other random-dot documents. But there are links to an interesting SIRDS FAQ, and lots of SIRDS that you can view right on your computer display. You'll also find plenty of information on how to make SIRDS.

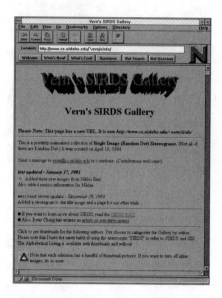

Figure 19.5 Vern's SIRDs document (URL: http://www.cs.uidaho.edu/~vern/sirds/)

★★★★ Le WebLouvre

URL: HTTP://mistral.enst.fr/louvre/

Topic: Art exhibition

Of Special Note: Strong collection of Impressionist art, and an on-line tour of Paris!

Though it has no official connection to the Louvre museum in Paris, WebLouvre is the standard for exhibiting visual arts on the Web. Clear and informative text accompanies most of the works in the museum's extensive collection. The text provides artists' biographies, descriptions of their techniques, and discussions of the works' subjects. (A recent addition, excerpts from performances of Baroque music, ranges beyond the scope of the visual arts.) You won't spend much time at WebLouvre before you conclude that this document was created by a person who is very much in love with art and wants the world to know why.

Developed and maintained by Nicolas Pioch, a Paris-based computer science instructor and computer consultant, WebLouvre includes an elaborate virtual tour of Paris, the museum has an especially strong collection of Impressionist art, though it has some Baroque, Restoration, and Modern works, as well. Artists' works are spread among several Web documents according to their place in the chronology of their creators' lives.

Take the WebLouvre's tour of Paris! Visitors can "wander" the city by themselves and look at pictures of the city, or follow a "guided tour" and see the same pictures with historical commentary attached. If you can't make it to Paris, this is the next best thing.

EXCELLENT

HOT TIP
Don't overburden slow trans-Atlantic backbone circuits: Access the WebLouvre's new mirror document, at HTTP://sunsite.unc.edu/louvre/. It's an up-to-date reflection of exactly what you'd find at the real thing in Paris.

When you arrive at the WebLouvre's welcome document, you see a brief introduction to the document and you're standing in front of the famous "Pyramid" at the Louvre's entrance. You're assigned a numbered pass, which tells you how many people have accessed the document so far.

Ostensibly, the WebLouvre is organized like a real museum, with virtual "rooms" for each exhibition, but the metaphor isn't carried very far. *Don't expect a clickable map!* When you scroll down, you'll see a list of hyperlinks that take you to the museum's fare (Figure 19.6), including the Famous Paintings exhibition, a medieval art exhibit, and a glossary of art terminology. All the graphics in WebLouvre download in compact JPEG files, a testament to Pioch's understanding of users of the Web.

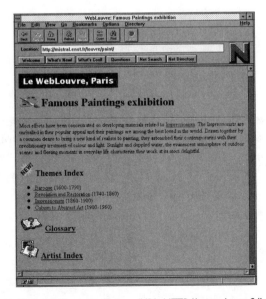

Figure 19.6 WebLouvre offerings (URL: HTTP://mistral.enst.fr/louvre/)

A very nice feature of WebLouvre is the Glossary of Painting styles, virtually an art history education in itself. Covered are the major periods of art history (Baroque, Classicism, Cubism, etc.), with brief, readable definitions.

🕷WEBMASTER

If you're planning a multi-document Web collection, take a look at the way Pioch breaks up the material into short, readable documents. Each document presents a manageable chunk of information, just enough to satisfy your curiosity without crushing you with details.

DANCE

Dance does not lend itself to display on the Web, since it is a three-dimensional form of expression. The best way to display such material on the Web is in video clips, which are unusable by many Web browsers because so much computer horsepower is required to run them properly. For these reasons, there are not nearly as many dance documents as there are visual arts documents, and those that exist are primarily places for dance fans to trade information.

★ **Frankfurt's Tango Home Page**

> **URL**:http://www.unifrankfurt.de/-garrit/english/tango/engl/tango/engl.html
> **Topic**:The Argentine Tango
> **Of Special Note**:A Tango discography on compact disks

Sporting good links to Tango pages elsewhere, and offering a couple of Tango discographies, this site is of interest to Tango aficionados despite its focus on the Tango scene in Germany (principally Frankfurt and Stuttgart). Not one of the best-developed sites on the Web, it's still of interest to those for whom Tango holds a special appeal.

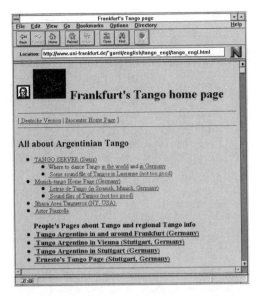

Figure 19.7 *Tango welcome document*
(URL: http://litsun35.epfl.ch:8001/~shawn/NOT-RESEARCH/Tango//index.html)

★★ Western Square Dance

URL: http://suif.stanford.edu/~rfrench/wsd/wsd.html

Topic: square dance and its fans

Of Special Note: An excellent example of a small community growing with the Web's aid.

The Western Square Dance document (Figure 19.8) is a good one, if you're into square dance. The document doesn't do a very good job of introducing novices to the dance, but it seems like an excellent resource for those with a background in the subject. The document provides links to lists of calls and square dance sound effects (but not in audio files), as well as links to the documents of smaller square-dance clubs. This document is another excellent example of a small community flourishing with the help of the Web.

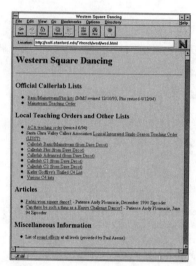

Figure 19.8 *Western Square Dance welcome document*
(URL:http://suif.stanford.edu/~rfrench/wsd/wsd.html)

MUSIC

A decent-sized graphics file and a audio file that contains a four- or five-minute song are about the same size, so both media have the potential to flourish on the Web. Sound files require special equipment, though, and so documents specializing in them are not as numerous as visual-arts documents. Many of the Web's music documents are collections of textual information *about* music—tour schedules, biographies, and so forth.

However, the documents that do handle sound clips are spectacular. If your computer has a sound board and a lot of free RAM and hard-drive space, your collection of CD-quality music can massively increase in size. Surf the Web in search of folk music, underground rock bands, and snippets from classical works.

★ **The Ceolas Celtic Music Archive**

> **URL:** http://celtic.stanford.edu/ceolas.html
>
> **Topic:** Irish music and culture
>
> **Of Special Note:** Lots of information about Irish music, and a link to an on-line Irish-interst newspaper.

Its title combines the Gaelic words for music (ceol) and information (eolas) to aptly describe the function of this Web document. Ceolas is a clearinghouse for all sorts of data about Irish music.

The Ceolas document is a good source if you're interested in Ireland or Irish Americans. Like the dance documents, Ceolas primarily is a collection of hyperlinks that point to tour schedules and artists' discographies, but it has a few embedded Irish tunes and a link to the *Irish American Times*, a Milwaukee-based newspaper that recently started publishing a Web edition.

The Ceolas home document (Figure 19.9) is loaded with links—many of them to remote documents. Be sure to check out the Internet Sources List hyperlink under the Resources header, which leads to a Web document that will take you to a variety of Irish-interest resources on-line.

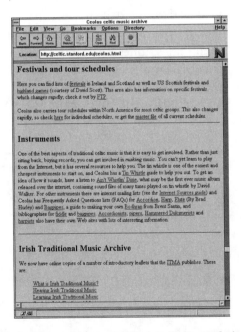

Figure 19.9 *Ceolas welcome document (URL: http://celtic.stanford.edu/ceolas.html)*

There's a long list of Irish groups and performers, but most of their hyperlinks lead to text files. It's good information, but doesn't take full advantage of the possibilities of the Web. There is also a link to the Digital Tradition, an archive of folk songs on line (see below).

As a newcomer to Irish music, I'd like to see some sound clips available with each of the bands and performers listed. Clips would foster interest in Irish music, and enable fans to preview artists' work before they went out to buy recordings.

WISH LIST

★★ Digital Tradition

> **URL:** http://web2.xerox.com/digitrad
>
> **Topic:** Folk music archive
>
> **Of Special Note:** A huge collection of folk music and a good search engine.

There's not much to this document except a lot of music and a search engine. If you're interested in folk music, both old and new, this is your document. There are hundreds of sound clips here, all of them free for the downloading and accompanied by music, lyrics, and some descriptive text.

At the welcome document, type a keyword in the box at the top of the document, or look at a list of song titles, tunes (the same tune often has more than one title) or keywords. A keyword search yields a hyperlinked list of songs in which your word appears (Figure 19.10). If you click the song you want to examine, Digital Tradition presents the lyrics with options to view the lyrics and play a sound clip. (Clips are available for most, but not all, listed songs).

Figure 19.10 Digital Tradition search results

Digital Tradition's search engine is a lot of fun. Put in a key word, and it search-es all song titles, plus all the lyrics, and gives a report of its hits in context. A search for "buss" yielded both "The Budling Song," in which the word had the meaning I had in mind—kiss. But it also turned up the line, "And it's cheer up, my lads, let your hearts never fuss / When you're integrating systems for the S-100 buss," from the song "S-100 Buss." They say those old Altairs were fun, but I had no idea.

EXCELLENT

★★★★ Internet Underground Music Archive

> **URL:** http://www.iuma.com/
>
> **Topic:** Garage-band music archive
>
> **Of Special Note:** Loads of garage-band music and a (mostly) slick user interface.

Looking for the latest from Asbestos Removal Crew or the Rubber Nipple Salesmen? How about the Barking Spiders? Then the Internet Underground Music Archive is your document. IUMA is to music what OTIS is to the visual arts—a venue for mostly unknown artists to get exposure.

Begin your tour of IUMA at the site selection document, where you choose from the three servers handling the archive. Though the three documents are not exactly the same—West coast concerts are not advertised on the European server—the archives are the same at all the sites, and you should be able to find any band or song on any server. Just cruising around any of the documents, sampling music is fun, though, and IUMA's excellent user interface makes it even more enjoyable.

IUMA's wecome document, regardless of which site you use, has seven graphi-cal buttons near the bottom which look like red labeling tape. Choose the button for artist, title, label, location or genre, or take a look at the "Fresh Catches" catego-ry, which contains the 15 newest bands in IUMA. There is also a very complete search engine that allows you to tailor a search any way you want.

It's not immediately obvious, but the string of letters at the top of each catalog document (Figure 19.11) are clickable—and each of the letters is linked to a particu-lar section of the catalog. For example, click on the "C" bead to see bands, artists, or labels that begin with that letter.

The lists of songs are IUMA's real attraction. Icons for sound files accompany each song listed, and you have a choice of playing a high-fidelity (but huge) MIDI-2 file, or a small but lower-quality Quicktime file. A lot of this music is so distorted that you won't miss much by choosing the smaller file.

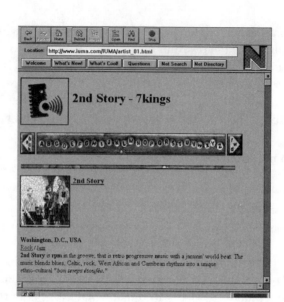

Figure 19.11 *IUMA catalog document (URL: http://www.iuma.com/IUMA/artist_01.html)*

Random surfing of IUMA brought me to the listing for Pterodactyl Presley, a "College/Indie/lo-fi/Rock" band from London. The description says that" This is an All-Action, Hard-Hitting, Hot Pumping, Supercharged Rock 'n' Roll Love Machine that includes recipes."

AWFUL

IUMA means well with its "Return to the Welcome Page" icon that appears at the top of every document, and generally such icons are a good idea. The icon in IUMA, however, returns you to the site selection document, leaving you to re-contact the server closest to you! The icons should be reconfigured to return you to the welcome screen of your current site.

WISH LIST

It would be nice if IUMA took a hint from OTIS and included a venue for commentary and discussion of bands in the archive. Such a forum would help the artists keep in close contact with their fans. Also, it would be interesting to see a Synergy-like project on IUMA, in which various musicians could overdub one another in collaboration on a song.

★★ Music Resources on the Internet

> **URL:** http://www.music.indiana.edu/misc/music_resources.html
>
> **Topic:** Links to music resources
>
> **Of Special Note:** A huge list of hyperlinks to on-line music resources.

This document (Figure 19.12) isn't much in its own right, but it contains links to every conceivable on-line music resource on the Web. Interested in the accordion? There's a link for you on this document. You say Croatian or fractal music is more your speed? Look here for links to match your interest.

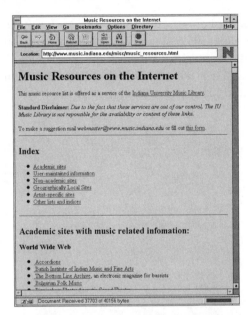

Figure 19.12 *Music Resources on the Internet document*
(URL: http://www.music.indiana.edu/misc/music_resources.html)

The document is not especially well-organized. You'd be best served to use your browser's text-search feature to find your subject, but the list is not so long as to prohibit you from scrolling through the list in search of things that strike your fancy. The Indiana University music library staff, which maintains this document, has included a form for you to suggest resources you think should be included.

THEATER

Most of the theater documents on the Web are home documents for performance troupes or university drama departments. Other documents are merely lists of information about performances, but some of those documents are much more interesting than others.

★ **On Broadway**

URL: http://www.cs.cmu.edu:8001/afs/psc.edu/usr/geigel/www/Theatre/on_bway.html

Topic: New York theater

Of Special Note: A real public service providing current New York theater information.

If you're into Broadway shows, you'll love this site. Joe Geigel, the maintainer of this document, provides a Web's-eye view of Broadway action, and updates it weekly. On Broadway (Figure 19.13) includes a hyperlinked list of shows playing in New York theaters. Click the name of the show you're interested in, and see showtimes, theaters, and ticket prices for that show.

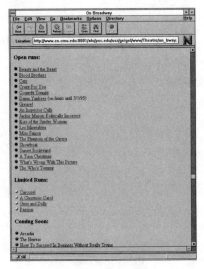

Figure 19.13 *On Broadway welcome document*
(URL: http://www.cs.cmu.edu:8001/afs/psc.edu/usr/geigel/www/Theatre/on_bway.html)

The welcome document also contains an Off-Broadway link, which leads to a document with links to the same information for off-Broadway shows, as well as a link to a list of other theater-related Web documents.

★★★★ **Shakespeare Homepage**

URL: http://the-tech.mit.edu/Shakespeare/works.html

Topic: The Bard's plays

Of Special Note: *Full text of all* of Shakespeare's plays, plus an excellent glossary of Victorian English!

The Shakespeare Homepage earned its four-star rating through intelligent use of hypertext to clarify a potentially difficult subject. What student of Shakespeare hasn't wished for a hypertext version of his plays? Such a version would enable them to verify the meaning of an archaic word or phrase without jumping to the margin or footnote and having to re-locate their place on the page. This MIT product is just such a product, and it is a valuable resource for anyone studying Shakespeare.

The welcome document includes a list of all of Shakespeare's plays as hyperlinks. Click one of the plays, and you see the list of characters in that play, followed by a list scenes, each hyperlinked to the full text of that scene. A link to the next scene appears at the bottom of each scene's text.

The real beauty of this edition of Shakespeare's plays is the hyperlinks to the glossary (Figure 19.14). What do the stage directions in Antony and Cleopatra mean when they say, "A sennet sounded"? A look at the glossary link under "sennet" reveals the answer: a flourish of trumpets.

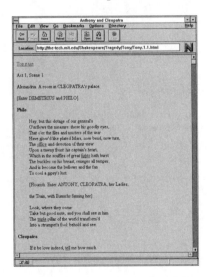

Figure 19.14 Hyperlinks in the text of Macbeth at Shakespeare Homepage
(URL: http://the-tech.mit.edu/Shakespeare/Tragedy/Macbeth/Macbeth.1.5.html)

🕷WEBMASTER

Take a look at how these plays are broken into parts to make reading and looking up passages more manageable. This wouldn't be nearly as easy with a big text file.

★★ **Theatre Central**

> **URL:** http://www.mit.edu:8001/people/quijote/WWW/theatre-central.html
>
> **Topic:** A list of theater resources.
>
> **Of Special Note:** The most complete collection of theater information I've found.

The Theatre Central document (Figure 19.15) belongs on every theater lover's hotlist. It's a well thought-out and apparently complete listing of hyperlinks to theater resources on line. Andrew Kraft, the maintainer of the document, has organized the resources by category: general, academic, theater companies, etc.

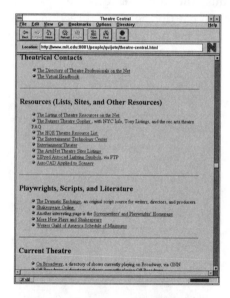

Figure 19.15 *Theatre Central document*
(URL: http://www.mit.edu:8001/people/quijote/WWW/theatre-central.html)

This document isn't outstanding by itself, but the collection of documents to which it leads is. This, after all, is the entire point of the Web.

FILM AND TELEVISION

Movie and TV fans keep the Web humming with information about their favorite stars and shows. The coverage is spotty—science fiction is well represented, but drama is not—but enthusiastic, even to the point of including sound clips and graphics for which, doubtless, no permission was secured. If you're a fan of a popular show, you'll love these Web offerings.

★★ Film and Video

URL: http://galaxy.einet.net/galaxy/Leisure-and-Recreation/Film-and-Video.html

Topic: Links to movie and video documents

Of Special Note: An elaborate list of links to on-line resources for movie fans.

This is another one of those documents we might call a "metadocument"—a document with information about other documents. If you're a film buff, you could spend hours accumulating URLs of the sites listed here and including them in your hotlist or home page. Instead, you can rely on this document (Figure 19.16) to provide you with links to the best movie and video resources on the Web (as well as in Gopher, FTP, WAIS and Telnet).

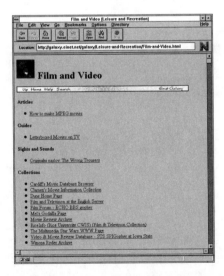

Figure 19.16 *Film and Video welcome document*
(URL: http://galaxy.einet.net/galaxy/Leisure-and-Recreation/Film-and-Video.html)

The Dune Home Page is here, as are the Winona Ryder archive and Mel's Godzilla Page. The document includes references to review databases and fan mailing lists. Take a look if you have any interest in movies, actors, or the Hollywood community.

★★★★ The Lurker's Guide to Babylon 5

URL: http://www.hyperion.com/lurk/lurker.html

Topic: Babylon 5, the popular science-fiction TV show

Of Special Note: A very comprehensive and well-organized collection of information.

Regardless of whether you're interested in *Babylon 5*, you need to take a look at this collection of documents. It's an the excellent example of the Web's ability to present information in a fun, useful way. Every bit of minutiae about the show, including, plot summaries, actor biographies, special-effects information, and development history has been accumulated and organized in such a way that it's interesting to even the rankest *Babylon 5* newbie.

The welcome document contains four important locations: a document describing the show's premise and background, a document about the people who make *Babylon 5*, a collection of episode summaries, and a page of hyperlinks leading to other Internet resources for fans. Click on the "Babylon 5 Universe and List of Characters" to see some examples of how well-organized these documents are.

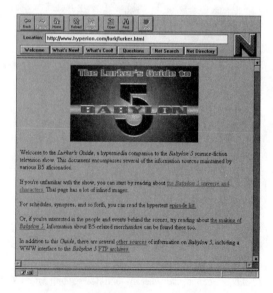

Figure 19.17 *Babylon 5 Universe and Characters document*
(URL: http://www.hyperion.com/lurk/lurker.html)

The universe and characters document (Figure 19.17) is a history of events that led to the scene in which *Babylon 5* is set—but it refers to things newcomers might not understand. Not familiar with the Earth-Minbari War? A hyperlink on those words leads to a full description of the war and its consequences.

🕷WEBMASTER

Note how well the documents in the *Babylon 5* collection are linked together. If a character's personality was developed significantly in a particular episode, there is a link in that character's biography to the summary of that episode. Dozens of links lead to comments from the show's writer. In short, the *Babylon 5* documents take full advantage of the hypertext medium, instead of just being a collection of nicely-formatted text documents.

★★ Star Trek: The Next Generation

URL: http://www.ee.surrey.ac.uk:80/Personal/STTNG/ (Watch those capitals!)

Topic: The second *Star Trek* television series

Of Special Note: Good background and character information for this popular TV show.

Though it suffers in comparison to the *Babylon 5* documents, the ST:TNG site is a good on-line source for information about the ongoing adventures of the Enterprise and her crew.

You arrive at the site's welcome document (Figure 19.18), and have a choice of hyperlinks. There are only four documents already located at this site, the hyperlinks on the welcome document are "relative links" that go to specific sections of the other documents. I found it useful to check out the Setting link first, then go to some of the episode summaries. By the way—the summaries are pretty basic— often no more than two sentences.

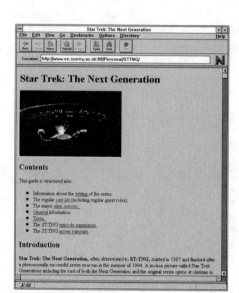

Figure 19.18 Star Trek: The Next Generation welcome document
(URL: http://www.ee.surrey.ac.uk:80/Personal/STTNG/)

**WISH
LIST**

Where are the graphics? Don't just tell us about the Klingons—show us one! A set of documents devoted to a show with images like those of ST:TNG should include a few of them on-line. Surely Paramount would grant a few permissions...

★★★ TV Net

> **URL:** http://tvnet.com/TVnet.html (Remember, capitalization matters)
>
> **Topic:** Television networks and stations
>
> **Of Special Note:** The Virtual Agent, a means by which TV professionals can display their resumés on-line.

TV Net is already a good resource for television fans, and it stands to get even better as more networks, stations, and shows establish their presence on-line. This document has a lot of information about contacting networks and stations by telephone and snail mail.

From the welcome document, you access other documents via a clickable graphic called an imagemap. Though this is a single in-line graphic (Figure 19.19), different parts of it are tied to different hyperlinks. The Networks button and the

Local TV button take you to entirely different documents, even though they are both parts of the same graphic.

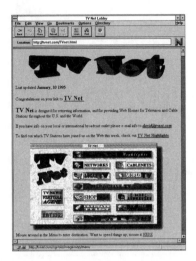

Figure 19.19 *TV Net navigation graphic*

The links to the major broadcast networks and most cable networks are pretty useless, in most cases providing only phone numbers and snail mail addresses. But be sure to take a look at the PBS listings. It seems that a lot of TV stations have opened some very sharp Web documents, probably because of their affiliation with universities. Two such stations, KQED-TV and KUSM-TV, have done such good jobs with their documents, I gave them their own listings below.

Also be sure to check out the Virtual Agent, an advertising forum for those who want jobs in TV. The facility isn't heavily used—there was only one resume on-line when I looked—but the idea is interesting.

★★★ The Ultimate TV List

URL: http://www.tvnet.com/UTVL/utvl.html

Topic: Television show information

Of Special Note: A list of resources for fans of a long list of television shows.

The Ultimate TV List is a collection of hyperlinks, but it's comprehensive and well-organized. The UTVL welcome document (Figure 19.20), confronts you with a series of hyperlinks. Choose "The List" first, and use your browser's text-search feature to look for the name of your favorite show, past or present.

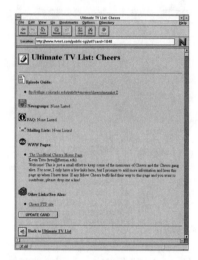

Figure 19.20 *Ultimate TV List welcome document (URL: http://www.tvnet.com/UTVL/utvl.html)*

A list of resources related to your show appear below the show's name including Web documents mailing lists, FTP sites, and whatever else is available. Everything but mailing lists are hyperlinked for easy access. Click the question mark icon to the left of the show's name to see another list of the same resources, plus a link to a form that allows you to add unlisted resources.

A hunt for my favorite show, *Cheers*, turned up an episode guide, a Web document, and an FTP site that contains such things like the show's theme song in an audio file and Norm-isms in text format. Though not all shows listed have resources—*The Simpsons* and *Star Trek* are two of the most heavily resourced shows—The Ultimate TV List is a great document for any fan of the small screen.

★★★ KQED-TV, San Francisco, California

URL: http://www.kqed.org/

Topic: KQED news, features and programming

Of Special Note: The full transcript of some good interviews and features, and well a laid-out programming guide.

Not only has this San Francisco public television station put its programming on-line, but it has put its *programs* on-line as well! Transcripts of documentaries and interviews populate the station's collection of documents. These documents are long enough to be interesting, but brief enough to be comfortably read on-screen.

To get to the on-line features, choose "San Francisco Focus" from the welcome document (Figure 19.21). You'll see two categories—Interviews and Features—and a number of hyperlinks under each. There were only two interviews and three features posed when I stopped by, but I found the Ken Burns interview and the "Swords in to Plowshares" feature about the Mare Island Naval Shipyard superb. You can almost imagine the way the scripts appeared on TV, with voice-overs interspersed with live quotes.

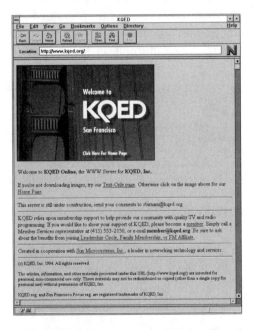

Figure 19.21 KQED welcome document (URL: http://www.kqed.org/)

The only thing missing from this television station's collection of documents is sound and video, things I think KQED will have no problem adding. Even if it were just sound effects that characterize a story's mood, sound clips would add a lot. It would be great if all quotations were available in recorded form as well.

WISH
LIST

★★ KUSM-TV, Bozeman, Montana

> **URL:** http://www.kusm.montana.edu/
>
> **Topic:** The goings-on at KUSM-TV
>
> **Of Special Note:** A very nice graphical programming calendar and consistent use of graphical design elements.

Since when is Montana on the leading edge of computerized information exchange? KUSM has done a superb job of presenting its programming on the Web. Like they say, in the global village, Bozeman, Montana and Manhattan are right next door.

The KUSM welcome document allows you to choose the Internet Program Guide hyperlink. Scroll down a bit to see the calendar for the current month—a composite of little in-line images, one for each day (Figure 19.22). Click on the day you're interested in to see the programming schedule.

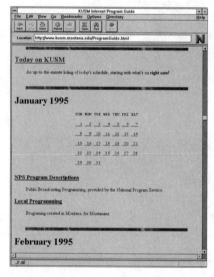

Figure 19.22 KUSM programming calendar (URL: http://www.kusm.montana.edu/ProgramGuide.html)

Granted, you're probably not interested in what was on TV in Bozeman last Wednesday, but I've included this site because it demonstrates how a graphical interface can make things more appealing.

CHAPTER 20

The Environment

We abuse land because we regard it as a commodity belonging to us. When we see land as a community
to which we belong, we may begin to use it with love and respect.
—Aldo Leopold

Contributors to the Web include many people working to protect and better understand the natural environment in which we live. Environmental Web resources range from reports of hard scientific research into the ways humankind and the rest of the Earth community interrelate, to displays of nature-related photographs and essays. An elementary school student and a graduate-level researcher will find themselves equally satisfied by the resources on the Web.

This chapter is organized in terms of the types of organizations that run the Web document collections described. Various government entities, especially some divisions of the U.S. Department of the Interior, have put together some nice places to visit, as have colleges and universities. The collections run by private individuals and by non-profit organizations are often not as slick as the government or academic documents, but they are useful nonetheless. Give all of these sites a try.

HOME
PAGE

You will notice that the division of the environmental resources is not perfect—academic sites often do research for federal agencies, and university students often run non-profit environmental action groups. It is appropriate that this blurring of distinctions takes place, as the environment is universal to everyone and doesn't divide itself neatly across various areas of responsibility.

ACADEMIC RESOURCES

Web sites maintained by university students and faculty are prime sources for hard scientific data about environmental engineering and ecology research. These sites—with a couple of exceptions—aren't a lot of fun, but they are informative and usually readable. In most cases, document writers have written their reports on the level of *Popular Science*. If you have some understanding of scientific and engineering principles, you can probably find some value in the academic documents.

Many of these documents also include links to pages full of references to other useful Web resources. Find your favorite ready-made hotlist, put its URL on your home page, and have an easier time finding the environmental Web documents you need.

★★★ Information Center for the Environment—U.C. Davis

URL: http://ice.ucdavis.edu/

Topic: A combination of friendly, general information about the environment and hard scientific data

Of Special Note: Links to the Long Term Environmental Research project and a collection of documents about early environmentalist John Muir.

The Information Center for the Environment gets no points for originality of design—the welcome page (Figure 20.1) is little more than a little text and a group of hyperlinks. It's the documents those hyperlinks lead to that make ICE appealing. Some of them take you to pages designed for elementary school students and their teachers, while others lead to the welcome pages of large-scale scientific consortia such as the Long Term Environmental Research Project of the National Science Foundation.

The basic links are interesting to everybody, not just the students for whom they are designed. Don't miss the John Muir exhibit (Figure 20.2), which includes biographical information about this famed environmentalist icon, excerpts from his writings, and statements about him by his friends. The exhibit also includes a page of suggestions about how to celebrate John Muir Day—a holiday in California.

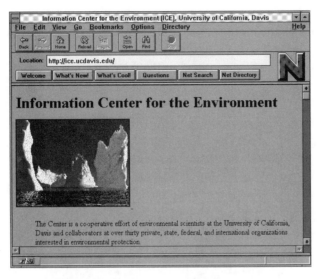

Figure 20.1 *ICE welcome page (http://ice.ucdavis.edu/)*

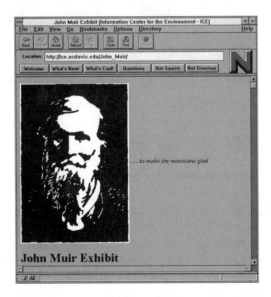

Figure 20.2 *John Muir Exhibit welcome page (http://ice.ucdavis.edu/John_Muir/)*

More technical but equally impressive is the Long Term Environmental Research project welcome page (Figure 20.3). This page contains information, including graphics, about a huge effort to study world environmental conditions, and features links to dozens of computers affiliated with the project in North America and Antarctica.

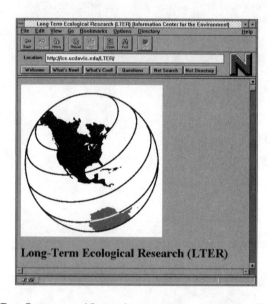

Figure 20.3 *Long-Term Environmental Research project welcome page (http://ice.ucdavis.edu/LTER/)*

★★ MIT EAPS Home Page

URL: http://www-erl.mit.edu/eaps/homepage.html

Topic: Academic research into environmental topics

Of Special Note: Some nice examples of applying various technology to earth science and environmental research.

MIT has been known for the clear and intuitive user interfaces on its computing resources for years, and this Web site upholds the tradition. The welcome page (Figure 20.4) is a listing of the various laboratories and research groups affiliated with the Department of Earth, Atmospheric and Planetary Sciences, complete with hyperlinks to each. The subsidiary pages list links to resources and descriptions of research projects, making MIT EAPS a real treasure if you're researching issues in environmental science or are just interested in reading about current research.

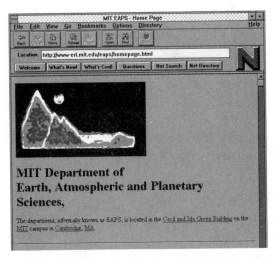

Figure 20.4 *MIT EAPS welcome page (http://www-erl.mit.edu/eaps/homepage.html)*

Take a look at the Earth Resources Laboratory link. On this page (Figure 20.5), you'll find descriptions of graduate and undergraduate research ("UROP" stands for Undergraduate Research Opportunities Program), and links to demonstrations of some exciting projects. Click the GPS Research link to see what's being done with Global Positioning System satellites.

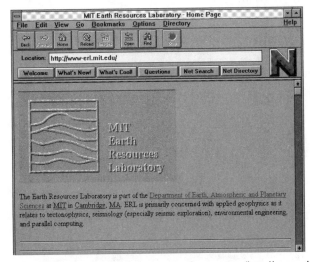

Figure 20.5 *MIT Earth Resources Laboratory welcome page (http://www-erl.mit.edu/)*

AWFUL

The maps in the GPS exhibit are in PostScript format, which is fine for downloading and printing but a real hassle for on-screen viewing. The maps should be available in JPEG format.

★★★ UCLA Center for Clean Technology Home Page

URL: http://cct.seas.ucla.edu/

Topic: Environmentally responsible engineering

Of Special Note: Readable write-ups of research into making modern society more compatible with the environment.

It's not light reading, to be sure, but the UCLA Center for Clean Technology documents clearly present information about ways to make traditionally messy processes—garbage disposal, for instance—more Earth-friendly. A few more graphics would make the collection of documents more visually appealing and even easier to understand, but the exhibit is apparently still under construction so such features may be available soon.

Dropping into the CCT welcome page (Figure 20.6), you see a little blurb about the Center's mission and history, and can choose from six subject headers describing various project categories, including Pollution Prevention, Combustion and Air Toxics, and Water and Wastewater Treatment. For example, the Combustion page, shown in Figure 20.7, deals with the problems of making fossil fuel engines run more cleanly.

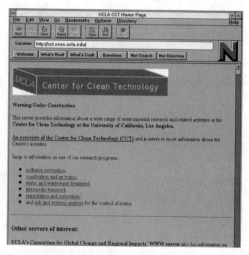

Figure 20.6 *Center for Clean Technology welcome page (http://cct.seas.ucla.edu/)*

Be sure to follow the hyperlink labeled "an Overview of the Center for Clean Technology." There's a link on the Overview page to an article about "Bugs that Eat Bombs," an interesting paper about disposing of explosives with bacteria.

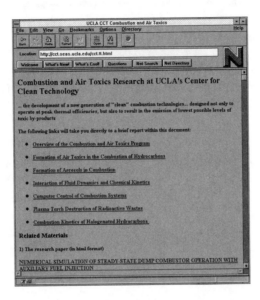

Figure 20.7 *Center for Clean Technology combustion and air toxins document (http://cct.seas.ucla.edu/cct.tt.html)*

ENVIRONMENTAL ACTION GROUPS

Different groups have varying plans for helping the environment's cause, but most of them include some sort of educational plank in their mission statements. They try to educate as many people as possible about the importance of the natural environment and raise awareness of the harm that can be done by careless people. Previously, environmental groups had to rely on making presentations in schools and publishing small magazine on-line. The Web makes such education efforts easier and cheaper by allowing groups to post their information on-line and making it easily accessible to those interested.

Environmental Web sites may, for the present, be preaching to the choir. Many Web users already favor protecting endangered species and reforming the way the federal government deals with environmental issues.

★★ EcoNet

URL: http://www.igc.apc.org/igc/www.eco.html

Topic: Environmental information, particularly environmental legislation and regulation.

Of Special Note: The Environmental Scorecard, a reasonably up-to-date record of how Senators and Representatives voted on environmental bills.

Part of the Progressive Directory, a site devoted to liberal thought on a variety of issues, EcoNet is a good place to look for information about what the United States government is doing regarding the environment. It's also another collection of links to other sites devoted to discussion of environmental issues.

The EcoNet welcome page (Figure 20.8) is a list of hyperlinks to other resources. Choose **General Environment** to get to a list of general resources, most of them away from the EcoNet site. Click **Environmental Scorecard** (Figure 20.9) to see a collection of information on how Senators and Representative voted on environmental legislation. The voting information is not presented in a mere list— first you must click the region of the country you're interested in. This clever way of organizing information is both visually appealing and prevents you from being overwhelmed by unneeded information.

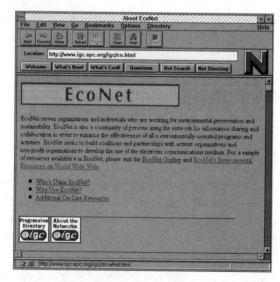

Figure 20.8 EcoNet Welcome Page (http://www.igc.apc.org/igc/en.html)

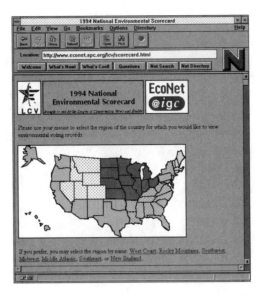

Figure 20.9 *EcoNet Environmental Scorecard welcome page (http://www.econet.apc.org/lcv/scorecard.html)*

★★★ EnviroWeb

URL: http://envirolink.org/

Topic: Environmental information clearinghouse

Of Special Note: The EnviroProducts directory is an on-line collection of "green" goods and services for sale.

While EnviroWeb isn't for you if you're interested in the scientific aspects of the environment, it's a great resource if you're looking to gain a layman's understanding of environmental issues and get a hint of the potential of on-line marketing of environmentally friendly products. Maintained mostly by college students, EnviroWeb is part of the EnviroLink network, a grass-roots effort to put environmental information on the Internet.

To see how EnviroWeb is promoting environmentally sound products and services on the Web, jump from the welcome page (Figure 20.10) to the EnviroProducts directory (Figure 20.11). The document displays company names along with their logos, which are hyperlinked to product descriptions and ordering instructions.

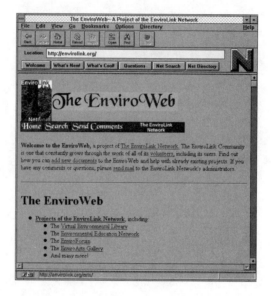

Figure 20.10 *EnviroWeb welcome page (http://envirolink.org/)*

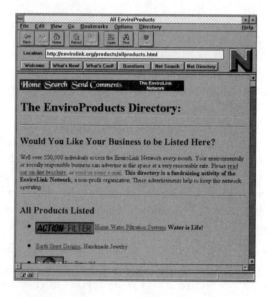

Figure 20.11 *EnviroWeb EnviroProducts Directory (http://envirolink.org/products/allproducts.html)*

Also check out the Virtual Library (Figure 20.12) link from the welcome page. It's more of a reference tool than a library, since it mostly contains links to other sites and brief statements about the environment, but it's useful nonetheless.

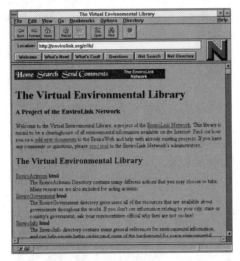

Figure 20.12 EnviroWeb Virtual Library (http://envirolink.org/elib/)

Take a look at the campus activism page. There is a form for visitors to fill out, theoretically to foster debate about environmental issues. There were no discussion items posted when I visited, but the potential for lively debate, as in a Usenet newsgroup, exists.

★★ Save the Manatee Club

> **URL:** http://www.satelnet.org/manatee/
> **Topic:** Florida's endangered manatees
> **Of Special Note:** Adopt a manatee!

Now here's something new. Did know you can adopt a manatee (a warm-water mammal that's in danger of becoming extinct) by means of your Web browser? The Save the Manatee Club lets you computer just that!

Before you rush off to equip your machine with more disk space to accomodate your massive new pet, realize that the Adopt a Manatee program is a fund-raising effort by the Save the Manatee club. You donate money to the club; they assign you a manatee.

The Save the Manatee Club welcome page appears in Figure 20.13. From this page, you can follow a hyperlink to the Adopt-A-Manatee document, or to documents that contain more information about the animal Florida chose to emblazon on its license plates.

Figure 20.13 *Save the Manatee Club welcome page (http://www.satelnet.org/manatee/)*

★★★ Solstice: Sustainable Energy and Development Online

URL: http://solstice.crest.org/

Topic: Alternative energy sources and conservation of energy.

Of Special Note: A really nice search engine with an alternative interface that doesn't require a forms-capable browser!

To maintain our current standard of living, we need to find alternatives to burning fossil fuels. We need to develop sustainable energy like solar or geothermal power, and Solstice exists to distribute information about such resources.

The Center for Renewable Energy and Sustainable Technology does a lot toward the goal of decreasing our dependence on fossil fuels with its Solstice Web site. Just as electronics hobbyists in the first half of the twentieth century relied upon amateur radio magazines to spread information about the latest technology, those interested in solar power, wind power, biomass energy, and geothermal steam have a forum on the Web.

One of the nicest things about the Solstice welcome page is its snazzy graphical navigation icons, some of which appear in Figure 20.14. The site is well-organized, the welcome page asks you to choose your area of interest from several options so you are not bogged down by too many choices.

Figure 20.14 *Solstice welcome page (http://solstice.crest.org/)*

The Environment page (Figure 20.15) is an example of the subject-specific pages available from the welcome page. Like ERIN's pages, these documents ask you to choose from among several sub-categories. On the Environment page, options include such things as Forests and Biodiversity (Figure 20.16) and Ozone Depletion. These links lead to pages containing lists of articles and other on-line resources.

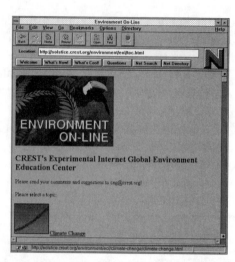

Figure 20.15 *Solstice environment page (http://solstice.crest.org/environment/eol/toc.html)*

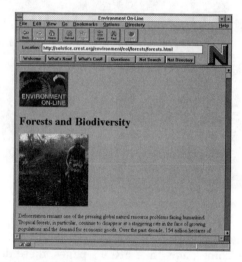

Figure 20.16 *Solstice forests and biodiversity document*
(http://solstice.crest.org/environment/eol/forests/forests.html)

There's also a nice search engine to use if you know what you need and don't want to browse around for it. Click "full-text search" in the paragraph of text above the navigation icons, and enter your search terms in the box. It even accepts Boolean operators, which are explained on the search page.

🕷WEBMASTER

There's a hyperlink to a "Simple Search" page on the search form for those using browsers that can't handle forms. Though most new browsers are forms-capable, it's courteous to accomodate those whose browsers can't display fancy boxes.

GOVERNMENT RESOURCES

You can't beat these government sites in terms of the sheer volume of information they provide. Nearly every U.S. government office, and an increasing number of such offices abroad, has a collection of Web documents, and most have hyperlinks to Gopher and WAIS resources. The very best government documents have good graphics and full-text articles in HTML format, while the worst (the ones not included here) have little more than a picture of their boss and some all-but-useless data about the department's function.

Also, many of the government Web sites include search forms that enable you to search their collections of data for a key word. These forms require a forms-capable browser, such as Netscape or NCSA Mosaic version 2.0.

★★★★ Australian Environmental Resources Information Network

URL: http://kaos.erin.gov.au/erin.html

Topic: The environment in Australia and world-wide.

Of Special Note: One of the best laid-out environment sites. Hyperlinks contribute a lot to the documents' organization, instead seeming like afterthoughts.

While the United States government has a lot of mostly independent Web sites dealing with the environment, Australia has organized its on-line environmental research materials into one coherent group. Enter through the main Environmental Resources Information Network (ERIN) welcome page, and explore the Australian government's offerings.

On the welcome page (Figure 20.17), check out the five stacked (and hyperlinked) pictures that together depict the entire natural environment (Figure 20.18). Organizing the main "branches" of the site's Web "tree" this way is helpful, since it breaks up resources by functional area, but shows that individual aspects of the environment are integral to the whole.

EXCELLENT

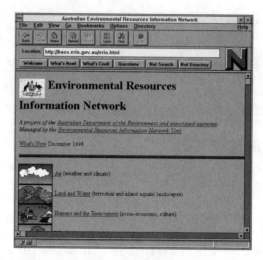

Figure 20.17 *Australian Environmental Resources Information Network welcome page (http://kaos.erin.gov.au/erin.html)*

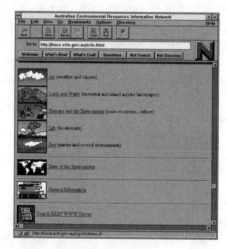

Figure 20.18 *ERIN's offerings (http://kaos.erin.gov.au/erin.html)*

ERIN's maintainers organize their resources around parts of the natural environment, such as air and water. For example, click the hyperlinked "Air" picture to see a page containing hyperlinks to weather resources, climate resources, and pages of links to other meteorological and climatological sites around the world (Figure 20.19). The weather and climate information pages are really tables of contents—lists of hyperlinked topic headings for such things as the Greenhouse Effect. These topic links lead to lists of articles, which are mostly clear and informative (and presented in Web format, not as clunky text).

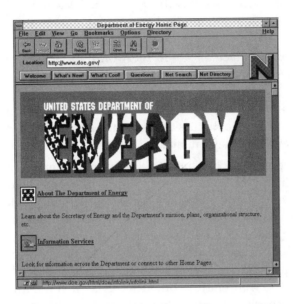

Figure 20.19 ERIN's Air page (http://kaos.erin.gov.au/human_env/human_env.html)

Though you can have a good time wandering around the ERIN site, you'll appreciate its search engine if you're researching a particular topic. Click **Search ERIN WWW Server** on the welcome page and type a key word into the box. ERIN presents a list of resources that deal with that subject—and provides a hyperlink from each list item to the resource itself.

🕷️ WEBMASTER

ERIN earned its four-star rating not so much because of the information it contains (though its information is great) as for its way of organizing that information. The welcome page presents visitors with a set of clear choices, and usually the visitor must go through a couple of intermediate menus before getting to an article, map or table. This is not as cumbersome as it sounds, as it's much better to have someone pick from a series of short menus than require them to slog through a huge list full of arcane terminology.

★★ Boulder Community Network Environment Center

URL: http://bcn.boulder.co.us/environment/center.html

Topic: Environmental issues of special concern to the citizens of Boulder, Colorado

Of Special Note: An electronic community organized around environmental issues.

This isn't the most spectacular site in the world; in fact, there aren't even any graphics here. Messages everywhere state that the site is under construction, and ask visitors to volunteer their time and ideas. The reason I chose to include the Boulder Community Network was the idea behind it: an on-line forum for residents of a community to discuss enviromental issues on the level at which they are affected, and at which they can make a difference.

The site's welcome page has links to lists of on-line environmental resources, information relating to the Boulder area, and lists of hot local enviromnetal issues. (Actually, all these lists are on the same page, but the links make it easy to jump right to the index you need.) Be sure to take a look at the index of on-line resources, where hyperlinks lead to such things as a list of Boulder-area hazardous-waste generators. Also look at the environmental issues section, where links lead to full-text copies of local legislation of environmental interest. It would be nice if this site had some sort of search engine, but it looks as if it's maintained by a few volunteers who probably have other things to do.

EXCELLENT

Think about the difference a site like this could make in the community. People too busy to attend local government meetings can keep up with issues, and those who already follow local government can get information, such as the full text of bills, that's not available in newspapers. Web sites like this one are the beginnings of the much-touted "electronic town hall."

★★ U.S. Department of Energy

URL: http://www.doe.gov/

Topic: Research and resources of the U.S. Department of Energy.

Of Special Note: A searchable on-line bibliography of declassified DOE documents.

The DOE site has some of the nicest graphics you'll see and a lot of good information, but without a search feature the information is virtually useless.

Though a search page exists, it did not work as of late December, 1994 and until it's running researchers will be better served by their local library.

The exception to this search engine problem is the link to OpenNet, a partial list of declassified DOE reports and other documents that is fully keyword-searchable. Accessible from the DOE welcome page (Figure 20.20), the OpenNet database yields lists of documents that match your query. Though the full text of the documents is not on-line, and you can't order copies via the Web page, OpenNet provides electronic mail addresses and phone numbers for the documents' keepers. Be sure to look at this feature if you think you need DOE publications.

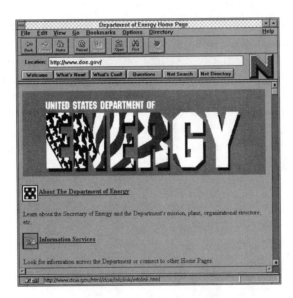

Figure 20.20 U.S. Department of Energy welcome page (http://www.doe.gov/)

If you have an idea which DOE laboratory might have the information you need (there aren't all that many so you should be able to guess), follow the Information Services link from the welcome page. The information page contains links to the Web pages of DOE sites nationwide.

Also take a look at the News and Hot Topics page, which has links to DOE press releases and schedules for demonstrations and lectures. It's nice that the site's maintainers put all the information into HTML format and didn't leave it as plain text.

★★ U.S. Environmental Protection Agency

URL: http://www.epa.gov/

Topic: Research and resources of the U.S. Environmental Protection Agency.

Of Special Note: A nice WAIS interface that lets you search a database of EPA documents.

The EPA site is everything the DOE site is not. This collection of Web pages lacks fancy graphics, and seems haphazardly organized. On the other hand, the EPA site has a very good search engine that lets you quickly find what you want, and in most cases see the full text on your screen.

The EPA welcome page (Figure 20.21) contains one search form, a hyperlink to another, and hyperlinks to several pages that describe the EPA's mission and operations. You will find the text search on the welcome page useful if you're researching EPA documents or activities. Be aware that this engine searches only summaries of EPA documents—it is not a full-text search. Nonetheless, you can call up a list that contains something useful if you use a sufficiently general search term. Search results take the form of hyperlinks, which usually lead to lists of other links that go to each of the various elements of a document. For example, a report might contain a text file and several spreadsheet files for you to download.

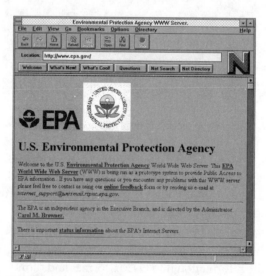

Figure 20.21 *U.S. Environmental Protection Agency welcome page (http://www.epa.gov/)*

Even Access EPA, a document that amounts to a FAQ document about the EPA, is searchable. Access EPA has information about EPA experts in various fields, and is a good place to start your exploration of this large and useful government agency.

🕷WEBMASTER

Note how the search dialog boxes don't make you click the "Submit Query" button after typing your key word—they let you hit the return key. Some search engines require you to use the mouse, which is a bit of a slow-down.

You can reach the Mid-Atlantic Integrated Assessment project (Figure 20.22) from the EPA welcome page for a good idea of the sort of information the EPA has available. The MAIA project deals with the environment of the Mid-Atlantic states, and the EPA has a lot of maps and table on the Web. It's especially interesting to those researching the environment of the Mid-Atlantic states, but MAIA provides everyone with a glimpse of the sort of environmental research material that's out there.

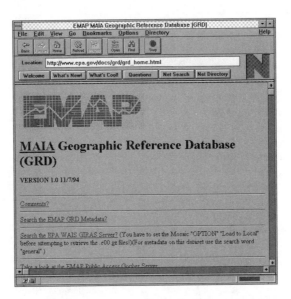

Figure 20.22 U.S. Environmental Protection Agency EMAP facility
(http://www.epa.gov/docs/grd/grd_home.html)

★★★ U.S. Fish and Wildlife Service

URL: http://www.fws.gov/

Topic: The wildlife of the United States, and the government's efforts to manage it.

Of Special Note: Clearly organized descriptions of the problems facing North American animals, plus the full text of some important Congressional legislation.

If its Web site is any indication, the U.S. Fish and Wildlife Service has a clear idea of its function and how to go about performing it. The FWS site doesn't have the scientific information of some of the other sites, but it explains specific environmental problems is layman's terms. Most of this site is basic enough to be understood by elementary school children.

From the welcome page (Figure 20.23), be sure to follow the hyperlink to the Endangered Species page. From there, you can access the full text of the 1973 Endangered Species Act or see a list of animals on the endangered list. Other hyperlinks lead to pages about fish and fishing, the migration of endangered birds, and the National Wildlife Refuge System.

Figure 20.23 *Fish and Wildlife Service welcome page (http://www.fws.gov/)*

Knowing the FWS page would be visited by a lot of Web novices, the site's maintainers have included a "Help!" icon at the bottom of the welcome page.

Though it doesn't provide help for the FWS site specifically, it leads to a page of hyperlinks to a series of Web and Internet primer pages. This is a courtesy other Web sites should offer.

Click the Hot List icon at the bottom of the welcome page, and see a list of the Web's best resources, particularly those of interest to environmental researchers. Designed as a jumping-off point for FWS employees using the Web, the Hot List is a great place to look for sources of information and is one of the features that distinguishes this site from the other government sites.

USEFUL RESOURCE

PRIVATELY MAINTAINED RESOURCES

I suppose this is what the environmental movement, and the Web, ultimately boil down to. These sites are maintained by individuals or small groups of friends to promote their positions on the environment. There are no imposing federal logos, no pleas for money. These documents are just free expression in a very pure form.

They're also useful and entertaining. Where better to learn about growing crops without chemical pesticides than from an organic farmer? And what could be more fun than a magazine put together by a group of people with a common interest and posted to the Web? These documents are models. Some day, many experts will have their own enjoyable, informative home pages.

★★ Bear Essential

> **URL:** http://www.teleport.com/~orlo/
>
> **Topic:** An on-line magazine for environmental debate and reflection.
>
> **Of Special Note:** Some well-written columns.

We all get magazines in the mail. You may even get small, privately published "'zines"—magazines that deal with unknown authors or topics of very narrow interest. The problem with 'zines is that they have no advertising and are usually published by amateurs, which often makes for some sketchy products.

The Web can make virtually any document look good, and publishing on it is free for those with the right connections, that is, anyone affilated with a university. Since university students comprise most of the 'zine scene, it's only natural that they move their publishing efforts to the Web. Bear Essential is an example of such a migration.

A collection of essays about the environment in general and the Pacific Northwest in particular, Bear Essential (Figure 20.24) is the Web version of a paper magazine. It features essays about environmental issues, and could stand to have some more drawings or photographs included with its generally good articles.

It makes sense that environmentalists begin publishing their magazines and other literature on-line. After all, aside from the electricity needed to run computers, Web distribution is an impact-free way to communicate data.

Figure 20.24 *Bear Essential welcome page (http://www.teleport.com/~orlo/)*

★★ Don't Panic; Eat Organic

> **URL:** http://www.rain.org/~sals/my.html
>
> **Topic:** Organic farming
>
> **Of Special Note:** A clever presentation of information and hyperlinks, oddly reminiscent of rebus puzzles.

This page carries carried the simple-is-good doctrines of organic farming into cyberspace. It communicates information effectively, even if it leaves something to be desired in the area of grammar.

Information about pest control and crop cultivation is here, plus some cool-but-irrelevant links to documents that show real-time traffic reports from California freeways. There are also lists of other organic-farming experts and resources. If you're into raising plants with minimal environmental impact, give Don't Panic; Eat Organic a visit.

CHAPTER 21

Government and Politics

> The basis of our government being the opinion of the people, the very first object should be to keep that right; and were it left to me to decide whether we should have a government without newspapers, or newspapers without a government, I should not hesitate a moment to prefer the latter.
> —Thomas Jefferson

The philosopher Montaigne once insisted that true democracy could only occur in a relatively small country, where the citizens could stay in touch with one another. When the American republic was founded, Europeans sneered at the effort—the country was too big to function as an effective democracy, they said. That's one of the reasons Americans have consistently viewed communication technologies as a panacea for democracies—the newspaper, the telegraph, radio, television, and most recently, the Internet, have all been viewed as democratizing agents, a means by which the voice of the people could be heard.

With the rise of the World Wide Web, the dream of a democratizing technology may have finally come true. Traditionally, Americans have learned about and debated the policies of their government through electronic media such as television and radio. But these are top-down media; networks decide what you'll see and hear. But the cost is modest enough that just about anyone can set up a Web site and leave it going full-time to promote any opinion imaginable. By the same token, cash-strapped state and local governments, as well as community organizations, can make information available to the citizenry at very low cost.

Will advanced computer networking shift the balance of power from the state back to individuals and communities? You be the judge. This chapter surveys and

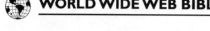

ranks selected Web sites that make government information accessible. Let me know whether you feel empowered after trying a few of these sites.

REFERENCE SITES

Governments produce huge amounts of text, which seems to be their main product besides compounding the public debt. There are gems to be had amidst the fluff, if only one could find them. And that's where government information reference sites come in. This section samples a couple of reference site offerings.

★★ FedWorld

> **URL:** http://www.fedworld.gov/
>
> **Topic:** A directory of on-line resources, Web and otherwise, provided by the federal government.
>
> **Of Special Note:** Intuitive organization and convenient hypertext links to listed resources.

It's not exciting. It's not especially pretty (FedWorld contains only one graphic). But it does its job well. FedWorld is an easy-to-use and fairly comprehensive directory of federal government on-line services. With listings for everything from the Bureau of Labor Statistics to the Senate Gopher service, FedWorld is the place to look for obscure government departments and bureaus.

You arrive in the FedWorld welcome page (Figure 21.1). Scroll down the page until you find the "Index of Subject Categories," and click the subject that interests you. You jump to a more complete listing (on the same Web document) of subjects that begin with the letter you chose. In most cases, the only listing is the subject you picked from the index. Click the subject you want, and a list of hyperlinked relevant resources is displayed.

Most of FedWorld's hyperlinks lead to non-Web documents, typically Gopher sites or FTP servers. Bear that in mind if you're expecting lots of glossy graphics and nice page layout.

AWFUL

FedWorld commits one of the cardinal sins of database design: it includes information twice. There's no reason to require you to choose from an index, then choose again from an almost identical list of subjects. If FedWorld expands, the two-step selection process will make more sense.

Figure 21.1 *FedWorld welcome page (http://www.fedworld.gov/)*

★★★★ **Consumer Information Center Home Page**

URL: http://www.gsa.gov/staff/pa/cic/cic.htm

Topic: On-line access to the valuable consumer information resources of the General Services Administration (GSA).

Of Special Note: For free, download reams of valuable information on cars, college, housing, health, and much more.

Knowledgeable consumers of government-produced information have known for years about one of this country's best-kept secrets: The General Service Administration's (GSA) Consumer Information catalog, which lists dozens of very valuable booklets on a wide variety of consumer issues. An example: "Preparing Your Child For College," a 49 page treatise that's surely the best thing available on the subject. Thanks to the Consumer Information Center's Home Page, the best of the CIC offerings are available through the Web, and for free.

HOT TIP

Have you ever wondered how you can compare bank interest rates meaningfully? You'll find out how in "Making Sense of Savings," in the Money area. If you're still thinking about college, check out "Buying Treasury Securities," which tells you how to buy zero-coupon bonds—and includes the addresses of Treasury offices near you.

🕷WEBMASTER

CIC's home page is a textbook example of effective hypermedia design. The clickable map, modeled on an Interstate Highway road sign, conveys its purpose immediately. Large icons, backed up by text in case you miss the visual symbolism, provide guidance to helpful features and additional information. A very fine job!

WISH LIST

One drawback to the CIC home page, as you'll eventually discover, is that the on-line versions of GSA's documents don't include tables and graphics—just ASCII text. Obviously, it would be expensive to scan in the graphic information, but it would be well worth doing—some of the documents aren't very useful without the graphics (there's a guide to identifying constellations, for instance, that doesn't make much sense without the pictures).

★★★ State WWW Servers

> **URL:** http://www.law.indiana.edu/law/states.html
>
> **Topic:** A directory of states' on-line services.
>
> **Of Special Note:** An interface like FedWorld's, but more streamlined.

Maintained by Indiana University, this page provides links to all sorts of state agencies and departments. Contrary to its title, not all of the resources listed here are true Web sites—a lot of them are Gopher or Telnet facilities. Nonetheless, this page (Figure 21.2) is the place to go when hunting for information about state governments.

It's organized as a hierarchical list, with agency and department names listed under state names. Some states aren't listed at all, while California is represented by dozens of hyperlinks. There's no search engine, since this site is organized for people looking for information about a particular state, not a subject. The search feature of your browser is adequate for looking up the state you want.

<sp>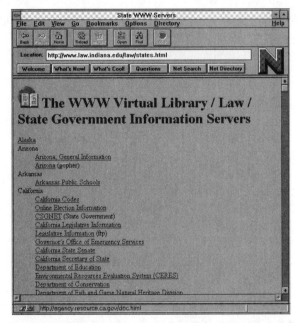</sp>

🕷WEBMASTER

FedWorld's maintainers could learn something from a visit to the State WWW Servers page. Instead of cramming everything onto a single page and using relative references to move visitors around, State WWW Servers lists each bit of data once and fits it logically into the collection.

Figure 21.2 *State WWW Servers welcome page (http://www.law.indiana.edu/law/states.html)*

EXECUTIVE BRANCH

It seems that nearly every agency in the Executive Branch has its own Web server. Some of these are downright boring, with no more information than the boss's picture and office address, while others are packed with useful and sometimes fun data. Browse these sites to see what you think—it's a lot easier than traveling to Washington and tramping all over town.

★★★★ Central Intelligence Agency

> **URL:** http://www.ic.gov/
>
> **Topic:** The Central Intelligence Agency, past and present.
>
> **Of Special Note:** The CIA World Factbook, a nifty reference almanac.

Those looking for something out of a John Le Carre novel had better look else-where: the CIA site has more in common with your encyclopedia than with LeCarre's spymaster, Smiley. But encyclopedias are still useful, right? Such is the case with the CIA site—lots of information, darned little international intrigue. Are they recording your email address when you access the server, perhaps for further analysis? Makes you wonder, doesn't it?

Figure 21.3 CIA welcome page (http://www.ic.gov/)

There are two main hyperlinks on the welcome page (Figure 21.3). One leads to the CIA World Factbook, described below, and the other goes to the Factbook on Intelligence, a hodgepodge of factoids and pictures about the CIA and its history. Be sure to follow the "We are often asked..." hyperlink. It leads to what is probably the oddest FAQ you've ever seen, with questions like, "Does the CIA spy on Americans? Does it keep a file on me?" and "Does the Central Intelligence Agency engage in assassinations?". The answers are pretty pedestrian (The answers to all of the above questions amount to "No"), but they're fun reading anyway.

The title leads you to believe that this resource might contain information like Fidel Castro's hat size or Kruschev's favorite bubble gum flavor, but alas, no. The CIA World Factbook, accessible from the CIA welcome page, is a great place to turn for answers that previously would have required an atlas or almanac.

USEFUL RESOURCE

From the index page, choose the country you want and move to a document featuring a map of the country and information about it. The information is truly exhaustive: administrative divisions, treaties signed, literacy rate, life expectancy, national holidays, major political parties, you name it, it's listed. You can reach a number of other resources, such as world maps, from the index page.

★★ Department of Education

> **URL:** http://www.ed.gov/
>
> **Topic:** The Department of Education and its publications.
>
> **Of Special Note:** A keyword-searchable database of press releases.

This site loses points for cramming all its mission statements, goals and departmental programs onto its welcome page (Figure 21.4), but makes up for its sloppiness by offering a good searchable press-release database and some nice resource pages for researchers seeking grants.

From the index at the top of the welcome page, you can choose from several hyperlinked topics, most of which are relative references leading to other places on the welcome page. Be sure to follow the Press Releases and Funding Opportunities hyperlink, which leads to a chronological list of Department press release titles. Instead of browsing through all the release titles by hand, click the **keyword search** hyperlink and use a search form. This is supposed to be under development, but I found that the searches ran quickly and brought up a lot of hits. Also take a look at the Selected Speeches page. Though the archive is not searchable, it's a list of some of the speeches given by the Secretary of Education, and is organized by date and place of the speeches. The speech archive is not exhaustive, but if you're looking for the full text of a particular speech, it's worth looking here.

"A Researcher's Guide to the U.S. Department of Education" is a good example of how to put together an informational booklet in hypertext form. The first page of the Guide is its table of contents, which allows readers to jump to any chapter of the book or begin at the beginning and read all the way through. At the bottom of each chapter are three buttons: one linked to the next chapter, one linked to the previous chapter, and one that leads back to the table of contents. Though there aren't a lot of hyperlinks embedded in the Guide's text, it presents its information efficiently.

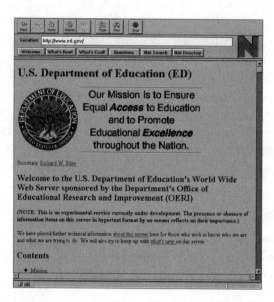

Figure 21.4 *Department of Education Welcome Page (http://www.ed.gov/)*

★★★★ Internal Revenue Service

> **URL:** http://www.ustreas.gov/treasury/bureaus/irs/irs.html
>
> **Topic:** Downloadable IRS tax forms.
>
> **Of Special Note:** A good search facility to ease finding the forms you need.

There's been a lot of talk about the sticky web of tax law. The IRS Web site does little to clarify the tax code, but it does a lot to ease collecting forms and instruction books. At the very least, it will save you a trip to the post office and get you a copy of Adobe Acrobat Reader, a pretty cool program.

The basic idea here is a simple one. The IRS has encoded tax forms in a consistent computer format, and provides the program needed to print it and a search engine so you can locate the forms you need without delay. You download Adobe Acrobat Reader, install it on your machine, download the needed form files, print them with Acrobat, fill them out and mail them in. With the IRS site and some sort of tax-preparation software, you can do your tax forms without ever leaving your computer until that final trip to the mailbox.

The IRS welcome page (Figure 21.5) is mundane but useful. Click **Frequently Asked Questions** to see a list of common tax questions and their answers, but click **Tax Forms and Instructions** to access the real action. The Tax Forms and Instructions page has three important hyperlinks on it. **View a list of all tax forms**, **Search through tax forms by keyword**, and **Get the Adobe Acrobat Reader**. If you don't already have Acrobat, download the Acrobat software first. Then follow the hyperlink to the search page.

In the search box, enter the name of the form you want, such as **1099** or **1040**.You'll get a list of hyperlinks that have to do with that form, typically this year's and last year's versions. Click those hyperlinks to download those files. The files contain both the forms and the corresponding instruction books, so they can be lengthy.

HOT TIP

Note the warning on the Tax Forms and Instructions page. It says that because of color-coding, versions of certain tax forms that may be downloaded from the IRS site may not be used for filing. Use these forms for practice only, and get the colored forms from the library or post office.

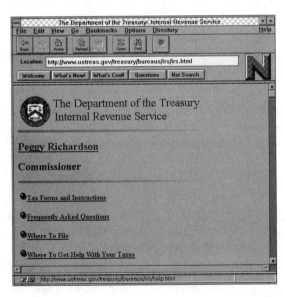

Figure 21.5 IRS Welcome page (http://www.ustreas.gov/treasury/bureaus/irs/irs.html)

HOT TIP Want more tax info? Check out Taxing Times (http://www.scubed.com/tax/tax.html), a volunteer effort of W. J. Proffer. You'll find the entire text of the U.S. tax code, transcripts from Usenet tax discussion groups, instructions on accessing information from the IRS, and more.

★★★★ Small Business Administration

URL: http://www.sbaonline.sba.gov/

Topic: Government aid for entrepreneurs.

Of Special Note: A really informative, albeit hidden, tutorial about buying a franchise.

The Small Business Administration works to help entrepreneurs start, finance, and grow new companies. Since a lot of startups deal with new technologies, it's appropriate that the SBA chose to set up a Web site to distribute information about its educational and financial services. The quality of the SBA's Web offerings belies the agency's reputation for ineffectiveness.

When you drop into the SBA welcome page (Figure 21.6), you see an impressive three-part graphic. Click the leftmost part, labeled **SBA Resources**, to find the SBA office near you. However, the really cool stuff is lower on the page. Click **Starting Your Business** to read about help with getting started, click **Financing Your Business** to read about loan guarantees, or look at **Expanding Your Business** to see about help in SBA growth.

EXCELLENT

The SBA site has a good-looking button bar at the bottom of each of its documents, which makes it easy to move to different sections of the site—say from Financing to Expanding. Unfortunately, the functions of the buttons aren't obvious from their pictures. There should be some text with each graphic to cut down on guessing.

WISH LIST

There's a great tutorial about franchise businesses hidden in the "Expanding Your Buisiness" section. Click the **Franchise Workshop** icon at the bottom of the expansion page, and work through a class on franchises. The class even includes several quizzes so you can monitor your progress. There are only two problems with this tutorial—the lack of hyperlinks for navigation from section to section without going back to the table of contents, and the fact that it's hidden. You should be able to access the Franchise Workshop from the welcome page.

Figure 21.6 *Small Business Administration welcome page (http://www.sbaonline.sba.gov/)*

★★ State Department Travel Warnings

URL: http://www.stolaf.edu/network/travel-advisories.html

Topic: Detailed information about the safety of traveling in various countries

Of Special Note: A nice set of links to other foreign-affairs issues sites.

Yes, this is a front-end for a Gopher server, but what a Gopher server! Virtually every country in the world is listed on the welcome page (Figure 21.7), and a single click brings up a text page full of information about the nuts and bolts of traveling there. The report includes information about wars, domestic disturbances, outbreaks of disease and crime, as well as administrative information about needed papers and embassy locations.

For example, clicking the hyperlink for Haiti brings up a report that includes information about the recent U.S. military action there, and warnings that visitors, because of their relative wealth, are targeted by criminals. The document warns of "random violence, sporadic disturbances and criminal acts" throughout the country—information any traveler would want. Details of getting to Haiti also appear on the document, as do embassy addresses and telephone numbers.

Don't miss the links to other travel and foreign affairs sites, either. The Perry-Castaneda Map Collection at the University of Texas and the Travelers' Tales Resource Center are both a lot of fun.

In case you're wondering why this site is housed at St. Olaf College, in Northfield, Minnesota, it's because St. Olaf is the official Internet and Bitnet distribution point for the State Department's travel warnings. With the coming wave of privatization, you'll see more private organizations contracting with the U.S. government to distribute public information.

🕷 WEBMASTER

The State Department's Travel Warnings welcome page provides an excellent example of how *not* to design a Web document. There's a huge, bandwidth-gobbling world map, which misleads you into thinking that it's clickable (it's not). The big State Department logo takes up the rest of the screen; it could have been run in-line with the document's Heading I text, but they didn't think of that. As a result, you'll have to page down before you get an idea of what's offered. Also, the lengthy list of countries could use some organization into world areas, with table-of-contents hyperlinks.

Figure 21.7 *State Department Travel Warnings welcome page*
(http://www.stolaf.edu/network/travel-advisories.html)

★★★ Welcome to the White House

URL: http://www.whitehouse.gov/

Topic: The White House, its occupants, and the rest of the government to boot.

Of Special Note: A really cool, albeit marginally functional, clickable map of Washington with embedded hyperlinks to other government on-line services.

It's to be expected in this age of the visual presidency, but unless you choose the text-only display option at the White House or have a fast connection, you'll spend more time there than several presidents did. This site is absolutely loaded with pictures, and while they're generally good, they're huge. Be prepared to go grab a jellybean or two while you wait for the graphics to load.

Termed "An Interactive Citizens' Handbook," the White House site's designers evidently understood that their baby would attract more traffic than, say, the Standards Bureau's server. So they built a lot of basic educational information into the site, and included references to other government resources. The White House site is a good jumping-off point for other federal resources. One can only wonder why the welcome messages from the President and Vice-President on the welcome page (Figure 21.9) are represented by pictures of lecterns with no one behind them.

The parts about the First Family contain mainly rah-rah sixth-grade civics text stuff ("Hillary Clinton, who has always found time to work with the children of the community, joins in on the fun at a local school with two young artists), but they might be fun to check out with a child. There's also an audio file featuring Socks the Cat.

The best part of the White House site is the clickable map of Washington, found under the Executive Branch link from the welcome page. Divided into six quadrants, you select the part of the city you want, and get a more detailed map of that area from which you can select the bureau or department you want.

The clickable map assumes you know where in the city your department is located, or that you know what its building looks like. This is fine for the Capitol, but not good when dealing with more obscure government entities. The map should have labels.

AWFUL

Follow the **Publications** link from the welcome page. You'll find a list of White House resources, including press releases, speeches, and background documents. The press release database is keyword-searchable.

USEFUL RESOURCE

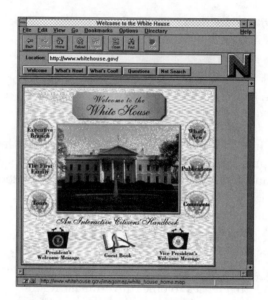

Figure 21.8 *White House welcome page (http://www.whitehouse.gov/)*

LEGISLATIVE BRANCH

Unlike the Executive Branch, which has scores of agencies, the Legislative Branch consists only of Congress and its supporting agencies, very few of which maintain Web sites. The available legislative sites are pretty diverse, though—the Library of Congress is one of the best museums on the Web, the Will T. Bill site is a great front-end for a database of legislation-in-process, and Rep. Peter DeFazio's site is a pacesetter for politicians going on-line.

★★★ Library of Congress

URL: http://lcweb.loc.gov/homepage/lchp.html

Topic: Library of Congress resources and exhibits

Of Special Note: Links to the Library's on-line catalogs, plus some great exhibits of historical photographs and texts.

The Library of Congress technically still serves as an information archive for legislators, but its appeal to Web users goes far beyond that. The LOC is a top-notch place to do on-line research, obviously, but on top of that it's a real cultural hotspot. Visit the LOC even if you have no interest at all in finding a book or paper. Think of it as a museum with a big reference section.

When you drop into the LOC Site (Figure 21.9), you see a picture of the original library building and a whole slew of hyperlinks. They're so disparate, I've included just a brief word about each.

American Memory: Depression-era photos, accounts of American folk life and Mathew Brady Civil War photos may be found here.

Exhibits: On-line versions of current LOC exhibits. Very cool.

Country Studies: A collection of facts about a few countries. Stick with the CIA World Factbook.

POW/MIA Database: A searchable archive of information about Vietnam War POWs and MIAs.

LC MARVEL: The Library's Gopher-based search engine—the card catalog.

Most of the information you get from the search engines is metadata—data about data. In the case of the POW/MIA database, you have to either arrange for your local library to borrow LOC documents, or pay for copies. It seems the LOC just has so much stuff, it can't get it all on-line.

It would be wonderful if a Web-based search engine for at least some of the LOC's collection were established. Gopher interfaces are clunky and awkward.

WISH LIST

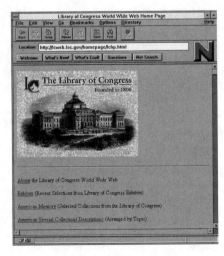

Figure 21.9 Library of Congress welcome page (http://lcweb.loc.gov/homepage/lchp.html)

★★★ Representative Peter DeFazio

URL: http://darkwing.uoregon.edu/~pdefazio/index.html

Topic: Representative DeFazio, Oregon, and its fourth Congressional district.

Of Special Note: Lots of information about DeFazio, and links to the full text of some important legislation.

It's nice to see federal legislators using new technology to distribute information to their constituents. Maybe some day we'll see an end to those annoying, self-aggrandizing newsletters sent out by Congresspeople at taxpayers' expense. The Web is the ideal replacement—production costs for a Web site are much smaller than those of a newsletter, so Web sites can be larger and contain more information. Web sites also save paper, since many newsletters are thrown away with junk mail.

Representative Peter DeFazio, of the fourth Oregon district, is one of the few legislators to have already embraced the Web, and he's done so very well. Not only can you use this site to see voting records and statements of opinion, you can visit it and learn something about DeFazio personally. His Web site contains the sort of thing that would be dropped from a newsletter for lack of space, and it's that material that makes DeFazio human.

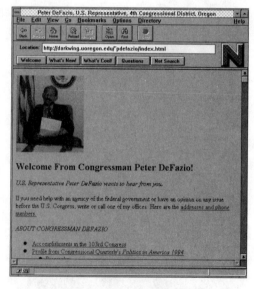

Figure 21.10 *Representative Peter DeFazio's welcome page*
(http://darkwing.uoregon.edu/~pdefazio/index.html)

Drop into DeFazio's welcome page (Figure 21.10), and see a list of hyperlinks to all the standard Congress stuff—voting records, a biography, and statements of opinion. But you'll also find things you wouldn't get anywhere else. For example, when I visited DeFazio's site, there was a video file available in which the Congressman talked about the upcoming Rose Bowl. On some of the other pages, there were links to the full text of legislation—like the huge GATT treaty—that would never in a hundred years find their way into a newsletter. DeFazio and his staff have made this page into not only a promotional tool, but a valuable resource as well. More legislators should follow his lead.

★★★★ Thomas (U.S. Library of Congress)

URL: http://thomas.loc.gov/

Topic: A wide range of information concerning U.S. laws and lawmakers.

Of Special Note: Full text search capabilities for House and Senate legislation

Introduced with great fanfare by the new Speaker of the U.S. House of Representatives Newt Gingrich, Thomas—named after Thomas Jefferson—includes the full text of bills from Congress, access to the House's Gopher system (which contains information about lawmakers, committees, and hearing schedules), the full text of the Congressional Record (not implemented at this writing), an essay on the legislative process by a House counsel, and much more. If you'd like to know more about what goes on in the U.S. Congress, this is the place to find out.

EXCELLENT

In line with a conservative House leadership that wants to remove power from Washington and return it to the states (and ultimately to the people), Thomas (Figure 21.11) is a growing enterprise. Future enhancements will include the Library of Congress' Bill Digest files, and summaries and chronologies of legislation. These will be fully integrated with the full text of bills, resulting in a powerful analytical tool for anyone concerned about existing or pending legislation.

Try the full-text searching capabilities. As you'll discover, the search engine is WAIS-like; you type one or more search words, and click the Start Query button. (Actually, the search engine was developed by the Center for Intelligent Information Retrieval at the University of Massachusetts, Amherst). The result is a new Web page with relevancy rankings (1,000 is the top score). You can also search by bill number.

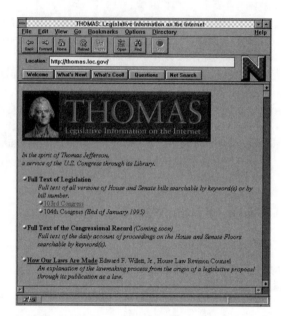

Figure 21.11 *Thomas (http://thomas.loc.gov/)*

★★★ Will T. Bill

URL: http://www.unipress.com/will-t-bill.html

Topic: Congressional legislation-in-progress.

Of Special Note: Get a report on any congressional bill via a nice front-end for a WAIS database.

Like the IRS site, Will T. Bill does a single, utilitarian task, but does it well and with style. Will T. Bill lets you look up any Congressional bill and see a report of its status. For the outside-the-Beltway crowd, the Will T. Bill page (Figure 21.12) has links to definitions of *bill* and *resolution*, but, oddly, no other legislative terminology.

The search form is very complete. Select from a list of bill types (Senate bill, House bill, joint resolution, etc.), enter the bill's name or number if you have them, or enter the names of the sponsoring congresspeople. You can even enter keywords from the body of the bill—this WAIS server does a full-text search.

Put Will T. Bill on your hotlist if you're even a little bit interested in the progress of certain legislation through Congress. This site is to C-SPAN junkies what Quotron is to investors.

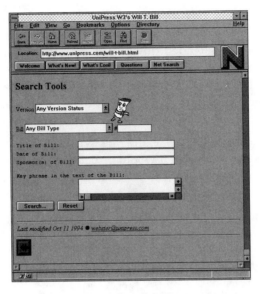

Figure 21.12 Will T. Bill search form (http://www.unipress.com/will-t-bill.html)

JUDICIAL BRANCH

The Judicial Branch, the smallest branch of American government, does not maintain any Web sites. To fill the void, Cornell University's Legal Information Institute has stepped in to provide an excellent searchable database of recent Supreme Court decisions.

★★★★ Supreme Court Decisions

URL: http://www.law.cornell.edu/supct/

Topic: Supreme Court opinions since 1990

Of Special Note: The full text of all opinions (those of the Court, plus concurring and dissenting opinions) since 1990, and an excellent search facility for finding the opinion you want.

Certain things were meant to be put on-line; mainly, those things that are large, and awkward to handle in printed form, and of little use to all but a few people. Supreme Court decisions fit that patter, and the Legal Information Institute of Cornell University has done a world-class job of getting recent Supreme Court decisions onto the Web.

From the welcome page (Figure 21.13), you must choose from several options. Unless you know at least one of the parties in the case you want, or know the year in which the decision was handed down, you'll want to choose the **Indexed by Topics** or **Keyword Search** hyperlink. Bear in mind that the keyword search facility looks only at the syllabus of the cases (the summaries of the decisions prepared by the Court). When the engine completes your search, you'll be presented with a link to the full text.

WISH LIST

The LII server delivers the full text of the syllabi and decisions in text form, which is ugly but okay for this job. It would be better if the opinions were in hypertext form, and links to cases and law to which the Justices refer were embedded.

🕷 WEBMASTER

Have you noticed how most of the four-star sites in this book do one thing, but do it very well? That's one appeal of the Web. It's not necessary to fit a variety of things into one package, as it is in the case of a newspaper or real-life museum. The Web can have distinct sites for each of a million different arcane tasks, and each of those sites can be excellent at its small task. Division of labor is as important for information management as it is for human workers.

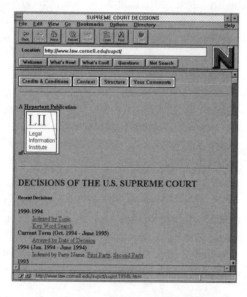

Figure 21.13 Supreme Court Decisions welcome page (http://www.law.cornell.edu/supct/)

POLITICAL PARTIES, MOVEMENTS, AND COMMENTARY

The Web has already begun to establish itself as a forum for the most important activity in our government—the exchange of information and opinion among citizens. While some of the ideas expressed in these Web sites may strike you as bizarre, remember that that's the point of the First Amendment—that people can express their opinions, no matter how far they are from the mainstream.

It seems that those on the fringes of American politics have been the first to grasp this new medium, too. These sites, include one for a small political party, two devoted to political lampoon, and one designed to spur interest in establishing a new island nation in the Carribean. There are no official sites for either major U.S. political party.

What is the American political scene if not an occasion for debate? These Web sites facilitate that aspect of our system of government.

★ Libertarian Party

URL: http://www.lp.org/lp/lp.html

Topic: The U.S. Libertarian Party's organization and opinions.

Of Special Note: Full text of party platforms for 1990, 1992 and 1994.

Only one graphic, no sound and no movies—the Saturday-morning cartoon crowd will feel left out here. All you'll find at the Libertarian site (Figure 21.14) is a well-organized presentation of the party's structure, history, and opinions. This structure makes the Libertarian site distinctive: the organizers could have fit most of the site's data onto a page or two and relied upon relative links and browser-based text searches, but instead chose to break up the data and build good index pages.

Take a look at the pages for the current party platform. Note how the index page is long enough to include many different category headings, but not so long as to be unreadable. The index page makes it easy to get to the information you need quickly.

Neither the Republican nor the Democratic Party seems to have a dedicated Web site, so the Libertarians get credit for being first to take their platform into cyberspace. Whether you agree with its politics or not, isn't it great that a small, cash-starved party can take its cause on-line and immediately be exposed to hundreds of thousands of Web users? It's tough to predict how widely available information resources will change our government, but there's little doubt the dynamics of running parties and campaigns will be different in the fairly near future.

Figure 21.14 *Libertarian Party welcome page (http://www.lp.org/lp/lp.html)*

★★ Oceania: The Atlantis Project

URL: http://unicycle.cs.tulane.edu/oceania/

Topic: Oceania, a country-in-the-making.

Of Special Note: The constitution and laws of Oceania.

Perhaps you've heard of the company-in-a-box, a hypothetical computer-based corporation that has no real assets of its own. Well, Oceania is a country-in-a-box. Right now, it's the governmental equivalent of vaporware—a country that doesn't exist yet, but might someday and is being hyped now. Its Web site (Figure 21.15) is devoted to distributing information about this proposed man-made island in the Carribean and selling things to help pay for building it.

For those who aren't interested in buying into a would-be country, the appeal of the Oceania site is the country's constitution and body of laws. (High school teachers, take note!) While understanding the function of government on a theoretical level is important, it's often hard for students to follow the old-style language and complexities of the U.S. Constitution, let alone the laws. The Oceania constitution and laws are written clearly, and are fairly simple. I can imagine an interesting classroom exercise in which students create a model of the government of this virtual state.

Figure 21.15 The Oceania welcome page (http://unicycle.cs.tulane.edu/oceania/)

★★★★ The Right Side of the Web

URL: http://www.clark.net/pub/jeffd/index.html

Topic: Conservatism and republicanism.

Of Special Note: Lots of links to other conservative-interest Web resources, plus audio clips of prominent liberals saying unflattering things.

The Right Side of the Web is a virtual cornucopia of conservative iconography. Rush Limbaugh is well-represented here. The Republican "Contract with America" is included in full, with check boxes that are supposed to be filled in when various parts are passed. A picture of Ronald Reagan is on the welcome page (Figure 21.16), with the caption "The greatest president of this century!" Needless to say, Jesse Jackson wouldn't feel at home.

🕷WEBMASTER

Whatever your feelings about the Right's politics, take a look at the welcome page's design—it's excellent. The lead in-line graphic displays quickly, giving you some text to ponder right away. New features and key resources are right up-front. The big graphic—Ron's mug—comes in last, and you can read the page while it's downloading. A fine job.

If you're interested in other conservative resources on the Web and the rest of the Internet, follow the link to the Right Side's directory. Also look at the Rush Limbaugh page, and be sure to try out the audio clips page. If you can't laugh at the clips, regardless of your political feelings, you're taking all this stuff too seriously.

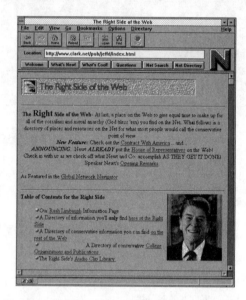

Figure 21.16 *The Right Side of the Web welcome page*

EXPERIMENTS IN ELECTRONIC DEMOCRACY

As the previous portraits suggest, the Web is providing increased access to the Federal level of government, but the most important political impact of the Web may be felt at the community level. Throughout the United States, **freenets**—on-line services that are most often based in libraries—are providing free access to civic resources, library card catalogs, and the wide Intenet. Increasingly, they're the local for interesting experiments in electronic participative democracy.

KEY TERM

Typically, freenets are designed as model "towns" that you can "walk through," stopping wherever you please—at the mayor's office, for example, to read announcements and leave suggestions.

USEFUL RESOURCE

A fine essay on community networking, written by Apple Computer librarian Steve Cisler, can be found at ftp://ftp.apple.com/alug/communet /ComNet6.93.txt. It's highly recommended for anyone interested in the problems and potential of community networks and freenets.

★★★★ **Minnesota E-Democracy Project**

URL: http://free-net.mpls-stpaul.mn.us:8000/govt/e-democracy/

Topic: Minnesota electoral campaigns, candidates, and issues

Of Special Note: A truly innovative feature is the E-debate among senatorial and gubanatorial candidates.

Sponsored by the Twin Cities Freenet, this service (Figure 21.17) seeks "to provide public access to campaign information in electronic form and to help create an electronic public space for voters to discuss the election issues that they feel are important." As one of the first experiments of its kind in the U.S, it's an important first step towards the electronic enabling of participatory democracy. Citizens will find information on voter registration, voter guides from a variety of organizations, searchable campaign releases, an email forum on Minnesota politics, and election results. By November 15, 1994, the service had been accessed more than 40,000 times.

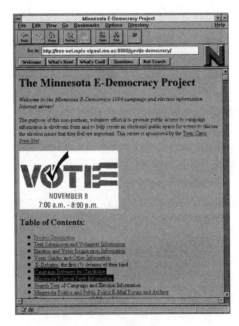

21.17 Minnesota E-Democracy welcome page (http://free-net.mpls-stpaul.mn.us:8000/govt/e-democracy/)

CHAPTER 22

Business and Shopping

For thousands of businesses these days, the home page is where the heart is.
—Peter H. Lewis

There's been a lot of talk about the ways in which the Internet, or some part of it, will change world commerce. It's tough to predict exactly what sort of changes will take place, and it's not likely things will change drastically for some time. Most likely, just as the mail-order catalogs of the nineteenth century did not eliminate real walk-in showrooms, on-line business will simply complement more traditional ways of exchanging goods and services.

Still, it's clear that on-line Web shopping is poised to explode in popularity, once procedures have been finalized for encrypting credit card data (see Chapter 30, Web Issues, for a discussion of security concerns). Until then, you'll find consumer information, on-line marketing efforts, the beginnings of on-line shopping malls, and electronic store fronts aplenty. Take a look—you may be examining the way many of us will shop in the future.

CONSUMER INFORMATION

Consumer information is the kind of thing that belongs on the Web. When it's in a library, buried behind tons of other data, very few people bother to look it up. When it's on television, few people watch because it's not on when it's needed and it can make pretty dry TV. The Web is a giant place for consumer information, since the information is both easy to find and attractively presented.

It's hard to separate particular Web data into this category, since most of the information out there could be categorized as useful by some consumers at one point or another. The two consumer information sites listed here are really very different. The Federal Trade Commission site specializes in distributing government data about consumer issues, while the Nolo Press site is really a sales tool for their collection of books. Explore the Web's commercial and informational sites with an eye toward how they might help you make more informed choices.

★★ FTC Consumer brochures

URL: http://www.webcom.com/~lewrose/brochures.html

Topic: Government information about common consumer problems.

Of Special Note: Dozens of clear, informative brochures from the Federal Trade Commission.

You know the "government documents" section of your local library that's stuffed with brochures and pamphlets about the most nit-picky of arcane subjects? Chances are you avoid that section, if for no other reason than fear of being buried beneath mountains of yellowing paper and plastic spiral bindings. But, when you need information about some obscure aspect of the law or government policy, there's probably no better place to look than a government document.

The Federal Trade Commission has done a real service by putting some of its informational pamphlets on the Web. Though there's no search engine and the writing in these short works won't win any prizes for creativity, you should look to this site for information about starting your own business, avoiding scams, and other trade-related topics.

Some examples of brochures you'll find at the FTC site include:

- Art Fraud
- Getting Business Credit
- Canadian Gemstone Scams
- How to Dispute Credit Report Errors
- Funerals: A Consumer's Guide
- Generic Drugs

Each of these pamphlets is about three pages—long enough to contain the information you need but short enough to comfortably read on-line. Most brochures also include ways to get more information.

★★★★ Nolo Press

URL: http://www.digital.com/gnn/bus/nolo/

Topic: The law for non-lawyers.

Of Special Note: Some informative (and sometimes funny) excerpts from Nolo's line of do-it-yourself legal manuals.

Nolo Press exists for the same reason computer book publishers exist—to explain a technical subject to people who aren't experts in that field. Nolo, a California company that has been publishing books for more than 20 years, has gone on the Web to further its mission of explaining the mysteries of the law. They say handling legal problems without a lawyer is a lot like choosing an over-the-counter medication instead of visiting the doctor: not a good idea for a serious difficulty, but perfectly legitimate for a minor problem. Nolo's Web site (Figure 22.1) is clean, well-organized, and a lot of fun.

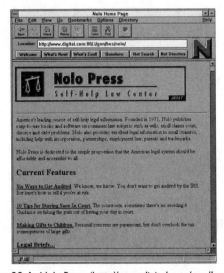

Figure 22.1 *Nolo Press (http://www.digital.com/gnn/bus/nolo/)*

You can get useful legal advice at this site that, were you to hire a lawyer, would cost several hundred dollars. Of course, Nolo's stock in trade is its body of self-help legal books, and the documents on the Web site are really just tastes of the material in its various books. The site offers to sell you the books on-line, but you won't feel pressured to buy and, unless you're facing a no-kidding lawsuit, you'll get plenty of enjoyment and information out of the snippets on the Web.

Some of the things you'll find at the Nolo site include:

- A list of the top 29 reasons not to go to law school (actually, the site lists only a few, but they're funny).

- A guide to protecting your home from burglars when you go away for vacation.

- A guide to getting your neighbor to turn down her stereo, including steps from merely asking her to turn it down to filing a suit for nuisance.

🕷 WEBMASTER

Note that Nolo offers instructions for ordering via fax and snail mail for those who are (rightfully) nervous about sending their credit card number via electronic mail. It's nice to be considerate of the cautious, and such care likely will net Nolo a few sales from people who otherwise would have passed up the chance to buy.

ON-LINE MARKETING

These companies have nothing for sale—they're just establishing their "presence on the Web."

★★★★ Sun

URL: http://www.sun.com/

Topic: Sun Microsystems' products, services, history and organization.

Of Special Note: A large collection of information about Sun's popular computer products.

Sun Microsystems has done its Web site (Figure 22.2) right, and it's only fitting: some of the most famous Web sites in the world are part of SunSite and more than half of the computers that comprise the Internet are Sun machines. Any big company looking to establish itself on the Web should pay a visit to Sun's Web site. The pages are attractive and well-organized, and they serve the purpose of giving Sun a corporate presence in cyberspace.

Figure 22.2 Sun (http://www.sun.com/)

The easiest way to think of Sun's on-line material is as a marketing brochure handed out at a trade show. The site doesn't try to sell you anything directly, but it exhaustively describes Sun's wares and tries (successfully) to give you a good impression of the company, its products and its people.

A small start-up company won't be able to have a Web site like Sun's, but a large company with hundreds of products, services and development teams could learn a lot from this site. From the welcome screen, you can go to screens that list Sun's products (with hyperlinks to longer descriptions), look into their service policies or check out company history and information.

The option of looking at Sun's corporate history and activities is really cool. Normally, when you deal with a company, you work with their salespeople or service representatives and are either happy or unhappy with the way they treat you. There is little opportunity to find out what the company is all about during the normal course of business. The Web gives you the ability to easily put your interaction with the company in perspective, in terms of how long the company has

EXCELLENT

been in business and how it thinks about its customers and its community. Of course, if you don't care about these things, the Web also gives you the option to ignore them.

★★★ You Will

> **URL:** http://youwill.com/
>
> **Topic:** The products and research of AT&T and Bell Labs.
>
> **Of Special Note:** Audio files describing things AT&T thinks "you will" experience in the future.

Though it's not as elaborate as the Sun Web site (Figure 22.3), AT&T does a lot to boost its image among Web users with this site. It's based on an advertising campaign in which announcers and headlines ask if you've ever done some wildly futuristic thing, like send a fax from the beach or pay a toll without slowing your car. At the end, the ads say, "You will," leaving you with the impression that the clever people at AT&T are on top of the technological heap.

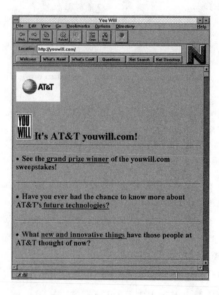

Figure 22.3 *youwill.com (http://youwill.com/)*

This site is pretty much a rehash of that campaign in Web format (in fact, the voice-overs from several of the commercials are included as audio files), but if you like to look at gee-whiz gadgets and technological innovations for their own sake, pay this site a visit. You'll find pictures and descriptions of AT&T's new products here alongside the services they promise for the years ahead.

Though AT&T doesn't go to the same lengths as Sun to tell you about its corporate character and history, it shines in the area of visitor interacting. You can send forms to AT&T, telling the company what you'd like to see in its future products and asking for information about what it's selling now.

ON-LINE SHOPPING MALLS

Credit-card transactions are just now becoming possible thanks to browsers with encryption capabilities like Netscape Navigator. These browsers let you send sensitive information like your credit card number without fear of being intercepted and illegally used. Many sites without facilities to handle secure transactions act like electronic catalogs where you pick out what you want, and phone or fax in your order.

Hundreds of on-line shopping malls and storefronts exist. Here, I've provided only a sampling of the many different kinds of on-line shopping resources out there. One of the things you'll notice is that on the Web, it's easy to establish a mall for a small interest group. In the world of bricks and mortar, it's impractical to build a mall containing only stores that interests environmentalists or sports fans, but on the Web, it's easy.

Some of the criteria by which I judged these sites were security, usability, and price range, as these are all questions you would ask before visiting a real-life shopping mall, too.

★★★ CommerceNet

> **URL:** http://www.commerce.net/
>
> **Topic:** A common "location" to begin your search for on-line businesses.
>
> **Of Special Note:** Lots of information about how electronic commerce might work in the future.

Just as a shopping mall is a structure in which you may look for the particular vendor you need, CommerceNet is a single on-line location at which you can hunt for a particular company. There are several hundred companies, people and organizations represented on CommerceNet, and the products and services they sell are as diverse as those you might find in a suburban megamall. Granted, their specialties tend more toward the high-tech realm than the occupants of a typical shopping center, but then the interests of the average Web user (at this point, anyway) tend more toward new technology than the average person.

Just as the character of a real mall is determined by the businesses that occupy it, the character of an on-line mall is set by the storefronts to which it has hyperlinks. Some of these storefronts are spectacular (be sure to check out the link to the FedEx package-tracking facility), but the structure of the mall itself is hard to judge. I gave CommerceNet its three stars on promises, in large part. Several parts of this mall were still "under construction" when I visited including a directory of products and services. However, CommerceNet's interface is attractive and easy to navigate.

★★★★ Commercial Sites Index

> **URL:** http://www.directory.net/
>
> **Topic:** A directory of businesses with Web presences.
>
> **Of Special Note:** A large database of commercial sites and a speedy search engine to look through them.

This is how it should be done. The name says it all—this is an index of commercial sites (Figure 22.4). You enter the welcome page, type in a word that describes what you want, and you get a list of hyperlinks to commercial storefronts that specialize in your subject. The interface is clean, fast, and doesn't impose itself on you when all you want is quick access to an on-line business. I gave this site four stars because it is the best way I've found to reach vendors on line. Think of it as the phone book, but in this case your fingers not only do the walking but the browsing, dealing and buying, too.

The companies listed here aren't all high-tech. I looked up "railroad," hoping to find a site related to model railroading, a hobby of mine. To my surprise, the Index came back with a hyperlink to the Atlas Model Railroad Company's site (a good one, by the way). The Commercial Sites Index is as useful as Lycos for those who want to hunt for commercial outlets.

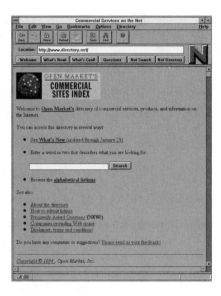

Figure 22.4 *Commercial Site Index (http//www.directory.net/)*

🕷WEBMASTER

Okay, one more time. Simplicity is good. Especially when your site is supposed to do something utilitarian like direct people to storefronts or distribute tax forms, you shouldn't clutter your site with electronic gewgaws that, while cool in their own right, are confusing. Stick to the basics for things like this, and save the wackiness for your home page.

★★ CyberMalls

URL: http://www.cybermalls.com/

Topic: On-line shopping for a variety of products.

Of Special Note: CyberWharf, a huge catalog of boats, boating supplies and boating information.

The Web is nothing if not an eclectic collection of information. The CyberMalls site fits the character of the Web very well, since it contains a group of stores dealing in products and services related to the state of Vermont, a complete boating showroom, and a record store. It's tough to figure out what those three shops have in common, but they're the components of the CyberMalls site and, for the most part, they're worth visiting.

Though the record store is nothing in comparison to CDNow or the Internet Underground Music Archive, the Vermont storefronts and, CyberWharf are good places to visit. Be sure to check out the powerboat and personal watercraft displays in CyberWharf—They're packed with good, fast-loading pictures, and clear text that appeals to any sailor, armchair, or otherwise.

★★ Downtown Anywhere

URL: http://www.awa.com/

Topic: A virtual Main Street—walk into any of hundreds of on-line businesses from this common front-end.

Of Special Note: A novel solution to the problem or unencrypted Web traffic.

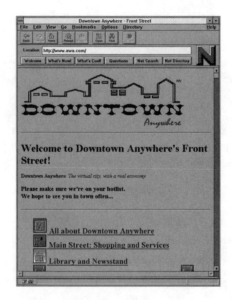

Figure 22.5 Downtime Anywhere (http://www.awa.com/)

Downtown Anywhere has a workable, albeit kludgey, solution to the problem of insecure transactions (Figure 22.5). Call a toll-free number and give your credit card number to become a "citizen" of Downtown Anywhere. As a citizen, you use your ID number to pay for things on line—Downtown Anywhere keeps your credit card number on file off-line, and only uses it when you purchase something. The credit card is never accessible on the Internet.

There are quite a few links to electronic storefronts on Downtown Anywhere, but they're hidden. To find the business sites, scroll way down the welcome page and click the link that says "Buy goods electronically." The main thrust of the welcome screen is to lure you to add your business to the list of hyperlinks.

It doesn't makes sense that links to stores—this site's reason for being—are buried under piles of advertising about why you should link your business to Downtown Anywhere. As a potential advertiser, you want it to be very easy for your customers to locate your storefront.

AWFUL

★★ EnviroProducts Directory

> **URL:** http://envirolink.org/products/
>
> **Topic:** Environmentally sound products for sale.
>
> **Of Special Note:** A sharp product-browsing screen, with embedded logos of companies that support EnviroLink.

As shopping malls go, this one is pretty small: fewer than 10 companies have storefronts here. The interesting thing about the Enviroproducts directory is what it says about the future of on-line retailing. It wouldn't be at all practical to build a real-life shopping mall to house only companies with products of interest to environmentalists, but on the Web, it's no big deal. Look for special-interest shopping centers to spring up all over the Web before long.

Whether you plan on buying anything or not, pay this site a visit for its educational value. Many of the vendors here sell products based on novel technologies, and it's fun to see the solutions they've come up with for the problems of energy management and pollution prevention. There are also a few environment-friendly jewelry and record storefronts on the EnviroProducts directory.

★ Shopping IN

> **URL:** http://www.onramp.net/shopping_in/
>
> **Topic:** A Web gallery of clothing and accessories
>
> **Of Special Note:** Some large pictures of various articles of clothing.

This is just a catalog of clothing vendors' stock, and a pretty shaky one at that. Shopping IN is too dependent on graphics that take a long time to load, and the text descriptions of articles of clothing are very limited. All you get is a picture of the item, a brief description (i.e., "Tank Top") and the name of the manufacturer. You're supposed to go through the site, clicking check boxes for the things you want. You "check out" by filling out a form with your address, and a bill is mailed to you.

One of the real shortcomings of this site is the fact that you don't really know what your purchase is going to cost, since tax and shipping are added to your bill later.

ELECTRONIC STOREFRONTS

There are hundreds of virtual storefronts on the Web, and it would be foolish to suggest that this is anything more than a list of a few of the good ones. The best way to find the sort of store you need is to visit a Web mall and look around. You're very likely to find a store that specializes in your topic of interest.

Don't forget the security issue of sending your credit card number over the Web. Most of these storefronts offer alternative ways of paying, such as by phone, mail or fax. You should use one of these payment methods unless the storefront supports an encrypted transaction method, such as Netscape's.

★★★★ CDNow

> **URL:** http://cdnow.com/
>
> **Topic:** A Web music store.
>
> **Of Special Note:** Album lists, artist biographies and a slick interface.

CDNow has hit the right formula for selling commercial music on-line in the same way the Internet Underground Music Archive understands distributing alternative music. Except for its somewhat high prices, CDNow is the ideal way to buy music until we can download entire albums and copy them onto compact discs ourselves.

At the heart of CDNow is a search engine that lets you enter whatever information you have about a piece of music. This engine can be slow when you're doing an elaborate search, but a faster telnet-based engine is also available. When the engine displays a list of albums that match your search criteria, you click the price of those you want to buy and the site adds them to your virtual "shopping cart." When you leave the site, there are several ways to pay for your purchases.

★★ Computer Express

> **URL:** http://cexpress.com:2700/
> **Topic:** A Web computer store.
> **Of Special Note:** A telnet-based catalog.

Philip and Lesley Schier have operated their on-line computer store since 1985, when it opened as part of Compuserve's on-line mall. Since then, the Schiers claim they've had more than 200,000 customers. Their store displays a variety of computer hardware and software, and lets you order it via electronic mail or, by phone or fax. Computer Express offers no encryption support.

Computer Express' rating suffered because so little of it is actually in the format of the Web. Aside from the welcome page, the entire operation is either gopher or telnet, which really detracts from the appearance of the site. Still, Computer Express offers a lot of things for sale, and if you can't tear yourself away from your machine long enough to go to the computer store, you'll want to give this site a visit.

★★★ Online Bookstore

> **URL:** http://marketplace.com/0/obs/obshome.html
> **Topic:** The name says it all; it's a Web bookstore.
> **Of Special Note:** A very useful book-search form.

There is something inherently pleasurable about going to a bookstore. Whether you go to make a purchase or just wander the aisles looking at things that interest you, the experience usually is relaxing and something you look forward to doing again.

It is not always possible to make leisurely trips to the bookstore, though. Sometimes you need a particular book right away, and don't want to waste time wading through piles of texts that invariably distract you from the task at hand. Or, perhaps you live way out in the country and can't devote an entire afternoon to a book-buying venture. On these occasions, services like the Online Bookstore are a very useful option.

If you know something about the book you want to buy, choose the hyperlink labeled "Bookfinder Service." This link leads to a search form on which you can write any information you may have about the book you want, and specify how you want it shipped and how you want to pay for it. The Online Bookstore lets you call or fax your credit card number if you're reluctant to send it over the Web.

The bookstore also features links to a number of interesting on-line essays, as well as links to the home pages of publishing houses, some of whom allow you to order directly.

CHAPTER 23

Staying in Touch: Electronic Magazines and Newsletters

All the news that's bits we print.
—*The Nando Times*

In addition to online versions of traditional publications, special interest magazines and newsletters have found a place to flourish on the Web. Groups too small to afford print publishing can set up a Web site. In the near future, the number of online publications will explode. And, as more and more people with varying backgrounds use the Web, we'll see fewer computer-oriented publications and more of general interest.

If you've forgotten what the star ratings mean, look at the box at the beginning of Chapter 19.

MAGAZINES

One of the appealing things about magazines is that they can be tailored to the tastes of a fairly small group of people. That is why we see magazines published for everyone from Italian-car enthusiasts to gerbil ranchers. Because a magazine doesn't have to appeal to the same huge readership as a metropolitan newspaper, it can neglect broad issues in favor of things that appeal to only a few people. And on the Web, not surprisingly, those interests center on the Web itself. That said, non computer special-interest magazines are beginning to appear on the Web, as well as quite a few magazines with general appeal.

★★★ HotWired

URL: http://www.wired.com/

Topic: The Internet, the Web, their associated cultures, and other contemporary movements.

Of Special Note: Club Wired, an electronic forum in which you can talk to the movers and shakers of the on-line world at prearranged times.

Published by the same people that put out *Wired* magazine, the well-known print publication about all things modern and especially those on-line, HotWired is an electronic magazine devoted to the same idea. The developers of the site are adamant that HotWired is not merely a conversion of *Wired* into an on-line format, and they're right. They've done more than most Web magazines to put the special features of their new medium to work. (See Figure 23.1).

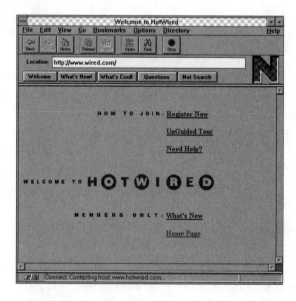

Figure 23.1 *Hot Wired (http://www.hotwired.com/Login)*

You have to register with the site before you can use HotWired—which takes only a few seconds and is free. After that, you can roam around the site, which contains full text from Wired features and a good selection of photographs. The text is inclined toward breathless statements about the electronic frontier, "way new journalism" and cyberspace, but it's generally informative and fun to read.

Don't miss Club Wired, a forum where you can "meet" famous people on-line. At preannounced times, authors, software developers and computer-industry leaders will "speak" in the forum and answer questions. When I visited, Neal Stephenson, author of the science fiction classic *Snow Crash*, had just wrapped up a presentation.

EXCELLENT

What do the hieroglyphs on the welcome screen mean? How are you supposed to know that "Coin" stands for on-line commercial services and "Renaissance 2.0" has to do with modern artistic movements? Sure, maybe it's part of the clubby atmosphere HotWired is trying to promote—those "in the know" about Internet and Web issues contrasted with everyone else—but the goofy terminology isn't welcoming to a novice.

AWFUL

★★★ MecklerWeb

> **URL:** http://www.mecklerweb.com/
>
> **Topic:** On-line magazines published by Meckler.
>
> **Of Special Note:** The Cowles/SIMBA media daily, a digest of computer news.

MecklerWeb (see Figure 23.2) claims to be "the first stop on the Internet." Well, it's true that an Internet and Web novice would benefit from a visit to this collection of on-line magazines and assorted other information, but that's not to say that a Web veteran wouldn't get something out of the experience as well. MecklerWeb is home to several publications, including *Internet World* and *VR World*, that may be purchased in printed form at newsstands.

Figure 23.2 *MecklerWeb (http://www.mecklerwebl.com/)*

Though the full text of the magazines doesn't appear here (Meckler is a magazine publisher), the size does contain information that you won't find in any magazine, either. Be sure to take a look at "This Week on MecklerWeb," where the Meckler webmasters post hyperlinks to cool sites they've found and news about the computer world. Also check out the Cowles/SIMBA media daily, a digest of computer news stories accessible through the News hyperlink on the welcome page.

Its good to see a site take time to explain the basics of Web navigation and protocol in beginner's terms. Because the Web is growing very fast, chances are good that some visitors to your site won't have a clue about Web basics.

EXCELLENT

★★★★ Pathfinder

URL: http://www.timeinc.com/pathfinder/Home_low.html

Topic: Time-Warner publications.

Of Special Note: Debate current news stories with the writers and editors of the magazines you read every day!

Pathfinder (see Figure 23.3) is Time-Warner's central Web site, with links to several on-line magazines. But it is not merely a common point from which you can find your favorite magazines. Pathfinder provides a forum for discussing the issues of the day, and Time-Warner writers and editors often get involved in the debates.

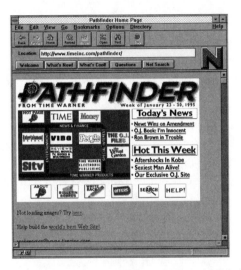

Figure 23.3 *Pathfinder (http://www.timeinc.com/pathfinder/)*

Pathfinder also includes links to clearinghouses of information about long-term news events. When I visited, O.J. Central was in operation, distributing background information about O.J. Simpson's alleged crimes and displaying a schedule of milestones in his trial. Pathfinder also includes reviews of books, movies, music, television, and multimedia products. Don't expect to find all the current articles in the print-based magazines; this site is a "teaser," offering (for the most part) a few current articles, archival resources, and background articles, such as Entertainment Weekly's list of Web hot spots. An exception: you'll find the full text of this week's *Time*.

Some of the magazines you can reach from Pathfinder:

> *Time*
>
> *People Weekly*
>
> *Entertainment Weekly*
>
> *Virtual Garden*, an on-line gardening magazine
>
> *Vibe*

★★★ PCWeek

URL: http://zcias3.ziff.com/~pcweek/

Topic: Computers, computing, and the computer industry.

Of Special Note: A nearly complete text of this popular computer-news weekly, and links to other Ziff-Davis periodicals on-line.

When a magazine goes on-line, it shouldn't do so in a tentative way. If a magazine is going to be on-line, its articles and columns should be on-line. If the articles and columns are going to be off-line, then aside from occasional advertisements on the print version, Web users should not be tantalized by a cut-rate Web version of the printed publication.

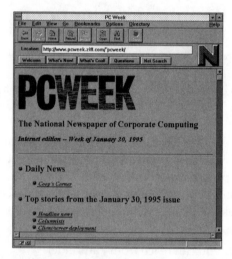

Figure 23.4 *PCWeek(http://www.pcweek.ziff.com/-pcweek/)*

PCWeek has gone on-line the right way. Ziff publishes this weekly computer- and information systems-industry publication in an Internet edition every bit as complete as the printed version. All the columnists, product reviews, and industry news are here. In fact, this version may even be better than the printed version: there are no advertisements to get in the way of the stuff you want to read. (Some people think ads are the best part of computer magazines, since they provide easy access to vendor information. The ads will probably be coming to the Web soon).

Consider *PCWeek* to be a harbinger of on-line trade magazines to come. Add a few hyperlinks to vendors storefronts and throw in a liberal dose of advertising, and you'll have a picture of a profitable, readable, environmentally friendly, and timely Web magazine without a print equivalent.

★★★★ Time

> **URL:** http://www.timeinc.com/time/magazine/magazine.html
>
> **Topic:** The full text of the current edition of *Time* magazine.
>
> **Of Special Note:** A report on how your Congressional representatives voted on recent bills.

This site (see Figure 23.5) leaves you with only one question: why in the world would anyone subscribe to the paper version of Time magazine after visiting this Web site? Well, okay, the Web doesn't make good bathroom reading. But aside from that, there's little in the print version that's not on the Time Web site. Advertisements are missing (thankfully) and unfortunately there are, few photographs here. But, the full text of all articles in the current issue appears here, and you can do a few things you can't do in print, like look up your Congressional representatives and see how they voted.

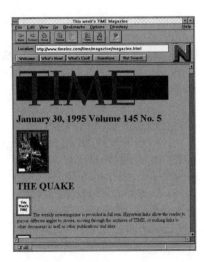

Figure 23.5 *Time (http://www.timeinc.com/time/magazine/magazine.html)*

From the well-organized welcome page, you can choose from among four main hyperlinks: This week's magazine, back issues, the voter's guide, and the Time masthead. Though you'll probably want to go right to the current issue, be sure to take a look at the masthead (the box in which the writers and editors names are listed) where, you'll find biographies for a lot of the Time staff—interesting reading if you want to know who's writing the news.

**USEFUL
RESOURCE**

There are other sites that let you see how your Congressional representatives voted on bills, but none so easy to use as Time's. All you have to do is enter your ZIP code into a box, and the search facility comes back with a table showing how your Senators and Representatives voted on about ten recent bills. The site also provides information about the bills, and electronic mail addresses for Congressional representatives so you can let them know what you think of their records.

**WISH
LIST**

Where are the photos? Many people people buy *Time* just to see color pictures of the things they've been reading about in newspapers all week. Its true that photos would seriously slow down the retrieval of a story, but maybe it would be possible to have a photo spread button at the bottom of each story so you could see the pictures if you wanted.

★★ Washingtonian On-line

URL: http://www.infi.net/washmag/

Topic: All things Washington, D.C.

Of Special Note: The list of restaurants. Do not read this if you're hungry!

Instead of trying to translate its stories and pictures into Web format, *Washingtonian* magazine (see Figure 23.6) took the information from its pages that fit best into the Web format and put it on-line. At the Washingtonian On-line site, you won't find long feature articles about news and newsmakers because they don't fit the medium. Another drawback: the Web isn't well suited (yet) to the kinds of design tricks the *Washingtonian* likes to perform. Still, Washington area Web users will want to add this URL to their hotlists. Instead, you'll get long lists of useful data about life in D.C. including:

- A guide to Washington-area private schools.
- A guide to specialized libraries.
- A list of area billiard clubs.
- A searchable database of Securities and Exchange Commission filings, including those made by Washington-area companies.

Most of the lists have hyperlinks to further information about each item. But don't expect lengthy articles.

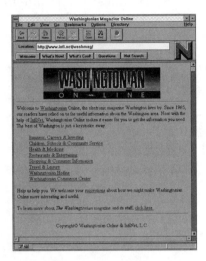

Figure 23.6 *Washington On-line (http://www.infi.net/washmag/)*

NEWSLETTERS

It's difficult to distinguish between magazines and newletters on the Web. In real life, a newsletter is usually just that: a page or two filled with news. On the Web, the information a newsletter carries can actually be linked to locations all over the world, with the welcome page just serving as a front end for other sites' data.

Here, an item is considered to be a newsletter if the body of information it contains is small, and if the publishers update it frequently. You might want to find a newsletter that pertains to your interests or line of work and refer to it frequently as it's helpful to have someone else combing the Web for information you might miss on your own.

★★ Cooley Alerts

URL: http://www.cgc.com/alerts/alerts.html

Topic: Recent developments in the law.

Of Special Note: Clear, relatively simple text easily understood by non-lawyers.

Cooley Alerts (see Figure 23.7) is similar to the Nolo Press site described in Chapter 22—it tries to explain legal issues to non-lawyers. A product of the California legal firm Cooley, Godward, Castro, Huddleson & Tatum, this site deals with more complex issues than Nolo Press and covers them more in-depth. Furthermore, Cooley Alerts does not try to sell you anything.

Figure 23.7 *Colley Alerti (http//www.cgc.com/slerts/alerts.html)*

There isn't a lot of information on the Cooley Alerts site, but what is available is good. When I visited, lawyers had posted four briefs about three different legal issues, including intellectual property, securities litigation, and venture capital issues. Each brief describes some history about the issue, and cites landmark cases that established precedent judges might use in the future. Cooley Alerts explains the issues in terms a businessperson would understand, emphasizing practical issues instead of legal theory. For example, the newsletter provides a bulleted list of three ways to determine a startup company's solvency, and describes how a cash-strapped company would affect the responsibilities of its directors.

You wouldn't expect to find graphics in a legal newsletter, and there aren't very many here. This site received a two-star rating because its information is limited in quantity and audience. Even so, it's worth a visit to keep on top of current legal issues.

★★★ Edupage

> **URL:** http://www.educom.edu/edupage.new
>
> **Topic:** News that deals with both higher education and computer technology.
>
> **Of Special Note:** Educom updates this page three times each week—it's current!

Yes, this is a text site. There are no pictures, no hyperlinks, and no sound clips. It's all plain text. But so is the *Wall Street Journal* (apart from a few charts and engravings), and its one of the best papers in the world. The value of a publication like Edupage is not its appearance (uncluttered and to the point), but its content.

Edupage compiles news related to computing issues into a single Web document three times each week. The articles are short summaries of news articles appearing elsewhere, so a quick scan lets you keep up with all the latest news about computing. If you're at all interested in the news that defines the Web and the Internet—educational institutions play a big role in both—make sure you put Edupage on your hotlist and check it every couple of days.

★★ GNN NetNews

> **URL:** http://gnn.com/cgi-bin/imagemap/HOME?384,94
>
> **Topic:** Internet and Web news and commentary.
>
> **Of Special Note:** Take a look at predictions of what Web sites will be hot in the future.

O'Reilly and Associates is known for its "Best of the Net" and "Best of the Web" awards. The company's newsletter is worth keeping an eye on, because who best to give you the news about the Web than the people who monitor its growth and development? This site includes news (a lot of it from Edupage), sports, commentary, weather, and, praise be, a comics page featuring the ever-popular Dilbert! This is a newspaper for Web surfers who like their news fast and clear, but accompanied by the humor that defines the Web in many ways.

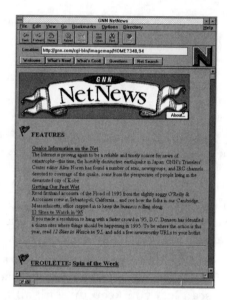

Figure 23.8 NetNews (http://gnn.com/cgi-bin/imagemap/HOME?384,94)

Don't pass up the chance to read the features in GNN NetNews. Here, from hyperlinks at the top of the welcome page, you'll see what O'Reilly and Associates experts think about various parts of the Web and the people and companies that run it. Effectively, this is a preview of "Best of the Web."

★★★★ Netsurfer Digest

URL: http://www.netsurf.com/nsd/index.html

Topic: The Internet, the Web, and the culture that's sprung from them.

Of Special Note: The Netsurfer Marketplace, a collection of ads offering products and services from a variety of vendors.

Published by Netsurfer Communications of California, Netsurfer Digest provides news, commentary, and opinion about the on-line world. Like Edupage, Netsurfer Digest is a Web version of a text-only newsletter distributed by email, so don't expect fancy graphics. But, there's a ton of useful information about the Web—specifically, new and interesting Web sites. Websurfer Digest offers what is probably the best overview of new Web resources that you'll find anywhere.

CHAPTER 24

Parents, Kids, and Education

*The main purpose of intellectual education is not the
acquisition of facts but learning how to make facts live
—Oliver Wendell Holmes*

The Parents section lists sites where parents and experts discuss and provide assistance with family problems. The Kids section lists resources for the young members of our community. (These resources are meant to be shared—the kids' sites are not for children alone. They'll get much more out of them when they're explored with a parent or teacher.

Finally, the education sites contain kinds of info that can benefit the entire Web community. Our colleges and universities are repositories of information, and their resources are useful to even the most junior students.

If you've forgotten the meanings of the star rankings, look at the box at the beginning of Chapter 19.

PARENTS

There are a lot of parents out there, and many of them deal with the same problems at one time or another. With the Web's ability to bring people together, parents have a new way of sharing information and helping one another through the often-challenging endeavor of raising children.

These sites include one with information of general interest to moms and dads, one specializing in the needs of parents whose children died before birth, and one of special interest to parents of handicapped or chronically ill children. The spirit of these sites is consistent, though: parents and experts who have dealt with difficulties before are reaching out across the Web to assist others.

★★★★ SANDS Information

URL: http://203.10.72.1/vicnet/community/sands.htm

Topic: Resources for parents of stillborn or miscarried children.

Of Special Note: A big collection of very specific information from people who deal with this highly emotional issue full-time.

A stillbirth or miscarriage terrifies and confuses everyone involved. Much of the Web concerns itself with the research and communication that may someday prevent such things from happening, but certain sites, such as Stillbirth and Neonatal Death Support (SANDS) (see Figure 24.1), deal with supporting and assisting those affected by unsuccesful pregnancies. SANDS gives people a new way to help one another in times of crisis.

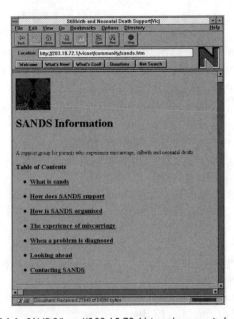

Figure 24.1 SANDS(http://203.10.72.1/vicnet/community/sands.htm)

SANDS consists of one document, arranged in outline form. A general index appears at the top of the document, the entries are hyperlinked to sections of the document. These sections, in turn, have more specific lists of contents, also hyperlinked, that refer to the actual information. The information you'll find at the SANDS site includes:

- A discussion of parents feelings after a miscarriage.
- An explanation of the technical aspects of naming and burial.
- A description of the sorts of counseling available.

This site received its four-star rating not on technical merit, but because it exemplifies the way in which a medium like the Web can be used to promote human interaction and support. Many of the Web sites reviewed in this book specialize in providing information about a particular issue, and many of these sites do a better technical job than SANDS, but few sites contain the sort of information that can help individuals in times of need and grief.

EXCELLENT

★★ Facts for Families

URL: http://www.med.umich.edu/aacap/facts.index.html

Topic: Family problems and solutions.

Of Special Note: More than 50 clear, well-written reports on common child and family problems.

A service of the American Academy of Child and Adolescent Psychiatry, Facts for Families includes a wealth of information about more than 50 family situations ranging from routine to dangerous. The text-based welcome page consists of a list of topics, each hyperlinked to a page of information about that topic. The reports were written by counselors, psychologists, and medical doctors, and each provides background information and possible solutions. Don't look for snazzy graphics, this site is serious business, and of interest only to those facing parenting problems.

Some of the topics covered are:

- Lead Exposure
- The Influence of Music and Rock Videos
- Stepfamily Problems
- Childrens Sleep Problems
- Children Who Steal

This isn't a site for do-it-yourself psychologists, but it is a good place to go for information if you think there's something wrong with a member of your family. These guides serve mainly as a self-screening tool for families, and each report advises you to get help from a professional if you've identified a problem.

★★ Parents Helping Parents

> **URL:** http://www.portal.com/~cbntmkr/php.html
>
> **Topic:** The special needs of ill and handicapped children and their families.
>
> **Of Special Note:** A big collection of software.

Founded in 1976, Parents Helping Parents (Figure 24.2) is a non-profit organization devoted to serving the interests of special-needs children and their families. The California-based organization works with doctors and families to help such children lead full and satisfying lives, and is known for its seminars and nationwide computer bulletin boards. PHP has now established a Web site to further its mission of distributing information and promoting communication.

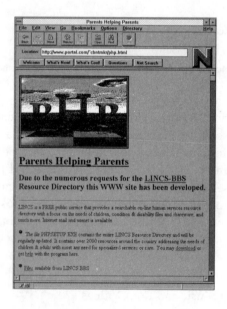

Figure 24.2 Parents Helping Parents (http://www.portal.com/~cbntmkr/php.html)

The site isn't too impressive by itself—it's really just a link to an FTP site and a collection of hyperlinks to other sites with similar interest. However, if you're interested in what is being done in terms of research and advocacy in the interest of injured and sick children, you should take a look.

Pay special attention to the FTP site, which contains text files having to do with the state of research into certain illnesses, and lists of hundreds of phone numbers to support lines and local computer bulletin boards. The site also contains programs designed to make it easier for handicapped people to use computers, including a "sticky keys" program for people who have difficulty with the keyboard. (This program lets you press the Shift key, release it, and press a letter key in order to get a capital letter on your screen.) The FTP site also includes programs and text files of general interest, such as mail readers and explanations of the ways of the Internet.

KIDS

It's the kids who are in elementary and middle school now that are going to really reap the fruits of the on-line revolution. These sites exist mainly to help kids with their homework, but in the process they can help them get used to clicking around the Web. Though these sites seem to have suffered from the poor Web accessibility in schools below the university level, they have the potential to be the fastest-growing segment of the Web before long.

★★ Kids'Net

> **URL:** http://rmii.com/~pachecod/kidsnet/ckids.html
>
> **Topic:** Kids eventually will us—and operate—this fun- and information-oriented Web site.
>
> **Of Special Note:** The "Wizards" room, where someday students will get homework pointers from each other and their teachers.

The concept is sound, but this site needs a lot of work and interest before it can start to catch on with its target audience of children 12 and younger. Kids'Net is supposed to provide children with their first on-line experience and get them interested in exploring the rest of the Web and Internet (see Figure 24.3). Kids'Net includes such potentially cool features as the Wizards page, where older kids will help younger ones with their homework and post the help for all to see, and the Computer Room, where students will learn to write HTML documents and expand

Kids'Net. The ultimate goal of Kids'Net's founders is to turn control of the site over to kids, and have them run their own on-line service.

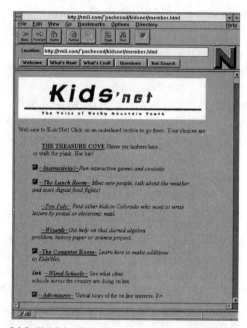

Figure 24.3 Kids'Net (http://rmii.com/-pachecod/kidsnet/ckids.html)

The best-laid ideas of well-meaning parents and teachers seem to be hitting a roadblock when it comes to interest from actual kids, though. In the Lunch Room, an area in which kids are supposed to chat, the only coherent message reads, "This is the first entry in this exciting new BBS. Come on kids, add your own." Presumably, Kids'Net will catch on after its been up a while and Web access spreads from government and higher-education sites to elementary and junior high schools.

In fact, giving Web access to such schools is another mission of Kids'Net. The site contains an appeal for corporate sponsors and programmers, which are needed to set schools up with the necessary equipment. Kids'Net offers to put companies' logos on its documents in exchange for money, equipment, and expertise. Though this site doesn't seem to have taken off yet, the potential is large and its good to see people using the Web for community-service reasons.

★★★★ Kids Web

URL: http://www.npac.syr.edu/textbook/kids web/

Topic: An on-line library of hyperlinks.

Of Special Note: One of the simplest and best laid-out, yet most complete, libraries you'll see!

Many parents use CD-ROM encyclopedias and other commercial multimedia products in efforts to provide their kids with the latest electronic educational tools. My advice to those parents: If you have a telephone line, save yourself a trip to the computer store and set your chidren up with a browser that has Kids Web (see Figure 24.4) at the top of the hotlist. This site, completely unaffiliated with Kids'Net, is a gathering point for links to some of the Web's finest resources on topics studied in elementary, junior high, and high schools. Though Kids Web contains no actual subject information itself, it has hyperlinks to resources in dozens of subjects, including astronomy, biology, chemistry, drama, government, literature, mathematics, and music. The site also features links to very useful on-line reference material, and to some fun stuff like sports sites. My only criticism of this site is its name—there's no way to argue that this site is useful only to kids.

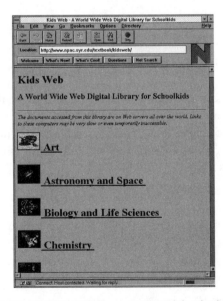

Figure 24.4 *Kids Web (http://www.npac.syr.edu/textbook/kidsweb/)*

Choose the topic that interests you from the list of subjects on the Kids Web welcome page. Youll be presented with a list of sites that specialize in that subject. For example, the biology list has links to several interactive frog dissections, a link to a page of references to dinosaur sites, and a link to something called the Rat Atlas (evidently a catalog of dissected rat parts.) Think of Kids Web as a reference librarian—it doesnt have any of the answers itself, but it's very good at telling you where to look.

🕷 WEBMASTER

Yes, Virginia, you can do a good job with a site that contains nothing but metadata. One interesting thing about the Web is that you can design your own interface for other people's information, and have your site be more popular than theirs. Kids Web is a value-added site, that gives you the convenience of having a lot of useful sites gathered together. Finding the sites you need in a reference emergency is a hassle, but sites like this make it easy.

★★★★ Kids on Campus

> **URL:** http://www.tc.cornell.edu/Kids.on.Campus/KOC94/
>
> **Topic:** A colorful directory of on-line resources.
>
> **Of Special Note:** A huge library of hyperlinks to other on-line locations.

The welcome page of Kids on Campus (see Figure 24.5) features a group of road signs, illustrating the "information highway" metaphor to kids. The signs feature directions designed to appeal to children, such as "Dinosaurs" and "Sound Studio." These links appeal to kids young and old, but it is the library section that makes Kids on Campus a truly useful resources.

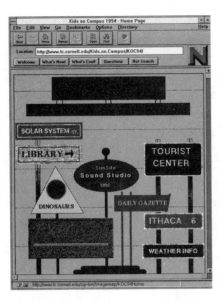

Figure 24.5 Kids on Campus (http:/www.tc.cornell.edu/Kids.on.Campus/KOC94)

The library page, updated freqently, includes a list of more than 50 general topics, such as finance, journalism, and software. The topic headings lead to listings of on-line resources in that field. For example, the journalism hyperlink led to a page of four sites containing information about newspaper and other media issues, each with a lengthy description and some hints on what you'll find there. This "expanded card catalog" will save you research time by focussing from your search to sites that are of value to you.

🕷 WEBMASTER

This site outshines a lot of the other library pages because it breaks up its information intelligently and lets you navigate freely. If the information at Kids on Campus weren't divided this way, either some information would have to be left out or the site would be so hopelessly confusing as to be useless.

The difference between this site and Kids Web is one of scope. Keep Kids Web in you hotlist for quick reference tasks; keep Kids on Campus there for more elaborate information-hunting jobs. You'll also wonder why this site has "kids" in its name, since it's so useful for grownups, too.

K-12 EDUCATION

We owe as much help as we can give to the people who go into classrooms full of kids and try to teach them what they need to know to live and work in our society. These sites certainly don't take much of the burden off of classroom instructors, but they might help a little and they could prove useful to students who have been turned off to learning by the seemingly dull research material in the school library. Instructors should also bear in mind the resources in the Kids section of this chapter—they're often just as good as these.

★★ IBM Kiosk for Education

> **URL:** http://ike.engr.washington.edu/ike.html
>
> **Topic:** IBM and its efforts to support education.
>
> **Of Special Note:** A great archive of educational software.

Unless you're studying the International Business Machines Corporation, this site (see Figure 24.6) isn't primarily concerned with issues of education. There's a lot of useful information here, particularly about computer science issues and IBM's efforts to share its expertise with schools, but this site is more of an on-line marketing tool than a real resource for scholars of any level.

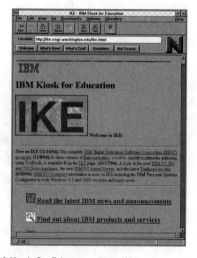

Figure 24.6 *IBM Kiosk for Education (http://ike.engr.washington.edu/ike.html)*

The one exception is the software available for downloading from IKE. Follow the **Download higher ed software** hyperlink from the welcome page, and browse the list of programs available in several formats. You'll find molecular-modeling software, stock market prediction models, planetarium simulators, and an Italian language tutor. Just click the name of any program you think you need, and IKE downloads it for you. If you're an educator, look here for software that might make your job easier.

USEFUL
RESOURCE

The site also features a database of IBM news and press releases, and gopher sites full of information about IBM's computers and software. Be sure to take a look at IBM's information about the new products of its various divisions. In short, this is a very useful site, just not one well-suited for the purpose of education.

★★ Dewey

> **URL:** http://ics.soe.umich.edu/
>
> **Topic:** A library of Web hyperlinks.
>
> **Of Special Note:** Descriptions of some cool on-line educational projects.

Dewey contains more references than Kids Web, but its organized badly and it might take a few clicks to get to the list of sites you need. Dewey, a project of Interactive Communications and Simulations at the University of Michigan, also includes descriptions of and links to several interesting ICS projects that use the Web to promote global communications among students.

To get to the actual Dewey library, you must either click two different hyperlinks on the welcome page or use the scroll bar. The first hyperlink, labeled "DeweyWeb Library," takes you to the bottom of the welcome page. There, a second hyperlink, labeled "Visit the library," leads to the actual library page. It would make more sense to have the library accessible with a single click, but until that happens, set your home page or hotlist to lead directly to the library page (http://www.umich.edu/~jmillr/WWW-libraries.html).

The library is a collection of hyperlinks; there is little actual information here. The hyperlinks aren't as well organized as they are on Kids' Web or Kids on Campus, but there are more of them. The library has three categories—on-line libraries, on-line galleries, and Web search facilities—but within those categories hyperlinks appear in no apparent order. You might want to visit this site and browse its links to see if any relate to your interests, but it's probably not a good idea to rely on Dewey as a fast way of finding specialized Web sites.

★★★ Education (K-12) Resources

URL: http://www.cs.fsu.edu/~durga/resources.html

Topic: Resources for students and teachers.

Of Special Note: A good list of links to other Web libraries.

Although Education (K-12) Resources take on too much for one site (the topic is education in general), They do a good job of providing teachers with a central place to exchange information with one another and hunt for Web sites to help with their lessons. The site is fairly well-organized and includes links to lots of other sites, including those of interest to educators as well as their students. For example, the site includes hyperlinks to the Department of Education site and the Smithsonian Natural History gopher.

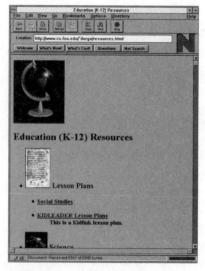

Figure 24.7 Education (K-12) Resources (http://www.cs.fsu.edu/~durga/resources.html)

Other links include:

- A bunch of Web libraries.
- Weather information.
- Penpal requests.
- NASA's Classroom Earth project site.

A teacher might not want to turn kids loose on the Web, since they might get lost among the links to sites of interest to educators when they're supposed to be looking for information about Saturn. It would make sense to separate the teacher-interest information from the research materials—combining the two makes the page confusing and hard to figure out.

HIGHER EDUCATION

Higher education institutions were among the first to go on-line, as professors and students communicated with colleagues and government researchers around the world. There are many Internet- and Web-literate people in academia, and quite a few on-line resources that cater to this community.

Because the academic community went on-line long before the Web came about, many of its on-line resources are not graphical. I've even included a gopher site here, because it's very useful to those in academia and just hasn't been converted to HTML yet.

★★ Academe

> **URL:** gopher://chronicle.merit.edu/
>
> **Topic:** The Chronicle of Higher Education
>
> **Of Special Note:** A searchable index of academic job openings.

Yes, this is a gopher site and the interface is correspondingly dull. On the other hand, the *Chronicle of Higher Education* supports this site, and its emphasis is on content instead of appearance. Like the popular journal of academic issues, this site carries information about all things related to academia. When I visited Academe, the issues included methods for teaching history, admissions standards for NCAA athletes, and personal-finance options for people employed in higher education.

If you're looking for a job in higher education, be sure to make Academe's job search feature your first stop. You can limit your search to any area of the United States, if you want, then type in a keyword— such as history or mathematics—and see a list of jobs available that meet your specifications. A search for history jobs in the South turned up 14 openings, and each listing was hyperlinked to a description of the job with contact names and addresses.

USEFUL
RESOURCE

Also be sure to check out the guide to the current issue of the *Chronicle of Higher Education*. The guide contains brief summaries of the articles in the current issue,

and could be useful if you're debating whether to buy the current issue. Sadly, there is no way to search the backlog of *Chronicle* summaries.

★★ American Universities

> **URL:** http://www.clas.ufl.edu:80/CLAS/american-universities.html
>
> **Topic:** Welcome pages of U.S. colleges and universities.
>
> **Of Special Note:** Easy to use with your browser's search function.

As more and more colleges and universities establish their presence on the Web, its useful to have a directory of their welcome pages. Typically, a university's welcome page has hyperlinks to various departments, the library catalog, and special resources at the university. American Universities (not affiliated with American University) alphabetically lists most of the higher-education welcome pages in the United States. It's a useful tool if you need something at a particular school, but don't know the URL of that particular resource.

HOT TIP

The best way to use American Universities is with your browser's search function. When you drop into the American Universities document, don't waste time scrolling through the list. Instead, call up your search function and enter the name of the school you want. The browser will find the school's hyperlink if it's on the list, and you'll have saved several seconds.

★★ Educom

> **URL:** http://educom.edu/
>
> **Topic:** Education and computer technology.
>
> **Of Special Note:** The Edupage electronic newsletter, described in Chapter 23.

Educom's welcome page says the organization is "transforming education through information technology." As an organization of computer companies, colleges, universities and individuals, Educom is dedicated to using computer technology to enhance the paper-oriented education system as it now exists. Educom organizes conferences, promotes on-line discussions, and publishes the Edupage newsletter, reviewed in Chapter 23.

All of these functions appear on this welcome page. There are hyperlinks to the latest Edupage and to back issues, and there are other hyperlinks to conference and seminar schedules. You also have opportunities to join Educom or contribute to the Edupage newsletter at this site.

CHAPTER 25

Just Plain Fun

It's like the information highway, but without the information.
—David Letterman

A lot of the sites in this book have been, well, kind of dry. You've seen sites that send you tax forms, teach you about manatees, or give you the text of Shakespeare's plays. Those sites are all useful, and perhaps fun in their own way, but they're not in the spirit of frivolity that permeates so much of the Web.

Computer people are notorious pranksters. Someone once gave me a disk, saying it contained "shareware." I put the disk in my machine and typed in the name of the only executable file listed on the disk. The words, "WARNING! Water Detected in Drive A!" appeared on my screen, and a convincing burbling sound came from the internal speaker. Both the sounds and the warning were the result of a prank program. I'd been had.

. The harmless fun lives on the Web as does the borderline, idiotic (humor is, after all; a matter of taste). There are sites containing plain jokes-and-stories, song parodies, cartoons, and "Top 10 lists." I've also included interactive sites,where you participate in the story. (If you've forgotten what the star ratings mean, take a look at the box at the beginning of Chapter 19.)

INTERACTIVE SITES

The technology of passive entertainment reached its pinnacle with television and motion pictures. Interactive entertainment, in which you play a part and don't just sit back and wait to be amused, is a budding genre that includes such things as hypertext fiction and interactive visual art.

The Web is a greenhouse in which these technologies are sprouting. Since it can not only handle text, pictures, video and sound, but also allow a reason to register a response to them, the web has all the components of successful interactive entertaiment. The sites listed below are some of the best interactive entertainment on the Web.

★★★★ The Doomsday Brunette

URL: http://zeb.nysaes.cornell.edu/ddb.cgi

Topic: Interactive fiction.

Of Special Note: One of the first Web implementations of a new artistic medium.

One of the benifits of new technology is the tendency of new forms of artistic expression to spring from it. We didn't have cave paintings until people figured out pigments and dyes; we didn't have finely detailed sculptures until metal tools came about; and we didn't have hypertext fiction until personal computers became widely available. The Web takes hypertext fiction—stories in which you make decisions about the path the plot takes—to new levels. Doomsday Brunette exemplifies the state of the art for hypertext fiction on the Web.

The Doomsday Brunette is the story of Zachary Nixion Johnson, a private detective in 2056. (Johnson's, mother was fascinated by late twentieth-century U.S. presidents, but could not spell.) He needs your help to solve his latest case, a drama that employs the hypertext capabilities of the Web to their greatest potential. This is interactive fiction: You choose your path through various versions if the story.

John M. Zakour, the creator of The Doomsday Brunette (if you're feeling postmodern, you might want to think about who's really the author of a hypertext story), uses this Web site as a marketing tool by only letting you see the first three chapters of the story. He wants you to download the full version (available in Windows format only), and pay $5.95 for the password that lets you see the rest of the chapters. It's not a bad idea: The Doomsday Brunette is a great story, the format is fun, and the price is less than you'd, pay for a detective paperback at the bookstore.

🕷WEBMASTER

Webmaster's, think of more ways to put the Web to creative use! We've seen the Internet Underground Music Archive present a way for musicians to bypass the music-publishing houses, so let's see the same thing happen for written text. And not just traditional texts, either: interactive hypertext works, as well. Such sites, will promote the arts and help a new expressive medium flourish.

★★ Inter-face

URL: http://www.well.com/Community/Inter-face/Inter-face.html

Topic: Mix-and-match face parts.

Of Special Note: A cool use of forms technology.

Get to know Anna, Jenny, John, Miko, PJ and Tom, the six people whose faces you get to work with at Inter-face (Figure 25.1). The idea is simple—you select which of the characters will provide the top, middle or bottom of a face, then click **Submit face** to send off your request and see the combined result. The results are pretty low-tech, since the site doesn't even try to blend the face parts together, and the original pictures from which the parts were taken aren't the same size. You'll get some goofy results—faces with black hair over their foreheads but red hair over their eyes, and little chins that don't match the rest of the face's proportions at all.

Figure 25.1 *Inter-face (http://www.well.com/Community/Inter-face/Inter-face.html)*

★★★ Tarot

URL: http://cad.ucla.edu/repository/useful/tarot.html

Topic: Tarot-card readings.

Of Special Note: Two different types of tarot readings, complete with interpretations.

For those who just aren't satisfied with fact-based information already on the Web, the Tarot site (Figure 25.2) will bring more information from the Other Side. Point your browser at this site to have your Tarot cards drawn and interpreted.

In one reading I got The Hermit, the solitary possessor of secrets, as the representative of my past. The Ace of Swords foretold my future, predicting "Excessiveness in everything." Perhaps most prophetic was the card drawn to represent my present—the Queen of Pentacles, reversed. This card indicates neglected duties and false prosperity. The Cards obviously know that I'm behind on my deadline!

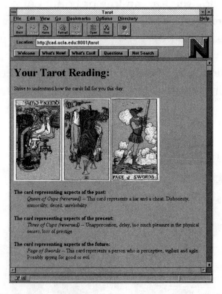

Figure 25.2 *My Tarot Fortune (http://cad.ucla.edu/repository/useful/tarot.html)*

There's also a more elaborate Celtic tarot reading feature, which involves more than a dozen cards and their attendant meanings. If you aren't enlightened about tarot, read the Tarot FAQ for basic information.

HUMOR AND GAMES

Computers have spawned two things—productivity software, like word processors and spreadsheets that helps you do more work, and games that help you relax after doing all that productive stuff. Web sites for both types of software are flourishing, but you'll enjoy visiting the humor and games sites a lot more.

Among the lighthearted sites, humor pages compete for your hours of time-wasting. Jokes, stories and (especially) lists beg for your attention, which you will proudly give if these sites make it onto your hotlist. A word of warning: do not visit these sites at work if you have a short-fused boss. There's no way to conceal the fact that these sites are pure entertainment.

★★ Dr. Fun

> **URL:** http://sunsite.unc.edu/Dave/drfun.html
> **Topic:** Dr. Fun cartoons.
> **Of Special Note:** An archive of past Dr. Fun cartoons, available for downloading.

David Farley, an amateur cartoonist who works full time in the computer labs of the University of Chicago, publishes a cartoon panel called Dr. Fun (Figure 25.3) on the Web five days each week. His cartoons are populated by elephants in toxic-materials handling suits and Nobel prize winners holding sticks of dynamite, and are reminiscent of Gary Larson's *The Far Side*. Dr. Fun doesn't appear in any books or other for-profit publications and is distributed solely via the Web and the Internet.

A link to Farley's archives appears on the Dr. Fun welcome page, and he makes it clear that he's quite liberal about the copyright restrictions on his work. You may use the archived cartoons for any non-profit reason you choose, so feel free to print out an especially funny panel and post it on your door. You can even use the cartoons in not-for-profit newsletters if you ask permission from Farley, so put his cartoons to good use.

USEFUL RESOURCE

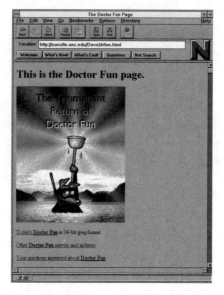

Figure 25.3 *Dr. Fun (http://sunsite.unc.edu/Dave/drfun.html)*

★★ **Games Domain**

>**URL:** http://wcl-rs.bham.ac.uk/GamesDomain/
>
>**Topic:** Computer game help.
>
>**Of Special Note:** "Walkthroughs" of tough games, for those who are stuck or like to cheat.

They say that games negated any productivity gains brought about by the micro-computer revolution. Who hasn't sat at their machine, playing Myst or Doom in an electronic stupor, even when there was important work to be done? Games are part of the personal computer culture, and if you're open enough about your habit to talk about it, you'll want to stop by Games Domain (Figure 25.4).

There are no games available for downloading here. Instead, this site provides support for commercial games and acts as a jumping-off place for other Web sites. If you're unclear about the rules of a game, look at the game FAQs. If you're completely stuck in a mystery or adventure (you just *can't* get the blue Mario to swim around the alligator), check out the walkthroughs. These two resources should get anyone older than 13 into video-game nirvana, players younger than that are already there.

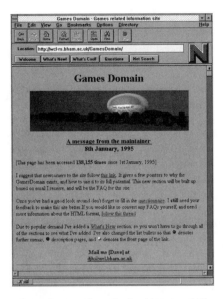

Figure 25.4 Games Domain (http://wcl-rs.bham.ac.uk/GamesDomain/)

🕷WEBMASTER

Check out the statistics pages at Games Domain. Visitors to a site want to know who's been there before them, and what those people have done. Though the Games Domain statistics format isn't the greatest, it's a start. Statistics pages are very useful, and belong on many Web pages of similar function.

★★ Giggle

URL: http://www.glasswings.com.au/GlassWings/jolly/giggle.html

Topic: A laugh a minute.

Of Special Note: Rocketship Ginger!

Giggle's purpose is "to reconnect people with their ability to have FUN!" Giggle makes a valiant stab at getting you to laugh, or at least introducing you to the quirks of Australian humor. Giggle is a monthly magazine containing jokes, trivia and an altogether odd serial about Rocketship Ginger a cartoon of Katherine Phelps (Figure 25.5).

Figure 25.5 Rocketship Ginger (http://www.glasswings.com.au/GlassWings/jolly/giggle.html)

EXCELLENT

Rocketship Ginger and her dog Rikki are the crew of the spaceship Polkadot as it travels through the galaxy encountering strange situations and concluding each episode in a comically inconclusive way. Rocketship Ginger has sound files attached that add a lot to the presentation.

Aside from "Rocketship Ginger," Giggle offers a variety of fun stuff. Don't miss "The Joke Assortment with Chewy Centres" or "The Rhinocerous in Maribeth's Living Room." Non sequiturs and general absurdity abound in this humor haven.

★★ Helpful Lists To Improve Your Life

> **URL:** http://www.umd.umich.edu/~nhughes/htmldocs/
>
> **Topic:** Letterman-style lists.
>
> **Of Special Note:** "How to Shoot Yourself in the Foot" has special appeal to programmers.

Internet humor has always included the sophomoric, and now there's a Web page specializing in poor taste. A sampling:

- Ways to Confuse Your Roommates (Number 15: "Kill roaches with a monkey wrench while playing Wagnerian arias on a kazoo").

- Ways to Annoy People ("Race the old woman for the last bus seat").

- Ways to Get Rid of Blind Dates (Number 8: "Stare at your date's neck, and grind your teeth audibly").

- Ways to Be Offensive at a Funeral (Number 2: "Tell the undertaker that he can't close the coffin until you find your contact lens").

- Ways to Annoy People in the Computer Lab (Number 50: "Two words: Tesla Coil").

★★ Jay's Comedy Club

URL: http://paul.spu.edu/~zylstra/comedy/index.html

Topic: Miscellaneous humor.

Of Special Note: A gigantic collection of lightbulb jokes.

Like any comedy club, Jay's includes an eclectic collection of humor on a variety of topics. Computer jokes and Star Trek humor (standard fare on the Web) abound here. There are also funny stories galore (follow the "Amusing Stories" hyperlink from the welcome page) and a decent collection of top-ten lists.

What really makes this site stand out, though, are its collections of light bulb jokes. If ever you wanted to insult some obscure affinity group, this is the place to go for ammunition. Jay stocks lightbulb jokes about nuclear engineers, pre-med students, jugglers, database programmers, and just about every political, religious, and national group you can imagine. And, if you can't find the right lightbulb joke here, there are hyperlinks to other joke sites.

★★★ Wrecked Humor Page

URL: http://www.cs.odu.edu/~cashman/humor.html

Topic: Humor and general silliness.

Of Special Note: The Canonical Lists. Do not visit this page in a crowded office or a solemn computer lab.

The Wrecked Humor page is far from ruined, because it collects some of the best humor you'll find on the Web. A case in point is the Canonical Lists page, which is hyperlinked to the Wrecked Humor welcome page. Check out the list of country & western song titles, and be sure to take a look at the list of National Hockey League team names. Also visit the "Songs and Parodies and the like" page, which has a link to "The Ballad of O.J. Simpson," and the "Top Ten Lists and Similar Humor" Page, where the "6 Things You Don't Want to See at the ATM" list resides.

🕷 WEBMASTER

Do not, for any reason, put any sort of text in a drop-down menu box like the one on the Wrecked Humor welcome page. It looks bad, and it's hard to read. Maybe the programmer was going for some kind of silliness effect, butit was lost on me.

WEIRDNESS

Think of the sites in this section as a sort of an on-line daytime talk show. They've got ghosts. They've got aliens. They've got UFOs. They've got carnivorous bunny rabbits. They've got a guy who rates couches for comfort. In fact, they seem to have at least one of everything!

These sites could be considered the Web at its weirdest. They're not really good for anything, but they're a lot of fun and in a limited way, you get to make new friends as their owners share their personalities with you.

★★ Archive X

> **URL:** http://www.declab.usu.edu:8080/X/
>
> **Topic:** Ghost and UFO stories.
>
> **Of Special Note:** Coming soon: the Ghost Hunter's Guide!

Archive X is a gallery of the weird, housing ghost stories, information about UFOs and science fiction, all giving new meaning to the phrase "ghost in the machine."

You'll be intrigued by the ghost stories—tales of hauntings and visits from the dead, punctuated with helpful interjections like, "This freaked me out and freaked him out as well." (A whole lot of freaking out goes on in these stories.) If this stuff doesn't scare you off, take a look at some of the two dozen or so links listed here. The site: curator promises that he'll post a Ghost Hunter's Guide soon, and which I'll certainly be back to see.

★ **Devilbunnies**

> **URL:** http://www.xmission.com/~snowhare/
>
> **Topic:** Adorable rabbits, or so you think.
>
> **Of Special Note:** The FAQs. You won't understand anything without them (and very little with them).

All of the following statements are true (or so this page maintains):

- Devilbunnies are cute and fuzzy, and are indistinguishable from conventional bunnies.
- Devilbunnies communicate not with words and emoticons like most Web citizens, but with words and odd text inserts like "<fluffle>" and "<giggle-hop>".
- Devilbunnies like to kill human beings in order to eat their toes.
- Human beings can fight the Devilbunnies with fireman's axes and shotguns. To quote the Devilbunnies rule sheet, "Omega weapons that will kill every-bunny in a 10,000 mile radius are no-nos."

If this is your kind of humor, go for it. This site sprang from the Usenet newsgroup alt.devilbunnies, a forum in which people assume human or devilbunny personas and go about doing battle with one another. You may wonder what exactly motivated the Devilbunnies cadre to develop the elaborate scenarios in which they enact their war, and maybe that's part of the point. Regardless, pay this site a visit in the spirit of human diversity.

★★★★ **Useless Web Pages**

> **URL:** http://www.primus.com/staff/paulp/useless.html
>
> **Topic:** The worst of the Web.
>
> **Of Special Note:** Links to all the bizarre sites you can imagine.

Some people make it their life's work to understand some obscure aspect of literature or theology. Other strive to help others by developing a cure for a certain disease. Paul Phillips makes it his mission to catalog the weirdest of the Web's weird pages. Visit his site, and see ...

- Joe's Couch Rating page (Joe rates and reviews all his friends' couches).

- National Texture Administration (featuring an exhibit called "Man: The Texturing Animal."

- Band Name Server (a new band name every time you visit!).

- Shakespearian Insult Server (A new insult every time, thou weedy fool-born lewdster).

- Steve's List of all his T-Shirts (Steve lists and describes the shirts in his dresser drawer).

- Dots, Dots, Stupid Green Dots page (a must-see).

- The Page That Tells You How Many Time's It's Been Accessed (fun for the whole family!).

So what's next, The Cereal Name Server? The Parship Page? With man the "texturing animal" at work, it's anyone's guess.

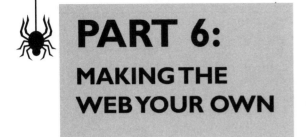

Using SmartPages

An ill-favoured thing, sir, but mine own.
—Shakespeare, *As You Like It*

When you start your graphical browser, you see the default home page. Chances are you've already changed this to something useful, like one of the starting points pages discussed in Chapter 16.

To get the most out of the Web, you'll eventually want to create your own home page, containing just the hyperlinks that you want to use on a daily basis. It may look homely, but who cares? It has the links you want. You can modify your browser so that it displays this home page, each time you start the program (or click the Home button).

The only problem with creating your own home page is that you must learn a little HTML. As Chapter 27 will show, it's not very difficult—no more so, certainly, than writing macros for word processing programs, which millions of people have done successfully.

AWFUL

If you're not quite ready to delve into HTML, the SmartPages provided on this book's disk might provide an interim solution for you

INTRODUCING SMARTPAGES

KEY
TERM

SmartPages, a unique feature of this book, are hyperlink-packed Web pages that you can use in place of your browser's default home page. They are a whole series of related, inter-linked pages on a wide variety of subjects. Using this book's SmartPages can increase your sense of control and knowledge of the Web's amazing resources.

The Connections Page

The Grand Central Station of your SmartPage collection is the Connections page (Figure 26.1). This is the page to use as your default home page (which you'll learn to do later in this chapter). It contains hyperlinks of general interest that you'll probably want to access frequently.

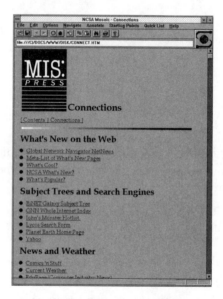

Figure 26.1 *The Connections Page*

What's New on the Web. Here, you'll find hyperlinks that keep you up-to-date on the Web's development:

- **Global Network Navigator NetNews.** The latest news on Web events and people.

- **Meta-List of What's New Pages.** An index of all the ways to find out about what's new on the Web.

- **What's Cool?** From Yahoo, a discriminating list of distinguished Web sites.

- **NCSA What's New?** A \"what's new" compilation from the folks who brought you Mosaic.
- **What's Popular?** From Yahoo, a list of the most popular hyperlinks accessed from the Yahoo subject tree.

Subject Trees and Search Engines. Here's quick access to the best subject trees and search engines:

- **EiNET Galaxy Subject Tree.** A sophisticated subject tree that incorporates a search engine as well.
- **GNN Whole Internet Index.** This subject tree contains selected high-quality hyperlinks; a good place to start if you're looking for the best.
- **John's Monster Hotlist.** One of my favorite subject trees, with emphases on weather, computing, the Internet, and the Web.
- **Lycos Search Form.** The best search engine by a wide margin, Lycos is the first place to start a key-word search.
- **Yahoo.** A wonderful, hyperlink-packed subject tree that's as cool as it is useful.

News and Weather. Do you need to subscribe to a newspaper? After checking out these links, you'll wonder!

- **Comics 'n Stuff.** A metapage listing over 50 comic strips available on the Web!
- **Current Weather.** An interactive, graphical map of the U.S.; click on an area to get a local forecast.
- **EduPage (Computer Industry News).** Succinct, well-written abstracts and magazine articles concerning developments in the computer and information industries, updated three times per week.
- **The News Page.** An incredible metapage, collecting hyperlinks to newspapers and magazines around the world.
- **Search Today's USENET News.** Don't waste time trying to plough through USENET for items of interest; use this service instead. It searches the dozens of megabytes of new USENET postings to find articles of interest to you.
- **Satchel Sports Page.** The latest sports news, scores, and stories.
- **Stock Quotes.** Quotations from today's markets, delayed only 15 minutes.

- **The Nando Times.** A great on-line newspaper from the Charlotte, N.C., *News & Observer*, focusing on national news.
- **This Week's Time Magazine.** Yes, the full text is here.

Reference. Whatever it is, look it up here!

- **Area Codes.** You type the location; the server gives you the area code.
- **AT&T 800 Directory.** Why call 1-800-555-1212? You can search here instead.
- **National Address Server.** If you're not sure of your correspondent's zip code but you do have the rest of the address, this site might be able to help.
- **NetFind.** This server might be able to help you find a person's e-mail address.
- **On-Line Webster's Dictionary.** So what's the difference between "epigram" and "epithet"? Find out here.

The Contents SmartPage

The Contents SmartPage (Figure 26.2) lists additional SmartPages, each of which contains a variety of hyperlinks focused on a particular area of interest (for an example see Figure 26.3). To get to the Contents SmartPage, click the **Contents** button at the top of the page. From the Connections SmartPage, you can access the Contents SmartPage by clicking the **Contents** button at the top of the page.

Please note that these SmartPages cover only a small portion of the Web's vast subject coverage; they don't even try to be exhaustive in their coverage. Their purpose is to provide a few interesting links to aid you in your exploration of the Web.

HOT TIP

As you're browsing through the SmartPages, think of how you can modify them to suit your own needs. It's easy to add a few hyperlinks to these documents! You'll learn how in the next chapter.

Here's a list of the SmartPages you'll find on the enclosed disk:

- **African-American SmartPage.** A variety of hyperlinks on African-American topics, including the AfroAmerican newspaper, AfriWeb, MelaNet, and much more.
- **Art SmartPage.** This SmartPage contains hyperlinks to art starting points, museums, and on-line exhibitions.

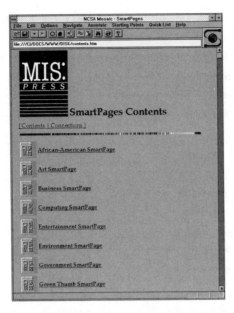

Figure 26.2 *Contents Page*

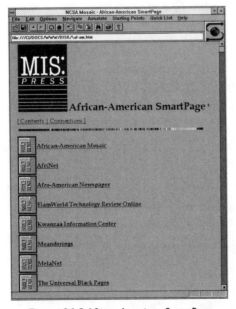

Figure 26.3 *African American SmartPage*

- **Business SmartPage.** On-line catalogs and shopping malls, as well as some interesting commercial sites.
- **Computing SmartPage.** Computer vendors, magazines, and user's groups.
- **Entertainment SmartPage.** Hyperlinks to sites of interest to TV and motion picture enthusiasts.
- **Environment SmartPage.** Green tips, environment-friendly businesses, and government information resources.
- **Government SmartPage.** Lots of hyperlinks to government agencies at the federal level.
- **Green Thumb SmartPage.** Gardens and gardening information—even a gardener's encyclopedia.
- **Instructional Technology SmartPage.** Lots of hyperlinks for anyone using computers for instructional purposes.
- **Investment SmartPage.** Stock market data, financial services firms, banks, and more.
- **K-12 Educators SmartPage.** A good Web start for anyone interested in K-12 education.
- **Kids' SmartPage.** Kids on the Web! Lots of fun stuff, including Calvin and Hobbes, games, and Kids' Net.
- **Law SmartPage.** The Constitution, law journals, and a very net-friendly law firm (Venable).
- **Management SmartPage.** Management schools and centers, management information, operations research, and more.
- **Medical SmartPage.** Information regarding general health and specific ailments.
- **Music SmartPage.** Everything you wanted to know about all kinds of music, including metapages to help you navigate the Web's musical riches.
- **Sports SmartPage.** Fishing, golfing, boating, ice hockey, and more.
- **Travel SmartPage.** Airlines, destinations, guidebooks, TravelWeb, even Club Med—let's go!
- **Wine SmartPage.** Wine reviews, and newsletters, even a virtual winery.

SmartPage Navigation

To access a SmartPage from the Contents SmartPage, just click the hyperlink. To return to the Contents SmartPage, click the **Contents** button at the top of the page. Alternatively, click the **Return** button at the bottom of the page. (You can also access the Connections SmartPage from any SmartPage by clicking the Connections button at the top of the page.)

INSTALLING SMARTPAGES

This book's SmartPages are provided in a self-extracting archive, which can be installed on any Microsoft Windows system. To install the archive on a Windows system, follow these directions:

1. Insert the enclosed disk in your floppy drive.

2. From the Program Manager's <u>F</u>ile menu, choose <u>R</u>un.

3. In the Command Line dialog box, type:

   a:\smart.exe.

4. Click **OK**.

Your system will switch to DOS, and the SmartPages will be decompressed. After SMART.EXE has finished running, you can make the Connections document your default home page, as explained in the following section.

USING A SMARTPAGE AS YOUR DEFAULT HOME PAGE

After you have installed the SmartPages on your computer's hard disk, you can make the Connections document your default home page. To do so, you must type the URL of this document correctly. If you store your SmartPages in the directory C:\\NETSCAPE, the URL of the Connections document would look like this:

   file:///c|/netscape./connect.htm

Note, the vertical line (|) character that is used in place of the colon is normally found after disk drive identifier. Also note that forward slashes, are used in place of the usual backslashes. If your browser doesn't load the Connections document correctly, check your typing carefully. Chances are you didn't include the colon, or

AWFUL

that you didn't type three slash marks, or you didn't use the vertical line character. Make sure you have typed the document's path correctly.

To change the default home page:

NCSA
MOSAIC

Use the Windows Notepad text editor to open the file **C:\\WINDOWS\\MOSAIC.INI**. In the [Main] section, look for the Home Page line. Erase the current URL, and carefully type the URL of the new Connections document, as described above. Save the file and exit.

ENHANCED
NCSA
MOSAIC

From the Options menu, choose **Configuration**. In the dialog box, type the URL of the Connections document, as described above, in the URL: area. Activate **Load Automatically at Startup**, and click the **OK** button.

NETSCAPE
NAVIGATOR

From the Edit menu, choose **Preferences**. In the Home Page box, type the URL of the Connections document, as described above. Click **OK** to confirm.

WEBSURFER

Open the Settings menu, and choose **Preferences**. In the Startup Document area, type the URL of the Connections document, as described above, in the URL box. Click **OK** to confirm.

SUMMARY

This book's SmartPages let you replace your browser's default home page with a series of interlinked pages, which offer dozens of useful hyperlinks. The "Grand Central Station" of the SmartPages is the Connections document, which contains many useful links to sources of Web information, Web search engines, news, sports, weather, and reference. The Contents document provides you with point-and-click access to SmartPages in a variety of areas of interest. They're far from exhaustive, but they're only intended to illustrate what you can do when you learn enough HTML to modify them. And that's the subject of the next chapter!

FROM HERE

- Learn enough HTML to create your own home page—or modify the SmartPages—in Chapter 27.

- Want to make your documents available for others on the Web? Check out Chapters 27 and 28, which fully explain what's required.

A Quick Introduction to HTML: Creating Your Own Home Page

All things are difficult before they are easy.
—Thomas Fuller (1732)

The previous chapter's Smart Pages provide useful default home page options for all kinds of people—but you're not all kinds of people, are you? If you'd like to create a default home page with just the hyperlinks you want, you've come to the right place. This chapter introduces just enough HTML to enable you to create your own home page to be the default home page for your Web browser. Your home page is *your* home page, designed to suit your needs rather than the lowest-common-denominator needs of the teeming masses. It's the ultimate customization for your graphical browser, and you'll find compete, step-by-step instructions in this chapter.

This chapter tells you how to create your own home page, and make it the default home page for your browser. However, this page won't be available for other Web users—it's yours alone. In the following chapter, you'll learn more about making your documents available for others to access.

HOME
PAGE

447

INTRODUCING HTML

The HyperText Markup Language (HTML) is exceptionally easy to learn. Anyone can learn enough HTML to create a simple document. Even if you've never done any computer programming, you'll find that it's a piece of cake.

Understanding HTML

HTML is not a programming language, which provide instructions in a sequence so that the computer can perform an action. Instead, HTML lets you *declare* what the parts of a document are, such as the title, the heading, a numbered list, and the author's address. This isn't the same as a word processor's formatting capabilities, though, and you should understand the distinction. A word processing program specifies precisely how a given unit of text should appear (including font, font size, line spacing, and alignment). In HTML, you merely identify the parts of your document; it's up to the graphical browser to determine *just* how to display these parts on-screen.

EXCELLENT

   The beauty of HTML is that, when properly written, the code can be read by any graphical browser, which is more than you can say for most word processing programs. Were I to create a document in Microsoft Word 6.0 for Windows, you'd have a tough time viewing it with Microsoft Word 5.0, which uses an earlier (and different) file storage format. HTML avoids these problems by declaring the structure of the document and leaving the specifics of formatting to the browsing software.

   An additional benefit of HTML is that its files are always plain text, with no special characters or binary code. These files are easy to exchange via Internet connections. What's more, you can display an HTML file in a text editor or word processing program for easy editing and updating.

What's in an HTML File?

**KEY
TERM**

An HTML document is an ordinary ASCII file (text file) that contains text and *tags*. A tag is an instruction that an HTML-capable browser can recognize and process; it doesn't appear in the document when you're viewing it on-screen. The tags tell the browser program what kind of text is found between the paired tags.

   Here's an example:

```
<H1>My very own home page</H1>
```

This is how Web authors code the Heading 1 titles that appear at the beginning of documents. Note the two tags:

- **Begin Tag (<H1>)** This code says, "Begin the Heading 1 formatting here."
- **End Tag (</H1>)** This code says, "End the title formatting here."

Note that HTML tags almost always come in pairs—a beginning tag and an end tag. The ending tag looks just like the beginning tag, except that it has a slash mark. The text between the begin tag and the end tag is marked for the browser as Heading 1.

If you leave off the ending tag, your browser will think that all the text that follows should be formatted according to the beginning tag. The result is very, very ugly. So remember—beginning tag, end tag.

AWFUL

HTML tags aren't sensitive to case, so it doesn't matter whether you type the tags in uppercase, lowercase, or a combination of them.

HOT TIP

Spaces and Tabs? Ignored

An important point to realize about HTML is that it doesn't preserve spacing created with the Tab and Enter keys. In this respect, it's very different from an ordinary word processing program, in which you press Enter to start a new paragraph:

> Here's a very nice paragraph in a word processing program, displayed the way it appears on the word processing program's screen. When you come of the end of the paragraph, you press Enter.
>
> The word processing program starts a new paragraph after you press Enter. This second paragraph is separate from the first paragraph.

But that's not the way this text will come out in HTML. Here's what HTML will do with it:

> Here's a very nice paragraph in a word processing program, displayed the way it appears on the word processing program's screen. When you come of the end of the paragraph, you press Enter. The word processing program starts a new paragraph after you press Enter. This second paragraph is separate from the first paragraph.

To start a new paragraph with HTML, you must use the <P> command, to mark the place where you want a new paragraph to start:

Here's   paragraph No. 1. <P> Here's paragraph No. 2.

When a graphical browser such as Mosaic or Netscape displays this text, you'll see it as follows

Here's paragraph No. 1.

Here's paragraph No. 2.

The <P> tag doesn't have an end code (</P>)—at least, not in Version 1.0 of the HTML standard. Because this is a discrepancy, the new HTML standard, called Version 2.0, calls for the use of <P> at the beginning of a paragraph and </P> at the end. However, you can still use <P> to mark the break between two paragraphs, and 2.0-capable browsers will format the text correctly.

HOT TIP

There's another tag you can use in place of <P>:
 (short for "line break").
 breaks the new line and starts the following text at the left margin, like <P>. However, most browsers insert a blank line after a <P> tag, but do not do so after a <BR> tag.
 comes in very handy for breaking lines in a list, where you don't want blank lines between the items. You'll see an example of this in the next section.

In the same way that HTML ignores Enter keystrokes, it also ignores spacing entered with tabs. You can press the Tab key all you like, but browsers will simply ignore the spacing you create. This makes it tough to type tables, a point to which this chapter returns later.

HOT TIP

Because browsers ignore spacing entered with Tab and Enter, you can use these keys to improve the readability of HTML files when you look at them directly (instead of with a viewer). You'll see examples of this later in this chapter. HTML ignores the case you use to type tags, but most HTML authors like to type the tags in capital letters. This makes them easier to differentiate from the surrounding text.

What Does an HTML Document Look Like?

Take a look for yourself. Here's the entire ASCII text of WELCOME.HTM, a file you'll create in Chapter 29. As you'll see in Chapter 29, this document is part of The

Generic Web Site, a series of documents that you can open and modify to suit your needs. To modify this document, you'll delete the generic text and type in your own title. For now, though, let's look at the file:

```
<html>
<head>

    <TITLE>Welcome</TITLE>
    <h1>Welcome!</h1>
    <h2>Place your subtitle here</h2>

</head>

<body>

[<A HREF="info.htm">Info ]</A> |
[<A HREF="contents.htm">Contents</A>] |
[<A HREF="welcome.htm">Welcome</A>]

<p><IMG SRC="line_gra.gif"><p>

    Place some brief text here describing the scope and purpose of this
    document, but don't add too much. This entire document
    should be displayed in one or two screens.<p>

    <A HREF="doc1.htm"><IMG SRC= <doc.gif"ALIGN=middle>Click here to see Item
1</A><BR>
    <A HREF="doc2.htm"><IMG SRC="doc.gif"ALIGN=middle>Click here to see Item
2</A><BR>
    <A HREF="doc3.htm"><IMG SRC="doc.gif"ALIGN=middle>Click here to see Item
3</A><BR>
    <A HREF="doc4.html"><IMG SRC="doc.gif"ALIGN=middle>Click here to see Item
4</A><BR>

<p><IMG SRC="line_gra.gif"><p>
```

```
<A HREF="info.html"><IMG SRC="info.gif"></A>
<ADDRESS>Your Name (your e-mail address)</ADDRESS>
<ADDRESS>Last modified 1/10/95</ADDRESS>


</body>
</html>
```

And how does this code look on-screen? Take a look (Figure 27.1).

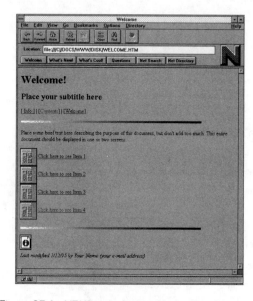

Figure 27.1 *HTML code displayed by browser (Netscape)*

WEB SECRET You don't have to become an expert in HTML to create Web documents. In practice, Web authors use very few HTML tags, mainly the ones in the above example. These tags do the things Web authors want done, such as providing hyperlinks (<A>), graphics <IMG SRC>, and line breaks (<BR>). Even without completely understanding what these tags do, you can type them, and view the results with your graphical browser. In short order, you'll understand what they do. And if you don't like typing the tags, you have two choices. You can easily copy the source HTML from any document you find on the Web (or on the disk included with this book), and use your word processor's copy and paste capabilities to copy and then modify the tags, or you can use an HTML editor, such as HTML Assistant, which is discussed later in this chapter.

THE PARTS OF AN HTML DOCUMENT

Now it's time for a bit of terminology. An HTML document is made up of two components:

- **Elements.** These are the tags that identify the components of a document's structure, such as the title, a heading, or a list.
- **Entities.** These are codes used to represent special (non-ASCII) characters. They're not used very often.

KEY TERM

Elements fall into two categories:

- **Head Elements.** Marked off by <HEAD> and </HEAD> tags, these elements (such as <TITLE>) contains information that does not appear in the on-screen display of the document. Instead, this information is used by browsers, often in different ways. The document's <TITLE>, for instance, appears on the title bar of most graphical browsers.
- **Body Elements.** These are the portions of your document that appear within the graphical browser's document display window. They include headings, paragraphs, lists, hyperlinks, rules (straight lines), in-line images, and more.

Here's the overall structure of an HTML document. Note that, to ensure conformity with all the browsers out there, you should encompass the entire structure in <HTML> and </HTML> tags:

Tag	Explanation
<HTML>	Begin HTML document
<HEAD>	Begin Head
(Head tags go here)	
</HEAD>	End Head
<BODY>	Begin Body
(Body tags go here)	
</BODY>	End Body
</HTML>	End HTML document

YOUR FIRST HTML DOCUMENT

The best way to learn HTML is to try it yourself. In the following pages, you'll create a new home page, which lists the hyperlinks you want to use on a daily basis. You'll then make this document the default home page for your browser.

Getting Started

Use your word processing program to create your home page, but remember two things. First, most word processing programs save documents using proprietary file formats, which are necessary to preserve the formats you choose. However, your graphical browser can't read these files—at least, not without introducing errors. Be sure to save your document using the "Text Only" or "ASCII" file saving settings of your word processing program. If you don't know how to do this, check your manual now before proceeding. Second, be sure to save your document with the extension .html (if you're using Windows, use .htm).

HOT TIP

If you're using Microsoft Windows, create your home page using the Windows Notepad utility. This program always saves files in plain ASCII text. (Macintosh users can use SimpleText.) If you do plan to use your word processing program, be sure to turn off the smart quotes feature that automatically inserts leading and trailing quotations marks. These aren't standard characters, they won't always show up correctly on other computers, and they just might crash an HTML interpreter.

Start your word processing program, and type the following:

```
<HTML>
<HEAD>

    <TITLE>My Home Page</TITLE>
    <HI>Favorite URLs</HI>
```

Note the blank lines after <head> and the tabs before the <title> and <h1> tags. This spacing has no effect on the way your document looks; it just makes the HTML document easier for people to read. It's optional, but most HTML authors feel that it's a good practice.

Save the file to your browser's directory or folder using the filename **myhome.htm** and close the file. (*Note*: If you're creating the file on a platform other than Microsoft Windows, name the file MYHOME.HTML.)

Be aware that you can't make even the tiniest typing error when you're typing HTML tags. If you add an HTML tag to your document and your browser won't display the tag, there's an error. You may have left out an angle bracket, or typed a file name incorrectly. Don't forget the slash mark in the end tag!

AWFUL

Viewing Your Home Page

Basically, graphical browsers are programs that let you view HTML documents as they're meant to be viewed—that is, *without* the funny-looking HTML commands and *with* all the pretty fonts and graphics. To see how your document looks so far (Figure 27.2), open it with your browser.

If you're using a word processing program, you may find that you must quit the program before your browser can access the MYHOME.HTM file. Should this happen, consider using the Windows Notepad utility instead. This utility permits other applications to open the file even while you're viewing it in Notepad's window. With the document displayed both by Notepad and your browser, you can quickly switch between the two to see the effects of your HTML tags.

AWFUL

To open your document with your graphical browser:

NCSA MOSAIC

From the <u>F</u>ile menu, choose **Open <u>L</u>ocal File**. In the File Open dialog box, use the directories and file lists to select the file you've created. Click **OK**.

ENHANCED NCSA MOSAIC

From the <u>F</u>ile menu, choose **<u>O</u>pen Local**. In the File Open dialog box, use the directories and file lists to select the file you've created. Click **OK**.

NETSCAPE NAVIGATOR

From the <u>F</u>ile menu, choose **Open <u>F</u>ile**. In the File Open dialog box, use the directories and file lists to select the file you've created, and click **OK**.

WEBSURFER

From the Retrieve menu, chose **<u>O</u>pen Local File**. In the File Open dialog box, use the directories and file lists to select the file you've created, and choose **OK**.

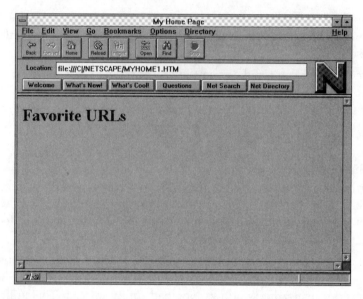

Figure 27.2 Getting started with MYHOME.HTM

Adding Subheadings and Body Text

Now try adding a couple of subheadings and some body text to your document. Open the **MYHOME** document with your word processing program, and add the new text that is shown in bold in the following:

```
<HTML>
<HEAD>

    <TITLE>My Home Page</TITLE>

</HEAD>

<BODY>

    <H1>Favorite URLs</H1>

    <H2>Network Starting Points</H2>
```

Click one of the following to explore new Web resources:<P>

<H2>Hot URLs</H2>

Here are some of my favorite URLs:<P>

<BODY>

Save your document, making sure you're doing so using your word processor's Text Only or ASCII saving option. Close the file, if necessary, and switch to your graphical browser. Click the Reload button to reload the file, and you'll see the document that's shown in Figure 27.3.

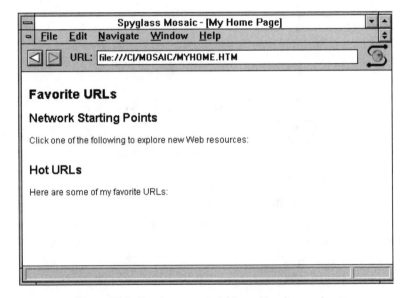

Figure 27.3 *Your home page: Adding subheadings and text*

Adding Anchors (Hyperlinks)

The most powerful capability of HTML is its facilities for incorporating hyperlinks into your documents. To create a hyperlink, you type an anchor, a special HTML command.

Every anchor must conform to the following pattern:

- It begins with an <a> tag, and ends with a </a> tag.
- You put the URL inside the first <a> tag, using the following pattern: <a href="URL">
- The text that comes between the <a> and </a> tags shows up on the screen.

Here's an example:

<a HREF="http://whitefoot.uncx.edu/www/sierra/backpack.html"> Backpacker's Home Page</a>

Try typing the following anchor under the Network Starting Points heading. It's NCSA's "What's New" page, which tells you about cool new Web resources. Be careful when typing and be sure to check your work.

<a HREF="http://www.ncsa.uiuc.edu/SDG/Software/Mosaic/
Docs/whats-new.html">What's New?</a>

Figure 27.4 shows the appearance of this anchor on-screen.

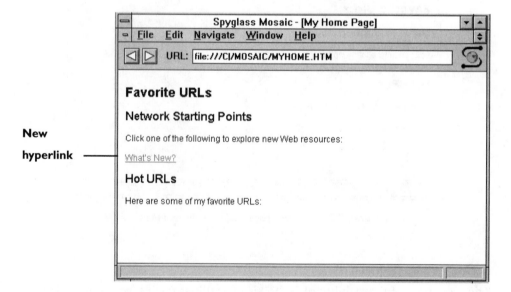

Figure 27.4 *MYHOME.HTM with hyperlink added*

HOT TIP

Be careful to type all the spaces just as they're shown in this example. Although HTML ignores extraneous spaces in ordinary text, you must put a space after <A, and you must *not* put any spaces within the URL. Also, don't forget the quotation marks.

Under the Network Starting Points section, add the following. They appear in most of the Smart Pages discussed in the previous chapter. Don't forget to put the <BR> tag after each anchor, or they'll all wind up on one line!

- **EiNET Galaxy**

    <A HREF="http://galaxy.einet.net/"EiNET Galaxy Subject Tree)</A>

- **John's Monster Hotlist**

    <A HREF = "http://wx.atmos.uiuc.edu/kemp/hotlist.html" John's Monster Hotlist </A>

- **Lycos Search Form**

    <A HREF="http://lycos2.cs.cmu.edu/lycos-form.html">Lycos Search Form(</A>

    Under the Hot URLs section, try typing these anchors now. If you'd like some suggestions, here are some useful URLs for your home page:

- **Current Weather**

    <A HREF=" http://rs560.cl.msu.edu/weather/interactive.html"> Current Weather </A>

- **On-Line Webster's Dictionary**

    <A HREF=" gopher://sfsuvax1.sfsu.edu:3015/7default%20SPELL" On-Line Webster's Dictionary </A>

- **The News Page**

    <A HREF="http://www.trib.com/news/news.html" The News Page </A>

When you're sure you've typed the anchors correctly, save and close the file. In your graphical browser, click **Reload** to see what your changes look like. Your screen should look like the one shown in Figure 27.5.

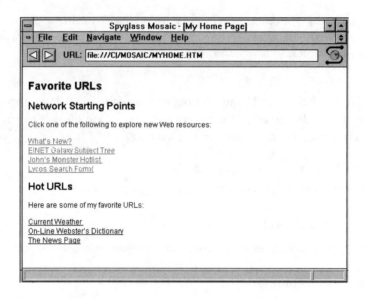

Figure 27.5 *MYHOME.HTM with more hyperlinks added*

HOT TIP

Be sure to test your anchors by clicking them while you're online. If you see an error message, open the document with your word processing program and check your typing carefully. If you're sure you typed the anchor tags and the URL correctly, it's possible that the URL isn't valid. (Web resources come and go quite frequently, you'll find.)

Adding an In-line Image

Your home page looks OK, but wouldn't an in-line image jazz it up? Graphical browser can read small GIF files directly. Using the graphics viewer that you've configured to work with your browser, you can obtain and resize a GIF graphic to use as an in-line image. Save the file to your graphical browser's directory or folder.

To include a GIF graphic in your document, use the following tag:

```
<IMG SRC="filename">
```

Filename refers to the exact name of the disk file. It can also be a URL, which is explained in "Accessing Additional Resources."

Try adding an in-line image tag to your home page, placing it just below "Favorite URLs." To add the image HOME.GIF, for instance, you'd type the following:

```
<IMG SRC="home.gif">
```

If you would like the graphic to appear on the same line with your document's H1 heading, place the in-line image tag within the H1 tags, as follows:

```
<h1><img src="mountain.gif">Favorite URLs</h1>
```

You'll see the results shown in Figure 27.6

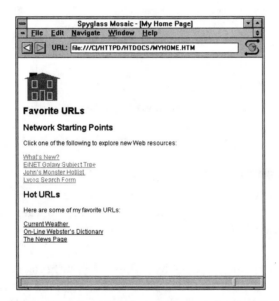

Figure 27.6 *Your Home Page: Adding an In-line Graphic*

Adding Rules

To divide the parts of your document, you can add rules (lines). To place a rule, enter a <HR> code where you want the rule to appear. In Figure 27.7, you see a rule that's been added after the H1 tag.

HOT TIP

Remember, keep it simple. It's tempting to add in-line images and rules all over the place, but doing so clutters up the screen, slows down document retrieval, and forces you to scroll to find the anchors you're looking for.

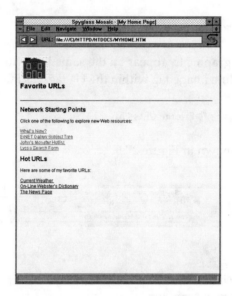

Figure 27.7 *Your Home Page: Adding a Rule*

Adding In-Line Images to Hyperlinks

While browsing the Web, you've surely come across in-line graphics that function as hyperlinks. They're easy to see, thanks to the blue border surrounding them. Often, these are used in lists of hyperlinks, to make it easier to click the item you want.

You can add in-line images to the hyperlinks in your home page. As an example, use one of the GIF icons supplied with this book, and place it in the same directory that houses your MYHOME.HTM document. Then, enter this in your HTML document.

```
<a HREF="http://www.ncsa.uiuc.edu/SDG/Software/Mosaic/Docs/whats-new.html"><IMG
SRC="search.gif">What's New?</a><BR>
```

Figure 27.8 shows how your home page will look after adding icons to all the items on your list.

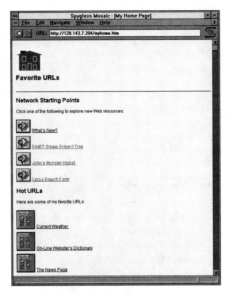

Figure 27.8 *Finished home page*

**KEY
TERM**

You've just used a *relative link* (in the tag <IMG SRC="search.gif">). This tells your browser to look in the same directory for the file named "search.gif." Relative links are commonly used to load resources present in the same directory.

AWFUL

Some browsers won't pick up a relative link unless you have a server up and running on your system. If you've double-checked your work and your browser still won't read the in-line graphic, use an absolute file reference instead of a relative link. In an absolute file reference, you tell the browser exactly where the file is located on disk. Let's assume you installed SEARCH.GIF in the directory C:\MOSAIC\IMAGES. To tell your browser to use this file, use the following IMG SRC tag:

```
<IMG SRC="file:///c:\mosaic\images\search.gif">
```

Adding this to the <A> tags should clear up the problem.

Troubleshooting

If you're having trouble getting your document to work correctly, carefully check your typing against the completed file:

```
<HTML>
<HEAD>

    <TITLE>My Home Page</TITLE>

</HEAD>

<BODY>

    <IMG SRC="home.gif"><h1>Favorite URLs</h1>

    <HR>

    <H2>Network Starting Points</H2>

    Click one of the following to explore new Web resources:<P>

    <a HREF="http://www.ncsa.uiuc.edu/SDG/Software/Mosaic/
    Docs/whats-new.html"><IMG SRC="/images/search.gif">What's New?</a><BR>

<A HREF="http://galaxy.einet.net/"><IMG SRC="/images/search.gif">EiNET Galaxy Subject
Tree</A><BR>

<A HREF = "http://wx.atmos.uiuc.edu/kemp/hotlist.html"><IMG SRC="/images/search.gif">John's
Monster Hotlist </A><BR>

<A HREF="http://lycos2.cs.cmu.edu/lycos-form.html"><IMG SRC="/images/search.gif">Lycos
Search Form</A><BR>

    <H2>Hot URLs</H2>

    Here are some of my favorite URLs:<P>

<A HREF="http://rs560.cl.msu.edu/weather/interactive.html"><IMG
SRC="/images/doc.gif">Current Weather </A><BR>
```

```
<A HREF="gopher://sfsuvax1.sfsu.edu:3015/7default%20SPELL"><IMG
SRC="/images/doc.gif">On-Line Webster's Dictionary</A><BR>


<A HREF="http://www.trib.com/news/news.html"><IMG SRC="/images/doc.gif">The News
Page</A><BR>


</BODY>
```

CHANGING THE DEFAULT HOME PAGE

Once you've created your home page document, you'll want your graphical browser to load it automatically. Here's how to make your home page the default home page for future browser sessions.

To reset the default home page:

NCSA MOSAIC

Use the Windows Notepad text editor to open the file **C:\WINDOWS\MOSAIC.INI**. In the Main section, look for the Home Page line. Erase the current URL, and carefully type the URL of the new home page you want to use. Save the file and exit.

ENHANCED NCSA MOSAIC

From the Edit menu, choose **Preferences**. In the Preferences dialog, type the new URL in the Home Page text box, and click **OK**.

NETSCAPE NAVIGATOR

Open the Options menu, and choose **Preferences**. In the list box, choose **Styles**. In the Start With area, select **Home Page location**, and type the URL.

WEBSURFER

Open the Settings menu, and choose **Preferences**. In the Startup Document area, type the URL of your new home page in the URL box.

HTML DO'S AND DON'TS

HTML is an easy language to use, but you'll find that many Web authors commit the following very common errors.

1. **Don't try to emphasize text by coding it as a heading.** You'll run across Web pages in which items in a bulleted list are coded as heading 1 <H1> or heading 2 <H2> in an attempt to make them look bigger on-screen. This doesn't look good with many browsers.

   The wrong way to emphasize text:
   ```
   <UL>
   <LI><H1>The first item in a list</H1>
   <LI><H1>The second item in a list</H1>
   </UL>
   ```

   The right way:
   ```
   <UL>
   <LI><B>The first item in a list</B>
   <LI><B>The second item in a list</B>
   ```

2. **Don't put emphases (such as boldface or italic) within hyperlinks.** Again, some browsers might not be able to handle this.

   The wrong way to emphasize text within a hyperlink:
   ```
   <A HREF "http://www.com"><B>A Document</B></a>
   ```

   The right way:
   ```
   <B><A HREF "http://www.com"> A Document</A></B>
   ```

3. **Don't forget the paired quotation marks in URLS.** Without both quotation marks, the URL won't work.

   The wrong way to type a URL (just one quotation mark):
   ```
   <A HREF "http://www.com>Wonderful Document</A>
   ```

   The right way (paired marks):
   ```
   <A HREF "http://www.com">Wonderful Document</A>
   ```

4. **Don't leave out the slash mark in the end tag.** If you do, the format will apply to text that comes after the end tag, producing unappealing results.

   The wrong way to type an end tag (no slash mark):
   ```
   <B>South Australian Chardonnays<B>
   ```

   The right way:
   ```
   <B>South Australian Chardonnays</B>
   ```

5. **Don't write dangling links**. A *dangling link* is a hyperlink that is separate from the text to which it refers. Put the hyperlink on the text itself, as in the following examples:

   The wrong way to write a hyperlink:

   Click <u>here</u> to see the latest watercolor exhibit

   The right way:

   The latest watercolor exhibit

6. **Don't rely on the TITLE tag <T> to convey your document's title**. Many browers display the title inconspicuously on the title bar. Use the HEADING 1 tag <H1> to convey your document's title.

   The wrong way to write a title heading:

   <TI>The Rise and Fall of the Roman Empire</TI>

   <HI>Introduction</HI>

   The right way:

   <TI>Roman Empire</TI>

   <HI>The Rise and Fall of the Roman Empire</HI>

7. **Don't leave any spaces within an <A>... </A> tag.** This might result in unattractive underlining over blank spaces (called *nicks*) when the document is displayed by some browsers.

   The wrong way to space an <A> tag:

   <A HREF="URL"> <IMG SRC="TUFF.GIF"> Cool Stuff! </A>

   The right way:

   <A HREF="URL"><IMG SRC="TUFF.GIF">Cool Stuff!</A>

8. **Don't drive people nuts by using too many different in-line graphics in a list of hyperlinks.** In Figure 28.8, you see just two; they categorize the links in a nice way. Too many different icons cause visual disorientation.

The wrong way to use in-line graphics as hyperlinks (different GIF files):

<A HREF="URL"><IMG SRC="TUFF.GIF">Cool Stuff!</A>

<A HREF="URL"><IMG SRC="ROUGH.GIF">Hot Stuff!</A>

<A HREF="URL"><IMG SRC="STUFF.GIF">Amazing Stuff!</A>

The right way:

<A HREF="URL"><IMG SRC="STUFF.GIF">Cool Stuff!</A>

<A HREF="URL"><IMG SRC="STUFF.GIF">Hot Stuff!</A>

<A HREF="URL"><IMG SRC="STUFF.GIF">Amazing Stuff!</A>

HTML EDITORS

If you find typing HTML tags to be a tedious job, you may wish to use an HTML editor. Ideally, using such an editor would be as easy as using a word processing program. You choose the formats you want, and they would look the way browsers display them; the program would create and save the tags in the background. But that's not the way HTML editors currently work. You still see the HTML tags on-screen (see Figure 27.9).

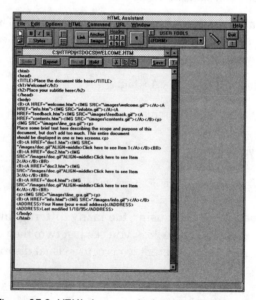

Figure 27.9 *HTML document displayed by HTML Assistant*

The point of using an HTML editor is that it's much easier to enter the tags. HTML Assistant, illustrated in Figure 27.9, exemplifies the benefits of using HTML editors. You can just click the buttons on the button bar to add headings, anchors, in-line images, and other elements. You can see the results immediately by clicking the Test button, which starts your browser and displays the document.

Here's a brief overview of some of the better editors now available for Windows and Macintosh users:

- **HTML HyperEdit.** Created by Steve Hancock, this freely distributable Windows editor can be found at http://www.curtin.edu.au/curtin /dept/cc/packages/htmledit/about.html.

- **HTML Assistant.** This popular Windows editor is illustrated in Figture 27.9. For more information, access http://cs.dal.ca/ftp/htmlasst/htmlafaq.html.

- **HTML Editor.** This shareware editor for the Macintosh is widely used and well liked; it's comparable to HTML Assistant. To obtain the program, use http://.

- **SoftQuad HotMetal.** Created by SoftQuad, HotMetal is more sophisticated than most of the available editors in that it resolutely checks your HTML to make sure that it conforms to the language's standards. As users quickly discover, however, the rules are set so strictly that most of the documents on the Web are in violation, so it's close to impossible to open and edit an existing document. An unsupported freeware version is widely available on the Internet. The supported and maintained version, HotMetal Pro, is available from SoftQuad (hotmetal@sq.com).

- **Microsoft Internet Assistant.** This add-on program for Microsoft Word for Windows enables Word users to create HTML documents easily. You just create and format your document; Word adds the HTML code and hyperlinks. This program also enables you to use Word as a Web browser. To obtain Internet Assistant, access http://www.microsoft.com/.

SUMMARY

It's a cinch to create your own home page. To do so, you'll need to learn a little HTML—but just a little. Create your document as a plain ASCII text file, and remember that almost all the HTML codes come in twos (a beginning code and an ending code). Be sure to type the anchors carefully. If your new home page produces error messages when you give it a try, there's probably a typo in there somewhere!

FROM HERE...

- Learn how to create your own Web site in Chapter 28.
- Weave your own Web in Chapter 29.

CHAPTER 28

Creating a Web Site

*There is a new profession of trail blazers, those who find delight in the task of establishing useful
trails through the enormous mass of the common record.*

—Vannevar Bush

So you want to become a Web information provider! Welcome to the club. In this chapter, you'll learn how to intelligently approach this exciting venture in a way that reflects positively on you and your organization. First, you'll consider whether the Web is really the right communication medium for your presentation (it does, after all, have some peculiar characteristics). You'll learn how to plan your web, choose your server software, and register your web so that others can find and access it.

This chapter provides an overview of web site creation. For the specifics of designing and creating documents to make available, see the next chapter. For instructions on installing WinHTTPD for Microsoft Windows, see Appendix C.

In this chapter and the following chapters, the term *web* (in lowercase) will refer to what is also known as a *web site*, a collection of linked documents that is stored on a single computer. You create a web; you put it on the Web.

Thinking about setting up a Web site? There's a ton of information available on the Web, all beautifully indexed at the WWW & HTML Developer's JumpStation (http://oneworld.wa.com/htmldev/devpage/dev-page.html).

HOME PAGE

KEY TERM

USEFUL RESOURCE

IS THE WEB THE RIGHT MEDIUM FOR YOUR MESSAGE?

The World Wide Web is a communication system unlike any other in human history. It's very different from sending up smoke signals, mailing a letter, making a telephone call, or even sending an email message. Here's a list of its rather peculiar characteristics:

- **You can't be assured that your audience will receive your message right away—or at all**. You put your web out there, do the best you can to publicize it, and sit back and wait. Perhaps the Internet community will beat a path to your server—and perhaps not. It's up to the Web's users, not you.

- **You can't control how users will navigate through your web**. Ideally, they'd start at the Welcome page, and follow the links as you've planned. In reality, that's not the way the Web works. They could very well start out in some secondary- or tertiary-level document, and navigate through your web in a way you hadn't anticipated. You can't fight this, and you shouldn't—the user's ability to control navigation is what makes the Web so interesting. But you'll need to provide background information and navigation aids to users so they can find out where your web came from, why it exists, and what else is available.

- **Your Web is accessible to millions of people, from all walks of life**. You'd better do a good job, because people far beyond your organization will access your web and draw conclusions about you and your organization.

- **You can't be certain that everyone will be using graphical browsers, and you can't control how graphical browsers will display the document's layout, including fonts, font sizes, and rules**. To avoid creating a poor impression, you must anticipate how your document might look when viewed with a variety of browsers.

- **If you create a valuable Web resource, an electronic analogue of "word of mouth" will spread your URL far and wide**. It will pop up in starting pages, hotlists, and manually-edited subject trees. You could very well find that your server is being overwhelmed with requests for information—and if people can't get through to your site, that could create a bad impression for your organization.

- **Your web will remain on the Net for as long as you keep it available, sending out the same message**. You'll need to think about maintaining your web and keeping it current. If your pages include hyperlinks to external URLs, you'd better be prepared to check them periodically to make sure they're still working.

- **Most webs are one-way communication media. Users access the web, browse or download information, and leave—but that's changing**. With the new forms capabilities of graphical browsers, important new opportunities have arisen for two-way communication. Users can leave messages and comments, fill out and submit forms, and—thanks to the new generation of secure servers—place orders with credit cards. The downside: creating an interactive web is still technically a formidable matter.

Is creating a web for you? If you're looking for a cheap way to advertise something or to grind an ax for your favorite political or social issue, the Web probably isn't a very good bet. Web users tend to respond very positively, though, to webs that provide interesting and useful information, even if it comes with a sales pitch or social message. At the heart of the Web is a community spirit—by making something of value available, every web author deepens the value of the Web for others. In short, if you think you've got something to offer that other Web users would appreciate, you're well on your way to creating a successful web.

One example of an effective web is CyberWeb's Virtual Library page, shown in Figure 28.1. CyberWeb is in the business of developing advanced web sites for businesses and organizations. Founded by former NASA Goddard Space Center astrophysicist Alan Richmond, CyberWeb contains a hubbub of WWW development activity. The page (and those linked to it) is crammed with information about HTML version 2.0, and even includes a form-based HTML 2.0 validation service—you enter your URL, and it checks whether it's 2.0-compliant.

EXCELLENT

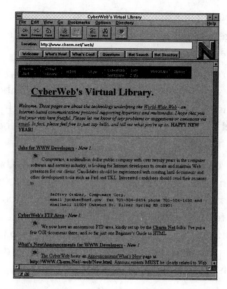

Figure 28.1 *CyberWeb's Virtual Library offers an appealing mix of information and advertising*

HOT TIP

The lesson that CyberWeb teaches is simple: *Think of your users' information needs, not your own purposes, when you're planning your web.* If you provide valuable and interesting information, users will listen to the rest of your message, even if it's a sales pitch, an advertisement, or a request for contributions.

PLANNING YOUR WEB

To create an effective Web presence, you need to plan carefully. Start by thinking about your purpose for creating a web? Then think about your audience—who will use your web, and why? Once you've thought about these issues, you're ready to state your goals. The following sections elaborate these points.

HOT TIP

Before you begin, remember the old adage "Don't reinvent the wheel." The world doesn't need another page bringing together Star Trek resources or another click art repository. Using the procedures introduced in Part Four of this book, use the Web's starting points, subject trees, and search engines to determine whether anyone has already accomplished what you're about to do. If so, you could create a simple, one-page document that includes links to the work that others have done. That's a lot less work!

Sometimes you might want to carry on anyway, even if there's another Web site that addresses the same information. Perhaps you feel that you could do a better or more complete job. Perhaps the other site hasn't shown any signs of activity in a while, and an email message to the site's Webmaster discloses that there's no plan to keep it updated. Perhaps the other site is located at the tail end of a very slow trans-oceanic connection. Under such circumstances, you may decide to proceed despite the existence of a competing site.

Knowing Your Purpose

Assuming no one else has created the Web resource that you feel is needed, it's time to focus on the purpose of your web. Given the peculiar characteristics of the Web as a communication, here are some defensible purposes:

- **Providing reference data.** Many of the best Web sites offer access to valuable data, such as glossaries of technical or computer terms, statistics on recent earthquakes, and information about upcoming Space Shuttle flights.

- **Providing on-line technical documentation.** For Web-capable customers, on-line versions of technical manuals offers many advantages when compared to printed media. For example, you can include training videos, and you can keep the documentation up to date.

- **Creating metapages.** These Web documents bring together URLs that have never been collected and would be difficult or time-consuming for others to assemble.

- **Creating an on-line catalog.** Junk mail wastes time and money, and takes up landfill space. In the future, many direct-mail catalogs will appear on the Web— and we'll be doing the environment a favor by patronizing the companies that make them available.

- **Creating an exhibit.** The Web is full of exhibitions of graphics, illustrations, fine art, photography, and even musical compositions. If you'd like to create your own exhibition, just make sure you've got permission from the artists or that the works are in the public domain!

These are just a few examples of good purposes for creating a web. The pages of this book are filled with many others.

Knowing Your Audience

To communicate effectively, you must know your audience. Given that millions of people the world over can access your Web site, that's a bit tough. But you should be able to specify just who would want to spend some time in your web, rather than just surfing on to the next destination. To refine your purpose, you need to ask, "Who is this web for?"

CyberWeb's page, discussed earlier and featured in Figure 28.1, stems from some careful and creative thinking about these questions. The page is designed for anyone with an interest in HTML programming, ranging from beginners to experts—there's something for everyone.

Making a Commitment to Professionalism

Please bear in mind that, in placing information on the Web, you're publishing documents that will reflect on you and the organization to which you belong. Your Web documents should meet the same standards you would apply to sales brochures, news releases, or other publicly-accessible information. At the minimum, this means that they will have letter-perfect spelling and grammar and an attractive appearance.

HOT TIP If you're creating a Web site at an organization such as a university or corporation, contact the person in charge of the Web to determine whether there's an internal style guide for Web documents. You may be able to use the organization's logo and other materials that will give your pages a finished, professional look.

Selecting Your Content

Once you've defined your purpose and audience, you're ready to consider what kind of information you'd like to make available. Here's a list of possibilities:

- **Hyperlinks to other Web sites.** Don't reinvent the wheel; provide links to information that's available elsewhere on the Web. Be sure to write *friendly links*. If a hyperlink takes the reader to a site outside your web, be sure to say so.

- **Hyperlinks to other documents in your web.** Try to break down the information you're providing into manageable "chunks" (see "Chunking," later in this chapter). You'll need to plan how the documents will relate to one another, and above all, how your users will navigate through them. Remember they may not enter your web at the Welcome page!

- **Text.** Most of the information you'll find on the Web is conveyed in text, but bear in mind that text isn't always the best way to communicate. If you can say it with a graphic, do so. If there's no other way besides text, write succinctly. For tips on dealing with lengthy text documents, see "Handling Lengthy Text Documents," in the next chapter.

- **Graphics.** A picture, or so the saying goes, is worth a 1000 words. But bear in mind that large graphics can take a long time to download on slow dialup connections, and not everyone's using a graphical browser.

- **Sound.** A brief sound clip or video can enhance your presentation. However, not every Web user's computer is equipped with the necessary software (a helper program) and equipment. Sounds should be used to amplify or repeat information that is available in other ways. And be friendly—tell your users how large the sound file is so they can decide whether or not they can load it.

- **Video and Animations.** Like sounds, videos and animations might be too large for many of your users.

- **FTP file archives.** Do you want to make software, text files, or other file-based resources available? If so, including access to an FTP archive is a good way to provide them.

WHAT ABOUT COPYRIGHTS?

If you're thinking about including text, sounds, graphics, animations, or any other material that was created by someone other than yourself, you need to think about copyright issues. Do you have the right to use the material?

The answer to this question is "probably not." The U.S. is a signatory to international copyright standards, which are very heavily biased in favor of the people who create literary, dramatic, musical, artistic, and other intellectual works, whether published or not. A work is considered to be copyrighted unless the creator has expressly placed the work in the public domain by making a deliberate statement to that effect. What this all boils down to is very simple: You cannot use someone else's literary, artistic, or musical expression without express written permission.

WHAT ABOUT COPYRIGHTS? (continued)

There are exceptions, of course. None of the following can be copyrighted: Names, titles, short phrases, catchwords or slogans, publicly-accessible information such as tide tables or the periodic table of the elements, facts about events reported in newspapers (as distinguished from the *expression* of these facts by a particular writer's choice of words), or any information about the world that could only be described in a certain way (such as how to format a disk with MS-DOS). In addition, U.S. copyright law mandates "fair use" of copyrighted material, which is generally taken to mean that you can reproduce a small portion of a written text for the purposes of commentary, review, or criticism. However, this does not apply to musical works, poetry, or artistic works.

If in doubt about whether you can use other people's works in your web documents, *ask for permission*. Before you include an icon, a sound, or a graphic, send that letter—and if you don't get a positive reply, leave it out!

If you ask an employee or a freelancer to prepare some text, graphics, sounds, animations, or videos for your web, make sure that this person understands that this work is contracted on a "work for hire" basis. Work prepared on this basis belongs to the employer or contractor, not the artist.

Note that these restrictions do *not* apply to any hyperlinks you include that take the user to someone else's Web site. Suppose Jane Smith has written an interesting essay and made it available on her web pages. The essay contains a copyright notice. You can include a hyperlink that points your users to Smith's web. You need not ask Smith for permission. If this wasn't the case, the Web couldn't exist.

CREATING YOUR WEB

You'll need to know some HTML, to create your web, but it's easy to learn. To help you get started quickly, this book offers a unique feature: the Generic Web Site, a multi-document web template that embodies high standards for web craftsmanship. To use the Generic Web Site, see the next chapter.

HOT TIP

Not sure whether your HTML is up to snuff? You can submit your document to an HTML checking service—an automated Web site that will return a document listing the errors you've made, if any. These HTML checkers aren't perfect, and they can't detect bad document design, but it's still worth taking a look! Also, see the section "Avoiding Common HTML Errors" in Chapter 27.

Here's a quick overview of the process you'll use to create your Web documents:

1. Use your word processing program or an HTML editor to create your welcome page.

2. Create the additional documents that you want to include in the web, if any.

3. Create or download the in-line graphics, sounds, and other multimedia resources you want to use, and test them.

4. Access your web documents with your graphical browser. You're sure to find errors.

5. Switch to your word processing program, display the HTML document that contains the error, and correct it.

6. Redisplay the document with your graphical browser to make sure you corrected the error.

You'll learn much more about this process in the following chapter.

CHOOSING YOUR SERVER SOFTWARE

KEY TERM

How will you put your web on the Web? You'll need an Internet connection and *server* software, a program that's designed to enable others to access your web pages.

What Kind of Internet Connection Do You Need?

To set up a Web server, you'll need a high-speed network connection or a dedicated line. A dialup SLIP or PPP connection won't do—and it's not merely because such connections are too slow. With most SLIP and PPP connections, your computer's IP address is assigned dynamically. This means that your IP address changes every time you access the Web. There's no way for other people to know which address they should use to access your documents.

Happily, the cost of permanent, high-speed data connections (called *dedicated lines*) is in free fall, and it's now quite feasible for a small business to think about setting up a Windows server with a 56 Kbps. On the horizon nationally, and available right now in many urban areas, is ISDN, which allows connections of up to 64 Kbps.

Introducing Web Servers

KEY TERM

In brief, a Web *server* is a computer connected to the Internet that has software which allows it to receive external HTTP requests. That sounds simple enough, but in fact servers do a lot of work. All Web servers perform three essential functions:

- **Locating and sending the requested resource.** Since HTTP integrates all the data types specified in the Multi-purpose Internet Multimedia Extensions (MIME) specification, this includes hypertext files (HTML), FTP-accessible files, Gopher menu items, graphics and sound files, and other resources.

- **Logging Web activity.** A server records the Internet address, time of connection, and file requests for each access that occurs. This information can prove invaluable for making your Web service more effective (for example, you can delete documents that are seldom or never accessed, and improve the more popular ones).

- **Protecting your system from unauthorized use** A Web server makes only certain files and directories available for outside access.

Increasingly, servers can perform advanced functions when configured to access external programs confirming to the CGI (Common Gateway Interface standard) such as the following:

- **Clickable maps and graphics.** You've seen plenty of these on the Web. Portions of the graphic are hyperlinks that the user can click to access relevant information.

- **User Authentication.** The server prompts the user to provide a login name and password, and rejects authorization if these are not supplied correctly.

- **Enabling searches of Web pages.** Using the <ISINDEX> tag in HTML, you can create an HTML document that prompts the user to enter a search word.

- **Forms for electronic mail feedback.** You can set up a Web page that lets users send you electronic mail messages.

- **WAIS searches of databases.** You can create a Web page that prompts the user to enter search terms and other options for a WAIS full-text search of documents stored on your computer.

- **Opening gateways to other Internet resources** including Telnet sessions and Archie searches.

- **Enabling Web access around firewalls.** Firewalls are security systems that insulate an organization's network from the Internet. To access the Web from within such a network, a *proxy server* that mediates between internal and external HTTP messages is needed.

- **On-line credit card ordering.** A very recent development, this lets users order goods and services and pay with a MasterCard (additional cards are soon to come). Advanced security features employ encryption to protect the user's card number. The server automatically contacts the credit card authorization service, obtains authorization, and responds to the user's request.

Server software is still in its infancy. Many of the features in the above list can only be implemented by people with advanced programming skills. By the time you read this book, however, this should change. The coming generation of servers will include easy-to-use, "point-and-click" installation of most of these features.

AWFUL

Which Server Software Should You Use?

Until recently, server software was available only for relatively expensive UNIX workstations. The tasks involved in installing, configuring, and maintaining a UNIX Web server are far from trivial, and best left to UNIX administrators with considerable software configuration experience.

HOT TIP

If you're working at a university or corporation with an established UNIX server, your best bet is to contact your site administrator to find out if you can put your Web pages on this system. You won't have to worry about the tedious details of configuring the CGI gateways; they'll take care of that for you, so you can concentrate on the content.

For people who don't have access to organizational UNIX servers, there's a significant new development: the availability of servers for personal computers, including the Macintosh, Windows 3.1 systems, and Windows NT systems. The availability of these servers has enormously expanded the opportunities for would-be Web information providers. The more powerful Pentium and Power Macintosh models provide all the horsepower a small-to medium-sized business needs to establish a Web server.

WEB SERVER SOFTWARE FOR PERSONAL COMPUTERS

Excellent servers are available for Macintosh and Windows systems on a free or a shareware basis.

SerWeb (ftp://emwac.ed.ac.uk/pub/serweb). Running on Windows and Windows NT, this server was written Gustavo Estrella, who appears to be doing his level best to avoid being contacted about this program. In short: It's a good piece of software, but don't count on much support! Further development is also open to question. SerWeb is available

WinHTTPD for Microsoft Windows. Available for Windows 3.1 systems only (not for Windows NT), this Windows port of the WinHTTP program is easily accessed by an HTML document included on this book's accompanying disk. Created by Bob Denny, this program is a very capable server package that implements most of WinHTTPD's advanced features, including forms capability. WinHTTPD for Microsoft Windows, is copyrighted but freely available for use and modification. One feature of WinHTTPD is that it contains several programming "hooks" for Visual Basic, which is encouraging Visual Basic programmers to develop lots of very useful accessory applications (such as ready-to-use forms generation accessories).

MacHTTP (for the latest information, see http://arpp1.carleton.ca/httpNotes/MacHTTP.faq.html). This is an outstanding Web server package for Macintoshes, with a version that's native to the Power Macintosh. Written by Chuck Shotten of the University of Texas's Health Science Center, MacHTTP is available on a shareware basis; if you like the program and decide to continue using it, you must pay the registration fee (currently $50-$100, depending on the use you will make of the program). Like WinHTTPD, this program is encouraging a lot of accessory program development.

Is there a drawback to creating your server on a PC or Macintosh? You should consider the following:

- **System Overload.** An individual or a small business probably won't run into problems with a PC or Mac server, as long as it's properly configured and connected to a reasonably fast (at least 56 Kbps) line. But large organizations should consider using the greater horsepower afforded by UNIX workstations.

- **Transaction Processing.** Looking to set up a credit-card ordering system? You'll need a server that's fully integrated with on-the-fly data encryption and other security services, such as Netscape's Commerce Server. At present, the only commercial servers that support credit card ordering run on UNIX workstations. That may change, however.

USEFUL
RESOURCE

IS LEASING FOR YOU?

Running a Web server can prove to be an expensive proposition, especially if it gets popular and you are forced to upgrade your system! An alternative is to lease space on a service provider's system. You provide the Web pages, and the service provider takes care of the rest. For more information, access http://www.charm.net/~web/Vlib-/Providers/Servers.html for a list of service providers that lease space for Web pages.

TESTING YOUR WEB

Once you've installed your server software and created the documents and other resources that you want to place in your web, it's time to test your work. Here's a quick rundown of the steps you should follow:

1. **Access your web from another computer.** This is the only way you can really tell whether things are working correctly. To do so, use another Web-connected computer, and use the following URL: HTTP:// followed by your computer's IP address (four numbers separated by periods), a trailing slash mark, and the name of your welcome page (such as HTTP://128.143.7.206/welcome.html).

2. **Test every hyperlink within your web**. Are all of them working? Do all of the in-line graphics display correctly? Chances are good that you'll find a mistake here.

3. **Test external hyperlinks**. If you can't gain access to one of these sites, it may be down temporarily, or it may have moved or disappeared. Try again later, and if you still can't access the site, remove the hyperlink from your web.

4. **Test your forms.** If you've included forms with your application, make sure the scripts are working correctly. Try out all the options you've enabled, such as sending mail, conducting searches, and accessing external resources.

5. **Repeat all of these tests with a variety of browsers and platforms.** Try accessing your site from a UNIX workstation, a Macintosh, and a Windows system, and try as many different browsers as you can. You may find that some of your documents look atrocious when displayed by certain browsers! A quick redesign can often solve the problem.

MAINTAINING YOUR WEB

Once you've made sure your web is working correctly, you needn't spend a lot of time maintaining it. But there are some tasks that must be done regularly (at least once per week or more often).

KEY TERM

1. **Eliminate stale links**. A *stale link* is a hyperlink in your document that has moved or disappeared. Periodically, check all the hyperlinks in your documents. If you see a messge informing you that a site has moved, update your documents so that they reflect the correct URL.

2. **Check usage statistics**. Most servers can compile statistics about document usage. You might consider making additional resoures available in the most popular areas, and deleting resources that very few people access.

3. **Check the server's error log**. Among the URLs listed in this log may be external sites that have moved or disappeared, or are just very busy and difficult to access. For the latter sites, you might consider warning your readers that these sites are busy and that they might not be able to connect—then they won't blame *you*.

GETTING THE WORD OUT

Once you've created your Web site, you'll need to publicize it. This isn't crass commercialism. Web users are eager to learn of new and interesting resources.

HOT TIP

Eager to publicize your new effort? Make sure you have extensively tested it before doing so. If there's something wrong with your web, you don't want your users—or customers— to be the ones to find out. See "Testing Your Web," earlier in this chapter.

Many of the Web's subject tree and search services actively solicit your publicizing efforts (see Figure 28.2). Here's where to advertise your Web offering:

- **NCSA's What's New** (http://www.ncsa.uiuc.edu/SDG/Software /Mosaic/Docs/whats-new-form.html).

- **comp.infosystems.announce** Post a brief notice of your Web offering to this Usenet newsgroup.

- **Aliweb** (http://www.ncsa.uiuc.edu/SDG/Software/Mosaic/Docs/whats new-form.html) Access this URL and follow the instructions.

- **Mother of All Bulletin Boards** (http://www.cs.colorado.edu /homes/mcbryan/public_html/bb/13/42/summary.html

This should be sufficient to get the word out. Before long, your site will be picked up by Web robots, too.

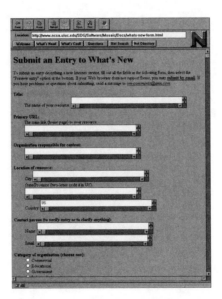

Figure 28.2 NCSA's What's New form

SUMMARY

Before creating a Web site, consider whether it's the right medium for your message. Plan your web carefully, and consider whether or not you're reinventing the wheel. Know your purpose and audience, choose your content carefully, pay attention to the design of the document, and be sure to check your spelling. Next, it's time to choose your server. If you work for a university or corporation, chances are that there's a UNIX workstation already set aside for Web documents. Otherwise, you can set up your own server, but you'll need a dedicated line. Excellent server software is available for Windows and Macintosh systems, although cuurently you need a UNIX workstation to set up credit card authorization and ordering.

FROM HERE

- Learn how to design and implement your web documents, in accordance with the best recent thinking on what makes a Web site work! See the next chapter.

- For instructions on installing WinHTTPD for Microsoft Windows server, see Appendix C.

CHAPTER 29

Weaving a Web: A Crash Course

> The web has spread from the grass roots, without a central authority, and this has worked very well. This has been due in part to the creativity of information providers, and the freedom they have to express their information as directly and vividly as they can. Readers appreciate the variety this gives. However, in a large web they also enjoy a certain consistency.
> —Tim Berners-Lee

What does it mean to weave a Web? Put simply, it means creating the documents that enable you to become a Web information provider. You can do this with just one simple page, and many people do. If you'd like to create an outstanding Web offering, though, read on; you'll find a very rich set of resources in this chapter for web weaving.

Admittedly, most would-be Web authors are quite content to put up a cobbled-together page, however poorly designed. That's fine for a college student or computer hobbyist, but if you're planning to create a Web site that's associated with your organization, such as a company or university, you'd better think twice about taking such a diffident approach. Your work will reflect on you and your organization. You'll be wise to see to it that your Web offering meets high standards.

This chapter helps you achieve these standards by offering a quick course in weaving a high-quality web. It guides you step-by-step through the creation of The Generic Web Site, a series of linked documents that embody the best principles of web design. An example is the generic Welcome page, which you can modify by typing in your own title and welcome text. (You'll see this page, and the others, illustrated in the next section.)

You can use this chapter in two ways:

- You can follow the tutorial step-by-step, typing the HTML and learning from doing. You can then modify these documents to suit your needs.

- You can open the completed documents, which are included on this book's disk, and are ready for your modification.

INTRODUCING THE GENERIC WEB SITE

The Generic Web Site is a series of linked documents that you can adapt for your uses. Designed with high Web standards in mind, it's ready for you to add your own text and logos. Simply by copying and renaming some of the files, you can easily expand this web in both breadth and depth or both, as explained later in this chapter. For now, though, let's take a look at the Welcome page (Figure 29.1).

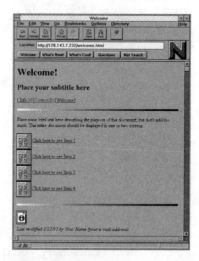

Figure 29.1 Welcome page (The Generic Web Site)

As you can see from Figure 29.1, this is a generic document that you can quickly and easily modify to suit your needs. You can supply your organization's logo or an illustrative graphic, type a more descriptive Heading 1 and a subtitle, add more descriptive text to the hyperlinks, and you're ready to go. You can even change the icons, if you like, to jazz things up a bit (Figure 29.2).

Figure 29.2 *Modified welcome page*

When you click on one of the four hyperlinks in the Welcome document, you see one of the generic documents at the second level of the web (see Figure 29.3). There are three more of these documents, keyed to the hyperlinks in the Welcome document. (If you wish, you can delete one or more of the links, or add additional ones. You can create additional second-level documents just by copying and renaming one of the files.)

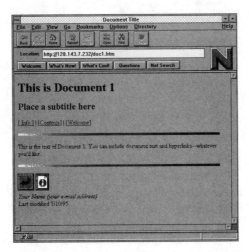

Figure 29.3 *Document at the web's second level*

Above all, this web is designed for easy navigation. At the bottom of the second-level documents, for instance, a Return button takes you back to the Welcome page. The top of *every* page of the web contains the following row of buttons, which are readable even by text-based readers such as Lynx.

- **Info.** Click here to see a page (Figure 29.4) that gives information about this web, including its scope and purpose. You can also place disclaimers here. The Information button at the bottom of every screen displays the same page.

- **Contents.** Click here to see a page (Figure 29.5) that lists all the documents in the web in alphabetical order, providing another convenient way to access the information this web contains.

- **Welcome.** This button displays the welcome page again.

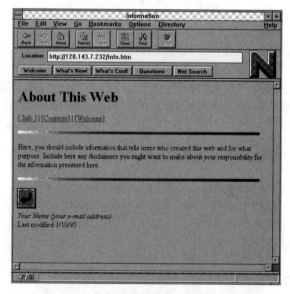

Figure 29.4 Info page

Want to add some depth to your web? One of the second-level documents has links to subordinate documents, one of which is shown in Figure 29.6. Notice that there's an additional icon at the bottom of this document, an up arrow. If you click this, you go back to the linked document at the second level. If you click the Return icon, you go back to the Welcome page. As with all the pages in the web, the

Contents, Info, and Welcome pages are immediately accessible using the buttons at the top of the document.

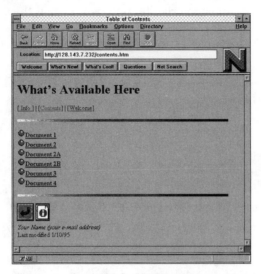

Figure 29.5 *Contents page*

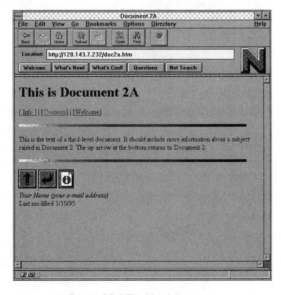

Figure 29.6 *Third-level document.*

That's the Generic Web Site. If you'd like to know more about how and why this site was created in this way, read on. You'll also find a tutorial that shows you how to construct the documents, in case you'd like to learn by doing. Perhaps the quickest and best way to use this material, though, is to install the Generic Web Site on your computer, and start adapting it to your needs!

INSTALLING THE GENERIC WEB SITE

The Generic Web Site found on the disk enclosed with this book. It contains the HTML files, the buttons, the arrows, and the icons that you see in Figures 29.1 through 29.5.

The Generic Web Site is stored in a compressed executable file, called GENERIC.EXE. To install this file on your computer, copy GENERIC.EXE to the directory where you keep (or plan to keep) your HTML files. (Note: If you're using WinHTTPD for Microsoft Windows, you *must* install this file in the directory c:\httpd\htdocs.) If you've already installed WinHTTPD for Microsoft Windows, this directory already exists because the program created it for you automatically. Switch to DOS, then switch to the directory in which you installed GENERIC.EXE, type **GENERIC**, and press **Enter**. The files will decompress. You can then open them with your browser.

FUNDAMENTALS OF WEB DESIGN

What rules and concepts underlie The Generic Web Site? You'll find out in this section.

**KEY
TERM**

One common mistake on the Web is to create documents that throw vast amounts of information at the reader in one huge, complex page. At the heart of effective hypermedia design is the concept of *chunking*, breaking information down into manageable units. Once you've chunked your information, you need to consider your web's *metastructure*—the overall plan by which the various documents will be organized. The following sections go into these points in detail.

The Art of Chunking

As a general guideline, most of your web's pages should occupy only one or two screens of text. There are legitimate exceptions, of course, a lengthy essay, meant to be read sequentially, can be provided in a single, multi-screen document (see "Handling Lengthy Documents," in the next chapter).

Just how you should chunk your information depends on what you're chunking, so an example might prove worthwhile. Suppose, you're putting together a web for a community youth orchestra. Now think for a minute about *what people want to know* about this orchestra. Tip: Use the journalist's "Five Ws" approach: who, what, when, where, why? With a piece of paper, brainstorm a list:

- Why is a youth orchestra worth having in our community?
- How is a youth orchestra supported?
- Who can play in this youth orchestra?
- When are the upcoming concerts, and what will the orchestra play?
- Who's the conductor? Who's on the management board?
- Who's in the orchestra?
- What do local civic leaders have to say about the youth orchestra and its contributions to the youth of this community?
- How can donors support the orchestra?

Once you've got your list, you're well on your way to developing your web. But there's one other important element—the metastructure—that you need to address before you begin.

Designing the Metastructure

A web's metastructure is the overall structure by which the various "chunks" will be linked together.

How you structure your web depends on the information you're providing, but some general principles can be stated nevertheless. Most people will expect to find a welcome page of some kind that states the web's purpose and provides links to documents containing the most important information. These documents, in turn, might contain links to less important information that only the truly curious would want to pursue. In other words, your users may be thinking of your information in terms of an inverted tree, as shown in the following diagram:

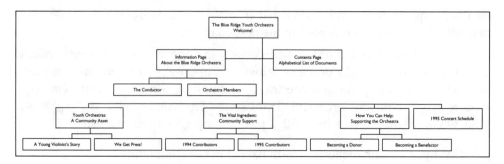

Need help organizing your web? If you're using Microsoft Word for Windows, you can use Microsoft Organization Chart, an OLE applet packaged with Word, to create charts like the one shown in the above illustration. Granted, a web isn't like an organization chart, as there are linkages among all the boxes in the chart, but this kind of software can provide a good start.

The following is an overview of the types of documents you'll find in the Youth Orchestra web:

- **The Welcome Page** ("The Blue Ridge Youth Orchestra: Welcome!"). This page succinctly states the scope of the web, indicates who created it and why, and provides links to the most important information that's available. It should be only one or two screens in length.

- **The Information Page** ("About the Blue Ridge Orchestra"). This page provides more detailed information about the creators and purpose of this web and why. It may also contain disclaimers that limit the Webmaster's responsibility for use of the information the web contains.

- **Contents Page.** Here's something useful that you rarely see on the Web. This page provides an alphabetized list of all the documents in the web and lets users access a page quickly, without having to figure out how to navigate through links to get there.

- **Second-Level Pages** ("Youth Orchestras: A Community Asset," "The Vital Ingredient: Community Support," etc.). These pages, directly linked to the welcome page, provide the most important information that users may want.

- **Third-Level Pages** ("We Get Press," "1994 Contributions," etc.). These Pages provide ancillary information that pertains to the second-level document one level above. (Some webs include more than three levels, but these can confuse the user.) These pages are substantive and can be more lengthy than the second-level pages.

This top-down organization might seem a bit rigid for a communication system as freewheeling as the Web, but it has its advantages. This web's welcome page would list the following topics (as hyperlinks):

- About the Blue Ridge Orchestra
- Youth Orchestras: A Community Asset
- The Vital Ingredient: Community Support
- How You Can Help
- 1995 Concert Schedule

This list of topics provides a clear, logical list of cues for information-seekers. Compare the above organization to a helter-skelter, disorganized approach that mixes information levels unsystematically:

- The Conductor
- Becoming a Donor
- We Get Press!
- Youth Orchestras: A Community Asset
- 1994 Contributors

Anticipating Multiple Points of Entry

The inverted tree design is a nice, logical layout, isn't it? Well, here's the bad news. You can't be sure just where readers will enter your web. Who knows how or why one or more of these pages will get linked, by accident or by design, to a hotlist, metapage, or starting points document somewhere? Users could come in at "Becoming a Benefactor," for instance, only to be confronted with a pitch for a $1,000 donation!

AWFUL

HOT TIP

Web surfers expect to encounter pages that are obviously at the second or third levels of a web, but they also expect to find links to documents that can tell them where they are, what all this means, and how to get around. *Every page of your web should contain hyperlinks—or, preferably, navigation buttons—that take readers to the welcome page and to the information page.*

For effective Web design, in sum, remember that every document in your Web can and will be accessed by people who haven't yet seen your welcome page. Each

document in your web should contain cues that answer all of the following questions:

- What's all this about? Where can I find out what the purpose of this page is?
- Where did it come from? Who is responsible for this?
- How do I find useful information here?
- Is this information up to date?

This advice can be put into practice in a number of ways:

- **Navigation Bar.** You should provide a bar of navigation buttons at the top of every page in your web, to allow the user to find the welcome, information, and contents pages quickly. Some or all of these icons should be repeated at the end of the document.
- **Signature.** Every page should include the name and email address of the person who created it.
- **Date of Last Modification.** Each page should include the date when the document was created or last modified.
- **Cues and Clues.** For people who access the web from pages other than the Welcome page, provide information icons that access documents explaining the web's purpose and structure.
- **Contents Pages.** Provide a Contents page that lists all the pages in your web in alphabetical order.

The Generic Web Site puts these principles into action.

CREATING THE GENERIC WEB SITE

You'll find the TGWS files on the disk enclosed with this book. If you'd like to get some experience with HTML, you can type the files yourself. Feel free to enter your modifications along the way. However, you'll gain additional insight and experience with HTML if you follow the tutorials in this section.

To create your web pages, you can use your word processing program, such as Microsoft Word for Windows. However, it's best to use the Windows Notepad utility (NOTEPAD.EXE), which you'll find in the Accessories program group in Program Manager. Unlike most word processing programs, Notepad doesn't deny other applications access to a document while you're editing it. You can keep your HTML document on-screen while you're testing it with your graphical browser.

Once again, remember that Netscape for Windows is the only browser discussed in this book that can resolve relative links without requiring that you run a server. If you're using another browser to develop your web, the relative links may not work until you install and run the server software.

AWFUL

Creating the Welcome Page

A good welcome page succinctly conveys the web's purpose and provides efficient navigation tools. To create the welcome page, you'll create a document title, headings and subheadings, hyperlinks, navigation buttons, and a return address, as explained in the following sections. You can create this document with any word processing program or the Windows notepad utility. You'll save the file using the name WELCOME.DOC.

If you're creating HTML documents with word processing programs such as Microsoft Word, you *must* remember to save the documents using the programs' Text Only option. Otherwise, the program will insert formatting codes into the document that your browser cannot read, resulting in on-screen gibberish. A good way to avoid this problem is to create and save the file using Notepad, which always saves using a plain text format.

AWFUL

Adding the Document Title

With most browsers, the document title is shown on the browser's title bar—which many people won't even notice. The title that will register in most people's minds is the Heading 1 text (see "The Document Heading," below).

HOT TIP

Since spiders and web crawlers will pick up your document's title, make it as descriptive as possible. Include key words that describe this document's content. Because this is a generic document, the word "Welcome" is used here, but you should use a longer title such as "Welcome to the Blue Ridge Youth Orchestra."

Type the following in your blank document:

```
<HTML>
<HEAD>
<TITLE>Welcome </TITLE>
</HEAD>
<BODY>
</BODY>
</HTML>
```

Note that what you've typed contains the correct, overall structure of an HTML document. Everything is enclosed within <HTML> and </HTML> tags, and there's a distant <HEAD> and <BODY> section.

Adding the Document Heading

The document heading (created with the <H1> tag) is the one that most people will notice. Because most browsers display this text using a large font, you may wish to use a subheading with the <h2> tag, as follows:

```
<H1>Heading 1</H1>
<H2>Place a subtitle here</H2>
```

Type these two lines between the <BODY> tags, as shown here:

```
<HTML>
<HEAD>
<TITLE>Welcome </TITLE>
</HEAD>
<BODY>
<H1>Heading 1</H1>
<H2>Place a subtitle here</H2>
</BODY>
</HTML>
```

Creating the Button Bar

Experienced Web designers know that readers appreciate having a row of buttons across the top of the screen that are linked to the most popular, useful, or frequently-accessed pages in the web. With the buttons at the top of the document (rather than the bottom), you don't have to page all the way through the document to choose navigation options.

You'll run across many Web documents that use colorful icons here, but there's a good argument against this practice. As you know, every in-line graphic makes your document download more sluggishly. Moreover, people accessing your web with text-based readers such as Lynx cannot see the in-line graphics. And the more you place at the top of the page, the longer it takes to get to the heart of your document. These three points argue for a text-based button bar.

Here's the HTML that produces the button bar shown in the figures at the beginning of the chapter:

```
<A HREF="info.htm"> Info </A>
<A HREF="contents.htm">Contents</A>
<A HREF="welcome.htm">Welcome</A>
```

Note the spacing. To produce the effect shown in the figures, you must type this with the spacing that's shown. You can place these tags just after the <H2> line, as shown:

```
<HTML>
<HEAD>
<TITLE>Welcome </TITLE>
</HEAD>
<BODY>
<H1>Heading 1</H1>
<H2>Place a subtitle here</H2>
<A HREF="info.htm"> Info </A>
<A HREF="contents.htm">Contents</A>
<A HREF="welcome.htm">Welcome</A>
</BODY>
</HTML>
```

Adding a Rule

Straight horizontal lines, called rules, can add organization to your document by creating a visual barrier between sections, but don't overdo it. The more rules you add, the less space is left for the text. To add a rule, use the <HR> tag, just below the <H2> tag, as shown:

```
<HTML>
<HEAD>
<TITLE>Welcome </TITLE>
</HEAD>
<BODY>
<H1>Heading 1</H1>
<H2>Place a subtitle here</H2>
```

```
<A HREF="info.htm"> Info </A>
<A HREF="contents.htm">Contents</A>
<A HREF="welcome.htm">Welcome</A>
<HR>
</BODY>
</HTML>
```

HOT TIP   You can use a graphic as a rule. Just remember to surround the image reference tag with <p> tags, so that the graphic displays on a line by itself. In place of the <hr> tag, this tag displays a GIF file containing a nicely-shaded grey rule (see the figures at the beginning of this chapter). To add this tag, delete the <HR> tag and add a new line its place:

```
<p><IMG SRC="line_gra.gif"><p>
```

Adding Introductory Text

After the document heading, subheading, and rule, you should add a very brief explanation of the document's purpose. Keep this as short as possible.

Remember that your word processor's line breaks have no effect on the way a browser displays the lines. To start a new paragraph, use the <p> code, as in the following example:

```
Place some brief text here describing the purpose of this document, but don't add too much. This
entire document should be displayed in one or two screens.<p>
```

You can add this text just below the <HR> rule.

Adding a List of Hyperlinks

Rather than confronting the reader with a huge amount of text on the first page, it's better to start with a brief list of hyperlinks (see "Chunking," in Chapter 28). These links point to additional documents.

This section explains how to create these links. The two following sections show how to embellish them.

The hyperlinks you create will be **relative hyperlinks**, that is, hyperlinks to documents stored in the same directory as the welcome document. These hyperlinks don't connect to anything yet; you'll create the documents later.

To create a list of hyperlinks, you use the following expression:

```
<A HREF="doc1.htm">Click here to see Item 1</A><BR>
```

You can place several of these in a list, as follows, just below the rule:

```
<A HREF="doc1.htm">Click here to see Item 1</A><BR>
<A HREF="doc2.htm">Click here to see Item 2</A><BR>
<A HREF="doc3.htm">Click here to see Item 3</A><BR>
<A HREF="doc4.htm">Click here to see Item 4</A><BR>
```

Here's what your document looks like so far:

```
<HTML>
<HEAD>
<TITLE>Welcome </TITLE>
</HEAD>
<BODY>
<H1>Heading 1</H1>
<H2>Place a subtitle here</H2>
<A HREF="info.htm"> Info </A>
<A HREF="contents.htm">Contents</A>
<A HREF="welcome.htm">Welcome</A>
<p><IMG SRC="line_gra.gif"><p>
<A HREF="doc1.htm">Click here to see Item 1</A><BR>
<A HREF="doc2.htm">Click here to see Item 2</A><BR>
<A HREF="doc3.htm">Click here to see Item 3</A><BR>
<A HREF="doc4.htm">Click here to see Item 4</A><BR>
</BODY>
</HTML>
```

Using Navigation Icons as Buttons

If you want a really jazzy hyperlink list, use in-line graphics and make them click-able, as explained in this section. This book includes the file DOC.GIF, which displays an icon that looks like a document.

Looking for buttons, icons, rules, and other cool graphics to include in your documents? Check out http://www.gsia.cmu.edu/gifs/index.html. You'll find instructions on downloading a compressed copy of all the graphics contained in this archive. Do you like to create your own buttons? Check out http://www.uwyo.edu/cte/Internet.html, a Grand Central Station for clip art on the net.

In the following, you'll add DOC.GIF to each of the hyperlinks in your document, and make the icons clickable. Begin by deleting the IMG SRC tag that inserts the yellow ball graphic. To make a graphic clickable, move the IMG SRC tag so that it's within the hyperlink tag. The following adds a graphic (an icon representing a document) in front of the hyperlinks:

```
<A HREF="doc1.htm"><IMG SRC="doc.gif">Click here to see Item 1</A><BR>
```

Note the box around the buttons in Figures 29.1 and 29.2, earlier in this chapter. Displayed in blue by most graphical browsers, this box indicates that the graphic is clickable. When you click one of these balls, you initiate a hyperlink to the same document you would see had you clicked the hyperlink text.

Aligning the Buttons

If you look at the result on-screen of what you've created so far, you'll see that it isn't as attractive as it could be, as the text is aligned by default at the bottom of the buttons. To force the text to align in the middle of the graphic, add an ALIGN tag, as in the following:

```
<A HREF="doc1.htm"><IMG SRC="doc.gif" ALIGN=middle>Click here to see Item 1</A><BR>
```

This tag produces the buttons shown in the figures at the beginning of the chapter.

Adding Another Rule

To visually set off the hyperlinks, try adding another rule below them. Use your word processors copy and paste commands to copy the tags used to insert the first rule.

If the rule doesn't appear on a line by itself, you forgot to add the <p> tags before and after the IMG SRC tag that inserts the rule. Put them in, and reload the document.

Adding a Navigation Icon

Below the rule you've just added, you should include one or more navigation icons to help the user navigate among the various documents in your web. Since this is the top level, you don't need buttons to return to the welcome page, but every page should contain an icon users can click to get more information, as shown in Figure 29.1 (earlier in this chapter).

This icon is easy to add; it's just after the second rule. The following inserts the icon from the file icon.gif, and includes a hyperlink to the file icon.htm (you'll create this file later):

AWFUL

```
<A HREF="info.htm"><IMG SRC="info.gif"></A>
```

What if you're reading this document with a text-based browser? You'll just see a placeholder, with no indication of what the graphic means or what will happen if you click it. That's true of the previous graphics, except that all of them are associated with explanatory text for navigational icons, which will be plainly visible to all users. There's a way to provide explanatory text to people using text-based browsers, as the following section explains.

AWFUL

🕷 WEBMASTER

If you insert an in-line graphic hyperlink that has no explanatory text, you should add an ALT attribute to the IMG SRC tag. Doing so will increase your page's accessibility for people using text-only browsers, such as Lynx. In place of graphics, they'll see the text that follows the ALT tag. Consider the following tag:

```
<IMG SRC="info.gif">
```

This tag displays an icon, as you've just seen. Now consider this tag:

```
<IMG SRC="info.gif" ALT="[Info]">
```

With this tag, people who browse your documents with text-based readers will see the text "Info" instead of the usual placeholder.

Is this worth doing? Here's what Web maven Brigitte Jellinek has to say:

Although many people now have graphical Web clients, one of the strengths of the Web should be that it can be read using a wide variety of computers with all kinds of capabilities. I hope my Web server can also be read by a blind person using a text-only web client and a text-to-speech tool that reads the text out loud.

'Nuff said.

Signing Your Page

The last part of your page provides the electronic mail address of the person who maintains the web, as shown in Figure 29.1, earlier in this chapter. You can also add the date of last modification to this line. Now your page is finished!

Your address is easily added with the following (just type in today's date and your name):

```
<ADDRESS>Last modified 1/12/95 by Your Name (your email address)</ADDRESS>
```

HOT TIP

At the end of your welcome page, you may also wish to add the date you last modified the file. This is convenient for people who might be checking out your site to see what's new.

The Finished Welcome Document

Here's what the finished welcome document looks like. Note the addition of spacing and blank lines, which makes the file easier to read:

```
<HTML>

<HEAD>
   <TITLE>Welcome </TITLE>
</HEAD>

<BODY>
   <H1>Welcome!</H1>
   <H2>Place your subtitle here</H2><p>

   <A HREF="info.htm">Info</A>
   <A HREF="contents.htm">Contents</A>
   <A HREF="welcome.htm">Welcome</A>

<p><IMG SRC="line_gra.gif"><p>

Place some brief text here describing the purpose of this document, but don't add too much. This
entire document should be displayed in one or two screens.<p>
```

```
<A HREF="doc1.htm"><IMG SRC="doc.gif"ALIGN=middle>Click here to see Item 1</A><BR>
<A HREF="doc2.htm"><IMG SRC="doc.gif"ALIGN=middle>Click here to see Item 2</A><BR>
<A HREF="doc3.htm"><IMG SRC="doc.gif"ALIGN=middle>Click here to see Item 3</A><BR>
<A HREF="doc4.htm"><IMG SRC="doc.gif"ALIGN=middle>Click here to see Item 4</A><BR>

<p><IMG SRC="line_gra.gif"><p>

<A HREF="info.htm"><IMG SRC="info.gif" ALT="[Info]"></A>
<ADDRESS>Last modified 1/12/95 by Your Name (your e-mail address)</ADDRESS>
</BODY>

</HTML>
```

Creating Second-Level Documents

Now that you've created your welcome page, it's time to create the second-level pages. These are the documents referenced by the hyperlinks on the welcome page (doc1, doc2, doc2, and doc4).

These documents can be created quickly and easily using your word processor's editing and file saving commands. Begin by saving your welcome page, and then use your word processor's Save As command to save the welcome page to a new file, called DOC1.HTM.

In the new file that you've created, carefully delete the hyperlinks between the two rules without deleting the rules themselves. What's left is an area for this document's text. You can add some generic text so that you'll be able to recognize this document when you're testing the links.

There's just one more thing you should add—a way to get back to the welcome page. Let's add a Return button to the button bar at the bottom of the second-level document. To do so, just insert a new in-line graphic hyperlink (<A HREF="test.html"><IMG SRC="return.gif">) in front of the existing one, as follows:

```
<A HREF="welcome.html"><IMG SRC="return.gif" ALT="[Welcome]"></A>
<A HREF="info.html"><IMG SRC="info.gif" ALT="[Info]"></A>
```

The hyperlink you've added uses the button called RETURN.GIF, and accesses the document WELCOME.HTM. Here's what the completed file should look like:

```
<HTML>
<HEAD>
   <TITLE>Document Title </TITLE>
</HEAD>

<BODY>
   <H1>This is Document 1</H1>
   <H2>Place a subtitle here</h2><p>
<A HREF="info.htm"> Info ]</A>
<A HREF="contents.htm">Contents</A>
<A HREF="welcome.htm">Welcome</A>

<p><IMG SRC="line_gra.gif"><p>

This is the text of Document 1. You can include document text and hyperlinks—whatever you'd
like.<p>

<p><IMG SRC="line_gra.gif"><p>

<A HREF="welcome.html"><IMG SRC="return.gif" ALT="[Welcome]"></A>
<A HREF="info.html"><IMG SRC="info.gif" ALT="[Info]"></A>
<ADDRESS>Your Name (your e-mail address)</ADDRESS>
Last modified 1/10/95
</BODY>
</HTML>
```

Note: Don't use the
 (line break) tag in the bar of navigation buttons. Without

, all the buttons appear on one line.

Creating Copies of This Document

Save DOC1.HTM, and use your word processor's Save As command to make
copies of this document called DOC2.HTM, DOC3.HTM, and DOC4.HTM. Add
some text to each new copy that will identify the document (such as "This is document 2,") so that you can identify the page when you're testing hyperlinks.

While you're at it, create a fourth copy, named INFO.HTM. You can use this to
create the information page, discussed in the next section.

WHAT? THEY STARTED READING THIS AT THE SECOND LEVEL?

You'd better get used to the idea. Ideally, all of your users would enter your web at the welcome page, but that's not necessarily what's going to happen. Suppose somebody likes the information you've placed on one of the second-level pages, and puts the URL for this page on a hotlist, starting points document, or subject tree. All of a sudden, many— or even *most*—of the people accessing your web are coming in at the second level! That's why it's so important to include a Return (or Home) icon, to let users get to the top-level document in your web. It's also a good idea to include an Information icon on each page of your web.

Creating the Information Page

Every web you weave should include a page of general information about the site and why you created it. This section contains information about creating an information page (INFO.HTM).

At this point, the file INFO.HTM contains a copy of one of your second-level documents. To create the information document, erase the subheading and move the in-line graphic of the information icon to the line that used to contain the subheading. Also, remove the hyperlink from the information icon, so that it's just an ordinary, in-line graphic. Here's the completed code for INFO.HTM:

```
<HTML>
<HEAD>
    <TITLE>Information </TITLE>
</HEAD>

<BODY>
<h1>About This Web</h1>
<A HREF="info.htm">Info</A>
<A HREF="contents.htm">Contents</A>
<A HREF="welcome.htm">Welcome</A>
<p><IMG SRC="line_gra.gif"><p>


Here, you should include information that tells users who created this web and for what purpose.
Include here any disclaimers you might want to make about your responsibility for the informa-
tion presented here.<p>
```

```
<IMG SRC="line_gra.gif"><p>

<B><A HREF="welcome.html"><IMG SRC="return.gif" ALT="[Welcome]"></A></B>
<ADDRESS>Last modified 1/12/95 by Your Name (your e-mail address)</ADDRESS>

</BODY>
</HTML>
```

Creating a Contents Page

The Contents page has a very simple function—it offers a simple, alphabetized list of all the pages in your site. For example, this generic web site will have seven pages, each with its own title. You can list these titles in alphabetical order and provide hyperlinks to them. This could prove invaluable to people who lose their way in your web—they'll really appreciate it.

```
<HTML>
<HEAD>
   <TITLE>Table of Contents </TITLE>
<h1>What's Available Here</H1>
</HEAD>
<BODY>
<p><A HREF="welcome.htm"><IMG SRC="welcome.gif"></A>
<A HREF="info.htm"><IMG SRC="infobtn.gif"></A>
<A HREF="feedback.htm"><IMG SRC="feedback.gif">
<A HREF="contents.htm"><IMG SRC="contents.gif"></A>

<p><IMG SRC="line_gra.gif"><p>

<IMG SRC="ball2_ye.gif"><A HREF="doc1.htm">Document 1</A><BR>
<IMG SRC="ball2_ye.gif"><A HREF="doc2.htm">Document 2</A><BR>
<IMG SRC="ball2_ye.gif"><A HREF="doc2a.htm">Document 2A</A><BR>
<IMG SRC="ball2_ye.gif"><A HREF="doc2b.htm">Document 2B</A><BR>
<IMG SRC="ball2_ye.gif"><A HREF="doc3.htm">Document 3</A><BR>
<IMG SRC="ball2_ye.gif"><A HREF="doc4.htm">Document 4</A><BR>

<p><IMG SRC="line_gra.gif"><p>
```

```
<A HREF="test.html"><IMG SRC="return.gif"></A>
<A HREF="test.html"><IMG SRC="info.gif" ALT="[Info]"></A>
<ADDRESS>Your Name (your e-mail address)</ADDRESS>
<ADDRESS>Last modified 1/10/95</ADDRESS>

</BODY>
</HTML>
```

Adding Third-Level Documents

If you wish to add third-level documents, you can do so using the same Save As techniques introduced in the previous section. Copy a second-level document and add features to it, as explained in this section. The following illustration shows the revised plan of the web, with three levels:

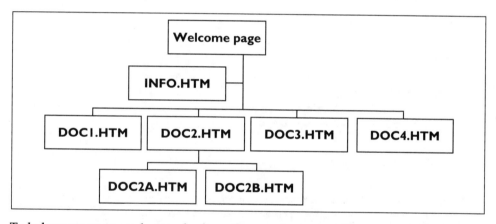

To help your users understand where they are in your web, you can include an up arrow, as shown in Figure 29.6, (earlier in this chapter). This arrow takes your readers back to the second-level document from which they descended (DOC2.HTM).

To create the third-level documents, use your word processor's Save As command to make one copy of DOC2.HTM. Then add the following IMG SRC tag to the navigation buttons at the bottom of the document:

```
<A HREF="doc2.html"><IMG SRC="up_arrow.gif">
```

After adding this tag, the button bar tags look like this:

```
<A HREF="doc2.html"><IMG SRC="up_arrow.gif">
<A HREF="test.html"><IMG SRC="return.gif"></A>
<A HREF="info.html"><IMG SRC="info.gif" ALT=" "></A>
```

Now save this document as DOC2A.HTM, and open it with your browser to make sure it's working correctly. If so, make another copy named DOC2B.HTM. Now you have created two third-level documents.

Here's how one of the third-level documents should look in your word processor:

```
<HTML>

<HEAD>
    <TITLE>Document 2A</TITLE>
<H1>This is Document 2A</H1>
</HEAD>

<BODY>

<A HREF="info.htm">Info</A>
<A HREF="contents.htm">Contents</A>
<A HREF="welcome.htm">Welcome</A>

<p><IMG SRC="line_gra.gif"><p>

This is the text of a third-level document. It should include more information about a subject
raised in Document 2. The up arrow at the bottom returns to Document 2.<p>

<p><IMG SRC="line_gra.gif"><p>

<A HREF="doc2.html"><IMG SRC="up_arrow.gif">
<A HREF="welcome.html"><IMG SRC="return.gif"></A>
<A HREF="info.html"><IMG SRC="info.gif" ALT=" "></A>
<ADDRESS>Last modified 1/12/95 by Your Name (your e-mail address)</ADDRESS>

</BODY>
</HTML>
```

Adding Hyperlinks to DOC2.HTM

At present, the third-level documents are not referenced anywhere in the web. Let's add hyperlinks to DOC2.HTM that display DOC2A.HTM and DOC2B.HTM.

Here's the text to add, in place of the generic text that's already in the document:

This is the text of Document 2. If you'd like more information on this subject, you can look at the <A HREF="doc2a.html">first</A> document below this one. You can also look at the <A HREF="doc2b.html">second</A> document below this one. <p>

MAKING THIS WEB YOUR OWN

Now for the fun part! The generic web you've created can be easily and quickly modified for many purposes. You can create an impressive web in short order simply by typing new text in the existing documents.

You can also extend the existing web, and in two directions:

- **Horizontally.** At the second and subsequent levels, you can add or remove documents. In this generic web, there are four documents at the second level, and two documents at the third level. You could modify this web so that there are only three documents at the second level, instead of four. Alternatively, you could add documents at this level. You can also add or remove documents at the third level.

- **Vertically.** Currently, there are three levels to this web: the welcome page (first level), the second level (DOC1, DOC2, DOC3, DOC4), and the third level (DOC2A an DOC2B). You could add a fourth or deeper levels if you wish. Don't add too many levels, though—a web more than four or five levels deep starts to get confusing.

HANDLING LENGTHY TEXT DOCUMENTS

At the second or subsequent levels of your web, you may wish to add text documents that are several pages in length. To make these documents more accessible and readable on the Web, you can use a very nifty HTML (discussed in this section) to create a list of hyperlinks at the beginning of the long document. Readers can click one of these links to go the the section within the *same* document that they want to read.

Figure 29.7 illustrates how this works. At the top of the lengthy documentis a list of hyperlinks, which functions in two ways. First, it provides a table of contents for the document, listing the document's major subheadings. Second, it provides a way to jump to these headings immediately. If you click "Nelson County Vineyards," for instance, you jump immediately to the portion of the document where the section on Nelson County begins (Figure 29.8).

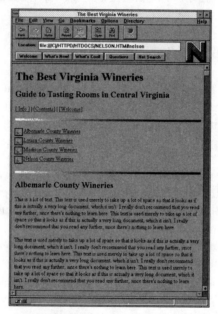

Figure 29.7 *Hyperlinks to sections of the same document*

AWFUL

To let readers jump to a specific place elsewhere in your document, use the <A> tag with the NAME attribute. Two tags are required to create the link The first tag marks the location to which the reader will jump, if the hyperlink is selected, and the second tag contains the hyperlink.

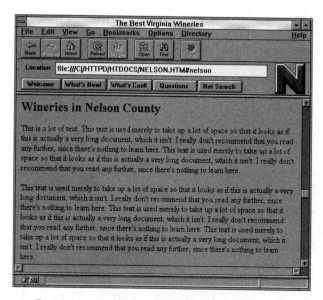

Figure 29.8 *Result of clicking "Nelson County" hyperlink*

To create the first tag (the one that marks the destination of the jump), use a tag such as the following:

    <A NAME="nelson">Nelson County Wineries</A>

You can make this tag part of an <H2> heading, as follows:

    <H2><A NAME="nelson">Nelson County Wineries</A></H2>

To create the hyperlink to this tag, use a tag such as the following:

    <A HREF="#nelson">Nelson County Wineries</A>

Note the pound (#) sign. This tag says, in effect, "Look in the document for the <A NAME> tag that matches "nelson."

You can jazz up this hyperlink in the usual ways. This is one of the hyperlinks that you see in Figure 29.7:

    <A HREF="#nelson"><IMG SRC="star.gif"align=middle>Nelson County Wineries</A>

To finish your lengthy document, be sure to add a link at the bottom of the document that allows the reader to return to the beginning.

HTML HORIZONS

In the previous three chapters, this book covered most of the HTML tags that you can use without having to worry about Common Gateway Interface (CGI) programming. However, some of the most exciting and useful HTML applications require such programming—for now. A new generation of HTML tools is on the way, which will make CGI programming unnecessary.

At the heart of these advanced HTML applications is the FORM tag. Essentially, the FORM tag accepts user input in text-entry and other input areas (see Figure 29.9), and produces output. The CGI scripting is used to direct that output. For example, you can create a script that sends the user's input to your electronic mail address and, at the same time, sends an HTML page to the user confirming the submission. Eventually, you'll be able to obtain user-friendly tools for creating forms and dealing with the output they create.

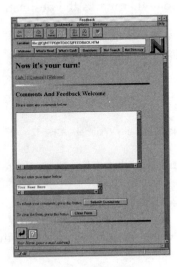

Figure 29.9 *Form displayed by FORM tags*

A harbinger of things to come is Polyform, created by Windows Webmaster Mark Bracewell. Polyform is designed to work with WinHTTPD for Microsoft Windows (WinHTTPD). Polyform provides a no-programming, point-and-click interface to Win-HTTPD that can route the output of FORM tags to your electronic mail account. For more information on Polyform, access http://www.portal.com/~cbntmkr/utility.html.

SUMMARY

This chapter describes a series of template documents and graphics files which have been woven together into a web you can modify for your own purpose. Based on the principles of Web hypermedia design, these files let you create a high-quality web in short order. You can follow this chapter's tutorials, which taken together constitute a crash course in web design, or just open the files on the disk included with this book and modify them to your heart's content.

FROM HERE

- Ponder the problems and controversies facing the Web in Chapter 30, Web Issues.

- Polish your crystal ball, and join in the speculation in Chapter 31, Web Futures.

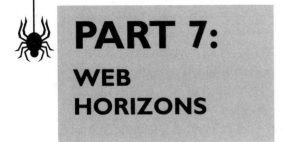

PART 7:
WEB HORIZONS

CHAPTER 30

Web Issues

> All that is human must retrograde if it does not advance.
> —Edward Gibbon, *The Decline and Fall of the Roman Empire.*

The Web is an amazing resource for many purposes, whether you're looking for erudition or entertainment, but it's far from perfect. This book has already pointed to several of the Web's shortcomings, including the difficulty of locating the information you want and the inadequacies of HTML. In this chapter, you'll learn more about some of the problems and issues facing the Web, including some drawbacks to the current version (1.0) of the HTTP protocol, the low quality of many Web offerings, the problem of copyright infringement, the problems of Web security, and the issue of universal access.

IS HTTP ADEQUATE?

The Web's underlying protocol, HTTP, makes the Web possible. But according to critics, it has many shortcomings. Here's a quick overview:

- **Inefficiency.** Currently HTTP wastes network bandwidth by requiring that a new connection be opened and terminated with each information request, even if it goes to exactly the same server. You can see this yourself when you access a URL containing text, in-line graphics, and additional objects. The browser initiates several independent contacts and downloads occur with the server. (It is as if you ordered a pizza with five telephone calls, one each for the dough, the sauce, the cheese, the pepperoni, and the anchovies.) The amount of network bandwidth consumed could be reduced substantially if HTTP created a single, virtual connection between the client and the server in which several objects could be transferred without having to renegotiate the connection for each one.

- **Lack of Security.** The current HTTP protocol enables simple authentication, in which the user is required to type a login name and password to access a server. However, this scheme is vulnerable to security abuses and is not sufficient for the development of Web commerce.

- **Lack of Indexing Information.** At present, there are no provisions made in the HTTP protocol for the exchange of information (such as document key words or copyright status indications) that could aid in the retrieval of Web information. This is a serious shortcoming. Were such information to be included, Web spiders and search engines could do a much better job of retrieving relevant documents.

Several efforts are underway to create a revised HTTP specification, to deal with these problems including a working group of the Internet Engineering Task Force (IETF). The organization most likely to achieve a workable standard, however, is the W3 Organization, a consortium of Web service providers that is discussed in the next chapter.

STANDARDS—OR "ISLANDS OF INTEROPERABILITY?"

The World Wide Web is at a crucial juncture in its history. Lacking a formal standards-setting body until late 1994, companies producing Web products have been sorely tempted to introduce their own proprietary additions to the Web protocols. The threat posed by such additions is that one firm's products might not work with another firm's products, creating what Mitch Wagner, writing in *Open Systems Today*, calls "islands of interoperability." At the worst, you would need a browser created by Company A if you wanted to access a server made by the same company; a browser made by Company B wouldn't work. This would be a disaster for the Web, many experts believe, because it would fragment the Web market just at the moment when an explosion of Web commerce is about to occur.

Is there danger that this fragmentation will occur? Some Web observer believe that Netscape Communications Corporation, the makers of the popular Netscape

Navigator browsing software, has crossed the line in incorporating non-standard features in its popular browser. For example, Netscape recognizes a tag, not included in HTML, that centers items on-screen. You won't browse the Web for long before you run into sites that urge you to use Netscape Navigator so that you can see all the available features.

Netscape Communications Corporation has received some harsh criticism for this move, but it's not completely clear whether it will fragment the Web market. The Internet's history is full of instances in which companies have unilaterally introduced innovative features, which have eventually found their way into public standards. As long as Netscape makes its innovations publicly accessible, fragmentation will not occur.

However, one area in which fragmentation is likely to occur is in secure encrypted communications, to be discussed later in this chapter. Two competing technologies have been announced by Netscape and by Spyglass, Inc. (the developers of Enhanced NCSA Mosaic.) To access a secure Netscape server, you'll need Netscape Navigator, just as you'll need Enhanced NCSA Mosaic 2.0 to access a secure Spyglass server. Just how this will work out in the Web's nascent commercial market is anyone's guess at this point.

ON-LINE TREASURES—OR TRASH?

There are treasures to be found on the Web—and a lot of junk, too. There's plenty of information available, but you must exercise judgment when you access it—all those documents *look* pretty in a graphical browser, but that doesn't mean they contain reliable information.

On the Web, anyone with a permanent Internet connection and a server can become an information provider. Many Web users fear that the Web will suffer the same fate as Usenet—a great system when it served a small, informed community, but plagued by a low signal-to-noise ratio once the Great Unwashed got on-line. That's an elitist notion, of course, and many would respond that it serves everyone's interest to have a variety of information resources available on the Web.

HOT TIP

There's one conclusion you can reliably reach from this debate: *caveat emptor* (let the buyer beware). Information you find on the Web should be greeted with skepticism (see the box, "Questions to ask about information on the Web").

QUESTIONS TO ASK ABOUT INFORMATION ON THE WEB

- **Who provided the information?** Was the document created by a company with a commercial interest, a public advocacy group with a biased angle, or an individual? If the document was created by an individual, is he or she qualified to provide this information?

- **When was it created?** Much information on the Web isn't updated as often as it should be. Check the last line of the page to find out whether the information provider included a "date of last modification." Email the page's provider, for information necessary.

- **Is it peer-reviewed?** The most authoritative print-based publications are peer-reviewed; that is, they are not published unless an anonymous panel of experts in a field decides that the work has merit. Some Web pages are peer-reviewed in this way. For an example, see the *MISQ Archivist* page at http://www.cox.smu.edu/mis/misq/central.html.

- **What references are provided?** Are any citations to publications or other Web documents provided to back up the author's contentions? Are the links up-to-date, and are they as authoritative as the current document?

CHALLENGES TO COPYRIGHT—AND FAIR USE

New technologies push existing laws into an uncharted arena, where it is far from clear just how these laws should be applied. Nowhere is this more evident than in the area of copyright. The Web makes it an easy matter to infringe on valid copyright claims. This fact has led to calls for more restrictive copyright laws, which could fundamentally alter the long-standing balance between the rights of copyright holders and the public's right to fair use of copyrighted material.

Do you violate copyright if you include a hyperlink to a copyrighted work? Although this matter has yet to be tested in court, the answer is almost certainly "No." Including a hyperlink does not constitute making an unauthorized copy of a work. It is comparable to including a bibliographic citation in a published work. Such citations do not require the author's permission.

Without question, some Web information providers are not sufficiently sensitive to intellectual property issues. Just because a work does not have an explicit copyright notice does not assure you that it's in the public domain; the work's author must expressly choose to place the work in the public domain. (A work in the public domain may be freely copied, modified, or resold without the author's permission.)

More than a few popular Web pages had made copyrighted materials available without the permission of copyright owners. An example is the famed Elvis Home Page, which ran into trouble with its Cyber Graceland tour. A letter from attorneys representing Elvis Presley Enterprises Inc. demanded that Elvis' songs and pictures of Graceland be removed from the Web. Andrea Berman, the creator of Elvis Home Page complied with this request.

But, isn't it permissible to reproduce copyrighted sounds, text, and images, so long as the purpose is not commercial? Berman had not sought any commercial gain by putting the Elvis sounds and pictures on the Web. However, her creation of a Cyber Graceland Tour could be seen to deprive Elvis Presley Enterprises of profits that it could pursue by creating a commercial Web service with the same focus. As with so many aspects of copyright law, it's a murky matter.

Copyright law may become less murky in the future, but in a way that many Web users won't like. A Clinton administration task force on intellectual property issues, the Information Infrastructure Task Force (IITF), has issued a preliminary report recommending changes to copyright law in light of new information technologies. The committee's recommendations could have grave implications for your right to fair use of copyrighted material.

Observing that computer networks allow easy duplication of digital material, the IITF seeks to preserve the market for copyrighted works by changing copyright law in the following areas:

- **Digital Transmission.** Digital transmission of a copyrighted work would be illegal, since it automatically makes a copy of the work. Thus you would not be able to email a copy of a copyrighted work to a friend, even if you paid for your copy and destroyed your copy of it.

- **Abolition of the "First Sale" rule.** In existing copyright law, a person who buys a copy of a copyrighted work has the right to sell or lend that copy without the copyright owner's permission. This would be abolished under the IITF's recommendations, because it is too easy for the work's posssessor to retain a digital copy of the work.

- **Creation of Copyright Circumvention Devices.** Creating a pgrogram or hardware device capable of circumventing copy protection schemes would be a crime under the IITF's recommendations.

The IITF's recommendations were strongly criticized by librarians, scholars, and networking advocates, who accused the IITF of uncritically accepting the position of the movie and recording industries. If information migrates from printed to electronic media, for example, libraries would not be able to lend works over a network; they would only be able to distribute physical copies of disks. Even more chilling with respect to the Web, it would become a crime to *browse* copyrighted material, since Web browsers download a temporary copy of the work. This would constitute the most radical revision in the history of copyright law, for it would, in effect, prevent the public from *reading* copyrighted material (current copyright law prevents the unauthorized *sale* of copyrighted material). The implications are frightening indeed for the public's right to access information.

Another alarming aspect of the proposed legislation is that, while it makes an offense of virtually all digital transmissions of copyrighted information, it does not protect on-line service providers from liability if one of their customers, illegally transmit copyrighted information through the providers' networkswithout the provider's knowledge.

WHAT IS "FAIR USE?"

Under current copyright law, you can make legal use of copyrighted materials under some circumstances. But be forewarned, the law is fuzzy.

The U.S. Copyright Act of 1976 (17 U.S.C. S107. Limitations on exclusive rights: Fair Use) holds the following:

"Notwithstanding the provisions of section 106, the fair use of a copyrighted work, ... for purposes such as criticism, comment, news reporting, teaching (including multiple copies for classroom use), scholarship, or research, is not an infringement of copyright. In determinging whether the use made of a work in any particular case is a fair use, the factors to be considered shall include —

1. the purpose and character of the use, including whether such use is of a commercial nature or is for nonprofit educational purposes;
2. the nature of the copyrighted work;
3. the amount and substantiality of the portion used in relation to the copyrighted work as a whole; and
4. the effect of the use upon the potential market for or value of the copyrighted work."

WHAT IS "FAIR USE?" (continued)

How do you know whether your use of copyrighted text is fair use or an infringement? Assuming your intended use is non-commercial, you'd be well advised to use very, very little of the work—a general guideline is 5% or less. What's more, the purpose of your use should be to comment on the copyrighted work, such as in a review or a scholarly article. If you're unsure whether your use falls under the fair use guidelines, play it safe—ask for permission!

CAN THE WEB BE MADE MORE SECURE?

When the Web was first developed, it was envisioned as an information exchange system for scientists. There were few security concerns in those halcyon days. As the Web evolves into the first genuine world information system, however, security concerns have come to the fore. These fall into three general areas: authentication, confidentiality, and integrity. The following sections examine each of these three areas of security, and discuss their relationship to evolving Web technologies.

Authentication

In brief, authentication refers to the process by which a person using a client program satisfies the server that he or she is a bona fide user of the system—that is, an authorized user who has an account and has agreed to use the system responsibly.

Most of the Web servers currently available provide only a basic level of user authentication, but better authentication facilities are becoming the norm. With NCSA's HTTPD server, it's possible to create four levels of user authentication.

- **Simple protection by password.** The protected document can be accessed only by a person possessing the correct password.
- **Protection by password; multiple users allowed.** The document can be accessed by more than one user, but each must have the correct password.
- **Protection by network domain.** The document is accessible only to those accessing it from within a certain Internet domain.
- **Protection by network domain—exclusion.** The document cannot be accessed by users from a specified domain.

Authentication may become more common simply as a means of finding out just who's accessing a given Web site. A case in point is HotWired, the online version of *Wired* magazine. When you access HotWired, you're asked to create a login name and password, and to supply your email address. You then receive an automatically-generated email message containing an authorization number, which you must supply to access the system. What's gained from this is a modicum of assurance that you aren't accessing the site using someone else's name and email address. HotWired wants to know just who's using their site, how often, and for what purpose—and then procedures assure that they will.

Confidentiality and Integrity

KEY TERM

Confidentiality refers to the protection of information from prying eyes while it is en route to its destination, while *integrity* refers to the protection of the information from tampering or alteration during its journey.

From the Web user's point of view, both confidentiality and integrity are supremely important. For example if you gave your credit card number and expiration date to a Web vendor you would like to be assured that nobody can intercept this information or tamper with it while it's on its way to its destination. The trouble is, current Web technology provides no assurance that this is the case.

KEY TERM

The answer to this problem is some type of *encryption*, which is the process of converting a *plaintext* message (a message that could be read by anyone) into *ciphertext* (a message that appears to be gibberish), by means of a *key*. Ideally, the message could be read only by the intended recipient, who possesses the key and uses it (in a process called *decryption*) to make the text readable again.

Bankers and diplomats have long used encryption to ensure the secrecy of messages, but the problem lies in how to get the key safely to its intended recipient. (The recipient needs the key in order to decode and read the message.) Traditionally, this has been done by courier. A new cryptographic method called *public key cryptography* eliminates the need to deliver the key, and raises the possibility that people who have never previously exchanged messages could send encrypted messages to each other.

Public key cryptography provides a method of encrypting a message that does not require the sender to convey a key to the recipient. In public key cryptography, the encryption key differs from the decryption key so that people can keep their encryption keys private. When the message is received, the receiver uses a private decryption key to decode the message. This method is secure as long as it is not possible to derive the secret decryption key from the public encryption key.

Several schemes are now available that employ encryption to assure confidentiality and integrity during the transmission of credit card information. Spyglass, Inc., the makers of Enhanced NCSA Mosaic, promise to include encryption in the next verison of the program. Netscape Navigator, already available from Netscape Communications Corporation, provides automatic encryption when contacting Netscape's secure servers.

Netscape may have the lead well in hand. In January, 1995, just as this book was going to press, Netscape announced an agreement with MasterCard that will enable on-line vendors to accept encrypted credit card information and receive nearly instantaneous credit authorization for MasterCard purchases.

WHAT'S A "FIREWALL"—AND WHY IS IT NEEDED?"

Concerned about potential security problems arising from Internet connections, many organizations have set up *firewalls*. In brief, a firewall is a device—generally, a router or a computer—that serves as an intermediary between a corporate network and the Internet. The firewall prevents unauthorized outsiders from logging on to computers within the internal network. This is often necessary to prevent malicious use by computer crackers and criminals.

The problem with firewalls is that they necessitate a tradeoff between the Internet's usefulness and security. The more secure the system, the harder it is for legitimate users within the organization to gain access to external Internet resources. At the extreme, a company with a high level of paranoia may offer only one connection to the Internet—a firewall system with absolutely no connection at all with internally-networked computers. However, this completely insulates employees from Internet electronic mail and other information resources.

One solution to the security/usefulness tradeoff is a *proxy server*, a program that mediates between internal users and the Internet. The proxy server can be configured to prevent external access, while permitting internal users to access external resources.

KEY TERM

HOT TIP

If you're using a Web browser within a network protected by a firewall, you may need to configure your browser to access one or more proxy servers. Among the Web browsers discussed in this book, Netscape Navigator is by far the best program to use under such circumstances. The program can negotiate with proxy servers to allow you access to external Web resources. You can also configure Netscape to work with Gopher, FTP, Usenet, and WAIS proxy servers, a unique feature among today's browsers.

> **USEFUL RESOURCE**
>
> For more information on firewalls, see the excellent Firewall FAW at http://fiver.sns.com/firewalls/firewalls.faq.html.

ACCESS ISSUES

If the Web is laying the foundation for the Information Superhighway of the future, there are grounds for concern that the society of the future will have two classes: the information "haves" and "have nots." Imagine what our society would be like if only the well-to-do had telephones and electricity. Universal access to these neccessitites of modern life is assured by federal regulation, but it is by no means clear that universal web (and Internet) access will be regulated in the same way.

THE WEB TODAY: OVERWHELMINGLY MALE, OVERWHELMINGLY WHITE

Whatever the Web may become in the future, it's currently very far from attracting a balanced spectrum of society. According to surveys conducted by Georgia Tech's Graphics, Visualization, & Usability Center, over 90% of Web users are male, and 87% describe their race as white. What is more, Web users are technically-oriented professionals or university students on a technical/professional track: the two largest user categories are people working in technical fields (27%) and university students (26%), with researchers, managers, and consultants not far behind. These patterns may change as computer use becomes more widespread, but for now the Web does not come close to attracting a cross-section of the societies it serves. Internet advertisers have taken note: *The New Yorker*, an upscale magazine if there ever was one, notes that the Internet's affluent, technically-savvy users "are people *The New Yorker* would appeal to," according to a senior vice president. The magazine has established a presence in the Electronic Newstand, a Web-accessible Gopher site.

What does "universal access" mean? A Clinton administration proposal defines universal access in institutional terms. Service could be considered universal if all the nation's classrooms, libraries, hospitals, and clinics were connected to the information superhighway.

Will universal access be achieved? There's a formidable barrier in the way, called the *last mile problem*. An infrastructure of high-bandwith backbone networks already exists, but the only existing means of connecting these networks to homes, schools, and offices is the local telephone system, which does not possess sufficient bandwidth to support an integrated services network capable of delivering multimedia. Wiring this "last mile" will cost an estimated $125 to $400 billion.

About 60% of U.S. homes have two last-mile delivery systems, a twisted pair telephone line and an analog coaxial cable that provides cable television. Since it is very unlikely that any of the current telecommunications players would contemplate the massive capital investment required to extend fiber optic or other high-bandwidth cables to millions of service delivery points, the interim solution to the last mile problem will very likely involve converting local telephones to digital signalling or modifying cable TV systems to permit two-way exchanges of computer data.

With established service to 98% of U.S. households, the telephone system offers excellent penetration. The technical problem lies in the limited bandwidth of the twisted pair wires that provide service delivery to the home. The existing analog telephone system can carry computer signals by means of a modem, but modems in common use today achieve data transmission speeds of only 14.4 Kbps. By the early twenty-first century, the telephone system will convert to digital signals using the ISDN standards, which will permit the simultaneous use of an existing twisted-pair cable for noise-free voice as well as 64Kbps data exchange. This is an improvement over the current system, but the limited bandwidth is insufficient for envisioned applications such as high definition television (HDTV) and distributed computing. With an estimated capital investment of $130 billion in twisted pair installations, telephone companies are very unlikely to contemplate upgrading their last-mile delivery system, which contains enough wire to run to the moon and back several hundred times. Replacing all of this wire with fiber optic would require the largest capital investments in human history. One conclusion: Don't expect a fiber optic cable to show up at your house anytime soon.

In contrast to the telephone system with it huge capital investment in antiquated cabling, cable TV systems currently bring high-bandwidth coaxial cable close to 97% of U.S. homes, and provide service to more than 60% of these homes. But these systems were designed with a broadcast model of transmission, in which signals emanate from the central office and travel to home TV sets in one direction only. Interim technical solutions allow computer data to traverse cable TV networks to specific TV sets, but are heavily biased toward one way data delivery. Providing enough upstream bandwidth may require the extension of a second coaxial cable to each service recipient.

A likely outcome of the last mile problem is a series of mergers between the regional Bell operating companies (RBOCs) and cable TV companies. In this way, a telephone company could acquire the delivery system it needs to implement integrated digital services, while cable TV companies could acquire the expertise and switching systems that they would need to offer local telephone service.

Will the efforts of private communications firms distribute Web access throughout our society? Some public advocacy organizations fear that an electronic version of "redlining" may surface. Redlining is an illegal banking practice in which certain neighborhoods, populated by poor or minority residents, are marked off as bad risks for home loans. Certainly, cable and telephone companies are likely to install high-bandwidth services in affluent neighborhoods before they get around to wiring everyone else—and, in the absence of regulation they may *never* get around to wiring poorer homes.

SUMMARY

The Web isn't free from problems, including the HTTP protocol itself, which has been rightly criticized for its inefficiency. Like all new technologies, the Web is pushing existing laws into new areas, and that's especially true of copyright law. If you're thinking of putting information on the Web, you should be aware of potential areas of copyright infringement. The Web's security problems, including security, confidentiality, and integrity, can be dealt with by authentication and encryption schemes, but there's no single universal method of supplying these. Finally, it's by no means certain that the Web will reach all segments of our society, threatening to create a two-tiered society of information "haves" and "have nots."

FROM HERE

- Take a look at the Web's future in Chapter 31, Web Futures.

CHAPTER 31

Web Futures

The good news from Washington is that every single person in Congress supports the idea of the information superhighway. The bad news is that nobody has any idea what that means.
—Representative Edward J. Markey

It's crystal ball time: Where's the Web headed? This chapter takes a look at very likely short-term prospects, including continued explosive growth and increasing commercialization, and examines iffier propositions concerning digital cash and the Web's relationship to the future "Information Superhighway."

WEB GROWTH

You've probably seen the gushing statements in newspaper articles about the Web, calling it "The fastest-growing communications system in human history." While that's true, it's worth remembering that the Web is growing within the Internet, which is itself growing at a phenomenal rate. Still, the numbers for the Web are pretty impressive. In the past year, the Web outpaced Gopher to become the second most popular Internet tool (see Table 31.1) the first, if you measure popularity by the number of transmitted bytes, is FTP. But what's even more impressive is the Web's growing numbers of users. According to a story in *Investor's Business Daily* in January, 1995, there will be 22 million Web users by 1998.

Table 31.1 World Wide Web vs. Gopher Traffic on the NSFNET Backbone (millions of bytes transmitted per month)

	WWW	GOPHER
Dec 92	78	34,247
Jan 93	122	43,238
Feb 93	512	60,897
Mar 93	3,613	79,024
Apr 93	8,116	89,074
May 93	17,298	103,870
Jun 93	35,701	111,881
Jul 93	48,728	139,006
Aug 93	50,779	148,795
Sep 93	75,401	198,096
Oct 93	122,174	250,785
Nov 93	172,340	291,133
Dec 93	225,443	309,691
Jan 94	269,129	374,681
Feb 94	347,503	396,066
Mar 94	518,084	480,690
Apr 94	671,950	517,625
May 94	799,163	555,708
Jun 94	946,539	567,479
Jul 94	1,056,081	555,089
Aug 94	1,311,822	651,846
Sep 94	1,593,463	751,454
Oct 94	2,152,956	864,259
Nov 94	3,126,195	867,043
Dec 94	3,475,374	778,290

Source Merit NIC Services

THE NEXT WEB STANDARD: THE W3 CONSORTIUM

A potential problem looms with the rapid growth of the World Wide Web. In pursuit of profits, companies may try to create proprietary communication standards, which are incompatible with other firms' efforts. This is a high-risk game: If you win, the entire industry is forced to pay you license fees, and that's big money. If you lose, you're out of business. Either way, though, users are the real losers, since they'll have to cope with a plethora of incompatible products.

Is that where the Web's headed? Not if the W3 Consortium has its way. A joint project of the Massachusetts Institute of Technology and the European Laboratory for Particle Physics (CERN), the W3 consortium plans to deliver a revised HTTP specification by mid-1995. This specification will provide enhanced features for Internet data security, privacy, and information retrieval.

Tim Berners-Lee, one of the Web's founders, heads the W3 Consortium, and attributes its development to the industry's perception that coordination was needed. "The decision to form the consortium came at the urging of firms investing increasing resources into the Web, whether in creation of software products, selling information, or for sharing information within their own companies, with business partners and the public," Berners-Lee told a *Communications Week* reporter. "We must make sure we all continue working together. When there are large commercial forces at work, we must make sure we have team spirit."

What does the W3 Consortium have in mind? Above all, downward compatibility with existing Web technology, says Berners-Lee: "We want to allow a rapid evolution [of the Web] that will include new features yet maintain the architecture." Specifically, the Consortium plans to focus on four areas of innovation: automatability (replacement of manual procedures with automatic ones), extensibility (ability to incorporate new data objects and concepts while maintaining downward compatibility), scalability (the ability of the Web to withstand continued exponential growth), and privacy (Web mechanisms for authentication, confidentiality, and integrity).

When the W3 Consortium finishes its work, the Web is likely to be more efficient and more interactive than it is now. Changes to the HTTP protocol will likely permit the automatic duplication of frequently-accessed documents, so that they multiply across the network, which will automatically decrease network overloading. In addition, changes are planned that will integrate the Web more tightly with electronic mail, and addition, conferencing capabilities are planned. These innovations will cement the Web's role as *the* interface of choice to the resources of the Internet.

EXCELLENT

COMMERCIALIZATION OF THE WEB

Right now, there's an explosion of commercial activity on the Web, which was formerly the exclusive habitat of academic and scientific types. Companies all over the world are finding that the Web is an excellent place to provide on-line documentation (especially for highly technical products), to market their products and services, to advertise, and to sell. The sections to follow detail these developments.

🕷 WEBMASTER

Doesn't the commercialization of the Web violate Internet mores and customs about commercial use of the network? In the past, the National Science Foundation's Acceptable Use Policies forbade commercial use of NSFNET, which formerly served as the sole Internet backbone. To provide an alternative to NSFNET and open the Internet for commercial use, a consortium of Internet service providers created an alternative "AUP-free" backbone for commercial Internet traffic. NSF plans to withdraw Federal support for NSFNET, which will soon be retired. Much of the aversion to commercial activity on the Internet comes from Usenet, where advertisements run counter to the purpose of Usenet's thousands of topically-organized discussion groups. Crass commercial advertising is not welcome on Usenet, because it gets into peoples' faces—you can't avoid seeing the subject line "Make Money Fast!" On the Web, advertising is inherently less problematic. Users don't see a company's ad unless they deliberately access the site—in which case they're probably interested in what the company has to offer and willing to put up with the marketing pitch. It's the Web that's making the commercialization of the Internet possible.

Providing On-line Documentation

Companies need very little arm-twisting to see the merits of one Web application—providing technical specifications and on-line documentation.

A manager at Hewlett-Packard estimates that his company currently maintains between 30,000 and 40,000 printed documents to describe the company's more than 20,000 products. Making these documents available on the Web will shorten the distance between the company and its customers—and what's more, coupling these documents with multimedia (sounds and video) can improve their quality. Hewlett-Packard's well-designed Web site shows how one company has made product information accessible to Web users (Figure 31.1).

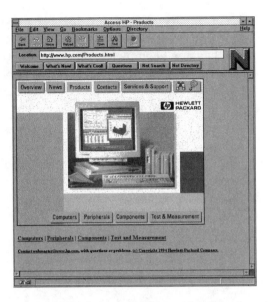

Figure 31.1 Hewlett-Packard product information page (http://www.hp.com/Products.html)

Another company that has utilized the Web to distribute information is GE Plastics, a $5 billion subsidiary of General Electric. GE Plastics manufactures industrial-grade plastics used in a variety of industries. The company logs about 80,000 customer calls per year on its customer support line, but the company wanted a better way to get complex technical information to its customers, and the Web fit the bill perfectly. The company's new Web site (http://plastics@www.ge.com) makes over 1,500 pages of technical documentation available. The page has received between 2,000 and 4,000 accesses per day since its installation.

Marketing

By any standard, marketing on the Web is an incredible bargain. The costs involved are minor, compared with traditional marketing. What's more, there is evidence that Web marketing is more successful than marketing in other media—ten times the success at one-tenth the cost, according to one gushing report. And there are some very appealing success stories, such as Racquet Workshop, a tennis equipment store in Houston, which receives 100,000 accesses of its Web home page every month.

That said, you won't be able to rush out and find a company that's getting rich through direct sales at its Web site. At present, most of the more than 6,350 firms marketing on the Web (as of January 15, 1995) are doing so to establish "presence," and many of them are doing so out of fear that they'll be left behind, in a technological *tsunami* that they don't completely understand. But presence can pay off. A Digital Equipment Corp. (DEC) spokesman recently estimated that the firm's Internet presence had led indirectly to "hundreds of thousands of dollars" worth of sales.

For now, there's widespread consensus that getting on the Web makes good sense, even if you're not sure of the results. "People come to the Internet for information, so companies that post a lot about their products are going to succeed," says Cliff Kurtzman, president of Tenagra Corp, a consulting firm that helps companies establish a Web presence.

Figure 31.2 Silicon Studio (http://www.studio.sgi.com/)

But Web marketing is a very different proposition from marketing in traditional media. In traditional media, such as newspapers and magazines, marketing is a one-to-many proposition. According to Web marketing experts Donna L. Hoffman and Thomas P. Novak of Vanderbilt University, that's not an accurate picture of Web marketing realities, in which users demand interactivity, and sometimes even take over some marketing functions themselves! Products such as Ford Probes, Barbie Dolls, and Legos have consumer-originated product information sites on the

Web. Hoffman and Novak conclude that "high-touch" services, offering lots of user interactivity and materials of interest, will be the most likely to succeed on the Web.

What does all this mean in practice? Take a look at the Silicon Studio, Silicon Graphics' Web marketing page. Silicon Graphics produces workstations that can be used for professional graphics development, and their home page is a cornucopia of resources of interest to graphics professionals. The Studio offers libraries of valuable information and technical tips on animation, and 3D modeling. What's more, it's designed to be highly interactive. If you join the Studio, you'll receive periodic updates. Through membership, you can work collaboratively with other members to build the Studio's resources.

EXCELLENT

Advertising

Advertising is coming to the Web, and why shouldn't it? One of the mechanisms that can be used to support Web information services is the sale of advertising space. Take a look at the *San Jose Mercury-News* home page (Figure 31.3), and you'll see the Coldwell Banker real estate ad at the bottom. Unlike the ads on the Prodigy on-line service, which can take up as much as half the screen, this ad is relatively discreet and well-mannered; you don't get the sales pitch in your face unless you click the in-line image.

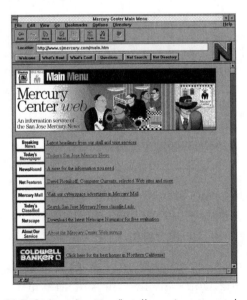

Figure 31.3 On-line advertising (http://www.sjmercury.com/main.htm)

Few Web users are likely to object to advertising that's handled this tastefully, but it's far from certain that future advertisers will be so restrained. If they're not, they're likely to find their efforts counter-productive. Web users share many of the Internet's broad disinclination towards crass commercialism, so a company that wants to send the right message to this technically savvy audience will be well advised to exercise restraint.

On-line Shopping

For years, we've been hearing that the computer age will usher in a completely new kind of shopping, one in which you sit in front of your computer rather than traveling to a store. Efforts to create on-line shopping malls in existing on-line services, such as Prodigy and CompuServe, have not met with glittering success. People like to see, handle, and try out the things they're thinking about buying—and they want to meet and talk to real human beings, to see if they can trust the vendor. Does on-line shopping have a better chance on the Web?

The current on-line shopping market—$120 million this year—is miniscule in comparison with the $2.5 billion annual sales of cable television's Home Shopping Network. (The $120 million figure includes current on-line services such as Prodigy and CompuServe.) Both of these are, in turn, a tiny slice of the $2.1 *trillion* a year that Americans spend in retail shopping stores. On-line shopping hasn't arrived—yet.

Nobody knows whether the Web will ignite an explosion of on-line commerce, but it's clear that plenty of companies are betting that it will, and there's a stampede underway to establish a Web presence. According to one recent survey, more than half of the corporate home pages on the Web are less than two months old.

Speaking of Home Shopping Network, guess who's on the Web? The Internet Shopping Network (http://www.internet.net/) is one of the Web's several "shopping malls," where the products and services of many firms are on display (600, in this case). ISN, which is a wholly-owned subsidiary of the Home Shopping Network, focuses on computer software and hardware, and seems to offer some great deals. According to ISN, prices are low because they don't have much overhead, thanks to the Web. To make a purchase, you call an 800 number; the company doesn't accept electronically-submitted credit card information.

Not every Web merchant has misgivings about unsecured electronic submission of credit card information. An example is Hot Hot Hot (http://www presence.com/H3/__5a499f0f/h3-home.html), an on-line catalog of hot sauces. As you browse the catalog, you can click the sauces you want; the order form automatically keeps track of the amount you've ordered. When you submit the order, you see a page informing you that you can pay in a variety of ways, including sending your Visa or MasterCard information unencrypted through the Internet. (There's a message explaining that, in the firm's view, this isn't much more dangerous than letting your Visa card out of your sight at a restaurant.)

Digital Cash

Pull out your wallet or open your purse, and take a look at that good old greenback dollar. If certain starry-eyed entrepreneurs get their way, it's about to be replaced with electronic transactions over the Web that have no paper equivalent, as the implications could be significant indeed for the protection of individual privacy.

A technology called *smart cards* already exists, which forms the basis for the use of electronic transactions on the Web. A smart card is a tiny computer that keeps track of how much money you have. You start out by downloading some "cash" into the card at the bank, which you then "spend" by inserting the card into machines at places like gas stations, pizza parlors, and retail stores.

The U.S. Internal Revenue Service isn't too happy about smart cards, because thanks to the development of public-key encryption technology, it's possible to design smart card systems in which the transactions are secure—and at the same time, they're untraceable. A smart card really is like cash in this sense. After you download your digital cash, there's no way the bank—or the IRS—can figure out exactly what you do with it.

How does all of this pertain to the Web? Basically, the computer you use to access the Web can serve as the smart card. All you need is the software, which is already available, thanks to DigiCash (http://www.digicash.com/ecash/ecash home.html). From the DigiCash home page, you can download software for Macintosh, Windows, or UNIX systems that will let you use DigiCash. For now, DigiCash offers its testers $100 in free "Cyberbucks," which can be used to purchase goods and services in dozens of Web sites.

Your cyberbucks work just like real money, except that you never see cash. To begin, you download some "coins" from the DigiCash on-line bank, and your e-cash client program keeps track of the withdrawal. When you browse the Web and find something you want to buy, you pay for it with cyberbucks; your client program deducts the amount you've spent, and the vendor receives credit. All the transactions are handled with public-key encryption to assure complete security, and the client software works with all the popular Web browsers.

If digital cash is such a great idea, why isn't it taking off? One reason is that DigiCash is still beta-testing its system. But there is strong resistance from the banking community, as digital cash would permit unlimited, untraceable transactions, opening up opportunities for criminal abuse that aren't available right now. With the current monetary system, kidnappers, drug dealers, money launderers, and other criminals can be traced through their transactions.

These concerns don't deter David Chaum, DigiCash's founder and president, who is concerned with an individual's right to privacy above all else. One thing's for certain, cash will disappear. What remains to be seen is whether digital cash systems will generate untraceable transactions—or whether, as the IRS would prefer, they're all traced and recorded. An IRS spokesperson stated that, so far as she was concerned, the ideal future would be one in which government surveillance is so complete that it would become unnecessary for citizens to file tax returns. Thanks to computer-tracked transactions, the IRS would know how you got every penny you made, and how and where you spent it—and tax you accordingly. This information would be freely available to other government agencies. Small wonder that Chaum, in a *Scientific American* article, stated that we have a choice before us: "In one direction lies unprecedented scrutiny and control of peoples' lives; in the other, secure parity between individuals and organizations. The shape of society in the next century depends on which approach predominates."

TOWARD THE INFORMATION SUPERHIGHWAY?

The advanced industrial powers have fallen in love with the concept of an *information superhighway*, a high-bandwidth, nation-spanning communications network that will deliver digital services to homes, schools, and businesses. Just as transportation infrastructures led to the explosive growth of economic activity, so too will the information superhighway, its advocates believe.

The superhighway metaphor is perhaps an unfortunate one, but it's meaningful for U.S. Vice President Al Gore, whose father spearheaded the introduction of the U.S. interstate superhighway system. The Clinton Administration's plans for the information superhighway's development call for cooperation between the private and public sectors in building the system. Private sector firms would construct and operate the backbone networks and "last mile" delivery systems, while the government would implement policies and pass laws encouraging private investment in the network. Gore challenged Congress and the telecommunications industry to deliver superhighway services to every community in the U.S. by the year 2000.

Does the Web shows us a glimpse of what the information superhighway will look like? If so, the picture is very different from the one favored by the information providers—motion picture companies, for instance—who have the most to gain from widespread one-way home delivery. In their scenario, potatoes would stay firmly planted in their couches, accessing information by means of a "smart" interactive television. A scenario in which the Web evolves into the information superhighway locates the network's point of penetration in the home computer, not the home TV set.

There's more at stake than just how the information comes into your house. There are two contrasting conceptions of the superhighway—the broadcast model and the community model, and they have dramatically different implications for the potential impact of the information superhighway on society.

The broadcast model is enshrined in the U.S. public's imagination, thanks to a series of devastatingly funny editorial cartoons that play off the theme "500 channels and there's still nothing on." But the implications aren't very funny. Service providers working with the broadcast model in mind could very well construct local delivery systems that allocate little bandwidth to upstream communications (messages that originate from the home). This would effectively prevent individuals from becoming the originators of information.

In the community model, the system's design emphasizes the value of allowing individual subscribers to *originate* information as well as *consume* information produced by others. The importance of Internet users' ability to make information available should not be discounted as one of the several reasons for the Internet's phenomenal growth. This information is not produced according to professional standards, but that has not stopped millions of people from going on-line to retrieve it. These information resources contain invaluable information for people working in specific fields—information that may prove vital to resolving a business or technical problem. They have also proven invaluable for individuals looking for information and assistance with matters of personal or social concern, such as information about ways to reduce the consumption of energy by computing equipment. It is unlikely that professional content providers would have much interest in developing such materials because they could not be sold on-line in sufficient quantities to repay their investment. An NII infrastructure biased against letting users originate information would work profoundly against public interest.

No one knows which model will prevail, and it's always possible that two systems will develop side by side. But one thing's for sure: The information superhighway is still many years away, and one rather cynical observer expresses doubt that we'll see it in our lifetimes. Delivering real-time multimedia services, such as video telephone service and movies, will require the installation of fiber optic cable to the home. The capital investment required is staggering, on the order of several hundred billion dollars. In comparison, the Internet-based Web is still a low-bandwidth system, providing only a glimmer of the technology to come.

SUMMARY

The Web's phenomenal growth has led many to believe that we are witnessing the birth of the "Information Superhighway." But the HTTP protocol will need some revision if it is to serve the Superhighway's role, namely, as a cornerstone of commerce, communication, education, and economic development. Thanks to the efforts of the W3 Consortium, some needed changes are on the way. In the meantime, commercialization of the Web is growing rapidly—companies are using the Web to provide documentation, to market, to advertise, and to sell their products and services. Decisions that are being made right now about how you pay for Web-purchased items could have significant implications with regard to privacy. No one really knows whether the Web will evolve into an information superhighway, but it does clearly show the social and economic benefits of the community model, in which all network participants can originate as well as consume information.

Installing and Configuring the Chameleon WebSurfer Sampler

The Chameleon WebSurfer Sampler disk, included with this book, contains everything you need to connect your Microsoft Windows system to an Internet service provider via dialup IP (SLIP, CSLIP, or PPP). It also contains WebSurfer, NetManage's Web browser. WebSurfer is designed to work only with the NetManage software. For an introduction to dialup IP, see Chapter 8.

INSTALLING THE CHAMELEON WEBSURFER SAMPLER SOFTWARE

To install the Chameleon WebSurfer Sampler disk included with this book, follow these instructions.

1. Place the disk in drive A.

2. In Windows' Program Manager, open the **File** menu, and choose **Run**. You'll see the Run dialog box.

3. In the Run dialog box, type the following and press **Enter**:

   a:\setup

   You'll see a dialog box asking whether it's OK to install the WebSurfer Sampler software.

4. Click **Continue** to install the software in the \NETMANAG directory. After copying the software, the setup program informs you that the installation is complete.

5. Click **OK**. When you switch to Program Manager, you see a new program group containing icons for launching the NetManage applications, including WebSurfer (see Figure A.1).

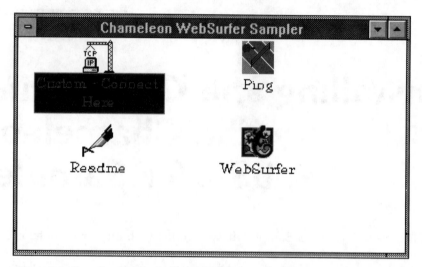

Figure A.1 *Chameleon WebSurfer Sampler Program Group (Windows Program Manager)*

CONFIGURING CHAMELEON

To configure Chameleon for dialup IP, you'll need to tell the program which configuration file to use and to supply the information that Chameleon needs.

Specifying the Configuration File

The Chameleon software requires that you name a configuration file, which specifies the script that the program uses to connect with your service provider. If the Chameleon Sampler disk contains a preconfigured script for the service driver you're using, count your blessings; you'll get through the instructions in this chapter in short order. If you must create your own script, you'll need to create a new, custom configuration file, as explained in the following instructions, and write a custom logon script, as explained later in this chapter.

To tell Chameleon which configuration file to use:

1. Double-click the **Custom** icon in the Chameleon Sampler program group. You'll see the Custom dialog box, as shown in Figure A.2.

Custom - C:\NETMANAG\TCPIP.CFG			
File Interface Setup Services Connect Help			
Interface:	PPP0 - COM2, 19200 baud		
Dial:	Listen for connections		
IP Address:	1.1.1.1		
Subnet Mask:	255.0.0.0		
Host Name:	<Put the name of this PC here>		
Domain Name:	<Put Domain here: example.com>		
Name	**Type**	**IP**	**Domain**
*PPP0	PPP	1.1.1.1	<Put Domain here: example.com

Figure A.2 *Custom dialog box*

2. Do one of the following:
   - If the Sampler disk contains a preconfigured script for your service provider, choose **Open** from the **File** menu. You'll see an Open dialog box. Choose the configuration file corrresponding to the service you want to use (see Table A.1 for a list), and click **OK**.
   - If the Sampler disk doesn't contain a preconfigured script for your service provider, choose **Add** from the Interface menu. In the dialog box that appears, type the name you would like to use to access the service. In the Type area, type **SLIP**, **CSLIP**, or **PPP**. Confirm your choice by clicking **OK** or pressing **Enter** in the list of configuration files that appears at the bottom of the Custom window and select the configuration you just created.

Table A.1 Configuration file names

SERVICE PROVIDER	CONFIGURATION FILE NAME
AlterNet (UUnet Technologies)	alternet.cfg
CERFnet	cerfnet.cfg
CICnet	cicnet.cfg
ClarkNet	clarknet.cfg
CRL	crl.cfg
CTS	cts.cfg
Cybergate	cybergate.cfg
Digital Express	digex.cfg
HookUp Communication Corporation	hookup.cfg
IgLou Internet Services	iglou.cfg
InterAccess	interacc.cfg
JVNCnet (Global Enterprise Services)	jvcnet.cfg
MRNet	mrmnet.cfg
Northwest Nexus	nwnexus.cfg
Olympus	olympus.cfg
OnRamp	onramp.cfg
PANIX	panix.cfg
PICnet	picnet.cfg
Portal Communications	portal.cfg
Prometheus Information Network Group	pingnet.cfg
PSI	psinet.cfg
The Internet Access Company (TIAC)	tiac.cfg
WLN Internet Services	wln.cfg

Supplying Information that Chameleon Needs

Now take a look at the information you've collected from the service provider, such as the IP address and the address of the domain name server (DNS). You'll need this information in the following steps, in which you supply the information that Chameleon needs.

To supply the needed information:

1. From the Setup menu, choose **IP address**. You'll see the dialog box shown in Figure A.3. If your service provider uses dynamic IP addressing, just type **1**, if necessary, in all four of the boxes. If you were given in IP address (such as 143.157.7.703), type the number in the four boxes. When you're finished, click **OK** or press **Enter**.

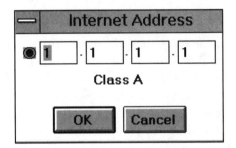

Figure A.3 *In this dialog box, you supply the IP address given to you by your service provider*

Now you need to tell Chameleon where your modem is located, what kind of modem you're using, and what modem speed to use.

2. From the Setup menu, choose **Port**. You'll see the dialog box shown in Figure A.4. In the Baud Rate area, choose the your modem's speed. For a 14.4 Kbps V.32bis modem, choose **19,200**. Choose **8 Data Bits, 1 Stop Bit, None** in the Parity area, and **Hardware** in the Flow Control area. Choose the Connection you're using (the port to which your modem is connected, and click **OK** or press **Enter**).

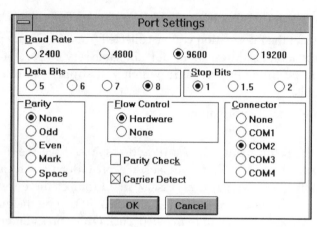

Figure A.4 *In this dialog box, you supply information about the port your modem is using*

Your next step is to identify your modem.

3. From the Setup menu, choose **Modem**. You'll see the dialog box
    shown in Figure A.5. The default settings should be fine, but make
    sure your modem brand is chosen in the Modem Defaults area. If you
    can't find your modem on this list choose the generic Hayes option.
    This setting will work for almost all recently puchased modems. Click
    OK or press **Enter** when you're done.

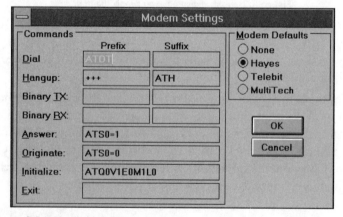

Figure A.5 *In this dialog box, you supply information about the modem you're using*

Next, tell Chameleon the telephone number that you dial to access
the SLIP, CSLIP, or PPP service.

4. From the Setup menu, choose **Dial**. You'll see the Dial Settings dialog box, shown in Figure A.6. If you'd like to be signalled when the connection is made, activate the **Signal When Connected** check box. If you'd like Chameleon to redial in the event of a busy signal or no answer, activate the **Redial After Timing Out** check box. Click **OK** or press **Enter** when you're done.

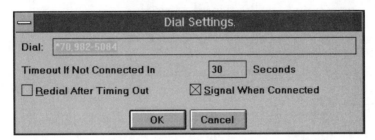

Figure A.6 *Dial Settings dialog box*

 If your phone line has the Call Waiting feature, you should disable it during dialup IP sessions. An incoming call will usually cause your session to fail with no obvious indication of the cause of the problem. To disable Call Waiting with most phone systems, type *70, (the comma is needed to introduce a one-second pause) followed by the phone number. Call your local telephone company to find out which code they use to disable Call Waiting.

You next tell Chameleon your login name and password.

5. From the Setup menu, choose **Login**. You'll see the dialog box shown in Figure A.7. In the User **N**ame area, type your user name (also called login name). In the User **P**assword area, type your password. Leave the Startup **C**ommand area as it is, unless you're accessing a service for which Chameleon doesn't have a preconfigured script. If you're writing your own script, type the startup command information your service provider gave you. For SLIP service, this is probably **SLIP** or **SLIPDEFAULT**, but it could be something else.

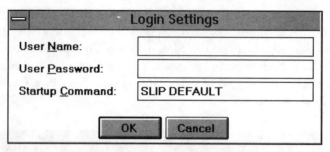

Figure A.7 *Login Settings dialog box*

Finally, give Chameleon the addresses of the DNS servers you'll be accessing. Generally, there's one default server and one or two alternates.

6. From the Services menu, choose **Domain Server**. You'll see the dialog box shown in Figure A.8. In the first line, type the default DNS server. If you were given a second DNS address, type it in the second line. If you were given a third address, type it in the third line. When you're done, click **OK** or press **Enter**. To save your configuration, choose **Save** from the File menu.

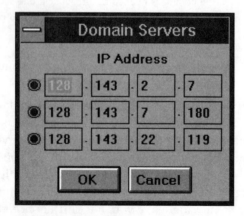

Figure A.8 *Domain Servers dialog box*

Logging On and Testing Your Connection

Unless you need to write a custom script, you're ready to log on! Be sure the configuration you've just customized is selected at the bottom of the Custom window.

Click **Connect**, which is all you have to do to set things in motion. After the connection is made, you'll see the Newt icon at the bottom of the screen.

To test your connection, use the Ping program, one of the utilities packaged with Chameleon. In the Chameleon Sampler program group, double click the Ping icon. When the Ping window appears, click **Start**. You'll see a dialog box prompting you for an IP address or domain name. Type the address of your mail server (such as post.cyber.com) and click **OK**.

WRITING A CUSTOM SCRIPT

Skip this section if you're using one of Chameleon's preconfigured scripts. This section is only for people who need to write a script because the Chameleon sampler doesn't include one for their service.

You can write a script successfully, but you'll need to pay careful attention to the minute matters of typing, including leaving spaces where needed. If you've ever done any computer programming, you know how careful you must be to get everything in the right order and follow all the rules.

A script is a way of telling Custom what to do after your modem makes contact with the service provider. It's really pretty simple. For PPP, the script has to enter your login name and password—that's it. For SLIP and CSLIP, it's a little more complicated because you have to enter the startup command. With dynamic IP addressing, the script has to get the IP address, too. But even in this case, the script isn't any big deal—it's only one line long!

Finding Out What Happens When You Log On

To get started writing your script, you'll need to see what happens when you contact your service provider. Switch to Program Manager, open the Accessories window, and start the Windows Terminal accessory program. Use the options in the Settings menu to set the communications options (port number and modem speed), the modem settings (modem type), and phone number. Then choose **Dial** from the **P**hone menu, and watch carefully what happens. You'll probably see something like the following. Respond to all the prompts using the information you were given, as illustrated by the text in boldface. Note that you have to press **Enter** after you supply your login name and password:

4CONNECT 14400

Welcome to Cyber City!

Login name:**wmi2x**

Password:***********

For many PPP services, that's all you need to log on, and your script—which automates the keystrokes you just typed—will be simple. Things get more complicated, though, if you're using SLIP with a service provider that uses dynamic addressing:

CONNECT 14400

Welcome to Cyber City!

Login name:**wmi2x**

Password:***********

CyberCity>**SLIP DEFAULT**

Initiating SLIP mode.

Your IP address is 129.70.222.10.

Matching headers to your compression

When you've finished logging on, there's no point in going on with Terminal, since it can't handle SLIP or PPP. For now, select all the text that you've seen, and copy it to the Windows Notepad utility and print it. Then switch back to Terminal, and choose **Hang Up** from the **P**hone menu. Exit Terminal by choose **Ex**it from the **F**ile menu.

Understanding the Two Basic Script Statements

To write an effective script, you have to tell Chameleon what to expect when it contacts the service, just like you did with Terminal. The script tells Chameleon to wait for a certain word or characters, and when it sees this, to do something (like supply your password). To put it another way, the script consists of two basic kinds of statements:

- **Expect Statements**. You type the word or the characters that Custom is supposed to wait for. For example, you can tell Custom to wait for "name:" and then have it enter your login name.

- **Send Statements**. These follow the expect statements and tell Custom what to send. An example of a send statement is ur, which means "send the login name and then press Enter." Take a quick look at Table A.2, which lists all the send statements you can use.

Table A.2 *Chameleon's Send Statements*

TYPE THIS STATEMENT:	TO DO THIS:
$n	send a new line
$r	send a carriage-return
$s	send a space
$b	cause a short "break" on the line
$t	send a tab
$1 - $9	pause the indicated number of seconds
$xXX	send the character with HEX code XX
$u	send the user id (login name)
$p	send the password
$c	send the SLIP COMMAND
$d	send the phone number
$$	send a "$" character
$f	define a prompt

Just one more point about the script language. The basic rule is that you begin with an expect statement, which must be followed by a send statement. Expect, send, expect, send, expect send—that's the way your script has to be written if you want it to work.

Planning Your Script

Now let's take a look at that simple logon procedure again.

CONNECT 14400

Welcome to Cyber City!

Login name:**wmi2x**

Password:***********

We want to write a script that tells Custom First, expect "name"; send the login name and press **Enter**. Next, expect "word"; send the password and press **Enter**. Piece of cake! Here's what the script looks like:

SCRIPT=name: ur word: pr

Please note that there's a space after "name:" as well as a space before and after "word:" And don't forget the colons! They're part of what you're telling Custom to look for.

Note Expect statements are case-sensitive. If you're telling Custom to expect "CyBerCiTy," you have to type the uppercase and lowercase exactly the way the letters appeared on your Terminal screen.

I'll tell you where you type the script in a minute, but there's more to learn if you're accessing a SLIP service with dynamic addressing. To get this address, you need additional expect commands, summarized in Table A.3.

Table A.3 *Expect commands for capturing dynamic IP addresses*

TYPE THIS STATEMENT:	TO DO THIS:
—	expect "-"
-n	skip an expect
-i	expect IP address (to replace your own)

Now take a look at that more complicated case again:

```
CONNECT 14400
Welcome to Cyber City!
Login name:wmi2x
Password:*******
CyberCity>SLIP DEFAULT
Initiating SLIP mode.
Your IP address is 129.70.222.10.
```

The first part of the above script will work just fine—it enters the login name and password, but then it stops dead. You need to add instructions that say, Expect "Cyber City>," and then send "SLIP DEFAULT," and then press **Enter**. Next, expect "address," and get the IP address.

Here's what the complete script looks like:

SCRIPT=name: ur word: pr City> cr address -i

The additions you've made to the script say: when you see "City>", send the SLIP command and press **Enter**. When you see "address", check for the IP address and get it!

It's pretty easy to write a script, but you may need to do some proofreading and make some corrections. Remember that the whole command has to consist of expect, send, expect, send, expect, send, etc. For some logon procedures, you may have to skip an expect. Here's an example: Some service providers require you to "wake them up" by pressing **Enter** when you first log on. Here's what you need to add to do this: **-n $r**. This says, "Skip an expect, and then press Enter." The completed script would look like this (for the simple PPP example):

SCRIPT=-n $r name: ur word: pr

Tip

If you're having trouble picking up the IP address, you might have to stick a "skip send" ($-) just before the -i, as in this example:

SCRIPT=name$u$r word$p$r City> cr address $- -i

Here's another adjustment you may have to make. Sometimes you need to tell Custom to wait a few seconds before doing something. For example, some computers don't like to have that initial Enter keystroke until they're good and ready. Here's a modification that adds two seconds ($2) before the initial Enter keystroke:

SCRIPT=-n 2r name: ur word: pr

Now—where do you type your script? In a Chameleon file called SLIP.INI. Open this file with Notepad, and scroll down until you see the interface name you typed in the Name area of the Add Interface box. As you'll see, Chameleon has put this name in brackets, added the default script, and ended it with the access type, as in the following example:

[Publix]
SCRIPT=login: ur word: pr
TYPE=PPP

To add your script, carefully delete the default script—don't erase the equals sign—and type yours. The result will be something like this:

[Publix]
SCRIPT=-n 3r name> ur word> pr
TYPE=PPP

Just one final reminder—most of the problems people have with Chameleon scripting is failing to get the expect-send syntax right. Look at the above example: it says "skip-an-expect (-n), send (3r ; expect (name>), send (ur); expect (word>), send (pr)."

SLIP.INI, as you'll see when you scroll through the file, has lots of scripts that can give you ideas for dealing with special logon situations. If you're having trouble getting your script to work, try copying one of the existing ones and modifying it.

When you're finished typing your script, proofread it carefully. Did you leave spaces before and after the "expect" text? Did you use the right pattern of uppercase and lowercase letters in the "expect" text? Did you include the right send commands? Is everything in the right order? Try describing in English what the script is supposed to do, and check it against what really happens when you log on. Does your script conform to the "expect, send, expect send (etc.)" syntax?

Finally, save **SLIP.INI** and exit **Notepad**.

For information on logging on and testing your connection, see the previous section. When you run your script for the first time, choose <u>**Log**</u> from the <u>S</u>etup menu to see an on-screen log of what's happening—this can be very informative! Click Connect to start the logon procedure. If you're trying out a script that uses dynamic addressing, double-click **Newt** so you can see whether Chameleon captured the IP address correctly. If something goes wrong, examine the Log window carefully— you should see where your script didn't do what you thought it would!

For more information on writing scripts for Chameleon, see the README.WRI file that's included on the Chameleon Sampler disk.

N o t e

APPENDIX B

Quick Reference Guide to Frequently-Used HTML Commands

This reference guide provides a handy subject guide to the most frequently-used HTML commands. If you're creating a document and you've forgotten which tag to use, look here. You'll find subject headings corresponding to the part of the document you're trying to create (such as a title, a rule, a bulleted list, or a paragraph). This appendix doesn't attempt to explain how to use HTML; please see Chapter 27 for an introduction.

ANCHOR

Usage: Creates a hyperlink.

Be sure to test your hyperlink to make sure it's working correctly. Watch out for syntax problems: If the hyperlink doesn't appear in Mosaic, you typed the anchor wrong (check to make sure you've got both beginning and ending quotation marks).

Beginning Tag:	<A HREF="put the URL here">
End Tag:	</A>
Example:	<A HREF ="http://jefferson.village.Virginia.EDU/rossetti/rossetti.html">The Rossetti Archive</A>

557

BODY

Usage: Demarcates the body of the document, as opposed to the header.

Surround all of the body with body tags.

Tip

Beginning Tag:	<BODY>
End Tag:	</BODY>
Example:	<HEAD>
	<TITLE>Document Title</TITLE>
	</HEAD>
	<BODY>
	This is the entire body of the document (short!).
	</BODY>

BOLD

Usage: Shows characters with a bold emphasis.

Use boldface sparingly. People may confuse a boldfaced entry with a hyperlink, may say disparaging things about you when, after clicking the boldfaced entry, nothing happens.

Tip

Beginning Tag:	<B>
End Tag:	</B>
Example:	Type <B>chmod +x Mosaic-sun</B> and press Enter.

BULLETED LIST

(see Unordered List)

FORCED LINE BREAK

Usage: Use this tag when you want to force a line break with no extra space between the lines (this is useful for typing a mailing address).

The <P> tag inserts a blank line, so this tag is useful when you don't want a blank line to follow a line break.

T i p

Beginning Tag:	
End Tag:	None
Example:	123 Mayflower Drive
	Centerville, IA

HEADER

Usage: Demarcates the header of the document, as opposed to the body.

Surround all of the header with head tags.

T i p

Beginning Tag:	<HEAD>
End Tag:	</HEAD>
Example:	<HEAD>
	<TITLE>Document Title</TITLE>
	</HEAD>
	<BODY>
	This is the entire body of the document (short!).
	</BODY>

HEADING 1

Usage: Major (Level 1) heading within a document; appears within the document view area as if it were the document title.

Use these sparingly—they're displayed in a large font size, and take up lots of room. Use the Heading 1 tag for the title of your document as you want it to appear within the document area (the Title tag appears on the title bar).

Beginning Tag: <H1>
End Tag: </H1>
Example: <H1>Biological Sciences</H1>

HEADING 2

Usage: Major (Level 2) subheading; appears in a smaller font size than Heading 1.

Use this tag for the major divisions within your document.

Beginning Tag: <H2>
End Tag: </H2>
Example: <H2>Environment and Ecology</H2>

HEADING 3

Usage: Minor (Level 3) subheading; appears in a smaller font size than Heading 2, but (usually) still larger than the normal font size.

This tag is needed only if you want to introduce divisions within a Heading 2 section.

Beginning Tag: <H3>
End Tag: </H3>
Example: <H3>Wetlands</H3>

HTML

Usage: Demarcates the portion of the document that's coded with HTML.

You must begin and end each document with an HTML tag.

Beginning Tag:	<HTML>
End Tag:	</HTML>
Example:	<HTML>
	<HEAD>
	<TITLE>Document Title</TITLE>
	</HEAD>
	<BODY>
	This is the entire body of the document (short!).
	</BODY>
	</HTML>

IN-LINE IMAGE

Usage: Displays a graphic within the document.

Keep your in-line images small. The larger the image, the longer the retrieval time.

Beginning Tag:	<IMG SRC="Put the URL here">
End Tag:	None
Example:	<IMG SRC="file:///c:\mosaic\blueball.gif">

ITALICS

Usage: Shows characters with italic emphasis.

Use italics sparingly.

T i p

Beginning Tag:	<I>
End Tag:	</I>
Example:	<I>The Rose Garden</I>, by Rossetti

NUMBERED LIST

(see Ordered List)

ORDERED LISTS (NUMBERED)

Usage: Creates a list of items that your browser automatically numbers.

Use an ordered list only if the items fit together in a numerical sequence, such as a list of steps to follow to achieve a goal. If there's no particular order to the list, use an unordered list (bulleted list). It's not necessary to end each line with a <P> tag, so long as

T i p

you precede each line with a <LI> tag.

Beginning Tag:	<UL>, and each item on the list begins with <LI>
End Tag:	</UL>
Example:	<UL>
	<LI> Place the disk in the drive
	<LI> Type **INSTALL**
	<LI> Press Enter
	</UL>

PARAGRAPH

Usage: Starts a new paragraph.

You don't need this tag if you're creating a list, but HTML won't start a new paragraph otherwise—even if you've started a new paragraph by pressing Enter.

HTML+, a revision of HTML that is currently underway, will require you to code paragraphs using a beginning code (<P>) and an end code (</P>), with the text of the paragraphs between these codes. However, you need not use these codes at present and HTML+ will be able to read HTML documents.

Beginning Tag:	<P>
End Tag:	None required
Example:	And so we've come to the end of yet another paragraph.<P>

PREFORMATTED TEXT

Usage: Preserves your line breaks and spacing, just as you typed them.

This is useful if you're typing a table.

Beginning Tag:	<PRE>
End Tag:	</PRE>
Example:	<PRE>

```
Course      Description
CS171       Introduction to HTML
CS181       Intermediate HTML
CS271       Advanced HTML
</PRE>
```

RULE

Usage: Adds a horizontal line to your document.

T i p

Use rules to separate the major sections of your document.

Beginning Tag:	<HR>
End Tag:	None
Example:	<HR>
	<H2>The Early Italian Poets</H2>
	</H2>

TITLES

Usage: Placed within a header, creates a title that is displayed on the title bar.

T i p

Surround with headers tags (<head> and </head>)

Beginning Tag:	<TITLE>
End Tag:	</TITLE>
Example:	<TITLE>The Decline and Fall of the Roman Empire</TITLE>

UNORDERED LIST

Usage: Creates a bulleted list.

Beginning Tag:	<O/>, and each item on the list begins with<LI>
End Tag:	</OL>
Example:	<OL>
	<LI>This is one item in the list
	<LI>This is another item in the list
	</OL>

APPENDIX C

Installing and Using WinHTTPD for Microsoft Windows

Accessible by means of an HTML document on this book's disk is a fine, full-featured Web server for Microsoft Windows 3.1 systems, called WinHTTPD for Microsoft Windows. An adaptation of NCSA's UNIX server for the Windows environment, WinHTTPD is a creation of Robert B. Denny of Alisa Systems. This company specializes in providing enterprise-wide email integration software for large corporate clients. As a service to the Web community, Mr. Denny distributes WinHTTPD, a copyrighted program, without charge so long as the program is used for non-commercial purposes. For information on commercial uses, please email Mr. Denny at rdenny@netcom.com. For more information on Alisa System's email products, check out http://www.alisa.com/mrkt/index.htm.

HOT TIP

Please remember that Mr. Denny provides WinHTTPD as a service to the Web community; don't pester him unnecessarily. Before sending email to Mr. Denny concerning this program, please be sure you have carefully read all the on-line documentation. In addition, check out the WinHTTPD Web site at http://www.alisa.com/win-httpd/.

WinHTTPD is extremely easy to install and use, as long as you're not planning to do anything fancy. Without any programming expertise or program configuration, you can make HTML documents available to people who access your site. These documents can include in-line images and links to larger graphics files, sounds, videos, and animations. Although WinHTTPD is capable of handling forms, clickable maps, or searches, you'll need some programming ability—or one of the many third-party point-and-click programs that are becoming available for WinHTTPD.

**HOME
PAGE**

You can install WinHTTPD for Microsoft Windows on any Web-connected Windows system with sufficient processing horsepower (at least a 486 running at 33 Mhz), but please note that doing so doesn't make much sense if you're accessing the Web through SLIP or PPP using dynamic addressing. For people using other systems to be able to access your documents, your system needs a permanent IP address. With dynamic addressing, your address changes each time you log on. This chapter will prove of interest, then, to readers who have or plan to get network access or dialup IP access with a permanent IP address. For more information on accessing the Web, see Part Two of this book.

EXCELLENT

WinHTTPD may be a freebie, but don't underestimate its capabilities. The program can handle 16 simultaneous accesses—up to 25,000 per hour on a 486 DX2 system—and it's fully capable of handling forms requests. In addition, the program's Windows CGI interface has generated a lot of third-party activity. A case in point: Polyform, a point-and-click forms script generator. Check out Alisa System's Web server for more information.

LEGAL STUFF

WinHTTPD for Microsoft Windows is copyright (c) 1994, by Robert B. Denny. Please observe the following stipulations on the use of WinHTTPD:

1. You may make and give away verbatim copies of the Standard Version of this Package without restriction, provided that you include this copyright notice and the following Liability Disclaimer in the documentation and/or other materials provided with the Package.

2. You may modify your copy of this Package in any way, provided you insert a prominent notice in each changed file stating when, how, and why you changed that file, and provided that you do at least ONE of the following:

(a) place your modifications into the public domain or otherwise make them freely available,

(b) use the modified package only within your corporation or organization,

(c) make other distribution arrangements with the Copyright Holder.

3. The name Robert B. Denny may NOT be used to endorse or promote products derived from this Package without specific prior written permission.

Source Code All right title and interest to the source code is hereby reserved by the Copyright Holder.

Disclaimer: THIS SOFTWARE IS PROVIDED BY THE AUTHOR "AS IS" AND ANY EXPRESS OR IMPLIED WARRANTIES, INCLUDING, BUT NOT LIMITED TO, THE IMPLIED WARRANTIES OF MERCHANTABILITY AND FITNESS FOR A PARTICULAR PURPOSE ARE DISCLAIMED. IN NO EVENT SHALL EITHER NCSA OR THE AUTHOR BE LIABLE FOR ANY DIRECT, INDIRECT, INCIDENTAL, SPECIAL, EXEMPLARY, OR CONSEQUENTIAL DAMAGES (INCLUDING, BUT NOT LIMITED TO, PROCUREMENT OF SUBSTITUTE GOODS OR SERVICES; LOSS OF USE, DATA, OR PROFITS; OR BUSINESS INTERRUPTION) HOWEVER CAUSED AND ON ANY THEORY OF LIABILITY, WHETHER IN CONTRACT, STRICT LIABILITY, OR TORT (INCLUDING NEGLIGENCE OR OTHERWISE) ARISING IN ANY WAY OUT OF THE USE OF THIS SOFTWARE, EVEN IF ADVISED OF THE POSSIBILITY OF SUCH DAMAGE.

PREPARING YOUR SYSTEM FOR WINHTTPD

WinHTTPD is very easy to install, so long as you carefully follow the instructions in this appendix. Above all else, please install WinHTTPD in a directory named c:\httpd; don't install the software in any other directory. If you run into trouble running the server software, please see the "Troubleshooting" section, later in this appendix.

For a trouble-free installation, please follow these directions carefully.

1. Using your graphical browser, access the file WinHTTPD.HTM, included on this book's disk. Follow the instructions in this document to download the file.

2. On your hard disk, create a directory called **c:\httpd**. *Please do not use any other name or location for this directory!* It must be located directly off the root. Please check your spelling: It must be called \httpd.

3. Copy the WinHTTPD file, **whttpd14.zip**, to the c:\httpd directory.

4. Use PKUNZIP.EXE to unzip the file. Be sure to use the -d switch so that the files are unzipped to the correct directory! (*Note*: If you use WinZip, the Windows interface to the PKZIP software, it will use this option automatically.)

5. The Common Log Format requires that times be recorded in GMT. Therefore, httpd must know what timezone your computer's local clock is set for. The TZ environment variable is used for this purpose. Using the Windows Notepad utility, add a line to your AUTOEXEC.BAT to set the TZ variable. Within the US, the syntax is as follows:

   ```
   SET TZ=sssnddd
   ```

   where sss is the 3-letter abbreviation for your standard timezone (e.g. EST), n is the standard time offset of your timezone from GMT (e.g. for Eastern, 5), and ddd is the 3-letter abbreviation for your daylight time (if your state has daylight time, e.g., for Eastern, EDT). For example:

   ```
   SET TZ=EST5EDT   (Eastern, daylight time)
   SET TZ=MST7      (Mountain, no daylight time)
   ```

6. The demo page and many examples in the documentation require the server to run back-end scripts in a DOS window. They will fail if you don't have enough environment space. Using the Windows Notepad utility, add a line

   ```
   CommandEnvSize=8192
   ```

   to the [NonWindowsApp] section of SYSTEM.INI.

7. Close Windows and restart your system before attemting to use WinHTTPD.

STARTING THE SERVER

To start WinHTTPD, follow these steps:

1. Create an icon for the server by dragging **httpd.exe** from the File Manager window to a Program Manager group window.

2. If necessary, start your Winsock-compatible TCP/IP software, and verify your Internet connection.

3. Double-click the **WinHTTPD** icon. If DNS is not available, it will take up to 30 seconds to complete initialization

Once the server has minimized itself to an icon, it is ready to go.

OPENING THE DEFAULT HOME PAGE

To test your server, open your browser and type the URL of your home page in the Document URL area. To do so, type a URL such as the following:

http://your.host.name/

If your computer's IP address is 128.143.7.256, you type the following:

http://128.143.7.256/

This URL accesses the default home page, index.htm, which is located in the \httpd\htdocs directly. You can also access any other HTML document in this directory by typing the document's name, as in the following URL:

http://128.143.7.256/welcome.htm

From WinHTTPD's default homepage, access the Server Demonstrations and Test page. This will familiarize you with the server's capabilities as well as test the features.

HOT TIP

TROUBLESHOOTING

If you're having trouble with WinHTTPD, the most likely explanation is one of the following:

- **Timezone environment variable not set.** You must add the SET TZ line to your AUTOEXEC.BAT file. See the installation instructions, above.

- **Insufficient memory and/or CPU power.** To run httpd and your browser together, you should have a 486/33 and 8MB of memory. Anything less will be agonizingly slow.

- **Insufficient DOS environment space.** You must add the line CommandEnvSize=8192 to the [NonWindowsApp] section of SYSTEM.INI. See the installation instructions, above.

- **Non-compliant or buggy Windows Sockets support.** Many of the ostensibly Winsock-compatible TCP/IP packages on the market have bugs or noncompliant features that make them incompatible with WinHTTPD. For the latest information, check out WinHTTPD's Web site, mentioned earlier in this appendix.

USING WINHTTPD

If you're able to access the index.htm document without difficulty, you're on the Web! You can now place your Web documents in the WinHTTPD default document directory, \httpd\htdocs.

If you would like to use in-line graphics with your Web documents, you can place them in the same directory with your HTML documents (\httpd\htdocs). When you reference these in-line images in your HTML documents, you can use relative links such as the following:

```
<IMG SRC="new.gif">
```

For better file organization, you may wish to place the GIFs in the \httpd\htdocs\images directory. If you do, use relative links such as the following:

```
<IMG SRC="\images\new.gif">
```

For more information on creating HTML documents for your Web server, please see Chapters 27, 28, and 29.

INDEX